The Media Enthralled

The Media Enthralled

Singapore Revisited

Francis T. Seow

with a foreword by

Henry J. Steiner

LYNNE
RIENNER
PUBLISHERS

BOULDER
LONDON

*To the memory of my father, Seow Chin Guan,
and to my mother, Pang Siew Peck,
my brothers, Gerald, Raphael, and George,
and my sisters, Gladys, Clare, and Rosalynde*

Published in the United States of America in 1998 by
Lynne Rienner Publishers, Inc.
1800 30th Street, Boulder, Colorado 80301

and in the United Kingdom by
Lynne Rienner Publishers, Inc.
3 Henrietta Street, Covent Garden, London WC2E 8LU

© 1998 by Lynne Rienner Publishers, Inc. All rights reserved

Library of Congress Cataloging-in-Publication Data
Seow, Francis T.
  The media enthralled : Singapore revisited / Francis T. Seow :
with a foreword by Henry J. Steiner.
  Includes bibliographical references and index.
  ISBN 1-55587-779-6
  1. Freedom of the press—Singapore. 2. Government and the
press—Singapore. 3. Online information services—Singapore.
4. Foreign news—Singapore. 5. Press law—Singapore. I. Title.
PN5449.S55S46 1997
323.44'5'095957—dc20   96-41596
                                                          CIP

British Cataloguing in Publication Data
A Cataloguing in Publication record for this book
is available from the British Library.

Printed and bound in the United States of America

The paper used in this publication meets the requirements
of the American National Standard for Permanence of
Paper for Printed Library Materials Z39.48-1984.

5 4 3 2 1

Contents

Foreword, Henry J. Steiner   ix
Preface   xi
Acknowledgments   xvii

1   The Bailiwick of Singapore   1
    A Glimpse at History, 2
    Vignettes on Indian Press Legislation, 2
    The Situation at the Straits, 4
    The *Singapore Chronicle,* 6
    The *Singapore Free Press,* 7
    The *Straits Times,* 7
    The *Malaya Tribune,* 8
    The *Singapore Tiger Standard,* 8
    The *Nanyang Siang Pau* and the *Sin Chew Jit Poh,* 8
    Some Extinct Publications, 9

2   A Handsel for the Media   11
    Press Legislation, 19

3   The Techniques of Repression: A Lesson Well Learned   22
    An Interlude, 22
    Singapore in Malaysia, 24
    Lee Kuan Yew and Journalists, 25
    Lee Kuan Yew and the *Utusan Melayu,* 28
    The Final Split, 35

4   The Subjugation of the Print Media: Two Important Cases   38
    Shades of Black Operations, 40
    The *Nanyang Siang Pau,* 42
    Habeas Corpus Applications, 48
    The *Eastern Sun,* 52

5   The Government's Case Against the *Singapore Herald*   56
    All About Reece, 62
    A Letter to the Editor, 64
    Prelude to the Prime Minister's Press Conference, 65
    The Press Conference, 66
    A Legal Notice of Demand, 72
    The "Save the *Herald*" Charade, 80

The Permit Revoked, 85
Of Overdraft and Guarantors, 87
The International Press Institute Conference, Helsinki, 88
The *Singapore Herald* Cooperative Rescue Effort, 95
The Final Curtain Falls, 99
The Foreign Media Reassured, 101
In the Aftermath, 101
Postscript on the *Singapore Herald,* 102

6   **The Divestiture of Control**   106
The Press Council, 108
The Socialist International Entr'acte, 109
The 1976 General Election, 111
The Divestiture Continues, 115
The Anson By-Election, 117
The Restructure, 119
The 1984 General Election, 125
Other Domestic Publications, 126
Political Organs, Newsletters, Etcetera, 128

7   **The Foreign Media**   140
Tallying Foreign Media Vexations, 140
The Foreign Media's Turn: The Circulation Restriction, 147
Time, 148
The *Asian Wall Street Journal,* 149
Asiaweek, 164
Far East Economic Review, 165
The *Economist:* A Missing Key Sentence? 171
The *International Herald Tribune,* 173
The Expulsion of Foreign Correspondents, 179
Requirement for Bond, Etcetera, 185
Singapore: A Salubrious Perch? 190
The Right of Reply Revisited, 191
Interviews with the Prime Minister, 194

8   **Inside the Web**   201
Official Advertisements, 202
A Special Relationship? 206
Media Blackout? 207
Self-Censorship, 208
The Tentacles of Censorship, 213
Letters to Editors, 215
Investigative Reporting, 217
Cartoons, Caricatures and Editorial Humour, 219
The Legal Weapon, 220
Conclusion: The Next Lap, 223

Addendum: Relevant Legislation   228

    Defamation Act, Cap. 75
    The Essential Information (Control of Publications and
        Safeguarding of Information) Regulations, 1966
    Judicial Proceedings (Regulation of Reports) Act, Cap. 149
    Internal Security Act, Cap. 143
    Official Secrets Act, Cap. 213
    Parliamentary (Privileges, Immunities and Powers) Act, Cap. 217
    Penal Code, Cap. 224, Sections 449 to 500
    Sedition Act, Cap. 290
    Undesirable Publications Act, Cap. 338

Appendix A: Newspaper Circulation   234
Appendix B: The Sunday Times, *May 22, 1988*   234
Appendix C: Asia Watch Response   236
Selected Bibliography   238
Index   244
About the Book and Author   254

Foreword

HENRY J. STEINER

The literature on human rights is rich in doctrinal and theoretical studies, as well as in reports of intergovernmental or nongovernmental organizations about a state's violations of those rights. We find less writing of a historical character that traces the evolution of state policies hostile to human rights and that explores in detail the strategies for implementing those policies. Such writing goes beyond a summary account of violations to give us their context and reasons. Francis Seow has given us such a book.

Mr. Seow is well suited to write with authority about the experience of Singapore during the reign of Lee Kuan Yew. He held a series of important positions in public life, culminating in his service as solicitor general during 1969–1971. Seow then entered private practice and served in 1986 as president of the Singapore Law Society. Arrested in 1988 under the Internal Security Act on allegations of receiving funds from the United States government to enter opposition politics, Seow was detained for 72 days before release.

Mr. Seow then contested the general elections and, although losing by a narrow margin, was offered pursuant to law a parliamentary seat as a nonconstituency member. Convicted and fined in absentia on a charge of tax evasion, he was disqualified from taking his seat and has since remained outside Singapore. From September 1990, Mr. Seow has been a visiting fellow with the East Asian Legal Studies Program and the Human Rights Program at Harvard Law School.

Tucked into this book's graphic details is a revealing account of the relationship between the press or other media and the government of the People's Action Party (PAP) with Lee Kuan Yew as premier. As Seow says, "Study of the subjugation of the Singapore media is a political study of Lee Kuan Yew in action." We learn of the changing attitudes of the independent press towards Lee, and vice versa. We learn of long-term strategies to curb the dissident press, ranging from withdrawal of advertising and expulsion of journalists to the tightening and recurrent invocation of national security laws and the employment of devices to shift control of newspapers from independent private hands. Most insidious of all strategies was Lee's effort, to some extent successful, to make newspapers their own censors. We wonder with the author why the press succumbed to this range of governmental pressures with relative quiescence, particularly in view of the tradition of an independent press to which Singapore had become accustomed.

Francis Seow's analysis of Lee's growing control of the press provides a different kind of insight into a political regime that has produced remarkable economic growth and that has witnessed relatively little violence, surely when compared with the many authoritarian regimes given to brutal repression of any opposition. In such circumstances, the world tends to ignore or forget the excesses. These excesses do not summon outraged attention as do systematic torture or disappearances. But their effect on a country can be profound and destructive of many fundamental rights.

Seow's narrative illustrates the extent to which Lee's strategies succeeded in repressing the expression of critical ideas and bringing Singapore into a situation of imposed uniformity. His study vividly illustrates why nongovernmental organizations like Article XIX play so vital a role in the human rights movement, and how important it remains that the world community be alert to the perils of censorship and control of political thought as well as to violations of basic rights to personal security.

Preface

This chronicle set against a historical background opens a rare window on the print media in Singapore—on its uneasy relationship with, and its eventual subjugation by, Prime Minister Harry Lee Kuan Yew, whose People's Action Party (PAP) formed the only government of Singapore, metamorphosing from a responsible internal self-government in June 1959 into a state government with special reserve powers within the Federation of Malaysia in September 1963 and, finally, into the government of an independent and sovereign republic of Singapore on August 9, 1965.

I was originally requested by Article XIX to write an account of "the history, current laws and impact of Lee Kuan Yew's increasing restrictions on freedom of expression in Singapore," which would be of "interest to audiences within and beyond the human rights community"; but the project grew beyond expectation and took final shape as this book, a methodical survey of the prime minister's war against the Singapore media and his skirmishes and battles with the foreign media. As far as I know, no one has attempted such a study before.

I was one of those serendipitous individuals whose service to Singapore straddled two disparate administrations, culminating in the position of solicitor general of Singapore. The Attorney General's Chambers, better known as the AG's Chambers, where I spent the best years of my professional life, provided a splendid vantage point from which to watch and enjoy the protean national scene. As one who walked the inner corridors of the citadel of power, it did not require any great acuity of perception to appreciate the myriad activities on the national landscape, or their undertows. I was present in Singapore during those tumultuous years and observed from the outset my prime minister's first subtle and, as he consolidated power, increasingly strident campaign against the print media. The voice media was always government-controlled.

Singapore's PAP government has been returned to power continuously in seemingly free and fair elections for more than three decades, during most of which Harry Lee Kuan Yew has been its prime minister. On November 28, 1990, he voluntarily stepped down in favour of his wooden but personable deputy, Goh Chok Tong, in whose cabinet he is now ensconced as senior minister and over which he continues to wield considerable power and influence. In this narrative, the expression "prime minister," unless otherwise indicated, refers to Harry Lee Kuan Yew himself, the indisputable genius of all the radical changes to Singapore's media law. This chronicle tells the poignant story of how a proud and free press was manipulated and finally brought to heel by a percipient and resourceful prime minister, who shaped it into an instrument of his political will and design. Or, to borrow his more trenchant words, the press was "subordinated to the over-riding needs of Singapore . . . and to the primacy of purpose of [the PAP] government."[1]

At the advent of internal self-government in June 1959, Singapore had a raft of free and independent English- and Chinese-language, as well as vernacular, newspapers, which, save for the venerable *Straits Times*, were owned or controlled by families or groups of individuals. But all this was to undergo a fundamental transmutation under PAP rule. The strategy employed by the prime minister in his campaign against the media is a uniquely Singaporean experience. Some of his tactics may be considered ex-tremely petty and even mean. For example, the withdrawal of official advertisements from intractable newspapers by government departments and statutory corporations, the denial of press accreditation facilities, or access to press releases and official publica-tions seem particularly heinous. But when these measures failed to retard journalistic exuberance, harsher measures were applied, as in the arrest, detention, or expulsion of journalists from Singapore, their prosecution under appropriate laws, or their arbitrary incarceration under national security laws. The selective use of the infamous Preserva-tion of Public Security Ordinance and its successor—the Internal Security Act (ISA)—against perceived political foes and dissidents, amongst whom were numbered owners of newspapers, editors and journalists, inevitably cast a long, dark shadow across any dissertation on the media in Singapore. For it created an ambience of fear that criticism was construed as disloyalty and dissension as subversion. An independent media is a vital player in any democracy, whose role therein is to report on the issues of the day fairly and accurately and, subject to the laws of libel and sedition, to analyze, interpret and record with objectivity news and events so that the public can make informed judg-ment on them. A media with a will of its own, however, can be tedious if a government has constantly to court it for support and endorsement of its policies and actions.

Domestic newspapers during the days of the British raj were not subject strictly to the blue pencil of the administration. But they had to be licensed annually under the press laws. The prime minister was not slow to exploit this colonial heritage, and, when-ever or wherever expedient, quote with approval this and the other practices of the raj. The threat of suspension or nonrenewal of the license had its moments of use but was not sufficient to control the press effectively. Lee initially tried wooing the press. But the press was not always consistent in its support of him and his government, such as the times when he had to face down the strident Malay-language newspaper, *Utusan Melayu*, the uncooperative family-owned Chinese-language newspaper, the *Nanyang Siang Pau*, or the feisty English-language newspaper, the *Singapore Herald*. In the cease-less strife for political longevity, hostile newspapers, to paraphrase Napoleon, are more to be feared than a thousand bayonets.

A study of the subjugation of the Singapore media is a political study of Lee in ac-tion. He was always wary of the media, especially of the Chinese and the Malay news-papers, which, he said, "bore more careful watching than the English-language press, as they make much more emotive and powerful appeals in the mother language" and "tug at the heartstrings" of their readers.[2] But the unruly domestic media was not suddenly or violently reined in. That would have been politically gauche and very un-Lee. A mas-ter plan for the suppression of the media was devised by him and time-implemented for maximum effect at critical stages. While professing his government a democracy, he introduced a plethora of laws systematically curbing freedom of expression under different guises. Newspapers were accused of "Malay chauvinism," encouraging "permissiveness" or other "undesirable Western values," "glamourizing" communism, "fanning the flames of Chinese chauvinism over language, education and culture," or of murky conspiracies with foreign individuals, groups and governments closely accompanied by arbitrary detention of journalists, editors and owners of newspaper companies under one pretext or another, but always in the name of security and stability. As a result, the independent Chinese-language *Nanyang Siang Pau* lost not only its owners but also its unique identity, while the two English-language newspapers—the politically correct *Eastern Sun*, whose bankers were the premier communist Bank of China, and the young and brash *Singapore Herald*, whose bankers, the Chase Manhattan Bank, were then the second-largest capitalist bank in the world—met their premature demise at the hands of the prime minister, whose own hitherto enviable reputation with the international media lay sadly shattered among the ruins of those newspapers.

In January 1973, as a first major step towards the subjugation of the print media, the Printing Presses Act was repealed and reenacted with profound amendments as the Newspapers and Printing Presses Act (NPPA) 1974, ostensibly "to safeguard public interest by ensuring that undesirable foreign elements do not gain control of our newspapers and use them against the welfare of our society."[3] Completely ignoring the egregious fact that the *Straits Times* had long been associated with foreign ownership and finance, the government noisily aired its distaste of newspaper companies receiving or being financed by foreign loans or investments without its knowledge or approval. That was the pretext for the change in the law; but the real raison d'être was to compel newspaper companies to convert themselves into public companies. The creation of different classes of shares and the compulsory divestiture of the owners' share-holdings heralded the end of private ownership of newspapers. "It is undesirable to allow any person or family to have monopolistic control of any major newspaper and . . . by spreading the ownership of newspapers as wide as possible . . . a free, healthy and responsible press will gradually be institutionalized in Singapore."[4]

The law smoothed the way for management control of the newspaper companies by persons approved or nominated by the PAP government. Warned the *Straits Times* editor-in-chief, who was later eased out of his powerful position: "Whatever the Singapore journalist's dreams, he cannot forget . . . the reality that . . . the [PAP] government could put anyone into or remove him from any position in a newspaper company."[5]

In October 1981, in the Anson by-election—created by the ill-starred elevation of PAP stalwart and Lee Kuan Yew's bosom political friend, C.V. Devan Nair, to the presidency of Singapore—opposition Workers' Party lawyer, J.B. Jeyaretnam, broke the PAP's stranglehold on political power, for which Lee and the government blamed the press, thus triggering further amendments to the law and accelerating the enthralling momentum over the media. In 1982, the government decreed the restructure of ownership of the English and Chinese newspapers and forced a marriage between the rival Chinese newspapers on the highly dubious but emotive ground that the long-term viability of Chinese newspapers was threatened by more Chinese-Singaporeans turning to read English-language newspapers, as more parents were sending their children to English schools. But, if so, no one paused to ask who had created this phenomenon in the first place. The two rival Chinese dailies were reluctantly merged to become wholly owned subsidiaries of a newly constituted holding company—Singapore News and Publications Ltd. (SNPL)—under a unified management and financial structure, allowing them to pool their financial and manpower resources to achieve the economies of scale essential for viability and—it was suggested—to also raise journalistic standards.

The final drama was played out in 1984, when the *Straits Times* group and the SNPL were merged into one gigantic publishing house, Singapore Press Holdings (SPH), presided over by a former senior cabinet minister and Lee's trusted political confidante. It was the largest industrial group and sixth-largest listed company on the Singapore Stock Exchange, with a capital base of S$1.4 billion (US$660 million). The reasons for the merger were said to be, amongst other things, to "avoid the costs of a long and hard circulation struggle and duplicated capital expenditure" and to overcome a "shortage of journalists."[6]

With the domestic media now the virtual mouthpiece of the PAP government, Singaporeans inevitably began to turn to foreign publications for critical and lively news on Singapore, which led Lee to initially warn the foreign press to "report on Singapore as outsiders for outsiders"; but the battle cry underwent a subtle change in stress into "do not interfere in the domestic affairs of Singapore." Lee's hypersensitivity to criticism or adverse and negative comments on Singapore and, in particular, of his and his government's actions and policies is proverbial. Foreign publications, however, were not subject to the press laws as their importation was covered by other legislation, such as the Undesirable Publications Act, Cap. 338. It, however, was not sufficiently efficacious. Thus, in 1986, when his increasingly stern admonitions continued to fall on deaf ears, the prime minister, with a breathtaking political élan, amended the NPPA to prevent or restrain critical reportage on Singapore by foreign publications through a simple device of restricting their circulation in Singapore. The relevant minister was invested with absolute discretionary powers to gazette the restricted circulation in Singapore of any foreign publication if he should deem it to be interfering in Singapore's domestic politics, with serious advertising revenue implications for the gazetted publication. It was a devilishly cunning move.

Sensitive to international percipience to an inordinate degree, the prime minister does not believe in retaliation by banning outright a foreign publication which offends him, unlike other governments in the region. It is important to him to deny the publication the moral high ground of trumpeting to the world at large that it has been banned. Eschewing such obvious lowly tactics, Lee decided instead to propel the foreign publication to practise through its pocketbook the art of self-restraint or censorship. The expensive message was swiftly learned when, in swift succession, *Time* and *Asiaweek* magazines, the *Asian Wall Street Journal*, and the *Far Eastern Economic Review*, each fell foul of this new law. The events and incidents relating to each publication are hereafter documented in some detail.

Singapore is a major advertising centre in Asia, with over 40 agencies. It boasts one of the highest English-language newspaper and publication readerships in Asia. "A viable publishing industry is an indispensable partner in the drive to make Singapore an international printing centre."[7] In moving against the errant foreign media, the government believed it would not affect adversely its grandiose plans to make Singapore the "information and knowledge centre" of Asia. Saith the minister for communications: "The restriction on circulation of the [*Asian Wall Street*] *Journal* has no effect whatsoever on our position as a printing and publishing centre. . . . the industry grew by 6 percent last year, while the domestic exports of publications grew by a phenomenal 37 percent last year. . . . the *Journal* continues to be printed in Singapore, notwithstanding its own solemn warnings to 'any business that wants to risk locating in Singapore.' This fact speaks for itself."[8]

Under the Goh Chok Tong administration, there were indications that the foreign media relationship was on the mend. But the appearance of improved rapport between the government and the foreign media was suddenly shattered when the government released an astonishing exchange of correspondence with the London-based *Economist*, in which it accused the prestigious weekly magazine of making fun of its "old-fashioned ways" and criticized its dilatoriness in recognizing the government's right to an unedited reply to an article on Singapore. The *Economist* was gazetted under the egregious Newspaper and Printing Presses Act, and, by virtue thereof, became an "offshore newspaper" and was required to, among other things, deposit a bond of US$125,000 and appoint a local representative to accept any legal papers in any future litigation. Its circulation was capped at 7,500. All this was not calculated to win friends. In January 1994, however, curbs on the *Economist's* circulation were lifted.

Notwithstanding its sterile environs, its petty feuds with the foreign media, and its rigorous laws and regulations circumscribing foreign journalists, Lee's ministry still clings to the belief that Singapore will be the best alternative media and information centre in Asia after 1997, when Hong Kong, the salubrious perch from which the western media "with [an] ineffable air of sublime confidence" view China and the rest of Asia, is handed back to the People's Republic of China.[9] The prospects of this occurrence now appear rather clouded with several imponderables, among which is the recently announced plan of the Malaysian government to turn its capital city, Kuala Lumpur, into Asia's communication centre by luring displaced Hong Kong journalists with relaxation of its press rules and regulations, including tax laws, and the provision of other attractive amenities. To service the needs of the media, among others, Malaysia is constructing the most advanced technological multipurpose telecommunications tower and other related infrastructures, and in 1996 put their own communications satellite in space.[10] The 421-meter tower will be the third tallest in the world. In tandem with this aggressive approach, the Malaysian government is vigorously promoting the free flow of information and "more tolerance for the diversity of opinions and views across our border."[11] Competition may yet refine the rough, ugly features on the face and body-politic of Singapore authoritarianism.

It piques the interest to reflect how a sophisticated Singapore electorate could accept almost unquestioned the reasons assigned for these infringements of their fundamental freedoms. Was it due to a siege mentality so relentlessly inculcated in their minds by Lee and his government following Singapore's sudden expulsion as a constituent state from the Federation of Malaysia—alone, ill-prepared and defenceless—into the harsh world of nations? Or, was it perhaps due to the ceaseless indoctrination of an omnipresent threat of subversion of the government, allegedly by communists or chauvinistic communalists? Or, to the belief in dark conspiracies so beloved of Lee, who would conjure up from time to time unnamed countries bent on destroying Singapore, envious of its stability, wealth and prosperity? Or, was it due to some other cause? This book, it is hoped, will provide some answers.

It is universally acknowledged that Singapore is a paragon of political stability and economic accomplishments, unique in the post–World War II era among new countries in the Third World. By virtue of its dazzling multidimensional achievements and its indisputable economic strength and vitality, it is the pacemaker in Southeast Asia and a nation exemplary well beyond the region, accustomed to receive foreign emissaries from all over the world anxious to learn of the "Singapore miracle"; many Singaporean leaders, especially the peripatetic longtime former prime minister, are periodically invited by foreign governments from Kazakhstan in the west to China in the east to be commercial or economic advisers to their governments to help replicate the Singapore miracle. Singapore wields an influence far greater than its size and population. For whatever is done in Singapore is seen as important to the region and the world as worthy of study and, sometimes, emulation.

Francis T. Seow

Notes

1. See Chew Kheng Chuan, "A statement of beliefs," *Far Eastern Economic Review,* October 22, 1987.

2. *Straits Times,* November 20, 1972.

3. *Hansard,* Parliamentary debates, June 29, 1977, col. 66.

4. *Singapore: Struggle for Success.* Melbourne: Allen & Unwin, 1984.

5. Peter Lim, quoted in *Straits Times,* April 23, 1982.

6. Joint press statement by the *Straits Times* group and SNPL, July 11, 1984.

7. *Hansard,* Parliamentary debates, June 29, 1977, col. 67.

8. Cecil K. Byrd, *In Singapore—A Survey of Publishing, Printing, Bookselling, and Library Activity.* Singapore: Chopmen Enterprises, 1970.

9. *Straits Times,* October 27, 1990.

10. *Hansard,* Parliamentary debates, March 20, 1987, col. 670.

11. *Straits Times,* June 25, 1993.

Acknowledgments

I would like to record my appreciation and thanks to the J. Roderick MacArthur Foundation, the London-based international organization against censorship, for funding Article XIX, for this interesting project, and to Aryeh Neier, then Executive Director, and Kenneth Roth, Deputy Director, Human Rights Watch, New York, for nominating me as the chronicler of longtime Prime Minister Lee Kuan Yew's campaign against the Singapore mass media, leading to its final subjugation. This may be an appropriate moment to express my profound gratitude to them for their compassion, encouragement and unfailing kindness towards me ever since I came to the United States in November 1988; my thanks also go to the staff of Human Rights Watch, New York.

I would also like to record my thanks to Henry J. Steiner, the Jeremiah Smith, Jr., Professor of Law and Director of the Human Rights Program, Harvard Law School, for his foreword. In addition, I am grateful to him and to William P. Alford, Henry L. Stimson Professor of Law and Director of the East Asian Legal Studies, Harvard Law School, for a congenial academic niche from which to carry out this challenging assignment. To Professor John A. Lent of Temple University, I am doubly indebted for his interest and invaluable oversight of my manuscript.

Former president of the Republic of Singapore, C. V. Devan Nair, and erstwhile editor of *Catholic News*, Edgar D'souza, proffered helpful comments on the manuscript, while my nephew Michael Lim and his wife, Jane, provided essential research materials with commendable urgency to enable me to update my manuscript; and my dear friend, Margaret John, provided me with inspiration that sparkled in both words and deeds; no one read the draft with greater care or inquiry or came up with more ideas and suggestions than she. To all of them, and to some whose names must regretfully remain anonymous for reasons too obvious to mention, I offer my sincerest thanks. But let me hasten to add that the final work is mine, and if there are any flaws or faults, they are mine alone, for which I accept responsibility unreservedly.

At the last moment, I managed to trace the indomitable John J. Hahn—better known to Singaporeans as Jimmy Hahn, the former managing director of the *Singapore Herald*—to Vancouver; Mr. Hahn played a major but increasingly futile role in trying to thwart the relentless repression of his star-crossed newspaper by a vengeful prime minister. I was rather concerned that he might understandably not wish to be reminded of the horribly humiliating days of the *Singapore Herald* saga, but he kindly agreed to peruse the chapter on this doleful episode in Singapore's media history—and returned it with the terse remark: "accurate and well-balanced." I thank him, too. Lastly, Frances D'souza, Article XIX's Executive Director, deserves mention for her assistance relative to the assignment.

F. T. S.

1 The Bailiwick of Singapore

For freedom of Press is the freedom of the people. The two are indivisible. The freedom of the Press is the freedom of individual, and the moment the liberty of the Press is restricted, freedom vanishes.

Leslie C. Hoffman[1]

The island of Singapore is but a minute speck on the atlas of the world. Shaped like the Isle of Wight, off the southern English coast, measuring about 639 square kilometres with a heterogenous population of about 3,002,800 Chinese, Malays, Indians, and other races,[2] it would have been largely ignored by history and the world but for its geostrategic position, straddling as it does the important crossroads of Asia and Oceania. Its position makes it a natural axis of ASEAN—an acronym for the Association of Southeast Asian Nations, now comprising Brunei, Indonesia, Malaysia, Philippines, Singapore, Thailand and Vietnam.

In June 1959, the People's Action Party (PAP), under the secretary-generalship of Cambridge-educated lawyer Harry Lee Kuan Yew, successfully contested Singapore's first general election, and formed the government. In September 1963, Prime Minister Lee Kuan Yew skillfully steered Singapore through the rocky shoals of opposition from a substantial segment of the population into a political union with the Federation of Malaya to form the Federation of Malaysia. But the ill-starred union was short-lived. On August 9, 1965, Singapore was booted out of the Federation of Malaysia into the world of nations as a sovereign and independent republic to fend for itself—without any natural resources and without the traditional economic safety-net of its Malayan hinterland.

Skillfully exploiting the bogy of communism and the Malayan fear of Singapore being "another Cuba," Lee caused the arrest and detention of numerous opposition political leaders and sympathizers, the most infamous of which was then Operation Cold Store. Bereft of its leaders, the formidable yet myopic opposition political party, the *Barisan Sosialis*—Socialist Front—which had split from the PAP over the question of merger with Malaya, was outmanoeuvred by Lee, and foolishly abandoned its parliamentary coign of vantage for a constituency of the streets, and became largely discredited. It boycotted successive general elections and, in the result, Singapore became a one-party state by default with the PAP as virtual political overlord.

In a relentless drive towards self-reliance, economic viability and independence, Singapore lost much of its old-world grace and charm, and, more especially, fundamental freedoms, in the name of nation-building and national security. Whatever the frailties of the British colonial administration, when it finally departed from Singapore it handed over to the victorious PAP virtually intact a sound governmental infrastructure, which included a body of laws and the concept of colonialism and freedom. It is trite but true that one cannot really lose anything which one has never possessed nor appreciate a loss which has never been known, possessed or experienced. This is an essay on one such precious loss—the freedom of the press.

A Glimpse at History

Modern Singapore began on February 6, 1819, when the farsighted lieutenant governor of Bencoolen, Thomas Stamford Raffles, acquired it as a trading station for the Honourable East India Company, under a treaty with the Sultanate of Riau-Johor, which, on August 2, 1824, ceded it in perpetuity to the company. From Bencoolen, Sumatra, Raffles administered the affairs of Singapore with a councillor in residence at Singapore as the chief local executive officer. Major William Farquhar, later major-general, who accompanied Raffles on this historic mission, became the first resident councillor. Singapore—together with Malacca, a British colony on peninsular Malaya first colonized by the Portuguese and then the Dutch—was subordinated to Fort William in the Bengal presidency in India, but, two years later, was incorporated into the Penang presidency. In 1830, the Penang presidency was abolished, and the three settlements reverted to the Bengal jurisdiction. In 1832, Singapore became the administrative seat of the three settlements, which, in 1851, were placed under the direct supervision of the governor general and the supreme government of India.

In 1858, the Honourable East India Company was abolished. The three Straits Settlements (SS)—which were popularly referred to in brief as "the Straits"—came under the administration of the new Indian government until 1867, when they were transferred to the British Crown, which administered them until the advent of the Second World War. In 1948, Singapore was politically amputated from the SS to form a separate Crown colony of Singapore whilst the settlements of Penang and Malacca became part of the Federation of Malaya. On August 31, 1957, the Federation of Malaya gained independence with Tunku Abdul Rahman Putra al-Haj as its first prime minister.

Vignettes on Indian Press Legislation

Jesuit missionaries brought the printing press to India in 1556 "as an aid to proselytism." Books and, later, newspapers were printed and published by private ventures. Although they were in the hands of "the compatriots of the rulers," the editors were nonetheless "often extremely critical of the administrators," and published robust comments on their administration.[3]

Initially, the East India Company did not exercise any control over newspaper publications in territories under its jurisdiction. But towards the end of the 18th century with the advent of the Napoleonic Wars, Lord Wellesley, the governor general of Bengal—better known to history as the Duke of Wellington—decreed severe restrictions on the printing and publishing of newspapers and prescribed penalties for the publication of seditious and defamatory matters, and, as a wartime measure, imposed rigid press censorship. Military intelligence indicated at the time that Napoleon was in correspondence with the restive Tipu Sultan of Mysore, and Lord Wellesley was concerned to prevent news of troop movements leaking through the press. Wellesley was also opposed to the establishment of a printing press beyond the immediate vicinity of Calcutta.

On May 13, 1799, the governor general in council promulgated a set of rules whereby the names and addresses of the editors and printers or proprietors of all newspapers were to be communicated to the government; all material meant for publication was to be submitted in advance to the government for inspection; and any violation of the rules was punishable by immediate deportation to England. The chief secretary to the government was nominated as ex-officio censor of the press.

Until 1813, the press in India remained exposed to constant threats of Wellesleyan censorship, though its execution after his lordship's departure in 1805 was only confined to periodic warnings. In 1813, Lord Hastings, a man of liberal disposition, was appointed governor general of India. He was opposed to the censorship of the Indian press imposed by Wellesley, and the press situation was reviewed. On August 16, 1818, censorship regulations were replaced with a press code of conduct. Editors were expressly enjoined to refrain from

- animadversions on the measures and proceedings of the Honourable Court of Directors, or other public authorities in England connected with the Government of India; or disquisitions on political transactions of the local administration, or offensive remarks levelled at the public conduct of public and judicial officers;
- discussions having a tendency to create alarm or suspicion among the native population of any intended interference with their religious opinions or observances, and also all controversial discussions on points of religion;
- republishing from English or other newspapers anything calculated to affect British power or reputation in India; and
- publishing any report containing private scandal and personal remarks on individuals tending to excite dissension in society.

Any infraction of the rules could lead to prosecution in court or cancellation of the licence of the offender and "deportation to Europe." In abolishing censorship, Hastings was relying on the "prudence and discretion" of the editors in their observance of the code. Editors were held "personally accountable" for anything they published in violation of those rules. As before, they had to send "one copy of every newspaper, periodical or extra" published by them to the chief secretary's office.[4] Hastings's reluctance to implement censorship brought forth ample freedom of thought and expression during his tenure of office. A profusion of critical and controversial articles on the Indian administration soon upset and alarmed the authorities. The recalcitrance of the *Calcutta Journal* in publishing certain outspoken articles led to the banishment from India in 1822 of its editor, James Silk Buckingham, by the government, which also took the opportunity of reviewing the press laws.

Since there was no provision in the existing press laws for punishing a defiant editor short of banishment, Hastings sought to introduce new measures of controlling the press. He requested the approval of the court of directors of the Honourable East India Company in London, which was displeased at the abolition of censorship and which had continued unsuccessfully to have it restored; but approval was yet to arrive when, on January 9, 1823, Hastings sailed for England. After his departure, John Adams, an erstwhile member of the governor general's council, acted as governor general. When the authorities in England indicated their consent to restrict the press in India and authorized the enactment of such laws as were deemed appropriate, Adams, "an administrator of the old school," lost no time in laying down a set of stringent regulations for the press.[5] They provided for the compulsory licencing of newspapers, journals and printing establishments. Under these new laws the licence of a newspaper was liable to be cancelled if it published any objectionable material. And for the offence of publishing a newspaper without a licence, the government could impose on its proprietor a maximum fine of 400 rupees.

In July 1828, Lord William Cavendish Bentinck became governor general. Soon after his arrival in India, Bentinck directed his private secretary, Andrew Stirling, to put up a detailed report on the press in Bengal to enable him to ascertain the influence it exercised on public opinion. The Stirling report showed that, with the possible exception of Bengal, Indian society was not yet prepared to "embrace a newspaper," which was "still a luxury to them."[6] Although Bentinck did not revoke the press laws of 1823, he pursued a liberal policy which was conducive to the growth of the press in Bengal. Sir Charles Metcalfe, who succeeded Bentinck in 1835 as governor general, continued the liberal policy toward the press in India and, on September 15, 1835, abolished many of the restrictions on the freedom of the press. Its abolition opened wide the floodgates of printing and publishing activity in India; but that belongs to another story.

The Situation at the Straits

Singapore was subordinated, as noted, to the presidency of Fort William in Bengal, India. As a result of statute 3 & 4 Wm. IV c. 85, 1833, Indian legislative acts were applicable to Singapore where they could expressly or impliedly be held to do so. The earliest Indian legislation germane to our discussion is Regulation III of 1823, which was referred to locally as the "Gagging Act." The Gagging Act prohibited the establishment of printing presses without licence and restrained under certain circumstances the circulation of printed books and papers. No person could print any book or paper, or keep or use any printing press, or types, or other materials, or articles for printing, without having obtained the previous sanction and licence of the governor general in council for that purpose.

The application had to be submitted to a magistrate of the jurisdiction in which it was proposed to establish such a printing press, specifying the real and true name and profession, caste or religion, age, and place of abode of every person or persons who were, or were intended to be, the printers and publishers and the proprietors of such printing press or types or other materials or articles, and the place where such a printing press was to be established. The facts stated in the application had to be verified, on oath or on solemn affirmation, by the persons named as the printers, publishers or proprietors, or by such of them as the magistrate might think it expedient to select for that purpose. A copy of the application, together with an English translation, if applicable, was then forwarded to the governor general in council, who, after calling for any further information which might be deemed necessary, would grant or withhold the licence at his discretion. If the licence was granted, the magistrate would deliver it to the parties concerned and apprise them, both verbally and in writing, of the conditions, if any, attached to such licence. Although the governor general in council reserved to himself the full power of recalling and resuming any such licence, the licence did not have to be renewed annually.

All books and papers printed at a press duly licenced by government had to have on the first and last pages, in legible characters, in the same language and character as that in which such book or paper was printed, the name of the printer and the city, town, or place at which the book or paper might be printed, and a copy would immediately be sent to the magistrate, whose duty was to forward it to the relevant department of government.

The circulation of any particular newspaper or other printed publication of any description could be prohibited by the governor in council at any time deemed expedient, whereupon immediate notice of such prohibition must be given in the *Government Gazette* in the English, Persian and Bengali languages. Any person who knowingly and wilfully circulated, or caused to be circulated, sold, or caused to be sold, or delivered out and distributed, or in any manner caused to be distributed such prohibited papers would on first conviction be punishable by a fine not exceeding 100 rupees, or in default thereof, imprisonment without hard labour for a period not exceeding two months; and for the second, and each and every subsequent offence, to a fine not exceeding 200 rupees commutable to imprisonment without hard labour, for a period not exceeding four months.

On August 3, 1835, the governor general in council passed Act No XI of 1835 providing that a printer and publisher of any "printed periodical work whatever," which contained public news or comments on public news within the territories of the East India Company, were required to make a simple declaration before a magistrate of the settlement within which such periodical was to be published, and as often as the place of printing or publication was changed. The names of the printer and the publisher and the place of printing and of publication had to be printed legibly on it. A failure to comply with any provision of the Act was punishable on conviction by a fine of S$2,500 and by simple imprisonment for a term not exceeding two years.

Although direct censorship of the press was abolished in Bengal in 1818, the freedom granted was relative, for it was replaced by rules limiting the material that an editor might publish. Insofar as Singapore was concerned, the proofs of the paper still had to be submitted to the resident councillor for approval before publication. In this respect, the *Singapore Chronicle*, the first newspaper to be published in Singapore—which, incidentally, bore the unmistakable imprint of Dr. John Crawfurd's style and interest—enjoyed an especial advantage in that Crawfurd was also the resident councillor.

In March 1833, the Indian government agreed to exempt newspaper editors in the Straits Settlements from submitting proof-sheets for approval to the governor before publication. The then resident councillor, Samuel George Bonham—later governor of Singapore—wrote to the editor of the *Singapore Chronicle* that the Supreme Government of India, on his recommendation, had sanctioned the discontinuance of censorship of the press in Singapore, so that proof-sheets need not be sent to him any more. The editor commemorated the event with an article on the subject,[7] in which he quoted the great English jurist, Sir William Blackstone, that to subject the press to the restrictive powers of a licenser was to make all freedom of sentiment liable to the prejudice of one man, and make him the arbitrary judge of controverted points.[8]

Consequent upon the infamous Indian mutiny in June 1857, the Indian government passed a law restricting the publication of seditious literature which might inflame public opinion, and imposing strict censorship on the press throughout all Indian territories for twelve months. Insofar as the Straits Settlements were concerned, it was a meaningless law, because at the time there was no vernacular press and the Straits were so far removed from the scene of action on the Indian subcontinent. The local press attacked the law as further proof of the Indian government's lack of understanding of the Straits Settlements' special position, and the inhabitants of Singapore agitated for its withdrawal. The law was never enforced in the Straits Settlements, and, in any event, ceased in June 1858; but it contributed to resentment and apprehension against the governor and the Indian government.

In 1867, the Honourable East India Company transferred its territorial possessions, including Singapore, to the Colonial Office in London. The transfer did not affect the Indian laws and regulations applicable to Singapore. Act No XI of 1835 continued to extend to Singapore until it was repealed by the Singapore Legislative Council in 1920.

During World War I, in February 1915, Singapore witnessed its own Indian mutiny involving sepoys stationed on the island. Censorship was so rigid that no news was permitted to leave the colony for a week "on the principle, perhaps, that suppressing the news meant suppressing the mutiny," so it was said.[9] Walter Makepeace, editor of the *Singapore Free Press*, writing on this particular episode of Straits history, noted that

> freedom of speech and freedom of the press are taken so generally as a matter of right by British citizens that the slightest attempt to curb them is resented, especially when the censorate's idea of the news, food of the grown-up man, is a ragout in which the foundation is so carefully disguised that it is not recognizable as fish, flesh, fowl, nor good red herring.[10]

The *Singapore Chronicle*

Five years after Raffles's acquisition of Singapore, Francis James Bernard, one of Singapore's earliest pioneers, established and published the first newspaper in Singapore, known as the *Singapore Chronicle*.[11] Bernard was the captain of the brigantine *Ganges*, a troopship which on January 28, 1819, had escorted Sir Thomas Stamford Raffles on his historic visit to Singapore. Bernard held many public appointments, including that of acting master attendant and magistrate. He married a daughter of Lieutenant Colonel William Farquhar, the first resident councillor of Singapore. In July 1823, Bernard applied through Dr. John Crawfurd, who had replaced Farquhar as councillor in residence, to the Bengal administration for official permission to publish the *Singapore Chronicle*. Copies of the first number of the *Singapore Chronicle* dated January 1, 1824, were sent to Fort William in Bengal for clearance. It was printed at irregular intervals at the London Missionary Society Press, where Benjamin Keasberry (1811–1873) is remembered as the pioneer of printing in Singapore. For the first two years, Crawfurd edited and contributed articles to the paper. Crawfurd's term as resident councillor ended on August 14, 1826. "As long as Crawfurd edited the *Singapore Chronicle*, the 'Gagging Acts' caused no inconvenience, but, later, blank spaces showed where the censor had been at work."[12] After Crawfurd's departure, the character of the paper changed under the hands of his successor, a critic of the government. Governor Robert Fullerton was one of those who was not particularly enamoured of press freedom, and silenced his opposition by threatening to deport him. But, fortunately, the governors who succeeded Fullerton were more tolerant. On September 30, 1837, the *Singapore Chronicle* ceased publication due to keen competition from a newly established newspaper, the *Free Press*, so called to commemorate the lifting of press censorship by the administration.

The *Singapore Free Press*

The *Free Press* was started by Edward Boustead, a merchant, George Drumgold Coleman, a leading architect and first superintendent of public works, and William Napier, a lawyer, in October 1835. It began as a four-page weekly, and continued as such until 1869, when it ceased publication. But, in 1884, moved by the same idealistic spirit as the original founders of the *Free Press*—that a "second newspaper was for the good of the place, and that it should not owe its inception to the need for profit"[13]—Charles Burton Buckley, the anecdotal historian, got together thirty-two other subscribers to acquire the old *Free Press*, and recommended publication under the same masthead as a weekly, with himself as editor and contributor of papers on the history of Singapore that eventually became the basis of his celebrated *Anecdotal History of Singapore*.

The weekly became so successful that, at the beginning of 1887, Buckley, together with four other well-known Singapore pioneers, John Fraser, John Cuthbertson, David Neave and T. Shelford, financed its conversion into a daily. William Graeme St. Clair was its first editor. Walter Makepeace was engaged as a reporter and assistant editor, and the first issue of the *Singapore Free Press*, as a daily, appeared on July 16, 1887. In 1895, W. G. St. Clair and Walter Makepeace became the proprietors of the paper, and, in 1916, on the retirement of St. Clair, the paper was converted into a private limited liability company. It was later acquired by the *Straits Times* group, and became an afternoon paper with the unchallengeable claim of being the oldest newspaper established in Singapore.

The *Straits Times*

In 1845, the *Straits Times* was started, together with the *Singapore Journal of Commerce*. Its first number appeared on July 15 as a weekly paper of eight folio pages with Robin Carr Woods—who came from Bombay—as the first editor. The *Journal of Commerce*, as its name implied, was devoted to matters of mercantile interest, and occupied a section of the *Straits Times*, which became a daily in 1858. On May 1, 1900, it was turned into a private limited company and, in 1950, became a public limited company. Meanwhile, towards the end of 1931, the first *Sunday Times* appeared—and became an instant success. The *Straits Times* grew in strength. It was free and independent but establishment-oriented, and claimed to be "the largest and the most influential newspaper in Singapore and Malaya," and over the years acquired lustre as a reputable newspaper of venerable vintage. But all this was to suffer a profound sea change in the seventies and the eighties.

The *Malaya Tribune*

Late in 1913, D.C. Perreau, a regular contributor to the editorial columns of the defunct *Daily Advertiser*, conceived the idea of an English daily paper to cater for the English-educated local population, underpinned by wealthy Chinese so that there would be "no need to dread financial results."[14] He passed the idea on to the talented and much respected Dr. Lim Boon Keng, a Queen's Scholar and legislative councillor, and to a scion of a well-known Malayan family, Alexander W. Westerhout. The result: on January 1, 1914, the *Malaya Tribune* was born.[15] Its *Sunday Tribune* made its debut on May 21, 1933. It provided much-needed competition to the *Straits Times* and its family of newspapers. It was ultimately acquired by the multimillionaire cinema magnate, *Dato*[16] Loke Wan Tho. It became the "most popular newspaper in Malaya"[17] with a rising daily circulation of about 13,000, when the Pacific War suddenly intervened. It resumed publication on October 15, 1945, but, compounded especially by the ravages of war, eventually succumbed to its own internal weakness. It was, incidentally, the *Malaya Tribune* which gave Sinnathamby Rajaratnam, later Singapore's first minister for culture, his leg up in his journalistic career as a cub reporter.

The *Singapore Tiger Standard*

The *Malaya Tribune* was succeeded in turn by an English-language newspaper, the *Singapore Standard*, better known as the *Tiger Standard*, which was started by the Aw family, which also owned the Chinese-language newspaper, the *Sin Chew Jit Poh*. S. Rajaratnam moved over from the *Malaya Tribune* to join it as a feature writer with a political column, "I Write as I Please," whose provocative articles were said to upset the Singaporean and Malayan establishments. He then crossed over to the *Straits Times*, where he was employed as a lead writer. During the 1959 general election, the *Tiger Standard* came under fire from the PAP, led by S. Rajaratnam, and folded up later that same year after the PAP came into power.

The *Nanyang Siang Pau* and the *Sin Chew Jit Poh*

The *Chinese Daily Journal of Commerce*, better known as the *Nanyang Siang Pau*, and the *Sin Chew Jit Poh* were two family-owned Chinese-language dailies, whose fates are considered below. They were founded on a clan basis. The *Nanyang Siang Pau* was started in 1923 by Tan Kah Kee, a rubber baron, industrialist and philanthropist in the Chinese Hokkien community, who became the only overseas Chinese to hold ministerial rank in the government of the People's Republic of China. He started the *Nanyang Siang Pau* to essentially promote his own manufactured goods and products, business and commerce; in time it became well established as the newspaper of Chinese business circles, as it was the only paper which provided reliable daily information on the prices of rubber and other local commodities, industry and finance. In 1937, the *Nanyang Siang Pau* was acquired by a business mogul, George Lee, a younger brother of the late tycoon, educationalist and philanthropist, Lee Kong Chian, and son-in-law of the illustrious founder himself. Until they were enjoined by the PAP government to divest their controlling interest in 1977, the newspaper was owned and controlled by the moneyed Lee family.

The *Sin Chew Jit Poh*, on the other hand, was established in 1929 by the legendary Aw brothers, Aw Boon Haw and Aw Boon Par, puissant figures in the Chinese Hakka community and founders of the world-famous panacea, Tiger Balm. It underwent the same divestiture fate as its rival. Until it was publicly listed in 1977, the newspaper was owned by the wealthy Aw family.

Some Extinct Publications

There were other English-language newspapers in Singapore, most of which were short-lived for disparate reasons but the common determinant being the economic ramifications: amongst them were the *Eastern Daily Mail* (1905–1906); the *Straits Advocate* in the eighties; the *Straits Guardian*, 1856, published on Saturdays "at the Reporters' Press," the *Reporters' Advertiser*, tri-weekly, gratis; the *Shipping Gazette*, 1858, at the Commercial Press; the *Straits Intelligence*, 1883–1886; and, at about the same time, the *Singapore Herald*[18] (which is unconnected to a subsequent paper of the same name which will be discussed shortly) and, in 1868, the *Straits Produce*, "one of the first papers of satire and humour."[19]

Several vernacular newspapers were at one time or another printed and published in Singapore. In 1888, there was a Tamil paper, the *Singai Nesan,* and, in 1876, an association of locally born Indian Muslims—called *Jawi Peranakkan* or the "Straits-Born"—started a Malay weekly under that name, which "claim[ed] to be the first Malay newspaper ever published."[20]

Among the Chinese papers, the pioneer *Lat Pau* was established in 1881 by See Ewe Lay, a progeny of a well-rooted Straits Chinese family and comprador of the Hongkong and Shanghai Bank. It was the first Chinese-language daily not only in Singapore but in the whole of Southeast Asia, and derived its name from the Malay word *Selat* or "Straits." It had a circulation of about 300 copies. *Lat Pau*, or *Straits News*, ceased publication in 1932 owing to stiff competition from other Chinese newspapers.[21] Another notable Chinese paper was the *Nan Chiau Jit Pao*, which was also founded by Tan Kah Kee, together with a number of supporters, in November 1946 with a capital of S$500,000. Tan Kah Kee was a major shareholder. Like many Chinese newspapers of the period, it was robustly involved in Chinese mainland politics. It was an important left-wing organ in the immediate postwar era, and ranked as one of the three most popular Chinese newspapers in Singapore, with a daily circulation of between 12,000 and 20,000.[22] It initially supported Republic of China President Chiang Kai Shek and the *Kuomintang* but, ultimately, shifted its support to the Communist leader, Mao Zedong, during the Chinese civil war. It became the pan-Malayan organ of both Tan Kah Kee and the China Democratic League, a left-wing intellectual group critical of the wayward rule of President Chiang Kai Shek. The *Nan Chiau Jit Pao* waged a lively war of words with the pro-Kuomintang newspapers but, after the Communist Party of Malaya (CPM) launched its armed offensive against the British government in 1948, the days of the newspaper were numbered. It was closed down by the colonial government in September 1950. Eu Chooi Yip, a left-wing political activist who worked on it as a journalist, escaped the security dragnet by seeking refuge in S. Rajaratnam's house and, later, fled to Beijing, China, where he remained until 1992.

The *Utusan Melayu*, a Malay daily in Arabic and romanized Malay, was one of the longest-lived, having been established in 1911.[23] It ceased publication in 1921; but, in 1939, another paper with the same name was launched, with which we shall deal hereafter.

The *Malaysia Malayali*, a Malayalam-language newspaper, was founded in 1933, edited and managed by I.V.K. Nair, a Muar rubber plantation manager. The paper enjoyed a small but steady pan-Malayan circulation. After about 3 years, it was sold to other interests. It ceased publication on December 25, 1988. The founder-editor, I.V.K. Nair, was the father of C.V. Devan Nair, who was to become the president of Singapore. It is noteworthy that it was the first time the name "Malaysia" was used in this or in any other context.

Notes

1. Editor-in-chief, *Straits Times*, April 21, 1959.

2. 1990 Census, *Singapore Yearbook 1992*. Singapore: Ministry of Culture Publications, 1993.

3. Anant Kakba Priolkar, *The Printing Press in India: Its Beginnings and Early Development*, Bombay: Marathi Samshodhana Mandala, 1958.

4. Abu Hena Mustafa Kamal, *The Bengali Press and Literary Writing, 1818–1831*, Bangladesh: University Press Ltd., 1977.

5. Ibid.

6. Ibid.

7. C.B. Buckley, *Anecdotal History of Singapore*. 2 vols. Singapore: Fraser and Neave, 1902.

8. Quoting Sir William Blackstone in Walter Makepeace, Gilbert E. Brooke, and Roland St. J. Braddell, eds., *One Hundred Years of Singapore.*, 2 vols., London: John Murray, 1921.

9. Ibid.

10. Makepeace, Brooke, and St. J. Braddell, *One Hundred Years of Singapore*.

11. C.A. Gibson-Hill, *The Singapore Chronicle, 1824–37, JMBRAS*, vol. xxvi, pt. 1, 1953, 175 ff.

12. Makepeace, Brooke, and St. J. Braddell, *One Hundred Years of Singapore*.

13. Ibid.

14. Ibid.

15. Walter Makepeace, "Institutions and Clubs: The Press," in Makepeace, Brooke, and St. J. Braddell, *One Hundred Years of Singapore*.

16. "The Most Popular Newspaper in Malaysia" was the paper's motto.

17. A Malay title, *dato* is also spelled as *datuk*.

18. *Singapore Yearbook 1992*.

19. Makepeace, Brooke, and St. J. Braddell, *One Hundred Years of Singapore*.

20. E.W. Birch, "The Vernacular Press in the Straits," *JSBRAS*, December 1879, p. 51.

21. For a fuller discussion of *Lat Pau* and other Chinese newspapers, see Chen Mong Hock, *The Early Chinese Newspapers of Singapore, 1881–1912*. Singapore: University of Malaya Press, 1967.

22. C.F. Yong, *Tan Kah Kee, The Making of an Overseas Legend*. Singapore: Oxford University Press, 1987.

23. Makepeace, Brooke, and St. J. Braddell, *One Hundred Years of Singapore*.

2 A Handsel for the Media

•
•
•
•
•
•
•
•
•

Freedom of speech is one of the most precious assets of a democratic country.

Wee Chong Jin[1]

During the 1959 general election campaign, with his political foes in disarray, Lee Kuan Yew and his cohorts, confident of broad mass support from the radical left-wing groups, including workers and Chinese school students, threatened to visit fire and brimstone not only on the political opposition but on every real and imagined opponent—the British colonialists, the expatriates, large commercial interests, "cine-moguls," the English-educated and many, many more—when his party took over power from the British colonial government. Very early on in the election campaign, perceiving the English-language press as inimical to their electoral prospects, Lee and his colleagues zeroed in on it, accusing it of conducting "vicious propaganda against the PAP."

On April 15, 1959, PAP speakers charged the English-language press at a lunch-time downtown rally[2] with misleading the English-speaking community by distorting the news, thus forcing the PAP to journey downtown to put their views directly to them, as the only information they had about the PAP was from the government-owned radio and the English press—the *Straits Times* and the *Singapore Standard*. "If you see what you read in the papers you will think that we are extremists and wild men," Lee charged. And, pointing to the other PAP speakers, he exclaimed, "See for yourselves. Are we wild men? Or, are those who say we are, mad men?" He said the assertion that the PAP leaders were wild men was an example of the "vicious propaganda conducted by the English press."

Citing the *Straits Times* news report of a police refusal to allow the PAP to hold its rally under the popular Empress Place "apple tree" as another example of press partisanship in the election campaign, he drew attention to its negative bold-typed heading, "PAP Told: No Apple Tree Rally,"[3] and complained that it was only in the last paragraph that a statement, in small type, said that the rally would be held across the river between Fullerton Building and Whiteaways. Lee alleged the composition was designed to mislead the people by giving the impression the PAP rally was cancelled. But the *Straits Times* headlined the rally of the Singapore People's Alliance (SPA): "SPA to Hold Rally Today." It was positive. It was clear. It showed, Lee said, that the meeting was on. Save for S. Rajaratnam, the former journalist, Lee, more than any politician in Singapore—then or now—appreciated the power and the influence of the written word. In this regard, Rajaratnam was a major contributing influence. Lee's irritability and impatience with the press may be seen in this early incident in which he was quick to perceive negative media reports on him and his PAP activities.

Lee told the largely English-educated crowd that he would like to make the Fullerton Building car park a regular rendezvous for PAP campaign rallies for them to hear the PAP views, because they would not find all of what the PAP speakers had said published in the *Straits Times*—the same kind of complaint which opposition political parties were later to make against him and his PAP government with much greater justification. PAP leader Yong Nyuk Lin[4] said: "The PAP believe in the freedom of the press which means objective reporting and the accurate dissemination of news. But what do we find in the *Straits Times*? When the SPA or the Liberal Socialists hold a rally and there are 600 people present they say 4,000 but, when thousands attend a PAP rally, they do not give the real figures."

Another PAP leader, Dr. Toh Chin Chye,[5] asserted there were only two important propaganda organizations to inform the English-educated of the political situation in the country—the radio and the English-language press. The English-educated did not attend mass election rallies, and all that they knew of the political situation was from what they had read in the morning papers. But these newspapers were not controlled by the workers but by the capitalists, who "only print what they want you to read to catch your support," and whenever the PAP put out public statements, or whenever PAP members made speeches, the "English press did not print them in full . . . They removed the commas, and put sub-editorial headlines so that you get a wrong impression of our policy statements." Paradoxically, these very complaints against the English-language media—which had so irked Lee and his PAP comrades—were to become a familiar refrain sung subsequently, however, by opposition candidates. The significant difference was that the *Straits Times* and the other newspapers in those days at least gave more exposure and coverage to PAP activities and statements than they are now allowed to give to the political opposition.[6]

Concerned at the PAP's attack on the media, which was specially focused on itself, the *Straits Times*, in a long editorial captioned "Threat to Freedom"—reproduced here in full not only for its prescient quality but for its topicality—declared:

Not for a hundred years has the freedom of the press in Singapore been in such danger as it is today. *If the People's Action Party is in a position to form a government, one of its first concerns will be to bring the newspapers to heel.* This is the only construction that can be placed on the statements of PAP leaders, including its chairman [Dr. Toh Chin Chye] and secretary general [Lee Kuan Yew]. If this conclusion is wrong, it is easy for PAP to say so. Its leaders need only affirm their respect for freedom of the press, their respect for the right to criticize, their respect indeed for the rights of all political opposition. They must not, however, qualify their affirmation with "buts." *Like the individual, the press is either free or not free.* It can comment and criticize, subject to the laws of defamation and libel, or it has no soul to call its own.

A censored press remains bad even when it produces good things. A free press remains good even when it produces bad things . . . a eunuch remains a mutilated being even if he possesses a fine voice. A great Socialist said that—Karl Marx. It may be that PAP's spokesmen do not mean all they say, or that they intend to do all that they threaten. They have said some quite monstrous things, not only about the press, and are likely to go on saying them, partly no doubt because they believe threats sometimes work but also because a strong section of their following expect it of them. There is occasionally a conscious "bold bad boy" pose about PAP leaders, as noticeable as their undress uniform of tieless white shirt and trousers. It would be foolish and reckless, however, not to pay PAP's leaders the compliment of believing that their threats, particularly against the press, are meant to be taken seriously.

It is ominous when the press is told, in an orgy of false witness by party leaders, that PAP believes in "objective reporting and the accurate dissemination of news." This has been the classic introduction to the repression of the press everywhere the press is in chains. *Dictatorships, whether of the Left or the Right, begin their suppression of the truth by confining the press to what they call "the accurate dissemination of news." The papers then disseminate news as the party and its leaders instruct, or the press does not publish at all.* It may seem fantastic that such a threat to freedom and liberty should confront Singapore in this day and age of political advance, but *PAP's leaders have made it quite clear that they do not understand the fundamental principles of the freedom of the press. It follows that they do not understand the first principles of the liberty of the people.*

Opposition to PAP policy, PAP spokesmen have said, entails the risk of becoming "a political casualty." There has been no definition yet of "a political casualty," the extent of the injury and the manner of inflicting it has been left to the imagination. But we must assume that this phrase introduces a new PAP conception of a government's powers, and of its right to act against those who do not share its views and who refuse to keep their silence. What other interpretation is there of this sort of threat? There is significance also of Dr. Toh's apparent conviction that the only newspapers which can be trusted are those which are in the hands of the workers. *Unmistakably PAP is hostile to a free press, to newspapers it cannot control.* The publications of the International Press Institute (Zurich) are replete with warning of the dangers to liberty which such a situation can quickly produce. *For the freedom of the press is the freedom of the people. The two are indivisible. The freedom of the press is the freedom of the individual, and the moment the liberty of the press is restricted, freedom vanishes.*[7] [Author's emphases]

On April 22, 1959, the next day, Rajaratnam led a headlong charge at the English press, singling out the *Singapore Standard* as "less intelligent [than the *Straits Times*] and [which] sometimes indulged in mental foolery."[8] He was followed by other PAP speakers. Kenneth M. Byrne[9] complained that "truth was all the time being tampered with," referring specifically to a news report in the *Singapore Standard* on "a split in the PAP and that Ong Eng Guan[10] wanted to resign," which he stated was not true, but which the *Singapore Standard* insisted it was. "Can you trust people like that?" he declared. Less than a year later, Ong Eng Guan was expelled from the PAP, and Kenneth Byrne ultimately was to find himself side-lined as High Commissioner to New Zealand for the greater part of his political life. He died a sorely disappointed man. Meanwhile, Ong Eng Guan, oblivious of what fate his comrade Lee Kuan Yew had in store for him, blithely pitched in, condemning the "British colonial press," which had, he said, attacked the PAP for the last four years, while he, as mayor, could only return the compliment "in a small and meagre way" by withholding official City Council advertisements in the *Straits Times*.[11]

On April 30, 1959, Rajaratnam widened the attack on the English-language press to take in the *Straits Times*: "Unlike the tenderfoots of the *Singapore Standard*, the veterans who run and control the *Straits Times* are very intelligent and clever people who have more political acumen. Like the *Singapore Standard*, the *Straits Times* too is very interested in the subject of the freedom of the press."[12]

Quoting passages from the *Straits Times* editorial "Threat to Freedom" and its reference to a statement by Karl Marx, he said: "It is on this point that the *Straits Times* differs from the *Singapore Standard*, which would have found it difficult to quote Karl Marx. It would have dismissed him as a lousy communist. But the *Straits Times*, when it suits its purpose, is prepared to call in Karl Marx, a dyed-in-the-wool communist."

Questioning the *Straits Times* concept of freedom of the press, Rajaratnam insinuated that it was necessary to find out who controlled the *Straits Times*. Contrary to its claim that thousands of people in Malaya owned it, Rajaratnam argued, the truth was the ordinary shareholders "own the *Straits Times* just as you own Fullerton Building."[13] Ordinary shareholders had no voting rights, no control over the policy of the company by resolutions at general meetings or by electing directors. They only had the right to receive dividends as and when the company chose to give them. A citizen of Singapore could at least vote out the government he did not want every five years. But the *Straits Times* shareholders could not remove the directors because there were two types of shares—ordinary and management. The 21,600 management shares were owned by people in England and a few companies in Singapore, he alleged.

Conceding that he was not fully acquainted with the facts, he nevertheless proceeded to name four persons who "really controlled the *Straits Times*. . . . They represent powerful British interests." For instance, the Hongkong and Shanghai Bank Corporation had "extensive interests in the *Straits Times*," which was in turn closely connected with Fraser and Neave Ltd., Raffles Hotel, Malayan Breweries Ltd., Metal Box Ltd., United Engineers Ltd. and the Singapore Cold Storage Ltd.—all of which were British vested interests, and considered "blue-chip." By controlling the management shares, between them they controlled S$5 million worth of property.

All the management shares were held by European directors who controlled the economy of the island in this way, except for the Singapore-based local bank, Overseas-Chinese Banking Corporation, whose subsidiary owned 490 management shares of the *Straits Times*. "On the whole, it was far easier for a local man to enter the gates of heaven than for him to become a director of the *Straits Times*," Rajaratnam added.

Now that he had exposed "the tie-up between the directors of the *Straits Times* and the other British firms," he said, the people could understand the kind of policy the *Straits Times* followed. The *Straits Times* had British economic interests backing it. These people wanted to make as much money as they could while they could. So, they thought, they could use an influential newspaper—a well-run newspaper like the *Straits Times*—to get the English-educated to act as auxiliaries for their interests, to fight their battle. But the *Straits Times* had lost this battle and were now preparing to move across the causeway. The *Straits Times* had scoffed at the PAP leaders as "wild, bad boys" because they were dressed like ordinary people. It only supported those who wore neckties, top hats and morning coats. "Don't be fooled by the *Straits Times*," he said. "When they talk about the freedom of the press, they don't mean freedom for you or me."

Answering Rajaratnam's tirade in an editorial, "Fancy and Fact," *Straits Times* editor-in-chief Leslie Hoffman said:

> A brief flash of honesty illuminated the lunchtime attack yesterday on the *Straits Times* by Mr. S. Rajaratnam, a PAP candidate and until the beginning of this month, a senior employee of the paper he was trying to besmirch. "I am not fully acquainted with the facts," said Mr. Rajaratnam. Yet he gave his ignorance full rein. It was quite a performance by an

imaginative mind released at last from the discipline of newspaper work. Mr. Rajaratnam drew a sinister picture of four directors of the *Straits Times* trust, interlocked with vested British interests, playing old hob with the true interests of Singapore. He dragged in the Hongkong and Shanghai Bank and "its extensive interests in the *Straits Times.*" The Hongkong and Shanghai Bank owns not a dollar's worth of the *Straits Times*, and never has. No company, in or out of Singapore, vested or unvested, exerts the slightest influence over the *Straits Times*.

The trust company of which Mr. Rajaratnam made mysterious play was formed, as other newspaper trust companies have been, to ensure that control of the paper shall not pass out of the hands of the journalists who edit and produce it. Mr. Rajaratnam knows that the *Straits Times* is controlled, edited and produced by the Malayan-born editors and executives with whom he worked, and who gave him his orders. If in the course of his four years with the *Straits Times* there had been a single instance of their authority being circumscribed by the directors, or of influence being brought to bear by anyone else, he would have known it, and he would have told of it. That is the complete answer to a flight of imagination of which, as a politician, he may be proud although it shames what may be left of the journalist.[14]

Dismissing the *Singapore Standard* as "journalistic trivia," Lee and his eager legions trained their heavy artillery on the *Straits Times*, which had disapproved of their exuberant harangues and threats of dire consequences against the press for allegedly partisan coverage of the election campaign. Notwithstanding the PAP's naked hostility, the *Straits Times* continued to give regular and ample publicity to it and the other political parties in the campaign.[15]

One of the main PAP platforms in the general election was independence for Singapore through merger with Malaya because, according to Lee: "In the context of 20th century Southeast Asian politics, island nations are political jokes."[16] Given the prevailing political atmosphere, the opposition, however, disagreed, assailing merger with Malaya. It was a dig at former chief minister David Marshall, in company with others, who had advocated complete independence. The *Straits Times*, expressing its own reservations on the issue of merger, condemned the PAP for menacing the press and the fundamental freedoms of free speech and expression. An angry Lee responded by threatening newspapers and newsmen in general, and picking out the *Straits Times* in particular, with arrest and detention for alleged subversion if they tried to "sour or strain" relations between Singapore and Malaya: "Any editor, leader-writer, sub-editor or reporter that goes along this line will be taken in under the PPSO [Preservation of Public Security Ordinance].[17] We shall put him in and keep him in."[18] Hoffman replied the next day:

The PAP has an infinite capacity for discovering sinister plots in the *Straits Times*. . . . It is no new experience for the *Straits Times* to be the object of the PAP's angry and vengeful regard. Yesterday, however, Mr. Lee shed new light on its intentions towards any newspaper it happens to dislike. A PAP government would like to "take in" under the Preservation of Public Security Ordinance "any editor, leader writer, sub-editor, or reporter" who, in its view, tried to "sour or strain" relations between the Federation and Singapore. The offence, said Mr. Lee, would be "subversion." This bears no relation to the argument with which Mr. Lee sought to explain in the Assembly his party's sudden regard for the Preservation of Public Security Ordinance. His justification then was that "as long as Emergency laws were necessary to security in the Federation," so long would they be necessary for Singapore. The island, he said, could not be turned into a rest camp for the Malayan Communist Party. It is a far cry from the M.C.P. to the *Straits Times*. *But the danger to freedom of the press in Singapore is very near, and very real.*[19] [Author's emphasis]

Five Singapore and Malayan newspapers protested to the Commonwealth Press Union that the PPSO was specifically directed against communist subversion.[20] Alarmed at Lee's naked threats against it, Hoffman essayed robustly and repeatedly to persuade him to the view that the question of subversion did not arise when a newspaper did its duty to report all sides of an election campaign. Lee's threats against the media, which were specifically focussed on the *Straits Times* and its "stooges," engendered a lively exchange of viewpoints in the letters column of that newspaper. British author-journalist Vernon Bartlett, writing as a columnist for the *Straits Times*, noted: "Mr. Lee Kuan Yew's attitude to press criticism is sinister."[21] In another editorial, "Think again Mr. Lee," emblazoned in bold types on its front page, Hoffman declared:

[N]ot since the Japanese conquered this island in February, 1942, has the press of Singapore faced such a grave threat as it does today. . . .

BUT MR. LEE PREFERS TO USE THE PRESERVATION OF PUBLIC SECURITY ORDINANCE INSTEAD OF THE SEDITION ORDINANCE.

A strange choice for a man who once opposed this same Preservation of Public Security Ordinance in these words: "What he [the Chief Minister] is seeking to do in the name of democracy is to curtail a fundamental liberty, and the most fundamental of them all—freedom from arrest and punishment without having violated a specific provision of the law and being convicted for it."

AND AGAIN:

"If it is not totalitarian to arrest a man and detain him when you cannot charge him with any offence against any written law—if that is not what we have always cried out against in Fascist states—then what is it?"

WHAT INDEED?

Mr. Lee cannot have his cake and eat it. He must choose between democracy and totalitarianism. And his supporters.

His supporters, like Mr. S. Rajaratnam, a former president of the Singapore Union of Journalists and a former member of the staff of the *Straits Times*.

Mr. Rajaratnam, writing in October 1955, in the *Singapore Journalist*, organ of the S.U.J. on "The Press and Mr. Speaker" had this to say:

"The Press is fair game for touchy politicians. In recent months the local press has been accused of wilful distortions of weighty and lengthy pronouncements by gentlemen who are struck by the fact that they do not read as well in print as they sound.

Believing as we do in free speech we think that politicians are perfectly entitled to air their views on whether a newspaper or a journalist has done justice to their speeches.

But it is a different matter when differences of opinion as to sub-editing could result in a newspaper or a journalist being denied facilities which were normally obtained in a free country.

It is to be hoped that when they (the Assemblymen) cry 'merdeka'[22] (with or without a clenched fist) they mean also 'merdeka' for the Press and Pressmen who have no objection to their ears being boxed.

All they ask is that they be allowed to carry on their pleasant and unpleasant duties of reporting and commenting with the greatest possible freedom.

There will not be that feeling of freedom if a newspaperman feels that he can be kept out of the Assembly by the Speaker whose decision cannot be questioned."

AND MR. RAJARATNAM SHOULD AGREE THAT NEWSPAPERMEN WILL NOT HAVE "THAT FEELING OF FREEDOM" IF THEY ARE DETAINED IN PRISON BY A GOVERNMENT WHOSE DECISION CANNOT BE QUESTIONED.

However that may be, Mr. Lee and Mr. Rajaratnam should know their newspapermen better.

Threats will not prevent a good newspaperman from publishing a story which he considers should be published or from commenting on an issue which is vital to the common good.

The *Straits Times* will continue to publish the news and honest opinion, whatever the consequences—even if the Preservation of Public Security Ordinance is invoked against individual newspapermen.

Mr. Lee and his comrades should think again.[23]

Realizing that he might have gone too far, Lee wrote a letter to the editor qualifying his threat to lock up only those newspapermen who worked on papers "owned and controlled by foreigners or foreign interests":

We of the PAP believe just as zealously in the freedom of the Press. If locally owned newspapers criticize us we know that their criticism, however wrong or right, is *bona fide* criticism because they must stay and take the consequences of any foolish policies or causes they may have advocated.

Not so the birds of passage who run the *Straits Times*. They have run to the Federation, from whose safety they boldly proclaim they will die for the freedom of Singapore.[24] [Author's emphasis]

Hoffman rejoined in another spirited front-page editorial, "Bird of Passage, Mr. Lee? I Stay":

It is about time Mr. Lee learned that others who do not subscribe to his ideologies can also be just as loyal to Singapore and to the Federation [of Malaya].

And if Mr. Lee considers it disloyal to move the headquarters of a newspaper which serves the whole of Malaya and Singapore to Kuala Lumpur, then I say his talk of merger with the Federation is MOCKERY, HYPOCRISY and UNTRUTH.

The *Straits Times* is a Malayan newspaper and if Mr Lee considers that a Malayan newspaper published in Kuala Lumpur constitutes the foreign press, then he should stop blathering about what he will do with editors who "sour up and strain relations" between the Federation and Singapore and say outright that he will ban Malayan newspapers from circulating in Singapore.

THE STRAITS TIMES INTENDS TO CIRCULATE IN SINGAPORE UNLESS IT IS PREVENTED FROM SO DOING.

And Mr. Lee should remember when he threatens—as he did last Wednesday—to deal with a publisher or editor "if he is a stooge of the white man" he is treading on very dangerous ground indeed.

Among his closest colleagues are two men, Mr. S. RAJARATNAM and Mr. K.C. LEE, who earned their living on the *Straits Times* for four years and two years respectively, who came uninvited to this newspaper to seek employment and who were given jobs on their qualifications as newspapermen and nothing else.

Neither of these gentlemen considered he was a stooge of the white man, as Mr. Lee so sonorously describes.

Nor were they considered stooges by their colleagues.

BUT IF THAT WORD IS FLYING AROUND, IT COULD WELL BE APPLIED TO THEM. And I would be the last person to use it on two colleagues whom I still regard as professionals in their field.

Mr. Lee's bully-boy tactics do him little credit.

HE SHOULD REALISE BY NOW THAT HE HAS TALKED TOO MUCH AND SHOULD HAND OVER THE MICROPHONE TO SOMEONE ELSE.[25]

Seeing that he could make little headway with Lee in Singapore, Hoffman took his crusade for freedom of the press to international assemblies and Commonwealth forums. Referring to the attack on the *Straits Times*, the London *Daily Express* noted "a blow at a newspaper in Asia is indirectly a blow at freedom everywhere."[26] The Australian Committee of the International Press Institute (IPI) observed:

> The ugly threat of Mr. Lee Kuan Yew to newspapermen in Singapore, and particularly to the *Straits Times*, is of grave consequence to Australia and to supporters of freedom everywhere. . . . Many politicians in free countries, sensitive to exposure of their weaknesses and failings by the press, thirst for the very powers which Mr. Lee Kuan Yew threatened to employ in Singapore. Such threats are a menace not only to newspapers and newspapermen everywhere but also to the already dwindling liberties of all free men.[27]

The IPI sent Armand Gaspard, as an observer, to Singapore to report on the threat to freedom of the press. But by the time he arrived there the People's Action Party was already firmly in the saddle of government. During his 18-day stay in Singapore, he met with the minister for culture, S. Rajaratnam, "all leading editors and foreign correspondents, diplomats, professors and trade union leaders." The talks were described as "friendly and informative" and the general tone of the discussions "optimistic."[28]

Meanwhile, at a University of Malaya forum, former chief minister and chairman of the opposition Workers' Party David Saul Marshall told a packed audience:

> The use of the Preservation of Public Security Ordinance against a newspaper would lead to the end of democratic government. At first this pronouncement of the secretary general of the PAP [Lee Kuan Yew] seemed an act of election madness, but we have now had it repeated and suggested that it is an issue in the election. What seemed at first as an act of election madness must now be diagnosed as the disease of infantile dictatorship—and this from a party that claims to be the only socialist party in Singapore.[29]

About a decade later, Lee used the provisions of the Internal Security Act—which had replaced the Preservation of Public Security Ordinance—against owners, editors and journalists of the *Nanyang Siang Pau* and other newspapers.

To return to the University of Malaya forum. PAP economist, Dr. Goh Keng Swee,[30] assured the forum that "the PAP believed very much in press freedom," but added: "In every independent country a foreign-owned daily newspaper has to be subject to certain limitations."

On May 28, 1959, the *Straits Times*, in another long editorial, concluded: "The freedom of the Press is no more and no less than the freedom of the people. This freedom now stands in peril in Singapore." Hoffman stoutly declared that Lee's threats would never prevent the press from doing its duty, and that the *Straits Times* would continue to publish honest news whatever the consequences. But, nonetheless, as a precautionary measure, the *Straits Times* shifted its headquarters to Kuala Lumpur and, as soon as the

PAP came into power, Hoffman also prudently betook himself there, from where he carried out his editorial duties for the rest of his working life. It contributed tangentially to the birth of the Malaysian edition of the *Straits Times*, bringing in its wake an amendment to the Printing Presses Ordinance prohibiting the sale and circulation in Singapore of Malayan (later Malaysian) newspapers.

In the meantime, the hard facts of economics decreed a modus vivendi be reached between the *Straits Times* group and the new PAP government. As author T.J.S. George pertinently observed: "The *Straits Times*, deciding that discretion generated the best re- turn on investment, bent like a bamboo to the wind from City Hall. Lee had made his first kill."[31] The victim, however, was by no means dead, only severely traumatized; but, before Lee could press his advantage home, he was distracted by the serious political shenanigans of radical left-wing elements within his own political party.

When the People's Action Party first took office in June 1959, the English-language newspapers published and in circulation in Singapore were the *Straits Times* and its Sun- day edition the *Sunday Times*, the *Singapore Free Press* and the *Sunday Mail*, the *Singapore Standard* and its Sunday edition (both of which ceased publication during the year).

The main vernacular language newspapers in circulation then were three Chinese newspapers, the *Nanyang Siang Pau* and the *Sin Chew Jit Poh* and their respective Sun- day editions, and the *Nanfang Evening Post;* the *Tamil Murasu*, a Tamil-language daily, which began as the organ of the Tamil Reform Association; and the *Kerala Bandhu*, a Malayalam-language daily.

There were also political party organs or journals, among which were the *Petir*, pub- lished fortnightly in Chinese and monthly in Malay, English and Tamil by the People's Action Party; the *People*, published monthly in Chinese, Malay, English and Tamil by the just-defeated Singapore People's Alliance; and the *Voice of the People*, published monthly in the Malay and the Chinese languages by the left-wing *Partai Rakyat*.

Press Legislation

It may be convenient here to pick up the threads on press legislation, prior to the PAP's assumption of political stewardship of Singapore. On October 27, 1919, the Legislative Council of the Straits Settlements passed the Printing Presses Ordinance, which re- pealed the Indian Act No XI of 1835, and enacted provisions to regulate the keeping of printing presses and the printing of documents. On March 1, 1920, the Printing Presses Ordinance became law.

"Newspaper" was defined as "any sheet of paper printed or published periodically in the Colony which contains public news or comments on public news." A licence to operate a printing press was required from the Colonial Secretary, who could withdraw it either per- manently or for such period as he thought fit. The printer and the publisher of any news- paper printed or published within Singapore must declare the names of the proprietors and of any changes in the proprietorship in the stipulated form. On May 12, 1930, the ordinance was amended to provide for the expiration of the licence at the end of each cal- endar year, as "the system of issuing a perpetual licence was considered unsatisfactory."[32]

In 1939, with war clouds darkening the Pacific horizon, the colonial government felt "a stricter scrutiny of and control over the activities of newspapers" was necessary. The ordi- nance was amended to enlarge the meaning of "newspaper" to include "any publication containing news, intelligence, reports of occurrences, or any remarks, observations or comments, in relation to such news, intelligence or occurrences, or to any other matter of public interest, printed in any language and published in the Colony for sale or free distribution at regular or irregular intervals, but does not include any publication published by or for the government." The definition of "proprietor" of any newspaper was also amended and, more importantly, a newspaper publishing licence was required, in addition to a printing press permit.[33]

No person could print or publish or assist in the printing or publishing of any newspaper in the Colony, unless the proprietor of such a newspaper had previously obtained a permit in writing under the hand of the Colonial Secretary authorising the printing and publication thereof. The permit was granted at the discretion of the Colonial Secretary who could refuse or revoke, or grant subject to conditions to be endorsed thereon. The permit or licence had to be renewed annually.[34] A refusal was subject to an appeal to the Governor in Council. The PAP inherited the Printing Presses Ordinance when on June 3, 1959, it assumed the reins of government.

Shortly afterwards, the PAP government introduced its first of many amendments to the ordinance. The amendment empowered the government to regulate the printing and publication of newspapers in Singapore, and the sale and circulation in Singapore of newspapers printed in Malaya. A proprietor of such newspapers was required to obtain a permit annually before he could lawfully distribute them. Malayan press law had similar provisions regulating the sale and distribution in Malaya of newspapers printed in Singapore. Newspapers which were being or had been brought into Singapore for the purpose of publication, sale or distribution in contravention of the ordinance or any condition imposed in respect of any permit were liable to seizure and detention.

During the debate in both the Singapore and Malayan legislatures, the *Straits Times* editorialized:

> It is plain that if the press were completely free, the matter of its freedom would not have to be discussed. It is no less plain that if the press were completely controlled, the manner of this control could not be debated. . . .
>
> The position today is that no newspaper can be printed and published without government permission. It needs a second permit for its sale in the other territory. These permits have to be renewed annually. They can be refused without reason being given, they can be withdrawn without notice, the courts have no jurisdiction and the newspaper no redress. The press is not free.
>
> It may be asked why the press should claim a greater freedom than the individual whose fundamental freedoms are restricted by legislation which permits detention without trial. The answer is simple, and it should be convincing. If a newspaper is subversive, if its editors are seditious, if the press stirs up communal strife—the activities for which personal freedom can be lost—the evidence is there in black and white. Newspapers cannot commit their crimes in secret. The printed word is never too terrified to testify.[35]

In moving the amendment, the minister for home affairs, Ong Pang Boon, was careful to assure an anxious media that the law did not threaten the freedom of the press: "The government, as a democratic government, will respect and maintain the freedom of the press."[36] The Printing Presses Act, Cap. 258,[37] was subsequently repealed, and re-enacted with amendments, as the Newspaper and Printing Presses Act, Act 12 of 1974, the passage of which marked a watershed in the uneasy relationship between Prime Minister Harry Lee Kuan Yew and the media. The Newspaper and Printing Presses Act (NPPA), together with its amendments, is discussed in the following chapters.

Notes

1. Chief Justice of Singapore in *Attorney General v Pang Cheng Lian & ors.*, 1 *Malayan Law Journal* 69, 74.
2. *Straits Times*, April 16, 1959.
3. A popular election rally turf.
4. Later minister for education.
5. Later deputy prime minister.
6. See also C.M. Turnbull, *Dateline Singapore: 150 Years of the Straits Times.* Singapore: Singapore Press Holdings, 1995.
7. *Straits Times*, April 21, 1959.
8. *Straits Times*, April 23, 1959.
9. Later minister for labour and law.
10. First and last mayor of Singapore, and short-lived minister for national development.
11. *Straits Times,* April 23, 1959.
12. *Straits Times*, April 30, 1959.
13. A government building housing the General Post Office and other government offices.
14. *Straits Times,* April 30, 1959. See also Turnbull's *Dateline Singapore: 150 years of the Straits Times.*
15. Letters, "Man-in-the-Street, Attacks on the Press unjustified; You can't help laughing," *Straits Times,* April 2, 1959. See also Turnbull, *Dateline Singapore: 150 years of the Straits Times.*
16. *Hansard,* Legislative Assembly debates, March 5, 1957, col. 1471.
17. The Preservation of Public Security Ordinance (PPSO) was replaced by the Internal Security Act in 1963, after Singapore merged with Malaya to form the Federation of Malaysia.
18. *Straits Times*, May 19, 1959.
19. Ibid.
20. John C. Taylor, "Lee Kuan Yew: His Rise to Power 1950–1968," unpublished M.A. thesis, San Diego State University, 1976.
21. T.J.S. George, *Lee Kuan Yew's Singapore.* London: Andre Deutsch, 1973.
22. A Malay rallying cry, meaning "freedom.'"
23. *Straits Times*, May 20, 1959.
24. *Straits Times*, May 22, 1959.
25. Ibid.
26. *Straits Times*, May 28, 1959.
27. Ibid.
28. *Straits Times*, May 27, 1959.
29. *Straits Times,* May 18, 1959.
30. Later minister of finance, etc.
31. George, *Lee Kuan Yew's Singapore*, 146.
32. Printing Presses (Amendment) Ordinance, 1930.
33. Ibid., section 2.
34. Ibid., section 6A (1), (2), and (3).
35. *Straits Times*, December 16, 1960.
36. *Hansard*, Parliamentary debates, January 14, 1960, cols. 108–110.
37. Statutes of Singapore, 1970 edition.

3 The Techniques of
: Repression: A Lesson
: Well Learned
·
·
·
·
·
·
·

Like the individual, the press is either free or not free. It can comment and criti-
cize, subject to the laws of defamation and libel, or it has no soul to call its own.

Leslie C. Hoffman[1]

Once, in an expansive mood, the prime minister proudly revealed to his audience that he had read the *Selected Works of Mao Tse-Tung,* and he discoursed on the importance of the Great Helmsman's dictum: "Always at any one time, define who is people, who is enemy, [who] will vary from time to time." Guided by that wisdom, Lee disclosed he was able to define pockets of perceived resistance to him and his government in the configuration of opposition politicians and dissidents, professionals, student activists, trade unionists and workers, among others—and had taken them on, one foe at a time. As his perception and skills sharpened, he had made use of one enemy to neutralize or eliminate another to achieve his political endgame. As he so volubly explained, he had made use of the communalists and the communists to fight the British colonialists and, later, the communalists to fight the communists:

> If you start fighting three chaps at one time you are likely to get mixed up. And three people going for you at the same time may be unpleasant business. . . . There are several foes; but to succeed, we fight only one. Don't fight them all: you will complicate things; it makes it difficult. We . . . decide after we have done all our calculations which is more dangerous to our survival and we fight that one foe and mobilise all resources to down that one.[2]

As will be seen, Lee has applied Mao's axiom with singular success in the context of Singapore's national politics. This essay deals with the subjugation of one perceived antagonist, the print media.

An Interlude

Because of dangerous rumblings of discontent within his political party, Lee had perforce to lower his sight on the media, and leave them momentarily in peace, while he sought to put his own party in order. Wherefore, it was necessary for him to tread his wary way through the uncertain political mire. Suppressing his instinctive distrust of the fickle media, he began to assume a more judicious posture, and strove to regain their goodwill and support in the inescapable forthcoming internecine intraparty political struggle, the campaign for merger with Malaya, and later for the laudable concept of a "Malaysian Malaysia"—but, as the events ultimately unfolded, especially when Singapore was suddenly thrust out of Malaysia to fend for itself as an independent and sovereign nation. Beleaguered, Lee needed all the support and goodwill of as many friends as he could muster from within and without the PAP.

Well aware of the fragility of his power, Lee's chiding of the wayward press was more muted than the early, heady days of 1959:

> In the past my colleagues and I have had occasion to state in no uncertain terms what we would have to do to expatriates who meddle in local politics, to colonial-owned newspapers and the expatriate newspapermen employed on the local paper. They took heed of our views. But they seemed to have found a new way of meddling with local politics by publishing tendentious and sometimes completely distorted reports of speeches, making mischief all round. We trust these misreportings so far were not deliberate. If they persist we shall have to revise our views.[3]

The inevitable fratricidal political combat was preceded by the expulsion of Ong Eng Guan, the minister for national development, and his supporters from the party. The party had barely recovered from this political avulsion when it split again to form the opposition *Barisan Sosialis*—Socialist Front—a motley collection of radical leftist elements within the PAP. It was a major political wound, and the resultant massive hemorrhage left the party critically weakened, for a time.

The Barisan Sosialis was a feared adversary with strong left-wing support; but many of its top and capable leaders were neatly arrested and detained in the infamous 1963 security operation Cold Store, with the tacit support of the British and the Malayan governments. The security operation netted in about 120 "troublesome and undesirable" persons, amongst whom were nine journalists from the Chinese-, Malay- and English-language print media. Notable among them were Said Zahari, Hussein Jahidin and Lee's future press amanuensis, James Fu Chiao Sian, each of whom we shall discuss in the course of this narrative. All the nine newsmen were detained not so much for their journalistic writings as for their trade union activities and known sympathies for the Barisan Sosialis and its leaders. All those 120-odd persons were tied by a common strand in their opposition to merger with Malaya. For example, Hussein Jahidin—as the then chairman of the Singapore Trades Union Working Committee—had invited representatives from more than a hundred civic organizations to oppose the referendum on merger. Two such proposed meetings were banned by the government.[4]

In stressing that it was the Internal Security Council (ISC) which took the consequential security action, which the Singapore government, for its part, "if left alone, would never have contemplated such sweeping action," the prime minister struck a characteristic pose.[5] The ISC was composed of an equal number of representatives from the British and the Singapore governments, with the Malayan government representative holding a casting vote.[6] The prime minister and the minister for home affairs were Singapore's representatives, without whose consent Operation Cold Store could not possibly have been launched. Be that as it may, Operation Cold Store, which heralded the advent of merger with Malaya, was a classic application by Lee of the Mao axiom in using the British and the Malayan governments to neutralize his erstwhile political comrades and enfeeble their party for his own agenda.

Whilst their leaders were languishing impotently in jail, the Barisan Sosialis was easily outflanked and outwitted by Lee, and thereafter began to slide down a disastrous slope to bottom out eventually as a caricature of a political opposition. With the impetuous exit of the Barisan Sosialis MPs out of parliament to take their struggle to the streets, Singapore became a one-party state overnight, and a pleased and triumphant Lee was able to resume suppression of perceived pockets of resistance.

Singapore in Malaysia

Singapore joined the Federation of Malaysia in 1963 under terms and conditions which had been carefully worked out and agreed to between the two governments. They provided, inter alia, that although the communications and information portfolio was to be a federal responsibility, the day-to-day administration of radio and television in Singapore, however, would continue to be discharged by Singapore. Recognizing the paramount importance of an outlet for the articulation of Singapore's viewpoints, Lee had shrewdly negotiated for this atypical provision to be included in the Malaysia Agreement. Soon afterwards, sharp differences arose between the Federal and the Singapore governments over the direction and emphasis of respective government policies. The Singapore government took to the airwaves to explain its position to the people, thereby fuelling resentment and bitterness among the Malaysian political élite. But in the strategic battle for the hearts and minds of the Malaysian people, the mass media was a powerful weapon. The Federal government, therefore, still held the ace in its hand.

On December 18, 1964, in a spellbinding oration as an opposition MP in the Malaysian parliament, Lee castigated the Federal government for trying to cast a "shroud of silence in the newspapers" over the PAP and its activities, and argued for an open society:

> Let us get down to fundamentals. Is this an open, or is this a closed society? Is it a society where men can preach ideas—novel, unorthodox, heresies, to established churches and established governments—where there is a constant contest for men's hearts and minds on the basis of what is right, of what is just, of what is in the national interests, or is it a closed society where the mass media—the newspapers, the journals, publications, TV, radio—either by sound or by sight, or both sound and sight, men's minds are fed with a constant drone of sycophantic support for a particular orthodox political philosophy? That is the first question we ask ourselves.
>
> Let me preface my remarks with this: that it is not only in communist countries where the mass media is used to produce the closed mind, because the closed society must produce the closed mind. I believe that Malaysia was founded, if you read its constitution, as an open society, constituting peoples of various communities, of various religions, of various languages, of varying political beliefs, in which the will of the majority will prevail, and in which a large dissenting minority will not be crushed and intimidated and silenced.
>
> . . . I would like to see minds stimulated and debate provoked, and truth refined and crystallized out of the conflict of different evidence and views. I, therefore, welcome every and any opportunity of a chance to agree, or to dissent, in order that out of thesis comes

synthesis—thesis, anti-major premise, anti-premise, synthesis, so we progress. . . . I welcome every opportunity to meet members of the opposition, and so do members of my party, over the radio, over the television, university forums, public rallies. We never run away from the open encounter. If your ideas, your views cannot stand the challenge of criticism then they are too fragile and not sturdy enough to last.

. . . Is this the open encounter? Is this the democratic system in which ideas compete for ascendancy, not brawn or the strength of one's phalanx, but the ideas? They crossed frontiers, they have brought men into space—and if we try to keep our men rooted, glued to the ground, fixed in an orthodox political society which resists change, the world will pass us by, and one day it will come down like a house of cards. It has not got the resilience, the sturdiness, the stamina.

. . . I am talking of the principle of the open society, the open debate, ideas, not intimidation, persuasion not coercion. . . .

. . . Sir, the basic fundamental we ask ourselves . . . is whether the duties of the Minister of Information and Broadcasting are to produce closed minds or open minds, because these instruments—the mass media, the TV, the radio—can produce either the open minds receptive to ideas and ideals, a democratic system of life, or closed and limited. But I know that the open debate is a painful process for closed minds. . . . But let me make this point: that 5 million adult minds in Malaysia cannot be closed—definitely not in the lifetime of the people of authority. It is not possible because whatever the faults of the colonial system, and there are many, . . . they generated the open mind, the inquiring mind.[7]

It was a brilliant speech but, like so many of Lee's speeches, it was spoken for the moment, to gain a momentary political advantage, to overcome or circumvent a temporary political inconvenience. It was not necessarily a firm statement of belief, nor of conviction. It was an expedience, which was as quickly discarded as it was easily forgotten when it no longer suited his political convenience.[8]

On May 27, 1965, concerned at the grave implications in the *Yang di-Pertuan Agong's*[9] address that he and the PAP were "an internal threat" to Malaysia, Lee passionately sought to convince the Federal government that the PAP believed in the Malaysian constitution and the fundamental liberties: "This is what we swore to protect, to preserve and to defend and this is what we have every intention of doing, . . . by every constitutional means open to us and given to us by this Constitution, the basis on which solemnly and in good faith we came into Malaysia."

The Malaysian leaders, however, were not convinced. His oratory had not somehow matched his actions. Seventy-three days after that impassioned speech on the fundamental liberties, Singapore and Lee were expelled from the Federation of Malaysia, to the relief of the Malaysian political elite.

Lee Kuan Yew and Journalists

Lee's disdain for journalism and journalists, at least where local journalists are concerned, is well known, and may be gauged from an observation which he made on August 29, 1972, at the Fullerton Square election rally: "I read reports of all the bright students going into engineering, the sciences, medicine, economics, and so on. The not-so-bright go to political science and sociology. When they cannot get a good job, they go on to journalism."

Upset at this gratuitous remark, the Singapore National Union of Journalists (SNUJ) deplored it as "uncalled for," observing that it was also an aspersion on his cabinet ministers, who were former journalists, to which Lee did not even deign a reply.[10] Neither did those cabinet colleagues concerned speak out against it or disapprove of it. The years that followed that grave, unwarranted aspersion had not seasoned nor improved Lee's viewpoint on the media.

On November 15, 1972, as the guest of honour of the Singapore Press Club, he delivered a blistering post-prandial speech on the media, noting that while a doctor, a surgeon, a lawyer or an engineer had to pass stringent professional examinations, and were bound by rules of conduct, a journalist did not:

> What amazes me is that this powerful instrument does not require of its practitioners special professional training nor codes of conduct to govern them. You can be a journalist without understanding the impact on the minds of millions when you write smut and circulate it through millions of copies to literate and semi-literate people.
>
> You can be a powerful influence for good or for bad by just having a good television personality. But special qualifications and acceptance of a code of ethics are not demanded.

The same observation could well be applied with equal—if not greater—force to politicians who are themselves not required to have any special qualifications or codes of ethics. And whose action and resolution in matters of state often affect for better or for worse not only the present generation but generations yet to come. In that same speech, he adjured the media that their duty was "to inform the people of what was happening in Singapore and in all parts of the world, of events relevant to Singapore, educate them not just in the three Rs, but continue the schooling process, inculcate values which would make Singapore a more cohesive society and viable nation, and entertain to sell without unnecessary salacious or blue jokes."

Where journalistic commentaries are considered irksome, the prime minister and his ministers have publicly castigated the journalist concerned, and, on one occasion, even to the extent of disclosing in parliament details of the journalist's academic and national service records.[11] On another occasion, Lee professed incredulity that a school certificate leaver—the *Straits Times* group editor-in-chief—was overseeing a host of university graduates. But the same observations could also be made of the editor-in-chief who replaced him. Another journalist, writing of her misgivings on certain aspects of the Corruption (Confiscation of Benefits) Bill, was publicly attacked by the law minister for "not having done her homework," and who unjustly insinuated that she had been influenced by a contemporaneous *Asiaweek* article.[12] It transpired that it was not the journalist who had not done her homework! Tan Teng Lang, in gentle reproof of this coarse display of arrogance, wrote: "While journalists should take responsibility and pride in their writings, such unwarranted exposure of their private lives, albeit not tantamount to harassment, nonetheless has the unintended effect of instilling uneasiness in the profession."[13]

For reasons which we shall shortly see, Lee's attitude towards the foreign and domestic press, never very complimentary, underwent a progressive change after 1971:

> Foreign correspondents are perfectly free to report what they like. There is no censorship but they must not interfere in national affairs. Singapore reporters are free to criticize in Singapore newspapers, but no one is free to use the Singapore press to sabotage or thwart

the primacy of purpose of an elected government. That is the job of a political party, not a newspaper. Singapore newspapers can report criticisms of the government by rival political parties but should not become propaganda sheets for them unless they state they are party papers.[14]

He began to propound and propagate a revolutionary doctrine that politics are only for professional politicians, and no person or group of persons, organizations or associations may comment on national politics without first joining or forming a political party. In other words, no one may comment on matters outside his own area of expertise or specialty. Needless to say, it was quickly picked up by his political minions, who not only actively promulgated these views but even began to mimic him in speech and mannerism. This political heresy was proselytized among the people with messianic vigour by his son, Lee Hsien Loong, and a cadre of followers as the new gospel. In August 1985, the first deputy prime minister Goh Chok Tong told a university audience: "We cannot have two forces [press and government] trying to influence the public in different directions . . . If they [journalists] think they've got superior views, then they should stand for election."

In 1986, the Law Society of Singapore and, again, in May-June 1987, 22 young professionals and social activists—in 1988, eight of them were re-arrested after their release, together with their lawyer—became the unwitting prey of this apostasy. The ninth person, Tang Fong Har, escaped re-arrest by being fortuitously out of the country at the time. The Law Society was attacked for its critique over the egregious amendments to the NPPA, while the 22 persons were accused of being members of a dangerous Marxist conspiracy.[15]

On February 26, 1988, the apostle Lee the younger preached the gospel to journalists at the Singapore Press Club lunar new year dinner. Brig. Gen. Lee Hsien Loong propounded: "If a journalist wishes to go beyond having a point of view and contenting himself with an article, and wants to campaign for an issue, then the right place to do it is in the political arena. Enter, take off your boxing gloves, it's bare knuckles."[16]

As can be seen, the young brigadier-general was well on his way towards acquiring the colourful language of the political street fighter. But, as the scales of the inane apostasy dropped off from the eyes of the flock, it became increasingly muted, and the populace was mercifully spared further proselytization, for a while. But, recently, Brig. Gen. George Yeo, the minister for information and the arts—who is increasingly moulding himself into a plastic copy of the prime minister—revived the guru's teachings that if a journalist uses the newspaper columns to campaign for an issue, and denies the minister or the civil servants the right to rebut it in those newspaper columns, or insists on having the last word after their rebuttals, then, he should "leave the newspaper and enter the political arena."[17] Given the tight media structure and degree of control over newspapers, editors and journalists today, it is difficult to see the emergence of any such wilful conduct or behaviour. When the *Straits Times* published a critique entitled "One Government, Two Styles"[18] by local columnist and author Catherine Lim, on the current prime minister Goh Chok Tong reneging on his promise of a people-orientated style of government, his press secretary overawed her and the *Straits Times*, to boot, in a blistering open letter in reply that she had strayed beyond the out-of-bounds markers on political debate and the role of the press[19]—which did not include demolishing respect for the prime minister and his government by systematic contempt and denigration. This fustian castigation of an honestly held opinion later received the seal of approval from the senior minister, Lee Kuan Yew, who laid it down that "only those elected can set the out-of-bounds markers. Politics are for politicians. Anyone else who wishes to comment on Singapore politics should first get himself or herself elected" by the people or forever hold his peace. The overawed *Straits Times* promptly discontinued the periodicity of Lim's commentary, which led the columnist to lament publicly that its discontinuance was "her greatest regret." She was "unable to persuade our newspapers to continue publishing my political commentaries after [the] controversy caused by two of them. I would have liked to share, to have gone on sharing, my views with my fellow Singaporeans."[20]

Lee Kuan Yew and the *Utusan Melayu*

The *Utusan Melayu*, the influential Malay-language daily, with its Sunday edition, *Utusan Zaman*, was founded in Singapore on May 29, 1939, and circulated across the causeway as a pan-Malayan newspaper. The paper ceased publication during the Japanese Occupation (1942–1945), but was revived after the liberation of Singapore. The owner-editor, Yusuf bin Ishak, was a puissant left-leaning Malay with access to the Malay political leaders across the causeway. The newspaper became a major focal point for Malay nationalism and the independence movement of Malaya. In 1951, Yusuf Ishak appointed a young leftist lawyer, Harry Lee Kuan Yew, as legal adviser to *Utusan Melayu*, a fateful appointment which not only opened the broad vistas of the Malayan and Singapore political landscapes to him but also provided him with indirect access to important political personalities.

Utusan Melayu deputy editor Abdul Samad Ismail, an astute Javanese-Malay political journalist and nationalist with impeccable ties to the political leadership in Indonesia, had been arrested and detained by the colonial administration for anti-British activities in 1948. When Samad Ismail was detained again by the British authorities in 1951, Yusuf Ishak retained Lee as his counsel.

Former *Berita Harian* editor Ahmad Sebi described the role played by the *Utusan Melayu* in the independence movements of Malaya and Singapore thus:

> The *Utusan Melayu* was the nerve centre of the intellectual movement in Singapore in the 1940s and 1950s, not because it was a newspaper organization founded and established by the people, but rather because of its direct and close ties with the independence movement of Malaya. Of the newspapers in the various languages in Singapore at that time the *Utusan Melayu* was the most authoritative and strident in its efforts to propagate the cause of independence. The *Utusan Melayu* attracted especially the liberal and radical among university students. It was this that led Lee Kuan Yew, who had just returned from London after completing his law studies, to become one of the legal advisers to the newspaper's company. It is undeniable that his rapport with the activists in the *Utusan Melayu* enabled Lee Kuan Yew to obtain national exposure and experience in controlling the trade unions and labour movements which culminated in the formation of the People's Action Party (PAP).[21]

Recognizing the importance of Malay participation in his future political design, Lee carefully cultivated the goodwill of Yusuf Ishak and Samad Ismail, among others in the paper. Subsequently, several members of the *Utusan Melayu* editorial and news staff went on to become cabinet ministers or to occupy high positions in the Malaysian and Singapore governments. Yusuf Ishak himself became the first locally born head of state and president of Singapore. Prominent in politics among the *Utusan Melayu* staff were news editor Othman Wok, who became Singapore minister for social affairs, and Yusuf's two journalist-brothers, Rahim Ishak and Aziz Ishak, who became a Singapore minister for state and Malaysian minister for agriculture respectively.

With his remarkable ability in making friends, Samad Ismail was able to establish an axis of rapport between the Chinese, Malay and Indian workers and the students, which he skillfully exploited for his newspaper and his own political agenda: "*Utusan* was his weapon to face his enemies. *Utusan* was the shield that protected him and his friends."[22] Using the paper to propagate the cause of Malayan independence and to ventilate social and labour grievances, he attracted a chequered crowd of politicians, intellectuals, trade unionists and student activists of all hues from the university and the Chinese schools, who shared a common yearning for independence. There was no doubt that during those volatile days before independence, not only the students but the political intelligentsia as well were beating a steady path to his door soliciting advice and counsel on the problems of the day. Among the legions who did were Hamid Jumat, later the Singapore Labour Party minister for local government, the United Malays National Organization (UMNO) leaders Lee Kuan Yew, S. Rajaratnam, Ahmad Ibrahim,[23] C.V. Devan Nair and Lim Chin Siong. It was thus through no fortuitous stroke that he was able to introduce the feisty labour leader C.V. Devan Nair, or the charismatic left-wing trade union leader Lim Chin Siong, among others, to Lee and the PAP. Wherefore, the prideful words of his journalist wife, Hamidah bte Haji Hassan—"A. Samad Ismail was *Utusan* and *Utusan* was A. Samad Ismail"[24]—appear no more than a mere statement of fact.

Thus, Samad Ismail, a man of many parts, played an important role in the founding, planning and organizing of the People's Action Party, and became one of its convenors in 1954. He represented the PAP at the memorable 1955 Bandung Conference in Indonesia. In the circumstances, it was not surprising to find that in the early years of Singapore's struggle for independence, *Utusan Melayu* was supportive of Lee. But by 1957, owing to differences of opinion with Lee, Samad Ismail broke away from the PAP. At about the same time, Samad Ismail's relationship with Yusuf Ishak was also showing severe strains, as both Lee and the leaders of the United Malays National Organization sedulously cultivated Yusuf Ishak for their own ultimate ends.

In 1956, Yusuf Ishak assigned Samad Ismail as *Utusan Melayu* representative to Jakarta, Indonesia, because the colonial authorities, alarmed at the direction of Malay nationalism, apparently had intimated to him that if Samad Ismail continued to run the paper, the *Utusan Melayu* printing licence would not be renewed. Samad Ismail's partisans, however, have held that he was exiled to Jakarta because of personal differences with Yusuf Ishak. It should not, however, be overlooked that Lee had by this time successfully won Yusuf Ishak over to his side, and was thus able to prevail upon him to curb Samad Ismail's activities and keep him out of the way until after the forthcoming general election. Whichever the reason was, Samad Ismail rusticated there until after the 1959 general election and until after Lee had been sworn in as premier. Samad Ismail's relationship with Yusuf Ishak was then at its lowest ebb. It was suggested that Yusuf Ishak had become resentful and envious of Samad Ismail's popularity with students and others who sought the latter's advice to his almost total exclusion. Some measure of Samad Ismail's popularity then might be gauged by the ready and easy access accorded to *Utusan Melayu* reporters and cameramen in interviews with Chinese student or strike leaders by a mere mention of his name during the notorious student camp-ins or industrial strikes, when reporters from other newspapers with similar assignments were denied access beyond the barricades or picket lines. It was all the more noteworthy when it is remembered that Samad Ismail is a Malay in what was a predominantly Chinese milieu.

Samad Ismail resigned from *Utusan Melayu* on his return from Indonesia, leaving a lasting mark and influence on *Utusan Melayu* and its staff, and on those who knew him. Among them was Said Zahari, the journalist who later, as editor of the still intensely independent *Utusan Melayu*, led a prolonged strike in 1961 by its journalists against the attempt to bring the newspaper under the control of UMNO, the ruling party. The strike was crushed, and when he later made a visit to Singapore he was barred from returning to Malaya on the ground that he is a Singapore citizen. In the notorious 1963 security dragnet Operation Cold Store, it will be recalled, he was one of several journalists, among a hundred others, arrested under the Internal Security Act for opposition to the creation of the Federation of Malaysia. He was detained without trial for more than 16 years, adopted as a prisoner of conscience by Amnesty International and, finally, emerged bloody but unbowed from detention, refusing to accept throughout his long incarceration the official allegations against him.

Sensing the shift in the political winds emphasizing Malay as the national language, the opportunistic *Straits Times* management started, in 1957, a daily in romanized Malay, calling it the *Berita Harian—Daily News—*and much later, a Sunday edition, *Berita Minggu—Sunday News*. It was an eight-page broadsheet, which was basically a translated copy, editorial and all, of the *Straits Times*. It was not originally intended to compete with *Utusan Melayu*, which used the *Jawi* script, but it provided a useful leverage to the PAP government in its campaign to reduce the powerful influence of *Utusan Melayu* on the Malay populace.

But, according to Professor Cheah Boon Kheng: "Most people regarded the publication of the *Berita Harian* as a far-sighted move of the *Straits Times* company to accommodate rising Malay nationalism in the wake of Malaya's independence on August 31, 1957."[25] After a promising start, the paper began to falter and experience a drop in circulation. L.C. Hoffman, the *Straits Times* editor-in-chief, then offered Samad Ismail the position of editor of the paper. It was timely, as his position in *Utusan Melayu* had become tenuous, and he had thoughts of leaving the paper on which he had stamped his unique personality. Under his direction, *Berita Harian* swiftly began to assume a character of its own, and began to reflect the Malay psyche and aspirations.

By the time Singapore became a constituent state within the Federation of Malaysia, *Utusan Melayu* had shifted support to, and was enjoying the patronage of, the Malaysian Malay political establishment. It was ultimately tied by ownership and management to the Malay political leadership of the ruling United Malays National Organization. As the influence of the United Malays National Organization waxed with its acquisition of *Utusan Melayu*, the influence of the PAP waned. Malay radicals within were mounting a challenge to the UMNO's growing influence in the paper. Both the Malaysian premier, Tunku Abdul Rahman, and the Singapore premier found themselves under constant and strident attacks from the paper. Although each had his own private agenda in mind, Lee saw it necessary to temporarily make common cause with UMNO leaders to counter the influence of the radicals. It was essentially a coalition of convenience. When PAP dissidents led by Lim Chin Siong revolted against Lee's leadership, and broke away to form the *Barisan Sosialis* in opposition, Samad Ismail apparently influenced the UMNO leadership in favour of the breakaway faction, a circumstance Lee has neither forgotten nor forgiven, as we shall soon see.

The *Berita Harian* now served an unexpected but useful role in displacing *Utusan Melayu* as the sole voice of the Malay *rakyat* or community, and removed any possible allegations that Lee and the PAP government were depriving the Malays of their language and culture. In August 1964, *Utusan Melayu* spawned a romanized Sunday version, *Mingguan Malaysia*, and emboldened by its success launched a separate daily, *Utusan Malaysia*, three years later. Preaching the political supremacy of the Malay race, language and religion, it became a gadfly relentlessly goading a hapless Lee and his government into political frenzy and frustration. In the existing fragile pan-Malaysian political relationship, there was very little that Lee could do to bring it around, let alone to his heel—and all his railing and ranting could not prevent it from plugging a stridently partisan Malaysian line. Lee suspected that the hand of Samad Ismail was in it and, considering him a man who "thrived on intrigue and manipulation," laboured hard to have him arrested as a communist by the Malaysian government at every turn; but, because of his powerful connexions, Samad Ismail was safe from arrest—though only temporarily. Meanwhile, in 1972, following the corporate split in the *Straits Times* group between Singapore and Malaysia, Samad Ismail became managing editor and deputy editor-in-chief of the *New Straits Times*.

Consequent on the proposal of the Dutch Labour Party to have the PAP expelled from the Socialist International for violations of human rights, many Singaporeans were arrested, among whom were the Singapore editor of the *Berita Harian*, Hussein Jahidin, and his assistant editor, Azmi Mahmood, on June 16, 1976, "for questioning in connexion with alleged communist activities." Hussein Jahidin was a former ISA detainee, but who the Singapore authorities must have considered sufficiently reliable politically to have entrusted as editor of *Berita Harian* in Singapore. Azmi was taken on as news editor of the Malay section, besides becoming a regular commentator on the weekly international affairs programme of the state-owned Radio and Television Singapore (RTS). Indeed, by most accounts, he was an unabashed supporter of the PAP government. His move to the *Berita Harian* must have had the tacit approval of the government, after security clearance by the Internal Security Department. But, in the ritualized TV appearance, both men "confessed" that they had attempted to "slant the news in their paper in a manner critical of the government" and "work up discontent and despair among the Malays and to influence them towards communism as an acceptable ally to solve their problems."

Hussein and Azmi had been at one time journalistic protégés of Samad Ismail, whom Lee in his mind-set regarded as, indeed, so powerfully Machiavellian that he could discern his figure casting dark shadows over Singapore from across the causeway. For Samad Ismail was reported to have once counselled Lee: "The art of leadership is to choose the target but to understand that 'the hand that throws the stone should never be yours.'"[26] They were accused of being under Samad Ismail's baneful influence, and acting as his proxies in pro-communist activities. Therefore, when they implicated him in their "confessions" on television as the mastermind of a communist complot, Samad Ismail expected the inevitability of his own arrest. Lee, who had prevailed long and hard with the Malaysian government to have him arrested as a "dangerous communist," saw him as the person largely responsible for the low ebb in the relationship between the two countries.

Now relocated to Malaysia with his family, Samad had powerful political friends there; and, as long as Tun Abdul Razak was prime minister, for whom he was a respected ghost speech-writer and adviser, he was safe.[27] Samad Ismail, when he was the chairman of the Singapore branch of UMNO in 1958–1959, had gained the confidence of the Malay political leadership, especially of Razak, then deputy prime minister. Upon Razak's death in 1976, Hussein Onn succeeded him as prime minister, retaining the emulous Ghazali Shafie as minister for home affairs, a man close to Lee and the PAP government, and who was not himself without prime ministerial aspirations. Ghazali required little persuasion to concur with the Singapore government's insinuation of Samad's "probable involvement," and obtained the agreement of Hussein Onn to detain him. Hussein Onn, a fine Malay patrician and an upright politician, strongly believed in the delegation of powers.[28] Until then, Ghazali had tried unsuccessfully to have Samad Ismail detained.[29]

Thus, on June 22, 1976, Abdul Samad Ismail was arrested on an order issued by the Malaysian minister for home affairs, Ghazali Shafie, "for direct involvement in activities in support of the communist struggle for political power in Malaysia." In this exercise, he had the assistance of the Singapore ISD.[30] The Malaysian home ministry statement declared: "Using Kuala Lumpur as the base of operations, Abdul Samad Ismail directed a programme at exploiting every possible grievance of the Malay community in Singapore fomenting inter-racial unrest, and to denigrate and ridicule Islam with finesse and subtlety in order to destroy the main obstacle to the acceptance of communist ideology by the Malays in Singapore."[31]

The official statement was notable for its generalities and the absence of any specificity of alleged misdeeds. Some 69 days later, on September 1, Samad Ismail, "wan and hollow-cheeked," appeared on public television looking "more martyr than monster," and shocked the nation with a "confession" that he was, among other things, a longtime "communist," and that the allegations against him of "actively indulg[ing] in the propagation of the communist ideology and in furthering the cause of communism" were "all true." But what the public generally failed to discern was that he was *reading* the "confession" before him,[32] and answering meticulously scripted questions by an interviewer, whose political credentials had previously been checked and approved by the Special Branch. No security organization could possibly afford to run the risk of a live or unrehearsed television presentation by a supposedly contrite political dissident.

Although Samad said he had been instructed in Indonesia in 1957 by Abdullah Sudin, a communist, to "penetrate" UMNO, he did not join the parent organization when he was living in Malaysia, for he had other priorities and, in any event, there was no immediate need, as "by 1964, UMNO leaders had consulted [him] regularly on party problems . . . invited [him] to give talks on the latest political developments and other political subjects to UMNO members . . . [and] even consulted [him] on such vital undertakings as planning for the general election."

> In my opinion, I was most successful with the younger generation of UMNO leaders. They were impressed by my ideas, and after I had gained their confidence, they constantly consulted me on various issues. Some of them developed a dependence on me. Through them, I managed to get closer to the core of the UMNO leadership, and through them I made the UMNO leaders that matter see things and resolve problems my way.[33]

Far Eastern Economic Review (*Review*) correspondent K. Das described Samad Ismail's TV appearance and performance thus: "Never in the history of television confessions—so plentiful in Singapore and Malaysia—had an audience been treated to the spectacle of a man, *patently a public enemy, cocking a snook at the government with such élan and sophistication.*" [Author's emphasis] That an experienced news correspondent could have perceived it as such is eloquent testimony to the professionalism of the Malaysian Special Branch,[34] which ex facie did not seem to be unduly interested in Samad Ismail's connexion with Hussein and Azmi, and vice versa. Pertinently enough, no reference was made in the script to the Singapore connection. Nonetheless, it could not be discounted that the whole TV presentation was a carefully orchestrated skit intended for a wider political purpose. The Special Branch investigations impacted on the Malaysian political leadership, and threatened for a time the beginning of a witch hunt for suspected communists within UMNO.[35]

Razak's death and Hussein Onn's delicate state of health had precipitated an UMNO succession struggle and created a situation of uncertainty, where various factions drew out their krises to reinforce their respective positions in the political succession. Samad Ismail's TV confession was clearly part of a determined effort by Ghazali to strengthen his hand. The finger of accusation began to point to Abdullah Ahmad, deputy minister of science and technology and former political secretary to Razak, and Abdullah Majid, deputy minister of labour and manpower and former press secretary to Razak, as being close to Samad Ismail and to the late prime minister. They were arrested under the ISA but not before resigning from the government. They were portrayed as wielding great political leverage, as powerful gatekeepers during the Razak administration, who checked and controlled access to the prime minister with no apparent diminution of powers in the subsequent Hussein Onn administration. Another victim was Khalil Akasah, the UMNO executive secretary, who was at the time away in Japan.

It is noteworthy that, in 1972, the urbane, highly respected and staunchly anti-communist home minister, the late *Tun* Dr. Ismail bin Abdul Rahman, had investigated a similar complaint against Samad Ismail, and had given him a clean bill of political health. It is reasonably safe to assume that *Tun* Dr. Ismail would, in his investigations, have had access to the secret files kept and maintained on A. Samad Ismail by the British and its successor in title, role and function—the Malaysian Special Branch, which also maintains close ties with the Singapore Internal Security Department, to which at one time it used to second a liaison officer. Oddly enough, no request appeared to have been made for those files, information or assistance until December 1975, even though the two security organizations work hand in glove with one another, a fact which the Singapore minister for home affairs publicly acknowledged in parliament. Thus, the resurrection of the accusation against Samad Ismail at that particular moment is pregnant with questions. It is also noteworthy that there was no suggestion that, as managing editor of the *New Straits Times*, Samad Ismail had tried to use the newspaper to propagate or influence the cause of communism. But, unlike *Tun* Dr. Ismail, Lee, who sees shadows around every corner, was convinced that Samad Ismail was an unrepentant important communist cadre, whom he had befriended during the exciting days of pre-independent Singapore, and whose communist party name was Laniaz, which Samad Ismail was said to have admitted was his party name.

On February 5, 1977, Abdullah Ahmad went on television to make a public "confession" of his secret proclivity for communism. He was followed two days later by Abdullah Majid who made a similar "confession," at the end of which both, apparently contrite pro-communists, pledged "loyalty to King and country."

Ghazali was one of several contenders in the UMNO for the post of deputy premier but, unlike the others, lacked a power base. The three men closest to the deputy premiership were the three vice-presidents of the UMNO—Dr. Mahathir Mohamad, deputy prime minister, Tengku Razaleigh Hamzah, finance minister, and Ghafar Baba, former agriculture minister and secretary general of the National Front. The two Abdullahs were political intimates of Mahathir and Tengku Razaleigh. With the removal of the two Abdullahs from the centre of power, their close associates would be tainted and this would open the way for Ghazali's own ascent to power. If Ghazali became prime minister, it would be welcomed in Singapore. Because of Ghazali's special relationship with Lee and the Singapore government, it would improve ties between the two countries and, more importantly, bring the Federation of Malaysia into Singapore's orbit of influence. Singapore would resume the traditional role of authority from where colonial governors used to proffer firm but subtle advice to the Malay sultanates in the administration of their affairs in peninsular Malaya. Relationship between the two countries had hitherto not been good, and part of the reason for it was laid at Samad Ismail's door. Thus, as long as Samad Ismail had ready access to the Malaysian cockpit of political power over which he wielded considerable influence, it was felt in Singapore circles that there could be no improvement in relationship.

The noisy allegations, malicious rumours and insinuations also threatened for a time the position of the other UMNO ministers. Rumours abounded that Dr. Mahathir and another UMNO leader, Musa Hitam, were communists. Harun Idris, the former chief minister of the state of Selangor, being prosecuted at the time, ascribed his legal and political woes to the machinations of communists led by Samad Ismail because he was one of the UMNO leaders who had refused to be influenced by Samad Ismail. Harun was then undergoing criminal prosecution, with two others, on two charges of forgery of stocks and shares worth M$6.5 million belonging to Bank Rakyat, and the abetment of criminal breach of trust arising out of the promotion of the Mohamed Ali–Joe Bugner world heavyweight title fight in Kuala Lumpur in May 1975.[36]

Other political personalities arrested at the same time were Tan Ken Sin, the executive secretary of the Malayan Chinese Association (MCA), and three opposition leaders, including two members of parliament. The MCA was, and is, a partner of UMNO in the political alliance. Tan, a former editor of the *Sin Chew Jit Poh*, Malaysia, went before the television cameras to make the customary "confession" of his communist past and his pro-communist activities in "encourag[ing] a group of editors and reporters with pro-communist inclinations to play up certain types of news, or to write certain types of features which would help to shape and influence the opinion of the readership in favour of the communist cause."

The Final Split

This might be a convenient place to digress and recall that, prior to the advent of the first PAP government in 1959, as a precautionary measure, the *Straits Times* group had transferred its domicile and operations to Kuala Lumpur, from where the *Straits Times* stable of newspapers were over the years separately published and distributed on a pan-Malayan basis under the same name. However, in 1972, following an industrial dispute with the European-dominated management sitting in Singapore, Samad Ismail—acting as editor-in-chief in the absence of the incumbent, Lee Siew Yee, who was then on leave—masterminded what Professor Cheah Boon Kheng described as the "Malaysian-ization" of the *Straits Times* group, a move that "led the Malaysian prime minister, Tun Abdul Razak, and [UMNO treasurer] Tengku Razaleigh, to direct the *Straits Times* management to transfer its entire Malaysian operation into Malaysian hands. Consequently, the *New Straits Times* was born and thereby severed the umbilical cord of its parent company in Singapore. . . . Shares were sold to the company's staff, the company was reorganized, with more Malaysians in editorial and managerial positions, and an entirely Malaysian board of directors."[37] It was an impressive corporate coup d'état. The company, the New Straits Times Press (Malaysia) Sendirian Berhad, was incorporated with UMNO and *bumiputra* interests acquiring 80 percent of the equity to set up the *Straits Times*, and take over the *Malay Mail* and the Malay-language *Berita Harian*, and their respective Sunday editions in Malaysia. Reading the signs of the times, the other Singapore-owned newspapers operating in Malaysia, the *Nanyang Siang Pau* and the *Sin Chew Jit Poh*, also followed suit.

For his contributions to national literature, in early 1976, Samad Ismail and five others received the literary pioneer prize from the new Malaysian prime minister, Hussein Onn, who had succeeded Razak. The citation stated: "Their work had instilled national consciousness in the people in their struggle for independence." After his release in 1981, Samad Ismail was appointed editorial adviser to the *New Straits Times* in 1983. On November 19, 1988, he was further honoured by being awarded the *Tokoh Wartawan Negara*—National Journalist Leader—for his outstanding contribution to the development of journalism in Malaysia, from the prime minister, Dr. Mahathir Mohamad. Not very long thereafter, the Malaysian king bestowed on him the *Darjah Panglima Setia Mahkota*, one of the nation's highest awards, which carries the title *Tan Sri*.[38] In July 1994, he was conferred the prestigious Ramon Magsaysay award for communication, journalism, literature and the creative arts. The awards board said that he had applied "his intellect and journalistic skills to champion national independence, cultural revival and democratic nation-building in Malaysia."[39] The award capped a long and distinguished—and one-time turbulent—career.

On November 28, 1990, a Singapore government gazette announced that the order of prohibition against entry into Singapore by A. Samad Ismail had been lifted. It was "one of the last acts" taken by Lee Kuan Yew, his éminence grise, before he handed over the reins of government to Goh Chok Tong.[40]

To return to *Utusan Melayu*. After Singapore's expulsion from Malaysia on August 8, 1965, it continued to publish and circulate in Singapore. But the playing field and the ground rules had changed drastically. But, in a spirit of seeming magnanimity, Lee publicly promised: "I am going to allow *Utusan Melayu* to carry on. I am not going to stop it. I am not going to ban it. It is going to carry on. But, unlike before, when it contravenes the law it will have to answer in a court of law."[41] However, on September 30, 1965, *Utusan Melayu* managing director Datuk Hussain bin Noordin was summoned to the Ministry of Culture where he met with the minister and the prime minister, who drew a median line across the Straits of Johor beyond which he hinted darkly *Utusan Melayu* crossed at its own peril. Datuk Hussain assured Lee that "*Utusan Melayu* would not publish articles prejudicial to the peace and security of Singapore."[42] Before he left, Lee pointedly gave him a copy of the Sedition Act as a parting gift, whose minacious provisions, Lee reminded him, were still the law of Singapore.

But on March 13, 1967, a PAP Malay MP, Rahamat bin Kenap, drew the attention of parliament, on cue, to "humiliatory articles" in *Utusan Melayu*, which, he alleged, were intended to cause political tension between Malaysia and Singapore, and that "clarifications" of those articles by Singapore government leaders were "invariably ignored" or "receive[d] scant coverage in the columns of the *Utusan Melayu* and, if they were published at all, were twisted about for specific purposes." The minister for culture, Othman Wok, rose to remind *Utusan Melayu* of that crucial September interview with the prime minister and of the parthian gift of a copy of the Sedition Act. The implications could not be clearer. *Utusan Melayu* prudently shifted its operations to Kuala Lumpur, but continued to circulate in Singapore until 1969.

The *Berita Harian*, well poised within the *Straits Times* group, stepped into the void left by the *Utusan Melayu*, and now serves the Malay readership in Singapore.

Notes

1. *Straits Times*, April 21, 1959.
2. Speech, Trade Union House, October 15, 1965.
3. University of Singapore Students' Union dinner, November 25, 1960.
4. *Straits Times*, February 2 & 5, 1963.
5. *Hansard*, October 14, 1959, col. 661. See also "The Fifth Column: Malaysia's communist threat," by C.C. Too, head of the psychological warfare section in the Malaysian government, *Far Eastern Economic Review*, December 7, 1989.
6. *Hansard*, October 14, 1959, col. 661.
7. *Hansard*, Malaysian Parliamentary debates, December 18, 1964, cols. 5075–5083.
8. See also Francis T. Seow, "Singapore's Closing Society," *Asian Wall Street Journal*, May 10, 1988.
9. His Majesty the King.

10. *Straits Times*, July 25, 1984.

11. *Straits Times*, March 31, 1988.

12. Tan Teng Lang, *The Singapore Press: Freedom, Responsibility and Credibility*. Singapore: Times Academic Press, 1990.

13. Francis T. Seow, *To Catch a Tartar: A Dissident in Lee Kuan Yew's Prison*, Monograph 42. New Haven: Yale Southeast Asia Studies, Yale Centre for International Area Studies, 1994.

14. See Chew Kheng Chuan, "A statement of beliefs," *Far Eastern Economic Review*, October 22, 1987.

15. *Straits Times*, February 27, 1988.

16. Roger Mitton, "The Long Story, What Role for the Press? Singapore's Answers, A Special Relationship," *Asiaweek*, September 25, 1992. See also Catherine Lim, "The PAP and the People—A Great Affective Divide," *Straits Times*, September 3, 1994.

17. *Sunday Times*, November 20, 1994.

18. *Sunday Times*, December 4, 1994.

19. *Far Eastern Economic Review*, February 15, 1996.

20. Ahmad Sebi, "Samad's Influence," in *A. Samad Ismail: Journalism & Politics*, ed. Cheah Boon Kheng. Kuala Lumpur: Singamal Publishing Bureau (M) Sdn. Bhd., 1987.

21. Hamidah bte Haji Hassan, "A Consummate Actor," in *A. Samad Ismail: Journalism & Politics*, ed. Cheah Boon Kheng.

22. Later Singapore's minister for labour.

23. Cheah Boon Kheng, "Introduction," in *A. Samad Ismail: Journalism & Politics*.

24. Hamidah bte Haji Hassan, "A Consummate Actor," in A. Samad Ismail, *Journalism & Politics*.

25. Dennis Bloodworth, *The Tiger and the Trojan Horse*. Singapore: Times Book International, 1986.

26. Tun Haji Abdul Razak bin Datuk Hussein died suddenly on January 14, 1976, in London, from leukaemia.

27. Hamidah bte Haji Hassan, "A Consummate Actor," in *A. Samad Ismail: Journalism & Politics*.

28. Harvey Stockwin, "Transcending all races," *Review*, September 17, 1976.

29. Ibid.

30. *Straits Times*, June 23, 1976.

31. See M. Rajakumar, "Malaysia's Jean-Paul Sartre," in *A.Samad Ismail: Journalism & Politics*, pp. 39, 42; and John A. Lent, "True (?) confessions—TV in Malaysia and Singapore," *Index on Censorship*, vol. 7 no. 2, March-April 1978, pp. 9–18.

32. A. Samad Ismail, "Radio and Television Malaysia interview," in *Straits Times*, September 2, 1976.

33. For ISD or Special Branch techniques of extracting confessions to order, see Seow, *To Catch a Tartar: A Dissident in Lee Kuan Yew's Prison*.

34. S. Husin Ali, "A Genuine Nationalist," in *A. Samad Ismail: Journalism & Politics*.

35. *Straits Times*, October 20, 1976.

36. Cheah, "Introduction," *A. Samad Ismail: Journalism & Politics*.

37. *Straits Times*, June 6, 1992.

38. *Straits Times*, Weekly Edition, July 30, 1994.

39. *Straits Times*, December 1, 1990.

40. Press conference, City Hall, Singapore, August 12, 1965.

41. *Hansard*, Parliamentary debates, March 13, 1967, col. 1188.

4 The Subjugation
of the Print Media:
Two Important Cases

We of the PAP believe just as zealously in the freedom of the press.

Lee Kuan Yew[1]

Harry Lee Kuan Yew, a master of the art of gradualism, often skillfully combines it with the politics of kite flying. Almost every self-serving radical political decision taken by him throughout his political career was carried out in at least two or three stages. Potent medicine, if given in one strong, large dose, oftentimes provokes violent reaction which may harm, and sometimes even kill the patient. The abolition of the jury system in Singapore's judicial infrastructure, with the inert aid of a cowering press, makes a fascinating case in point. The abolition was essentially a political decision, and had little to do with the jury system per se, which had worked "reasonably well," as even Lee himself had admitted, since its introduction in Singapore around about 1824—but which he later spurned as foreign crotchet. To minimise protests especially from the bar, at its abolition, he devised its abolition in two stages. Using the pretext of bringing the jury system into line with the practice of the majority of the states within the Federation of Malaya, jury trials for felonies and serious criminal offences in Singapore were abolished and restricted only to capital offences for which the punishment was death. Notwithstanding the misgivings of the legal profession, the first stage of the abolition was accomplished with reasonable ease in 1959.

In early 1969—a decade later—Lee resumed his attack on the jury system by proposing its complete abolition, labelling it an "Anglo-Saxon concept" which had "no relevance to Asia."[2] The proposal upset the legal profession spearheaded by David Saul Marshall, a very capable criminal lawyer and the first chief minister of Singapore. On April 24, 1969, at an extraordinary general meeting of the Law Society of Singapore, the lawyers expressed their "deep concern" at the proposal totally abolishing the jury system. The resolution and the sentiments of the bar were communicated to every newspaper, but not a single newspaper published them or discussed the abolition of the system of justice. By any standard, the abolition of the jury system would have been a media event. Through the quiet use of the Essential Information (Control of Publications and Safeguarding of Information) Regulations, the government was able to effectively stifle public debate on the abolition of jury trials.

David Marshall—a prime protagonist for the retention of the jury system—appealed in turn to the state-owned Radio Singapura "for a few minutes on the air," and to the state-owned TV Singapura "to hold a public forum on this very serious law to abolish juries," and, again, to the press to publish his "criticisms of the measure and warnings of the dangers ahead," without success. Floundering in utter frustration, he exclaimed: "The Singapore press is unique as constituting the only newspaper in the world which refuses to publish a special resolution of a special meeting of the lawyers of the country in respect of a matter of major public importance—not even newspapers in Communist countries would refuse to publish resolutions of their own country's lawyers."[3] "Such is the fear of the government that pervades our public life," he said—a truism which would be echoed down through the vale of years, and re-echoed by many more persons, both great and small, on this and other issues.

History repeated itself in the late eighties when the Law Society of Singapore was forced to take out a paid advertisement in the newspapers, which had given scant publicity to the extraordinary general meeting resolution of its members disagreeing with the government's momentous decision to abolish appeals to the Judicial Committee of the Privy Council, Singapore's ultimate court of appeal in London. An important and final tier of appeal in the judicial system of justice was being abolished without any serious discussion by or in the columns of the media. Oddly enough, the most distinguished defender for the retention of the Privy Council had been none other than the prime minister himself, who warned his own parliament of the dangers, if not the folly, of such abolition:

> I can only express the hope that faith in the judicial system will never be diminished—and I am sure it will not—so long as we allow a review of the judicial processes that takes place here in some other tribunal where obviously undue influence cannot be brought to bear. As long as governments are wise enough to leave alone the rights of appeal to some other superior body outside Singapore, then there must be a higher degree of confidence in the integrity of our judicial process. This is most important.[4]

Until fairly recently, there had been no replacement of this crucial avenue of appeal, a sad testimony to the indecent haste with which the government abolished a cornerstone of Singapore's judicial infrastructure.

As a curtain-raiser to the 1972 general election, Lee predictably raised a bogy, the bogy of communalism, which, as events unfolded, he expanded to include the goblin of communism and the spectre of foreign black operations. On April 28, 1971, using the "Seminar on Communism and Democracy" organized by pre-university students as his platform, Lee signalled the start of a massive crackdown on the print media,[5] which was to end only with the total and absolute subjugation of the media some years later. Without identifying them by name, Lee declared that "a Malay newspaper has been talking of nothing but Malay problems, and advocating *bumiputra*[6] policies." And a Chinese newspaper had been playing up "pro-Chinese communist news, and working up Chinese language issues."[7] They were, however, easily recognizable as the *Berita Harian* and the *Nanyang Siang Pau* newspapers. He next alluded to the English-language press's dubious sources of finance, particularly "one" English-language newspaper with its encouragement of "permissiveness in sex, drugs and dress-styles," and which, whilst paying "lip service support to national service," faulted it "on every count." It required very little imagination to conclude that he was referring to the spunky newspaper, the *Singapore Herald*, which was becoming a thorn in the side of his government. Lee accused those three newspapers of setting off "three different pulls in three contrary directions" that, unless checked, would tear Singapore society asunder. "*Any* government of Singapore that does not keep these divisive and disruptive activities in check is guilty of dereliction of duty," he added.

The *Berita Harian*—a paper which, Lee asserted, he reads "daily for Malay thinking"—apparently took the cue and made the necessary adjustments in its editorial policy, but the other two newspapers allegedly persisted in their respective editorial directions. Indeed, the *Nanyang Siang Pau*, far from being apologetic, reacted to Lee's speech with a provocative editorial, "Taking on the PM"[8]—thus unwittingly providing Lee with the necessary pretext to begin the massive crackdown on the press.

Shades of Black Operations

Soon after Lee's speech, four *Nanyang* executives and editorial staff were arrested under the ISA. Few people believed that they were communists or communalists or that its multimillionaire owner-publisher, Lee Eu Seng, and his newspaper were or could be a part of a communist black operation against Singapore. A spirited Lee Eu Seng waged a credibility war in the columns of his newspaper against the government, which greatly discomfited Lee and his government, a bold and brazen response which Lee had not expected. The resulting furor created a crisis of credibility for the government.

To close the serious yawning credibility gap, Lee had perforce to drag in another English-language newspaper, regarding which he disclosed he had corroborative proof of Chinese communist subversion, and to whose owner "not so long ago, Chinese communist agents in Hongkong had given nearly HK$8 million—equivalent to S$4 million." The newspaper maintained an anti-communist line. The communists, who were "very patient people" and, Lee asserted, who were "not in a hurry," allowed the paper to continue that policy. They were planning, "not for tomorrow, but for next year, for 10 years' time."[9] The communists wanted a foothold in the media through underwriting the newspaper, he claimed, as they knew that more and more students, both in English and Chinese schools, would read English-language newspapers.[10] His nuanced and extensive remarks left his listeners at the Sennett community centre in no doubt that he was referring, this time, to the English-language newspaper, the *Eastern Sun*. What he did not mention was that the loans had come from the Bank of China in Hongkong, which also has a duly registered branch in Singapore.

In a further attempt to obfuscate the growing issue, Lee proceeded specifically to name the *Singapore Herald* as the recipient of dubious funds, accusing it of "taking on" the government since it commenced publication the previous year. The largest shareholder of this newspaper was a Hongkong partnership—Heeda and Co., with two "dummy" names. Foreign capital coming to Singapore to start a newspaper, he expounded, did not "take the government on if it wanted to make money. It was only prepared to take the government on, if it was after something other than money, and was prepared to lose money." Lee deliberately chose to ignore the *Herald* code—which it had professed as a "pro-Singapore rather than a pro-government newspaper." For, to Lee, there were no such fine lines of distinction.

Lee revealed that the government had stopped official advertisements, and had denied it press facilities, but the *Herald* had carried on, nevertheless. Finally, realizing its position would become too exposed and untenable, its founder-editor, Francis Wong, had stepped down, and gone back to Kuala Lumpur. But Wong had stepped down so as to facilitate the entry of new investors, who were told that he was the stumbling block to continued government goodwill. One of the new investors was Hongkong publisher Sally Aw Sian, who had pledged S$1.5 million to the financially troubled newspaper.

After Wong's departure, Lee met with its new editor, Ambrose Khaw, and asked him about the newspaper's financial arrangements, and who had put in "the first lot [of money] from Heeda and Co., Hongkong." Khaw told him that it was Donald Stephens, the former chief minister of Sabah—a Bornean state within the Federation of Malaysia—and at the time Malaysian high commissioner to Australia; but Lee queried Khaw whether he "really believed that Donald Stephens would take S$1.5 million of his own money to lose it in a Singapore newspaper which took the Singapore government on." There were really two questions to Lee's query. But Khaw, unskilled and unprepared for this trick question, apparently agreed that this was difficult to believe, whereupon he asked Khaw whether he "really believed [Sally Aw Sian] the Hongkong publisher—a hard-headed business person—would put money in a sinking newspaper." Qualifying his negative reply, Khaw ventured to say that the newspaper was "only losing S$60,000 per month, and with more advertisements could break even." Lee then asked him: "Whose money is it?" to which he replied: "I don't know." Lee then told him: "Well, when you know, come and tell me." On the facts as enumerated by Lee, there was no or not sufficient evidence from which to draw the irresistible conclusion that either Donald Stephens or Sally Aw Sian or both of them, or, indeed, any other persons, had mounted a "black operation" through the *Herald* against Singapore. A black operation in the argot of the Internal Security Department means operations organized by foreign sources to cause disruption and trouble to Singapore, in which the operatives are working.[11]

Turning to what he called the "very strange case" of the *Nanyang Siang Pau*, Lee said that its general manager, Lee Mau Seng, had come down to Singapore from Kuala Lumpur in Malaysia after the notorious May 13, 1969, riots, and was followed in 1970 by editor Shamsuddin Tung Tao Chang. As *Nanyang* editor, Tung had "played up" crime in Singapore, and "played down" government news, whilst their Malaysian edition, on the other hand, had "played up" government and political news, but "played down" crime in Malaysia. They had "tried to bring in a known MCA [Malayan Chinese Association][12] activist from Kuala Lumpur to be editor of the Singapore news page." Later, they "worked up more and more communist news." As there was "something fishy," the government kept it "under surveillance." By February 1971, the *Nanyang* was apparently getting "bold," as nothing had happened, and it was "in too great a hurry." It engaged Ly Singko, "a well-known opportunist and Chinese chauvinist," who had been repeatedly warned by the government for writing chauvinistic editorials for the *Sin Chew Jit Poh*. But *Nanyang* offered him more money—what Lee called "danger money"—to come over "to work up, to stoke up heat over Chinese language, education and culture." In the result, the campaign began to "generate some heat among the Chinese-educated." No specifics were offered or cited for the allegations of Chinese chauvinism or adulatory-communist articles, only generalities.[13]

All these things were happening, according to Lee, because Singapore appeared to be doing "too well" and "some people wanted to sour up our ground." Singapore was an important centre in Southeast Asia. So, the capacity to generate emotions could have an unsettling effect, and be used to push the government one way or the other. This could be useful to whoever wanted to influence the government. "We would be foolish if we are not alert to all these furtive activities." With those damning introductory remarks began the infamous crackdown on the print media which was to reverberate down through the years.[14]

The following sections deal separately with each of the three newspapers against which Lee made allegations of black operations, which rocked Singapore society to its very core in sheer amazement and disbelief, and ended for good the pristine universal media adulation for Prime Minister Harry Lee Kuan Yew and his PAP government.[15]

The *Nanyang Siang Pau*

On May 2, 1971, at about 3 A.M., ISD officers forcibly broke down the door of the home of Lee Mau Seng, the former general manager of the *Nanyang Siang Pau* and second son of the late business magnate George Lee, whose family owned and controlled the pan-Malaysian Chinese-language daily, roused him from his slumbers, and took him unwillingly away.[16] Lee Mau Seng and his family were about to emigrate to Canada. At about the same time, two top *Nanyang* executives were picked up at their residences and detained under the ISA. They were the editor-in-chief, Shamsuddin Tung Tao Chang, and the senior editorial writer, Ly Singko. A third executive, public relations officer Kerk Loong Seng, was picked up the next day.

Shamsuddin Tung Tao Chang, a Chinese Muslim and son-in-law of a former Kuomintang (KMT) consul in Malaysia, had been a working journalist for many years and was known for his strong anti-communist views and articles published in Singapore and Malaysian newspapers. The government alleged that Lee Mau Seng, as general manager, had brought Shamsuddin into the newspaper, under whose editorship the *Nanyang* policy gradually changed to one of "glamourizing communism and stirring up communal and chauvinistic sentiments over language and culture." Lee Mau Seng was also accused of bringing Ly Singko into the *Nanyang Siang Pau* to "reinforce the new *Nanyang* policy." Like Shamsuddin, Ly had a "strong KMT background," and had been the chief editor of *Ih Shi Pao*, a Catholic-sponsored anti-communist newspaper. Although his children were educated in English schools, Ly had, nevertheless, taken, according to the government, a "militant Chinese chauvinistic line, especially on Chinese language, education and culture."[17]

A May 2 government statement on the arrests said:

> The *Nanyang Siang Pau* has made a sustained effort to instil admiration for the communist system as free from blemishes and endorsing its policies, while highlighting in the domestic news pages the more unsavoury aspects of Singapore life.
>
> The glamourizing of the communist way of life at this juncture of Singapore's history is made all the more sinister by the fact that both Shamsuddin Tung and Ly Singko are journalists with a *Kuomintang* and anti-communist background.

A study of the Singapore and Malaysian editions of the paper in the last six months shows that the policy in regard to Singapore was deliberate and calculated. In the Malaysian edition, no attempt is made to play up communist achievements or to stoke communal sentiments over Chinese language and education.

On the contrary, in the Malaysian edition there is general support for that government's educational policies. On the other hand, in the Singapore edition, not only are communist achievements played up but the impression is built up of Chinese language and education fighting desperately for survival against a hostile government.

None of the editorials which appeared in the Singapore edition to work up fears over Chinese language and education appeared in the Malaysian edition.

These propaganda changes first started in the last quarter of 1970, several months before the recent spate of news about China and the American ping-pong team visiting China in April 1971.

In its campaign to work up disruptive and dangerous emotions, the paper continuously echoes the pro-communist cry that Singapore's independence is "phoney" by maliciously referring to Singapore as having undergone 150 years of colonial fetters, and that Singapore has not "in fact enjoyed real political freedom."

In a deliberate campaign to stir up Chinese racial emotions, the paper sets the mood of tension, impending conflict and violence by persistently reminding its readers of the violence, turmoil, and unrest of the turbulent 1957–59 period of Singapore's history.

By April 28, the *Nanyang* had reached the stage in the campaign when it was prepared to use conscious falsehoods to whip up communal fears. In its editorial of that day, the paper, under the pretext of criticism, openly incited communal hatred against the government.

Having over the weeks depicted the government as the oppressors of Chinese education and language, it went one step further. It branded the government as "pseudo-foreigners who forget their ancestors."

This is the battle cry that was once used by Malay chauvinists in Singapore against their multiracial compatriots before the island plunged into communal violence.

The policymakers of *Nanyang* are determined and appear to be in a hurry to create trouble in Singapore.

While he was general manager, Lee Mau Seng, who does not read or write Chinese, employed two formerly anti-communist journalists to work up pro-Chinese communist news and stoke up emotions on Chinese language and culture which will, if unchecked, lead to a communal explosion.

Though Lee Mau Seng handed over the management of *Nanyang* to his brother, Lee Eu Seng, in February this year, he still maintained a close working relationship with Tung Tao Chang.

There are all the signs of what in Special Branch terms is called a "black operation."

Lee Mau Seng may have been emboldened by the belief that his family wealth gives him power and immunity. They may also be under the delusion that by posing as champions of Chinese language and culture they could inhibit the government from acting to stop them in their mischief.

The Singapore government must, and will continue to take action against all those who allow themselves to be used by outside sources to the detriment of Singapore. The government will not be deterred by the wealth, professional, social or political status, or the protective patronage of powerful groups outside Singapore.

The government has taken action to prevent these men who, under cover of defending Chinese language and education, are letting loose forces which will sharpen conflict along race, language and cultural lines.[18]

On May 3, 1971, Lee Eu Seng issued a personal statement on the arrests of his brother and the three *Nanyang* executives:

> As chairman and chief executive, I have always been responsible for the policy of *Nanyang Siang Pau* and . . . I have never allowed it to be influenced by any group or organization from either here or abroad.
>
> It is necessary to state very clearly that in Singapore, the newspapers have a clear and definite duty to bring to the attention of the government (since there is no opposition in Parliament to do so) the wishes, criticisms and legitimate grievances of the general public.
>
> If the government uses the Internal Security Act to silence all criticisms they are depriving the people of Singapore the right of expression and dissent.[19]

On the same day, in an editorial, *Nanyang Siang Pau* protested the arrests, called on the government to withdraw "all grave accusations," and demanded "the respect due to us as an independent newspaper" and "clarification . . . after careful study of the incident."

On the afternoon of May 3, 1971, a triumvirate of ministers—led by the minister for foreign affairs, S. Rajaratnam, the minister for culture, Jek Yuen Thong, and the minister for home affairs, Dr. Wong Lin Ken—met with anxious pressmen at a press conference, whereat Rajaratnam assured them that "the government was not against any newspaper which was critical of government," and that there was "no change in [its] liberal [*sic*] attitude towards newspapers."[20] This was an office which was eminently outside the portfolio of Rajaratnam as minister for foreign affairs or as acting minister for labour, but whose involvement therein was attributable to his experience as a former journalist and undoubted intellectual ability in decisionmaking. The ministry of home affairs was, and is, for the purpose of administration, responsible for the Internal Security Department, which however deals directly with the prime minister in national security matters. In the event and, aside from this cameo appearance, Dr. Wong Lin Ken was, thereafter, marginalized. The fact that the official statements were issued under the name of his ministry from time to time does not detract from this observation. His tenure as minister did not last long, and he returned chastened to academia, after being brutally told by the prime minister to his face: "I don't want a liberal in my cabinet."[21] Although a professor of history, he had never really stood high in the political estimation of the prime minister. He later committed suicide.

The minister most directly affected by the unfolding media drama was Jek Yuen Thong, whose ministry of culture oversaw and regulated the media in all aspects; but he, too, was relegated, as will be seen, to a minimal role. This was partly because he did not enjoy Lee's fullest confidence in handling the growing crisis. Although pushed to the edge of the swelling scene, he was sometimes allowed to make fleeting public appearances to mouth a few appropriate lines before yielding the scene to Rajaratnam or to Lee. In this grim drama of speech and movement, Lee was in all respects the director and leading star, ably supported by a trusted and capable lieutenant, S. Rajaratnam. On May 4, 1971, the *Straits Times* loyally editorialized the *Nanyang* arrests:

> The Singapore government's action must be judged not by the canons of freedom of the press, but the purpose of regulations expressly designed to maintain security, to prevent subversion and to guard against communal conflict. . . .

The paper's policy in Singapore, the government said, gradually changed until it glamourized Communism and stirred up "communal and chauvinistic sentiments." This is the essential accusation, although it is not proof—while it may invite suspicion—of what the Special Branch calls a "black operation" organized from outside the country.

. . .

The *Nanyang* complains in its editorial that its policy has been misunderstood, . . . And it is difficult to justify the assumption of "misunderstanding" with the disclosure that cabinet ministers on two occasions last year warned the paper's general manager that the *Nanyang's* policy had become a security problem. That is the whole gravamen of the government's case. It acted in the direct interests of security.

On May 4, 1971, in reply to Lee Eu Seng's statement, the ministry of home affairs (MHA) issued a terse but ominous note:

Mr. Lee Eu Seng, chairman and chief executive of *Nanyang Siang Pau*, who was away in Europe the past year and reassumed control of the paper in February this year in a statement issued yesterday asserts that he has always been responsible for the policy of *Nanyang Siang Pau*. The government has taken note of this.[22]

On May 5, 1971, the *Nanyang Siang Pau*, in a second editorial, "The Journalist's Bounden Duty," stated that it "categorically opposed racialism and that it had never supported communism," and replied *seriatim* to the "three grave accusations" in the government's earlier statement on the arrests.

Interestingly, a series of interschool debates, organized by the government-owned Radio and Television Singapore, and appropriately, if not coincidentally, entitled "That Local Newspapers Have Not Played an Effective Role in the National Life of Singapore" scheduled for the same day, was abruptly cancelled "because the topic is too hot at present."[23] The abrupt cancellation of the debate spoke volumes for the profile on the prevailing climate of uncertainty and fear in Singapore.

On May 13, 1971, Lee Eu Seng, undaunted, issued another statement denying again the prime minister's "three serious charges," and renewed his call for the release of the paper's four executives.[24] Stressing that he was forced to counter the charges by providing the facts, which would "prove conclusively" that the government's action was based on "wrong information," he asserted that, contrary to its allegations, Lee Mau Seng returned to Singapore on January 22, 1969, from Malaysia, *before* the May 13 riots of that year, because his wife was admitted into hospital because of a serious illness. Later that same month, the couple had left for Hongkong to seek further medical attention. Mrs. Lee died in November 1969. Among the preposterous allegations against Lee Mau Seng was that he had helped to incite the Malaysian race riots of May 13, 1969.[25]

Lee Eu Seng further asserted that he had engaged Shamsuddin Tung as managing editor, and not his brother, who did not know and had never met him prior to the engagement—but who had tried to employ another Malaysian journalist, Chen Hsien Tee, who, because of the immigration department's refusal to grant him a professional visit pass, had subsequently gone on to head the Department of Journalism at the Nanyang University. It was also he who had employed Ly Singko, and had personally negotiated the terms of Ly's employment, which was necessary because of a shortage of editorial writers. His brother had never met Ly prior to his employment. It was "absurd," he concluded, that the *Nanyang Siang Pau*, a multimillion-dollar organization with "no foreign capital participation, and widely known for its fierce independence should be mentioned in the same context as papers receiving foreign funds by the prime minister, who recently spoke on black operations."

Lee Eu Seng's statement, if accepted—and there was really no good or cogent reason why his statement should not be accepted—went a long way towards absolving his brother and the other *Nanyang* executives of any complicity in the alleged black operation, except that it would have been a grave blot on the ISD's escutcheon on infallibility and, more particularly on the prime minister's, under whom the ISD worked and still works, and from whom it took and still takes instructions regarding his fears of and beliefs in perceived pockets of opposition and subversion. Besides, an absolution of the *Nanyang Siang Pau* and its independent-minded executives would not have fitted in with the prime minister's long-range plan of converting a perceived pocket of resistance into a propaganda tool of government.

Unknown to most Singaporeans, the then acting ISD director had apparently reported to the prime minister that the four *Nanyang* executives were innocent of any conspiracy to disrupt the internal security of Singapore. Not long thereafter, he was replaced by a new director. Indeed, the government offered to release the *Nanyang* newspapermen if the paper agreed to change its editorial policy.[26] It, however, refused, declaring that "we are fighting for a principle," and accused the government of "depriving the people of Singapore of freedom of speech." Its circulation soared. For this act of principled defiance, Lee Eu Seng was to suffer the same fate as his younger brother and, through the machinations of his powerful homonym, lose control of his family newspaper as well.

All three *Nanyang* senior executives were detained without trial, allegedly for "glamourizing communism and stirring up communism," and for good measure "communal and chauvinistic sentiments over language and culture," despite the grim irony that Shamsuddin Tung was a Chinese Muslim and Ly Singko a Roman Catholic, both of whom had a long and consistent history of supporting the virulently anti-communist Kuomintang. Given the fact that Ly had sent all his children to English schools, the accusation against him of being a Chinese-language chauvinist went against the grain of the government's case. That there were gross inconsistencies and inherent contradictions calling into question the allegations against each of them did not faze Lee in the slightest. On May 15, 1971, Rajaratnam repeated the shopworn allegation that the *Nanyang* had "glorified the communist system" and had gone "out of its way to confirm the allegations of unfriendly external forces that Singapore is becoming a Third China."[27]

On May 22, 1971, the MHA announced that Lee Mau Seng and the *Nanyang* executives had admitted under interrogation to "glamourizing the communist system and working up communal emotions over Chinese language and culture."[28] The public announcement of their "confessions" coincided with the formal orders of detention made against them. But they were still denied their constitutional right of access to counsel.

The order of detention for a period of two years against Lee Mau Seng stated that "since 1970 [he] had consciously, knowingly and wilfully veered the editorial policy of the *Nanyang Siang Pau* to (i) one of glamourizing Communism, and (ii) stirring up communal and chauvinistic sentiments over Chinese language, education and culture." The allegations of fact were that:

1. Under your management control, the *Nanyang Siang Pau* had deliberately and systematically instilled admiration for the Communist system. This had been achieved by presenting the Communist system as one free from blemishes. And whilst endorsing its policies, you had highlighted in the domestic news pages the more unsavoury aspects of Singapore life.
2. You had utilised the *Nanyang Siang Pau* to arouse communal sentiments over the Chinese language, education and culture, and created the impression that Chinese language and education were fighting desperately for survival in Singapore against a government hostile to the Chinese.
3. In your campaign to work up disruptive and dangerous emotions, you had continuously echoed in the *Nanyang Siang Pau* the pro-communist cry that Singapore's independence was "phoney" by maliciously referring to Singapore as having undergone "150 years of colonial fetters" and that Singapore had not "in fact enjoyed real political freedom."
4. You had used deliberate falsehood to whip up communal fears and openly incite communal hatred against the government.[29]

Almost identical grounds and allegations were given in the orders made against the other three executives, Shamsuddin, Ly and Kerk.

On May 23, 1971, *Nanyang Siang Pau* ran a blank editorial column as a protest against the detention of their four executives.[30] At a conference, Lee Eu Seng—quoting the imperious words of the prime minister himself, "The Singapore government does not flinch from any face to face encounter when the truth is involved"—demanded that the four executives be brought to an open trial. "Let the government face the people. Or they could set up a public commission of inquiry into these so-called black operations in Singapore." This was the first of many fruitless calls to the prime minister to constitute an independent commission to inquire into his allegations of black operations. As to the government's charge that they had admitted glamourizing communism, Lee Eu Seng commented: "Nowhere do I detect anything of black operations in the statements."

Denying that it was ever the *Nanyang* policy to glamourize communism, Lee Eu Seng disclosed that a survey conducted by the newspaper in March among the residents in the Housing and Development Board (HDB) flats showed that readers would like to read more news about China and crime stories. "Is that influencing policy or is it reflecting what our readers want to read? In this particular case, I certainly detect McCarthyism, that is, guilt by association." As for stirring up racial feelings, he said: "Singapore consists of a majority of Chinese. And being a Chinese-language paper, we naturally would encourage the study of the Chinese-language." (Which, in fact, the Singapore government is vigorously promoting today.)

On May 25, 1971, the government produced a photocopy of a document, dated April 2, 1971, purporting to be an editorial directive, as proof that *Nanyang Siang Pau* had glamourized communism. The directive, said to have been sent to Lin Pin, the editor of the Important News Page, by Shamsuddin Tung on the instructions of Lee Eu Seng, read:

> The managing director has directed that as from today, all news reports about China, except those that are libellous and slanderous, should, irrespective of their length and importance, be translated in full and printed on the front page.

Should there be insufficient space on the front page, they may be printed in other pages.[31]

In a statement issued that night, Lee Eu Seng said he failed to detect anywhere in his directive an intention to glamourize the communist system: "It was issued at the peak of the international ping-pong competition when teams from Canada, Britain and U.S. were all invited to play in China. The world would be watching the coming events with great interest and, furthermore, by issuing a signed memo, it clearly showed there was nothing secret or sinister."[32] On May 26, 1971, the government made a weird one-sentence reply: "If this is so, then why did Mr. Lee give instructions to destroy this memo?"[33] No evidence was adduced to show that Lee Eu Seng had issued instructions to have it destroyed. One is thus vividly reminded of the classic non sequitur: "When did you stop beating your wife?"

Habeas Corpus Applications

On May 5, 1971, Lee Mau Seng, Shamsuddin Tung and Ly Singko were granted leave by the high court to apply for writs of habeas corpus against the minister for home affairs and the commissioner of police. On May 11, 1971, Kerk Loong Seng was granted similar leave by the high court. Their applications were grounded on the denial of their constitutional right of access to counsel.

On May 26, 1971, a preliminary hearing on the right of access to counsel relating to Lee Mau Seng's application opened before the chief justice.[34] At counsel's request, the three other applications were consolidated as the arguments were largely common to all. Counsel submitted that there was unlawful detention of his clients by virtue of the denial of the constitutional right of access. They had been held incommunicado for three weeks.

The attorney general, Tan Boon Teik, submitted: "It has always been our contention that [under the ISA] there will be no right to counsel during the preliminary detention. But as soon as detention orders were made the detainees were informed through their counsel that they could see their counsel." The preliminary detention covers a period of one month. Any further detention requires an order from the minister. Such an order of detention is made at the end of one month from the date of the suspect's arrest or sooner if the ISD's investigations are completed by then. It can, therefore, mean a denial of access for as long as one month. In the case at hand, Marshall was only given access to his clients 20 days after their arrest. In the result, the court adjourned the hearing to enable him to take his clients' instructions germane to their detentions and applications.

On June 8, 1971, at the resumed habeas corpus hearing, the four *Nanyang* detainees, in separate affidavits, repudiated "in very categorical terms" the official statement dated May 22 that they had "admitted glamourizing the communist system and working up communal emotions over the Chinese language and culture."[35] Lee Mau Seng affirmed that in 1968 he had planned to emigrate with his family to Canada, and had received Canadian immigration clearance in 1969, but their departure had been delayed by his wife's illness. He had re-applied in 1971 and, pending the arrival of new permits, had agreed to act in his brother's place so as to enable him to take an extended holiday. His association with the *Nanyang* commenced in January 1970 and ended in January 1971. His affidavit also exposed official efforts—during his brief stewardship—to control, meddle and manipulate the publication of the *Nanyang Siang Pau*:

I was deeply dissatisfied in the course of the following months by interference and attempted interference in the publication of the paper by Mr. Li Vei Chen, press secretary to the prime minister, who caused me and my paper a great deal of trouble because we refused to obey orders issued by him.

Because of refusal to comply with those unwarranted interferences, I incurred the wrath and displeasure of this officer, and the *Nanyang Siang Pau* came under a ban which prevented it from receiving government press releases and notices.[36]

It was self-evident that the press secretary to the prime minister, Li Vei Chen, would not have had the temerity to interfere or intervene in the editorial policy of newspapers without the knowledge, approval or instructions of the prime minister himself. It was equally evident that the *Nanyang* was not the only newspaper at the time being denied "government press releases and notices" because of noncompliance with official instructions or refusal to toe the line.

Shamsuddin, in his affidavit, stated it was "farcical" to suggest that he was "ever a party to a campaign to work up disruptive and dangerous emotions," whilst Ly Singko said that during the many hours of interrogation and one which lasted 40 hours,[37] he had at no time made such a statement, and claimed his detention was mala fide. Kerk said that, as a publicity relations officer, he had nothing to do with *Nanyang* editorial policy, and had never at any time sought to influence that policy.

Marshall argued that the "twin grounds" of glamourizing communism and of stirring up Chinese chauvinistic sentiments were incapable of being dealt with adequately and intelligently, as they had intentionally been left vague and unnecessarily obscure, leaving them only to "fight with shadows." The allegations of fact were entirely false, and lacked particulars, which were specifically required when one was to be detained, and in danger of losing his fundamental personal liberty. The news reports about mainland China were all translated from foreign and western news agencies and *Nanyang* had at no time endorsed communist policies "as a matter of editorial comment or views." On the assumption that they could be said to be held for "arousing communal feelings and inciting disaffection against the government," Marshall suggested a trial *in camera* under the Sedition Act would be the appropriate course. As the case against them was based on editorials in the *Nanyang Siang Pau* over a given period, they would be in a position to rebut those allegations and to produce copies of the offending editorials to vindicate themselves. The question of unwilling witnesses would be obviated and their number restricted. The thrust of the attorney general's submission, on the other hand, was that as the decision to detain them was an executive act, no court could inquire into the reasons a detention order was made unless mala fide on the part of the president of Singapore was alleged, and hence, failure to do so was fatal to the applicants' case. Judgment was reserved.

On July 13, 1971, the chief justice held, inter alia, that "the constitution had clearly provided beyond a shadow of a doubt the right of an arrested person to consult his lawyer if he so wished and that this right must be accorded to him by the relevant authority "within a reasonable time after the arrest."[38] As to the orders of detention being "illegal or unlawful," it was not open to a court in Singapore to examine the grounds and allegations of fact for the purpose of deciding whether or not some or all of them were so vague, unintelligible or indefinite as to be insufficient to enable the applicant (Lee Mau Seng)—and by extension to the three other *Nanyang* executives—to make representation against the order of detention. In brief, it was not a justiciable issue. A sorely disappointed Lee Eu Seng observed in disbelief:

> The judgment of the Chief Justice . . . shows clearly that the Internal Security Act over-rules the basic principles of human liberty without allowing any recourse to existing legal institutions.
>
> The Internal Security Act should only be utilised under the most exceptional of circumstances. This is not so in the case of the arrest of the four top executives of the *Nanyang Siang Pau.*
>
> It has been clearly shown that the original charges of "black operations" are totally unfounded.
>
> To detain people for an indefinite period of time without trial is a clear act of injustice and in this case clearly shows indifference to public opinion.
>
> Mr. Lee Kuan Yew during the course of debate in the [Legislative] Assembly in 1955 expressed similar sentiments, and I quote: *"If it is not totalitarian to arrest a man and detain him when you cannot charge him with any offence against any written law – and if that is not what we have always cried out against in Fascist states – then what is it?"*[39] [Author's emphasis]

On June 25, 1971, the Commonwealth Press Union, at its annual conference in London, unanimously called for the immediate release or trial of the four *Nanyang* detainees, and viewed "with disquiet [the Singapore government's] recent actions which run counter to established Commonwealth precepts and risk impairment of Singapore's progressive and liberal reputation in the eyes of other nations of the free world."[40]

The government's case against the *Nanyang* executives was at best tenuous. The prime minister had acknowledged that Lee Mau Seng did not read or write Chinese, which made it questionable whether he really knew or was aware of what was being printed or published. It was equally clear that he had not engaged the two *Nanyang* executives in employment. His administrative connexion with the *Nanyang* was recent and temporary, and only for the period when his brother took a long delayed and extended leave in Europe. More pertinently, the bulk of the "so-called offensive articles, which precipitated the press crisis of 1971, appeared long after his resignation from the paper"—a fact which he confirmed in a long letter to the *Hongkong Standard*, from Canada.[41] He had sold out all his interests in *Nanyang* to his brother in preparation for his departure for Canada, which spoke eloquently of his interest in the company. That Lee Mau Seng had resented the intrusive interferences of the press secretary to the prime minister in the publication of *Nanyang* was as understandable as it was never officially gainsaid; but that was not a good cause for his detention. Furthermore, Lee Eu Seng's public statements showed beyond doubt that Lee Mau Seng had been wrongly accused, and, given the evidence, the conclusion was irresistible that he had been mistaken for his brother, Lee Eu Seng. The case against Shamsuddin Tung, a Muslim, and Ly Singko,[42] a Roman Catholic, each of whom had a long history of anti-communism, of "glamourizing" communism and fanning the flames of Chinese chauvinism over language, education and culture, has already been touched upon. And the suggestion that Kerk, a public relations officer, was influencing the course of the *Nanyang* editorial policy and direction seemed too bizarre for words.

The nub of the *Nanyang* problem was that it was a fiercely independent newspaper, which was generously salted with wealth-engendered hubris, as it was owned by a family with substantial means, which had no need, and had in fact refused to kowtow to officialdom and its directives. Such a newspaper could work the masses against the government. With a crucial general election around the corner, the prime minister could not afford the luxury of a free and independent newspaper to queer his political pitch. On January 28, 1973, Lee Eu Seng's long-expected arrest finally took place for allegedly "using his newspaper to incite the people against the government over issues of [Chinese] culture."[43] The vengeful prime minister had not forgotten him: "People with long histories have long memories. And I happen to have a long memory."[44] As with the case of the other detainees, no charges in court were ever preferred against him. He was detained under the ISA for five years. With his arrest and detention, the government cancelled the publishing and printing permits issued to him, and reissued them in the name of Tan Chin Har, a senior editorial writer.[45] And while Lee Eu Seng was conveniently out of the way in detention, Lee introduced consequential amendments to the press law to deprive him of his shares in and control of his newspaper, the *Nanyang Siang Pau*.

In October 1973—two and a half years later—Lee Mau Seng was released on a restrictive order after making a "public statement admitting his past mistakes," pending emigration to Canada.[46] While en route to Canada to take up permanent residence there, he stopped over at Hongkong, where he disclosed in a press interview that he had signed a "Russian confession" to obtain his release. Ruefully, he said: "I never understood the meaning of raw power and the nuances of politics in Singapore until I was hit. This has been an education." It was an excruciatingly expensive lesson, which both brothers had paid for in terms of their liberty and precious possessions to a vindictive government. It is bizarre to recount today that this self-same government led by its capricious prime minister is committing the cardinal sins of "Chinese chauvinism"—if not of "glamourizing communism"—for which it had doomed the two Lee brothers.[47] Now, openly asserting the superiority of the Chinese race in Singapore in numbers, language and culture, Harry Lee Kuan Yew has completely abandoned the concept of a "Singaporean Singapore"—where all citizens irrespective of ethnic origins were referred to simply as Singaporeans—in preference for hyphenated-Singaporeans. Unctuously playing up to ethnic hubris and ego, Chinese-Singaporeans are constantly being urged to remember their Chinese roots, culture and ancient heritage, learn their native language, retain the *Nantah* or emigrant-pioneering spirit—which Lee had crushed in an earlier generation for his political agenda then—visit the motherland and invest in the land of their forebears, among other ethnocentric objectives and projects. Commuting between these two territories with rapturous and breathless frequency, Lee now champions the cause of Communist China and its Chinese leaders before America and the world, and recently brokered the historic meeting in Singapore between the People's Republic of China and the Republic of China with the promise of more such meetings to come. These are, indeed, more weighty matters than the *Nanyang Siang Pau* reporting on the international ping-pong games and other events in Peking. In recalling the tragic case of Lee Eu Seng and the *Nanyang Siang Pau*, one wonders whether the former senior minister, S. Rajaratnam, would still condemn these goings-on, as "going out of one's way to confirm the allegations of unfriendly external forces that Singapore is becoming a Third China?"[48]

On June 13, 1992, Prime Minister Goh Chok Tong observed that Chinese-language newspapers in Singapore had grown from 330,000 daily about 10 years ago to 450,000 copies today, and voiced the new sentiment that "[Chinese] newspapers and books have an important role to play in preserving and promoting traditions and values which are central to Singapore's long-term survival and growth."[49] This may portend the confirmation of a redefinition of the government's envisaged role for the Chinese media to underline the Chinese-ness of Singapore.

The *Eastern Sun*

On July 17, 1966, a new English-language newspaper with the promising name of the *Eastern Sun* commenced publication, but, for reasons we shall see, did not reach its full meridian and, Icarus-like, plummeted earthward in a premature burnout due to official pressure. *Datuk* Aw Kow, the managing director of the *Sin Chew Jit Poh* and a stable of other newspapers, was the owner and publisher. He recruited R. B. Ooi, an experienced Malaysian journalist with somewhat out-moded views on newspaper management, as editor to run the new paper, assisted by his own wife, *Datin*[50] Aw Kow, as manageress, using the premises of the defunct *Singapore Standard*. Owing to growing differences with her in administrative and editorial policies, Ooi left the *Eastern Sun* within a year or so, and was succeeded by an Indian expatriate editor. At the relevant time, all the senior editorial and management staff were foreigners, who were rightly alarmed at the way Lee had framed his allegations against the newspaper.

On May 14, 1971, in a front-page reaction to the prime minister's allegations that a "certain English newspaper" was associated with a black operation, the *Eastern Sun* declared: "This newspaper has always been, and still is anti-communist." That same evening, at a PAP branch anniversary dinner, in an obvious reference to media black operations, Lee cynically sounded a warning against "stoking up heat" over language, culture and religion: "Newspaper editors do not owe you a living. They do not owe your children jobs. But my colleagues and I do."[51]

The next day, a government statement detailed allegedly secret negotiations between *Datuk* Aw Kow, a progeny of the well-known Aw family, and avowed high-ranking officials of a Chinese communist intelligence service based in Hongkong in early 1964, as a result of which *Datuk* Aw Kow received a loan of HK$3 million, which he had used to establish an English-language daily newspaper in Singapore—the *Eastern Sun*. In fact, the negotiations were with the Bank of China in Hongkong, which had extended the loans to him.[52] The bank—which has a duly registered branch in Singapore—no doubt also lends to other customers who would try to get the loans on the best terms possible. Be that as it may, Lee's statement continued:

> In return for this loan, which was made available at a ridiculously low rate of interest of 0.1 percent per annum, with a repayment of the capital to commence after five years, Aw Kow agreed that the *Eastern Sun* would follow three basic principles laid down by the communist intelligence service officials, viz.
>
> - On major issues—no opposition;
> - On minor issues—neutral stand; and
> - To maintain fairness in editorial comments and the treatment of news.
>
> These requirements were only meant to be a modest start in their long-term political objective of gaining control of the press in Singapore.
>
> In September, 1965, a second loan of HK$3 million was again made available to Aw Kow on the same terms and conditions. This second loan was paid into Aw's account with

Chung Khiaw Bank, Hongkong, of which he is a director, between September 28, 1965, and December 24, 1965.

The *Eastern Sun* commenced publication on July 17, 1966, and at once incurred heavy losses in its running costs. Between January, 1967, and March, 1968, Aw Kow had a series of meetings with the communist officials in Hongkong and was again granted a subvention of HK$1.2 million.

This time Aw was told that a Chinese operator under their control would be infiltrated into Singapore. This nominee would act as adviser to the *Eastern Sun* and carry out unacknowledged duties on behalf of the intelligence service. Aw was to provide a cover position in his newspaper organization for this man.

The communist officials made it clear that their representative would feed news items of their own choice to the Sin Poh group of newspapers.

Back in Singapore in mid-1968, Aw Kow attempted to sponsor the nominee's entry into the Republic. All his attempts were frustrated.

The intermediary used by Aw Kow to contact and liaise with officials of the communist intelligence service based in Hongkong was his own personal secretary and former deputy editor-in-chief of the *Sin Chew Jit Poh*, Julius Yeh Sai Fu. Yeh was arrested and detained under the Internal Security Act on February 25, 1971, and subsequently released on March 24, 1971, after interrogation.

Several outside forces, for different objectives and working independently of one another, have sought to capture and manipulate the local mass media, as one of the most effective ways of influencing public opinion and creating political situations favourable to their interests.

The *Eastern Sun* was allowed to pursue a moderate editorial policy to gain respectability as a responsible paper.

It is very likely that none of the members of the editorial staff of the *Eastern Sun* was privy to this black operation, nor knew what their preliminary role was.

No one should believe that the patronage of outside powers will give him protection or immunity, whatever his social, professional or political status. Action must be taken once the Singapore government decides that the situation must be stopped from going beyond the limits of security control.[53]

At about the same time as the official release, Rajaratnam told a dinner audience that the government's "tussle with some newspapers did not involve freedom of the press but the freedom of Singapore." The *Eastern Sun* had, in fact, "behaved responsibly" and had "consistently supported the government." The prime minister's allegation was not that the paper had misbehaved but that its proprietor had received $4 million from communist sources "to use the *Eastern Sun* on behalf of outside interests when the time came."

On May 16, 1971, the editor and six senior expatriate staff resigned from the paper and, in a joint statement, declared:

> We have discussed at length with the directors of this newspaper the sources of finance, and we are completely satisfied that these sources do not influence the editorial policy of this newspaper, for which only we are responsible.
>
> We have been told by high officials of the government that the editor-in-chief and senior staff are in the clear and that the policy of the *Eastern Sun* is acceptable and positive.
>
> We are sure, and the management has assured us, that when we leave the *Eastern Sun* will have to close down because of the staff shortage.
>
> As journalists of long standing we would not like to see any newspaper close down. But we hope that the government understands that we cannot work under this pall of distrust.

If the prime minister does not vindicate us and we leave after our one month's notice expires, we stand accused of being part of a black operation.

Since many of us will be working in other countries which also are anti-communist we would like the prime minister either to vindicate us or prove that the *Eastern Sun*, under our editorial direction, was part of a black operation.

The editor stressed that "on a personal level, he had not received a single editorial direction from *Datuk* or *Datin* Aw Kow since he joined the paper as editor-in-chief two years ago."[54] Two months short of its fifth anniversary, the *Eastern Sun* set. The paper had been using newsprint imported from communist North Korea; but there was, however, no suggestion that it had been purchased at friendship prices—only the loans!

Assuming for a moment that the *Eastern Sun* was, indeed, financed by Chinese Communist intelligence sources for long-term mischief, two things immediately strike an observer. As has been noted, there was no law prohibiting foreign investment in or the underwriting of, or the receiving of funds by, newspaper companies in Singapore, of which the *Straits Times* group of newspapers was perhaps the most notable example; and, secondly, given that the dark negotiations with Chinese Communist officials were to undermine the future security of Singapore, why was *Datuk* Aw Kow, who, from all official accounts, was not only privy to but also involved in that nefarious conspiracy, not arrested? Or, at the very least, brought in for interrogations? And, if interrogated, what were the results of those interrogations? The authorities were significantly silent. Why were they not made public? Could it be that they were not supportive of the prime minister's allegations? Other persons before or since this episode were detained for very much less under the ISA, and their so-called evil deeds published to the world. *Datuk* Aw Kow, however, seemed to have borne a charmed life![55] The conclusion is inescapable that there was no or not sufficient evidence to support the official allegations of a nurturing communist conspiracy—and the premature departure of the expatriate editorial staff from the paper, resulting in the total collapse of the *Eastern Sun*, had thus saved the face of Lee and his government.

Notes

1. Letter, *Straits Times*, May 22, 1959.
2. See Francis T. Seow, "The rule of law is no cliche in Singapore," speech, Williams College, Williamstown, Mass., Septermber 15, 1995.
3. *Straits Times*, December 16, 1969. See J. Victor Morais, ed., *Selected Speeches: A Golden Treasury of Asian Thought and Wisdom*. Kuala Lumpur: J. Victor Morais, 1967.
4. *Hansard*, Parliamentary debates, 15 March, 1967, cols. 1294–1295.
5. *Straits Times*, April 29, 1971.
6. Ibid.
7. A Malay word meaning a "son of the soil," that is, an indigene.
8. *Straits Times*, May 4, 1971.
9. *Sunday Times*, May 9, 1971. See also the *Eastern Sun*, May 14, 1971.
10. *Straits Times*, May 12, 1971.
11. *Straits Times*, May 13, 1971.
12. Malayan Chinese Association, a Malaysian political party and partner in the Alliance coalition government.
13. *Straits Times*, May 13, 1971.

14. Ibid.

15. For an excellent exposition on Lee's crackdown on the media, see Anthony Polsky, "Lee Kuan Yew versus the Press," *Pacific Community, An Asian Quarterly Review*, vol. 3, nos. 1–4, October 1971–July 1972.

16. For further details of the arrest, see Simon Casady, "Lee Kuan Yew & the Singapore Media: Purging the Press," *Index on Censorship*, vol. 4, no. 4, 1975.

17. *Straits Times,* May 3, 1971.

18. *Straits Times*, May 3, 1971.

19. *Straits Times*, May 4, 1971.

20. Ibid.

21. *Straits Times*, May 5, 1971.

22. Ibid.

23. *Straits Times*, May 14, 1971.

24. See Lee Mau Seng's letter to the Editor, dated June 26, 1974, *Hongkong Standard*.

25. See Polsky, "Lee Kuan Yew versus the Press."

26. *Sunday Times*, May 16, 1971.

27. *Sunday Times,* May 23, 1971.

28. *Straits Times*, May 24, 1971.

29. [1971] 2 *Malayan Law Journal* 137.

30. *Straits Times*, May 27, 1971.

31. *Straits Times*, May 26, 1971.

32. Ibid.

33. *Straits Times*, May 27, 1971.

34. Francis T. Seow, *To Catch a Tartar: A Dissident in Lee Kuan Yew's Prison.* New Haven: Yale Southeast Asia Studies, Yale Center for International and Area Studies, 1994; on methods of ISD interrogation.

35. *Straits Times,* June 9, 1971; see also [1971] *Malayan Law Journal* 137.

36. Ibid.

37. *Lee Mau Seng v Minister for Home Affairs & anor* (1971) 2 *Malayan Law Journal* 137.

38. *Straits Times*, July 14, 1971.

39. June 26, 1974. See, also, "Chauvinism and Mr. Lee," *Hongkong Standard,* June 1, 1974; and Moira Farrow, "Newsman says 'Fear rules'," *Vancouver Sun*, October 12, 1974.

40. *Straits Times,* June 26, 1971.

41. After his release, Ly Singko and his family emigrated to Australia via Paris, where he taught at Sorbonne University. He died on February 17, 1996, aged 82 years, in Sydney, New South Wales.

42. Speech, Liquor Retailers' Association, Singapore, October 3, 1965.

43. *Straits Times,* January 29, 1973.

44. *Straits Times*, January 29, 1973.

45. *Sunday Times,* October 14, 1973.

46. *Far Eastern Economic Review,* December 3, 1973.

47. *Sunday Times*, May 16, 1971.

48. *Straits Times,* Weekly Edition, June 20, 1992.

49. A *datin* is the wife of a *datuk*.

50. *Straits Times*, May 15, 1971.

51. See also David deVoss, "Southeast Asia's intimidated press," *Columbia Journalism Review*, March-April, 1978.

52. *Sunday Times*, May 16, 1971.

53. *Straits Times*, May 17, 1971.

54. See Polsky, "Lee Kuan Yew versus the Press."

5 The Government's Case Against the *Singapore Herald*

I would like to see minds stimulated and debate provoked, and truth refined and crystallized out of the conflict of different evidence and views.

Lee Kuan Yew[1]

In July 1970, a new English-language newspaper, the *Singapore Herald*, sprouted on thorny ground, albeit after official approval and advice. But before it could bloom into the full promise of its local and foreign investors, it was caught in a maelstrom of controversy, nipped at its roots, and thus withered away. Given its journalistic lineage, its implausible beginnings and untimely demise are the stuff of an incredible saga of nefarious plots, sinister intrigues, and skullduggery involving a medley of foreign investors, a diplomat, and conspiratorial international bankers and financiers—aided and abetted by the international news media—all bent on subverting the stability of the Singapore government. Such a cloth could only be woven by the imaginative and resourceful prime minister of Singapore, Harry Lee Kuan Yew.

The lacklustre reputation of the once formidable *Straits Times* owed as much to an indifferent editorial and news staff as to a sycophantic desire to please the establishment. For some time, Lee had "not been happy with the paper's longstanding habit of filling its pages with endless government speeches—often reprinted with an embarrassing number of inaccuracies." When the idea of another newspaper was first mooted, the government agreed, albeit warily, to its publication, as it perceived the lethargic local press wholly dominated by the *Straits Times* group could do with a little "livening up."[2]

The idea of an alternative newspaper to the *Straits Times* fired the imagination of a number of professional and lay persons. Notable among the investors was a high-profiled Malaysian, *Tan Sri Datuk* Donald Stephens, a former journalist himself and at the time Malaysian high commissioner to Australia, whose participation in the venture was welcomed by the minister for foreign affairs, S. Rajaratnam—who knew him—on behalf of Singapore officialdom. It is pertinent to bear this salient fact in mind in the light of subsequent official disclaimers and allegations. "If you are putting up money given by Donald Stephens, we give the benefit of the doubt: we have our suspicions. And we will judge it by the policy of the paper"[3]; so Rajaratnam told the founder-editor, Francis Wong. Because of the sensitivity of Stephens's official position, Wong specifically informed Rajaratnam that his investment would be channelled through a Hongkong holding company, so as to avoid any possible embarrassment to all parties concerned. Be that as it may, for diverse reasons, one of which was said to be the notorious May 13, 1969, riots in Kuala Lumpur, many of the original investors decided not to proceed with their original intention.

Thus, seriously undercapitalized, the *Singapore Herald* began its operations. As all the promised capital failed to materialize, Stephens—a former chief minister of Sabah—became the inevitable major investor in spite of himself. Stephens's share-holdings in the *Herald* were originally held by a Hongkong nominee company, Heeda and Company, whose entire interest therein was absorbed subsequently upon voluntary liquidation by a Sabah-based company owned by him. Soon after the *Herald* was launched, it ran into distribution difficulties and insufficient advertising revenue. It was not easy to loosen the stifling grip of the entrenched *Straits Times* group on the advertising and media markets. No newspaper, alas, could have had more inauspicious beginnings.

Overarching its growing predicament, the zestful *Herald* soon revived the deep-seated suspicions which the prime minister had of its founder-editor, and inspired his implacable hostility, for he began to see in this brash newcomer a host of problems for the government. Lee beheld a "half-politician" in Francis Wong—a former editor of the defunct *Sunday Mail*, a newspaper in the *Straits Times* stable—whose journalistic credentials and integrity were suspect, and whose editorial direction first of the *Sunday Mail*, and now of the *Herald*, fed rich the gnawing suspicions he had of him—notwithstanding Wong's congenial relationship with other PAP leaders, including Dr. Goh Keng Swee and S. Rajaratnam.[4]

Wong was also friendly with two prominent PAP dissidents, James Puthucheary and S. Woodhull,[5] both of whom had deserted the PAP with many others to form the opposition Barisan Sosialis largely over the vexed issue of merger with Malaya, and whom Lee had branded as "pro-communists."[6] In a healing gesture, Wong acted as an intermediary between the PAP leadership and the "pro-communists" who were agitating against merger, and tried to plead their cause with Rajaratnam, who, for his part, had only entertained Wong's visit because of a misconception that it was a press interview on the issue of merger with Malaya. Wong endeavored to persuade Rajaratnam that Lim Chin Siong, the Barisan Sosialis leader, James Puthucheary and S. Woodhull were really "not communists" but "nice chaps," and that they all should "patch up this trouble [over merger]."[7] Wong's credentials, if not motives, were suspect as he was thought by Lee at the time to be "playing a role for somebody else." Or, as George Herbert put it more pithily: "He that lies with the dogs, riseth with fleas."[8] Notwithstanding his reservations, Lee ostensibly left the matter of approval to Rajaratnam, who gave Wong his official benediction, coupled with this sage advice:

> Remember, you are a Singapore newspaper. Over the years, there will come moments when a Singapore newspaper will have to take a stand 100 percent for Singapore. You must be prepared to take issue, make quite clear against anybody, what Singapore stands for. So, once I

am convinced that you are 100 percent for Singapore, you can be [as] critical as you like because then I will not have the slightest doubt that your criticism is as a good Singaporean.[9]

Thus, right from the very beginning, the Singapore government knew of Stephens's investment and involvement in the *Herald* venture. Indeed, there would probably have been more capital investments by Malaysian investors but for the reasons already mentioned. However that may be, Wong was circumspect enough to seek the advice and approval of officialdom on the acceptability of the *Herald*'s foreign investors and sponsors before launching the publication. And, as there was then no legal prohibition against foreign participation, the question of foreign investors was never really an issue. Indeed, the venerable *Straits Times* was widely known to have British or foreign interests. In the circumstances and even without official approval, Stephens's and the other sponsors' open investments in the *Herald* were anything but sinister. There was no need for concealment. Nevertheless, the prime minister—as was his wont—later sought to give it an ugly twist by unjustly charging that the Singapore government had been kept in the dark about Stephen's involvement, as well as the size of his investments, in the venture.

Lest foul tongues should whisper abroad of shareholders' interference in the publication of the *Herald*, whether by its foreign or local shareholders, Stephens and the other shareholders wisely executed the usual management agreement, stipulating that the editorial policy and direction of the paper would squarely be in the hands of the editor and the editorial board. But, as events turned out, all those precautionary steps did not help the parties thereto when Lee's dark suspicions finally reared their ugly head. Meanwhile, after the briefing, Rajaratnam reassured Wong: "It's good to have [another] Singapore paper. Let's forget the past."

However, the ghost of merger past still rankled and had not been laid to final rest, and continued to hover ominously over the founder-editor and the *Herald*, enshrouding them finally in the phantom cloak of black operations, for want of a better pretext. Unlike its rivals, from its inception the *Herald* almost immediately took a lively independent stance on matters of public moment, concerning which its readers' letter-columns carried on a spirited dialogue which offended the staid establishment. Suspicious to the point of paranoia, Lee had Wong and the *Herald* closely monitored, whose free-spirited approach and insouciant treatment of matters held sacred and inviolate by the establishment only served to reinforce Lee's increasing distrust of the "half politician."

The *Herald* editorial posture over the arrest of the *Nanyang* executives was not calculated to endear itself and its editor to a leery prime minister. Unlike the *Straits Times*, which, from well-remembered bitter experiences, spelled out all the politically correct words and phrases that the government had acted "in the direct interests of security," the youthful *Herald* had the temerity to reserve its political judgment, pointing out, not without some truth, that "nobody could know the full facts of the case."

Paying scant regard to the forceful "advice" of the press secretary to the prime minister, and refusing to "co-operate" with the authorities—which Lee termed as "taking on" the government—Wong's actions repercussed in an official policy of harassment. Lee directed all government departments to deny press facilities and access to official press conferences to the *Herald*[10] and, to underscore his displeasure, forbade it all official advertisements. Government departments and statutory boards were instructed to cancel their subscriptions, and not to reply to readers' letters of inquiry published in the *Herald*. Officials refused to speak to reporters from the *Herald*, PAP members of parliament returned complimentary copies, and even the president of Singapore was said to have cancelled his subscription to the *Herald*. Some headmasters told teachers and students not to bring the paper to school, and, in some misguided instances, to even pressure their parents to cancel their subscriptions. But, as will be seen later, these attempts to crush the *Herald* created a reactive momentum of its own. For all practical purposes, the *Herald* and its staff had become journalistic pariahs to Lee and his PAP government.

The official denial of the bread-and-butter advertisements compounded the *Herald*'s financial problems. Lee had intended that the withdrawal of official advertisements and the resultant loss of revenue would swiftly bring the *Herald* to heel. But he had not anticipated the extent and intensity of feelings aroused among its friends, supporters and well-wishers who mounted a rescue attempt of the *Herald*. Amongst them was a consortium of Asian publishers. Unwilling to see the only challenge to the monopoly of the *Straits Times* go down, it established a management pool to save the *Herald*. Foremost among them was the newspaper proprietor and publisher Sally Aw Sian, who negotiated the transfer of staff and professional expertise with several companies and newspapers, including *The Age* (Melbourne) and the Westminster Press Group. Finance was reportedly forthcoming from "publishing companies from four continents," each being asked to take up a US$50,000 share. The participation of Aw Sian in the *Herald* was well known to Rajaratnam and the authorities. There was no mystery surrounding it, but Lee, nonetheless, characteristically attempted to cloak her investment with an aura of enigmatic intrigue.

To placate the prime minister, Francis Wong was offered up as a sacrificial lamb, and was replaced by Ambrose Khaw, formerly of the *Straits Times*, who was to have been assisted by two expatriates recruited from the *Bangkok Post*—Dominic Nagle and Bob Carroll as managing director and advertising director respectively. It was a high price to pay for a remote hope that it would procure a reversal of the prime minister's hostility toward the *Herald*. In any event, the *Herald* criticized the prime minister's public quiz on its source of funds, and reproached him for having "unfairly lumped" them together with those allegedly involved in newspaper black operations. In a telling editorial, the *Herald* said:

> There are no mysteries about this newspaper and there never has been.
>
> The opinions which are expressed in our columns, the judgments we make about what to print and how to present it—all these are decided here in this office by journalists who have Singapore's interests at heart.
>
> No one has pulled any strings. No one has and no one will.
>
> *That, indeed, was the assurance which was given to responsible senior members of the government before Heeda Ltd, was accepted, and Heeda's investment was cleared by them.*
>
> *The assurance was also given to a "very high level" government official before Miss Aw Sian's capital was received.* [Author's emphasis]

Referring to Lee's comments about Miss Aw's investment, it said:

> She has invested in this newspaper in the firm conviction that it also will be a success.

There was nothing unusual in such an operation. Other newspaper publishers invest in newspapers and then as far as policy is concerned, leave them strictly alone to serve their communities.[11]

The paper rightly claimed that all four English-language newspapers in Singapore had foreign investments, and added: "The point is: 'Does that investment come from an acceptable source and does it influence our editorial policy? In our case the sources were accepted and they do not influence our editorial policy.'"

Referring to his meeting with Lee, Khaw said: "It is true I agreed that it was unlikely that hard-headed men and women would put money into a newspaper, as the P.M. put it, to lose it—but there was a qualification. I said to Mr. Lee that he was assuming that this paper was not commercially viable from the start and could never be."[12]

On May 12, 1971, Stephens, who was being deliberately dragged into the controversy by a calculating Lee, wrote him a personal letter from Canberra, Australia:

> I have just heard that you had mentioned me by name in a speech in which you condemned the *Singapore Herald* because I have put a considerable sum of money into the venture.
>
> I feel I should tell you that my only motive in putting money into the *Herald* was because I have been in the newspaper business before and because I believe Singapore to be a country where my investments would be safe.
>
> Jimmy Hahn, formerly of Reuters, whom I have known for many years, . . . suggested to me that there should be place for another high quality newspaper in Singapore. I agreed with him and having known Jimmy to be a hard headed business man I told him that I would consider putting money into the venture.
>
> . . . the newspaper business is one business I really know something about.
>
> To infer sinister motives on my part is most unkind and unfair of you and somewhat ironic because it was my faith and belief in Singapore that persuaded me to invest in the *Herald*.
>
> I have had nothing to do with the running of the newspaper and the only say I have had was during discussions before publication when the question of policy was raised. Broadly, the policy was that the *Singapore Herald* should be genuinely Singapore orientated, a Singapore newspaper. I also made a point about the paper being pro-government, your government.
>
> On this I was told by Francis that it would not be wise for the paper to be too openly for the government as it would then be taken not as an independent newspaper but as a mouthpiece of the government. But I believed that my point was fully taken. When it was found that for some good reason or other Francis Wong was getting on your nerves I agreed at once to his removal.
>
> That just about sums up my part in the *Herald*. . . .
>
> I have never asked the paper to publish anything or not to publish anything at all. And this was agreed very early in the talks which led to the publication of the *Herald*—no interference in the running of the newspaper by shareholders.
>
> I assure you once again that as far as I am concerned my only interest in the *Herald* has been to see it become a success commercially and would bring in good returns for my investments.[13]

Lee did not disclose receipt or contents of this personal letter, for it did not serve his plan then. Disclosure would probably have widened, if not deepened, the credibility gap. Together with Wong's letter, it would have put the matter of Stephens's investment in the *Herald* in perspective, and the situation to rest. During the 1972 general election, however, Lee found its disclosure opportune, and released it to the *Straits Times*, which published it on August 30, 1972, prompting Stephens to write from Canberra, Australia, to the editor:

> Mr. Lee Kuan Yew has, I understand, given you a copy of a letter I wrote to him when he decided to kill the *Singapore Herald* . . .
>
> I knew Mr. Lee well and wrote to him in good faith; I did mention the fact the reason that I had put what he has described as my "old age pension," my savings, in the *Herald* was because I did have faith in Singapore as a good place to invest at that time.
>
> This however did not mean that I had no faith in my own country as a place for investment the way Mr. Lee has twisted it to mean.
>
> Everything I have is in Malaysia. The reason I agreed to invest in the *Herald* was because those who were able to obtain a publishing licence after lengthy discussions with Mr. Rajaratnam felt, and I agreed with them, that Singapore being a city with a large English-educated population was ideal for such a newspaper and was therefore a good business venture.
>
> We had no other motive. Naturally those who initiated the publication of the *Singapore Herald* had plans for expansion to other areas once the *Herald* was on its feet. But the *Herald* was growing too much muscles to be tolerated.
>
> Mr. Lee's twisting of my words to make it appear that I had more faith in Singapore than I have in my own country is of course typical of the man.
>
> His allegations that I was in no position to raise the $1.5 million invested in the *Herald* and suggesting therefore I had obtained the money from elsewhere he knows to be untrue.
>
> The money invested was from my timber company, Nabahu Company, and the one and a half million invested was from this company.
>
> This timber company has been in operation for more than ten years and, although one and a half million dollars is a lot of money, this company did make large profits from its timber operations, and a one and a half million dollars loss did not cause it to be insolvent.
>
> I have other investments in Malaysia which certainly exceeds what was invested in the *Herald*.
>
> I may also mention that my company intended to invest only $250,000 in the *Herald* but others who originally had agreed to back the venture did not do so, and as someone who had faith in Mr. Jimmy Hahn and others who had got the *Herald* started, I continued to give it my support to the extent eventually my company was the major shareholder of the *Singapore Herald*.
>
> There are many other people who have invested in Singapore—British, Americans, Australians, Germans and others; does Mr. Lee Kuan Yew really believe that they have done so because they have no faith in their own country?[14]

In the meantime, on May 15, 1971, Rajaratnam continued to plug the black operations line, telling a dinner audience:

> Our tussle with some newspapers is symptomatic of the new turn in Singapore politics. . . . And black operations are part of this play. It is no fantasy. Let us not be befuddled by cries that the tussle we recently had with some newspapers involves freedom of the press. It involves the freedom of Singapore.
>
> The fact that the paper [*Eastern Sun*] has been friendly to us has not deterred us from revealing that it is a weapon being kept in the cold for future use.
>
> This should give the lie that our revelations in regard to the *Herald* is because it has been critical of us. We are a tough political party. We are quite capable of coping with criticisms— and most certainly criticisms from a newspaper to which we gave every encouragement and facility when it wanted to establish itself in Singapore.

We had our doubts then but decided to give it a chance to either confirm or dispel our doubts.

As it turned out, it became clearer to us that criticism had become a cover for eroding the will and attitudes of people in regard to certain fundamental matters.[15]

Rajaratnam said that he recalled that the "first issue of the *Herald* began with a series of seemingly friendly articles about the armed forces. Then came some letters and editorials, which eventually added up to a campaign against national service." He continued:

The paper knew full well as the government knew full well that national service was not popular. The *Herald* also knew full well that national service was vital to the future of Singapore. Any moron could have become popular by working up feelings over national service. If it wanted to establish itself as a paper fighting for the people against an oppressive government this was the right issue for the *Herald* to exploit.

There were also from time to time articles and letters, under cover of criticism, to work up agitation over our labour laws, the Internal Security Act, over communist detainees, over the permissive society and so on.

"The story is not yet over," he declared darkly. There were "financial ramifications" arising from this "one interesting fact"—financial interests in Hongkong, United Kingdom, Australia, Philippines and Korea were forming a consortium to save the *Herald*. Professing bewilderment, he said: "I do not know why so many countries should be interested in the fate of a small newspaper in Singapore," insinuating that one reason why Singapore had become an important target for black operations was that, contrary to general belief, it had acquired a new strategic importance. Hitherto, it was important only to the British. "But today and in the seventies, it will become important to many more big and not so big nations."

All About Reece

Late on the afternoon of May 17, 1971, *Herald* foreign editor, Bob Reece, and his Malaysian-born wife and features editor, Adele Koh, were ordered to leave the country within 48 hours by immigration officials.[16] No reasons were given. Another *Herald* journalist, sub-editor M.G.G. Pillai, whose visit pass expired on May 12, was also told that he had been refused extension. No reason was given.

Khaw depicted the immigration action, in a letter to Rajaratnam, as "obvious efforts to cripple a newspaper," and "morally indefensible and must be repugnant especially to a former journalist like you," and the refusal to renew his staff's work permits as "brutal," especially when there was a "lamentable lack of local talent."[17] In this connexion, he wrote twice to Rajaratnam appealing for an appointment to discuss work permit clearance, but even before he was given an appointment date, he was deprived of the services of those three persons. Another five *Herald* staff members were also awaiting renewal of their professional visit passes—some of which had already expired.

An official statement denied the next day that it was a "48-hour surprise" since Reece and his wife had known that they would have to leave the country on the expiration of their one-year professional visit passes. And that, on May 3, 1971, Khaw had informed Rajaratnam that Reece had tendered his letter of resignation dated May 1, which he had accepted, but had not disclosed this to the immigration authorities, when the *Herald* applied on April 29 for the extension of their professional visit passes, among others.

On May 18, Khaw courageously replied in a signed editorial "The Right to Live with Dignity," denying the paper was a threat to the security of Singapore: "Unless we defend ourselves publicly, we may be forced to disappear under a clinging morass of half truths, innuendos and downright inanity."

On May 19, at a press conference presided over by the prime minister himself, Rajaratnam reiterated that Reece had not been expelled from Singapore as he had known that his permit would not be renewed after May 7, and had been given an extra 10 days to pack up his belongings. "So, I don't know why it was said that he got 48-hours' notice to quit."[18] Furthermore, Rajaratnam said Khaw had told him that he had accepted Reece's resignation "with alacrity," after he had refused to go along with Reece's suggestion to come out with a "forthright editorial" condemning the government on the *Nanyang* arrests. But, according to Reece, he had tendered his resignation "as a result of dissatisfaction with conditions of service and a desire to return to freelance writing, based in Singapore."[19]

Rajaratnam then disclosed Francis Wong had informed him earlier that Reece, an expatriate, was brought in as foreign news editor. Hence, he said: "It is very odd that a foreigner should take issue in regard to a domestic issue. It confirmed our suspicion that Mr. Reece is not just a foreign editor." But Rajaratnam was careful to state that the "precipitated" departure of Reece and his wife had nothing to do with officialdom's suspicions about the *Herald* operations.

Reece described Rajaratnam's statement that he had resigned over the *Nanyang* arrests as "mischievous." He had thought of resigning and returning to free-lance writing for some time but had been persuaded to stay on by the management, which was corroborated by the *Herald* application for the extension of his visit pass.

Be that as it may, it is singular that Wong had kept Rajaratnam closely informed on even such mundane matters as the recruitment and employment of expatriate staff by the *Herald*, including their designations—just as Khaw sought Rajaratnam's clearance for the extension and issuance of work permits for old and new expatriate staff.

Khaw tried to explain that, although Reece's resignation had been accepted "with alacrity," the immigration's notice to him to leave Singapore within 48 hours was, nevertheless, "brutal"—and its acceptance was motivated by a concern for "the future of the company [which] could be jeopardized" because Reece's remarks on the *Nanyang* affair were known to have caused the government "obvious displeasure." The *Herald* had sought "a policy of appeasement" because its "commercial operation was dogged first by fierce competition, by ill-luck, and not least by ominous signs of implacable hostility towards this paper," which all added up to "a pattern of such implacable hostility that we ourselves . . . can't see the justice for this." And, before Khaw could say anything further, Lee rudely cut him off, and deftly deflected the issue:

> I don't have the whole afternoon. . . . I had nothing to do with the launching of this paper. Mr. Rajaratnam gave his blessings and I supported [him] because I have confidence in Mr. Rajaratnam's good judgment. And he gave his blessings despite certain misgivings. . . . Let me explain this: That the *Herald* would not have got off the ground if we didn't want it to get off the ground. That's to begin with. And Mr. Rajaratnam had reservations, I said,

"Well, never mind, you decide on it." And he will explain why. We gave it the benefit of the doubt—and said let it run.

With those chilling remarks, the controversy over Reece and his wife ended, only to surface briefly about a month later at the International Press Institute (IPI) conference in Helsinki, Finland. In the meantime, departing Singapore, Reece and his wife denied, in a joint statement, that they had any prior indication that their passes would not be renewed: "In the context of the black operations charges levelled by the government, we feel that our expulsion implicates us some way." They were pointedly even denied "two-week social passes" to visit Singapore.[20]

A Letter to the Editor

On May 18, 1971, the *Herald* published a letter date-lined May 16, Kuala Lumpur, from its founder-editor Francis Wong, setting out the origin of the newspaper, the reasons for his resignation, and his hope that the *Herald* "founded with the best of intentions would be given a chance to get on with the job." It was an important letter.

> I now work in Kuala Lumpur because it has become impossible for me to practise at home the only craft I possess.
>
> Mr. Lee Kuan Yew's recent references to the *Herald* could not but cause the public to suspect that the paper was founded by foreigners to make trouble in the Republic, and that I myself am some kind of foreign agent.
>
> To erase this unjust impression, I wish to place on record an account of the beginnings of the *Herald*, its relations with the government during the period when I was its editor and the developments which led to my resignation at the end of February this year.
>
> In particular, I wish to clear up the mystery which has been created around Heeda Ltd. and *Datuk* Donald Stephens, and to shed new light on the assertion that the *Herald* "took on" the government.
>
> The *Herald* had originally been conceived by three journalists—the present editor Mr. Ambrose Khaw, the late Norman Siebel, former *Straits Times* sports editor, and myself.
>
> *The Singapore government had been kept fully informed of the Herald's capital sources and the reasons for the need for Datuk Stephens to invest in the Herald through a Hong Kong holding company.*
>
> I and my associates had hoped to raise capital for the newspaper in Singapore, but our portfolio of potential investors began to crumble because of the May 13 riots in Malaysia and the resultant business uncertainties here.
>
> *Datuk* Stephens's name was then brought in by Mr. J.J. (Jimmy) Hahn, then general manager for Reuters in South-east Asia, who had joined me, and now managing director of the *Herald*. *Datuk* Stephens was Mr. Hahn's good personal friend—at that time a stranger to me.
>
> Together we presented the project to *Datuk* Stephens on a commercial basis and, on that basis entirely secured his participation.
>
> Naturally enough, *Datuk* Stephens asked many questions about our editorial policy. I said the journalists in our group felt that the Singapore government had the right answers on all the big questions and that this belief would be reflected in our paper.
>
> I added that the public utterances of the Prime Minister, my own conversations with other senior ministers and the fact that Singapore was stable politically and doing well

economically persuaded me that there would be scope for the kind of reasoned dialogue and debate that makes for lively journalism.

With regard to Malaysia, I said we had a duty to report the facts straight and interpret events from a Singapore standpoint, but had no interest in political sniping.

Datuk Stephens had thought those positions very reasonable and readily agreed that there should be an instrument of the board of directors giving me full control of editorial policy.

I was, and am, completely convinced of the *Datuk's* bona fides. *It occurred to me, however, that his open association with the firm might be exploited to embarrass our claim to a Singapore orientation. It struck me too, that the Datuk might find himself in an awkward position if, through no fault of his, we should incur the displeasure of the Malaysian government.*

And so I suggested that he make his investment through a holding company. The choice of the name Heeda Ltd. and the decision to register in Hong Kong were his; the original suggestion was mine. And there is no mystery to it at all than that.

Moreover, the Singapore authorities were put fully in the picture on common insistence.

On Mr. Lee Kuan Yew's charge that the *Herald* "took on" the government, I say this statement ascribed to us more courage or foolhardiness than we actually possessed. What is true is that—more out of considerations of survival than of heroics—we did not always do what we were told.

I resigned from the *Herald* because of government pressures to deny the newspaper all access to official news sources at a crucial juncture in the paper's negotiations with Miss Aw Sian of Hong Kong for additional finance.

A local group, and a group headed by Miss Aw, were just about to sign on the dotted line. To restore their [the new investors'] confidence it was necessary to normalize our relations with the government.

For this, there obviously had to be a price. I told my colleagues that if that price should turn out to be my resignation, then so be it.

The Prime Minister's statement on my resignation, however, implied that some kind of unsavoury plot had been nipped in the bud. I had long ago got over feeling bitter on my personal account. My only hope is that the *Herald* would be given a chance to get on with the job.[21] [Author's emphases]

It was a vital letter from and by a person who was *au courant* with its origin and policy, and its investors, and intimately involved in active management of the *Herald*. There was no official denial of its contents, contrary to the usual practice of the Singapore government. Thus Wong's letter should have settled the matter but, unfortunately, the *Herald* affair was not allowed to be treated as an ordinary matter. The prime minister was still searching for dark shadowy configurations, which were not there.

Replying to the prime minister's constant reiteration that the *Herald* had been "taking on" the government ever since it commenced publication, a *Herald* cartoon entitled "Some Contest!" succinctly depicted the real situation. It showed Lee manning a Singapore army AMX–13 French-built tank about to run down a small baby, labelled "*Herald*."

Prelude to the Prime Minister's Press Conference

On May 17, 1971, Lee and Rajaratnam[22] met with newspaper publisher and financier Sally Aw Sian, alone at City Hall, over the *Herald* newspaper's sources of funds.[22] She had flown in from Hongkong at Lee's request for the meeting. Lee and Rajaratnam also met with *Herald* managing director Jimmy Hahn and editor Ambrose Khaw, severally and jointly.

On May 18, their meeting with Miss Aw Sian resumed, with Jimmy Hahn present on this occasion, after which *Herald* bankers, vice-president and manager of Chase Manhattan Bank, Hendrik J. Kwant, and credit marketing officer, Robert Quek, were ushered in to join the meeting.

The management and manipulation of meetings wherein disparate parties—oftentimes unbeknown to one another—meet alone, severally and jointly with the prime minister and/or a cabinet minister at different times in different places in the same building, and whose colloquia are invariably recorded on tape or in writing, "in case there is any misunderstanding," during which the weight of authority is skillfully brought to bear on them, is a hallmark of Lee's orchestral skill. It is difficult for a persona thereafter to protest any subsequent change of mind or heart, or of being misunderstood, without being confronted by the tape or the written record. Or, as in this case, by the sudden production of confidential details of the *Herald* bank accounts and transactions before the relevant persons at the several meetings. Miss Aw Sian was initially alone, deliberately isolated from the *Herald* senior staff and its bankers, firstly, to ascertain from her the source of her funds; secondly, to convince her that, being the shrewd businesswoman she undoubtedly was, she could not possibly hope to make any money from further investment in the *Herald*, and certainly not in the face of official hostility towards it; and, thirdly, to obtain from her a commitment of disinvestment.

The next step was to cut the *Herald* off from its source of money supply by "persuading" its bankers, Chase Manhattan Bank—which was looking to Miss Aw Sian's participation to bail the *Herald* out of its financial difficulties—to stop their line of credit because Miss Aw Sian had decided not to invest further in the venture. And, lastly, to convince the *Herald* staff that there was no hope of any bailout by anyone.

Time and space are often of the essence, and the party or parties are kept separated and away from one another for as long as is necessary, and are given little or no time for mutual discussions on the matters for which they had been summoned by and to the prime minister's office. Once the set objects are achieved, a press conference is called—the press corps having been alerted beforehand by his press secretary to stand by—presided over by Lee, at which the awe-struck and dumbfounded dramatis personae are led out and exhibited to an assembly of reporters and a battery of cameras—and who, if experience is any guide, would merely nod or mouth the appropriate monosyllables to the prime minister's enunciation of events. Lee almost invariably dominates the press conference, during which he keeps the dramatis personae on a tight leash, cutting them off whenever they show signs of balking or straying from the agreed text or script.

The Press Conference

Comfortable with the results of the preliminary meetings, the featured press conference was staged soon afterwards at City Hall, with the minister for foreign affairs, S. Rajaratnam, the *Herald* editor, Ambrose Khaw, its managing director, Jimmy Hahn, and the Chase Manhattan bankers in attendance. Only Miss Aw Sian was absent. It is crucial to the success of the strategy that the press conference should follow immediately after the conclusion of the aforementioned meetings. No intervening period, adjournment or delay is allowed lest the parties have any second thoughts on the matter. This press conference is a classic Lee performance, and repays careful study.

Dripping with heavy sarcasm, a smiling prime minister began by professing his "only regret" at the absence of Miss Aw Sian, who had left for Hongkong that morning, from the conference, whose absence had deprived them of the "privilege of hearing how she had parted with half a million dollars of her money" in return for three *Herald* receipts—S$100,000 in February, and S$200,000 in March, both for shares, and S$200,000 on May 5 termed as a loan—signed by its cashier. "'Please sign that and say for a loan. No more for shares!'" she had, according to him, told the *Herald* cashier. She did not receive any share certificates. His sarcasm was unmistakable.

He had requested Miss Aw to stay back for the press conference so that the assembled reporters could ascertain for themselves whether they believed her story of how after "just meeting" Mr. Jimmy Hahn, through the introduction of Mr. Adrian Zecha, she had parted with S$500,000 as "additional equity." "If he had been Miss Aw Sian," Lee sniggered, "he would not have parted with S$500,000, just like that, without knowing the financial standing of the company."[23]

Turning to Aw Sian's financial rescue operation, Lee announced, with sardonic satisfaction, that she had declined to invest more funds in the *Herald*. He had arranged for Kwant, who did not know her, to meet with her at his office, unabashedly portraying the orchestrated encounter as a "favour" to the banker, so that he could hear from her own lips that she would not put any more of her money in the *Herald*. Jubilantly, he produced Miss Aw's note handwritten on his official stationery: "My investment in the *Herald* is limited to S$500,000 only. I don't intend to put any more money of my own money in it." He had extracted the note from her during their meeting: "I wanted to make quite sure it's in her own handwriting what her position was."

Although she personally was "worth a lot of money," however, Lee, made it abundantly plain he did not believe the money which she had invested in the *Herald* belonged to her, notwithstanding her assertion to the contrary—because of the "curious way" she did her business. "She looked a bit unhappy when I pressed her. But, being a lady, I thought, well, that's about as much as we could ask her." Nonetheless, he was pleased, if not almost relieved, when she indicated that she did not intend to "part with any more [of her money]."

With a triumphant smile lighting his lips, Lee announced the *Herald* would have to cease publication unless it could find S$4.5 million more to keep going. It must first make money to pay off an outstanding debt of S$4.5 million before any investor in the *Herald* could recover his own money. Hahn and the banker, Kwant, were asked to publicly affirm the sad financial situation of the paper, whereupon Lee exclaimed rhetorically: "The question is what foreign money is going in to hire a lot of foreign personnel, to run a losing newspaper."

Lee next deftly maneuvered the banker into making a further public affirmation that the accounts of its customer were overdrawn by S$850,000, that no further credit would be extended to it, and that a recommendation would be made for its foreclosure. The prime minister's statement that the bank had stopped honouring cheques totalling S$28,000 was publicly confirmed by the banker, who had earlier been hectored by him into disclosing the same. Lee, who had made known to the hapless banker in words and action what he had expected of the bank, prodded the banker to announce its future course of action, to which a discomfited Kwant feebly replied: "The time has come for us to make a decision," but, not entirely satisfied with the statement, Lee pressed on:

Lee: Otherwise, you would have paid out another $28,000 today, wouldn't you, on the overdraft? And that's another $28,000 plus which you'll be chasing. Or, you think, I did you a disfavour?

Kwant: No, Mr. Prime Minister.

Lee: You are quite sure I did you something to the good.

Kwant: Might be, Mr. Prime Minister.

Lee: Saved your bank money?

Kwant: I think what you have done was told us the facts of the *Herald* case.

Lee: I think that about sums up the case of the *Herald* before the story enters a third installment.

Smiles of triumph creased his swarthy face. By any yardstick, it was an impressive performance. It was an awesome exercise in publicly compromising the financial integrity of a major foreign bank in Singapore—reportedly the second-largest in the world at the time—and discrediting its customer, a struggling newspaper, whose main transgression appeared to have been, judging from the tenor of the press conference, to have crossed him in its editorial direction—and not some nebulous black operations.

For an island state, which prided itself as a significant financial capital of the world, it was a dismal display of the nonconfidentiality of bank-customer relationship, where a prime minister could summon for information and publicly interrogate the senior officer of the bank on the accounts of a customer, announce the stoppage of credit to and the honouring of the cheques of its customer. With no inkling of the bank's move until Lee announced it at the press conference, Jimmy Hahn might well be forgiven for wondering what the prime minister or his office had to do with the commercial operations or the financial problems of his newspaper. A reporter inquired of the prime minister whether the *Herald* would be published that week, to which Hahn interjected to say that it would still carry on until it was foreclosed. Bristling at that defiant interruption, Lee retorted: "The cheques are not being met. You've heard Mr. Kwant."

Asked whether the government had any inherent objection to foreign investments in Singapore newspapers, Lee, skirting the question, replied that the Singapore government had a very keen interest in knowing what foreign capital came in, for what purpose, and if it went into newspapers. It was very anxious to know whether it was coming in to make money, sell news, sell advertisements or for other purposes. Ambrose Khaw interrupted to observe the prime minister had used the word "operation" only once, and from the way the prime minister unfolded the story, he was talking in terms of a commercial rather than a black operation: "You are not persisting in this charge of 'black operations,' are you?" In an unequal exchange of obfuscated bullying, Lee attempted to silence Khaw by showing up his ignorance and, when it failed to dampen the irrepressible Khaw, told him bluntly that he was "not part of the press conference," but merely "a part of the *Herald* staff whose credit has been seized."

Lee: Mr. Ambrose Khaw, you told me—and it's all on tape—that you have nothing to do with the financial arrangement of the company and therefore you are not in a position to say yes or no. I am telling you these facts. You are not telling me. I have told you what the facts are, not you told me.

Khaw: Quite right.

Lee: I have assembled the facts from Mr. Hahn and from Miss Aw Sian. No, but he
        told me that [you] do not know anything about the financing. So, if you know
        nothing then you are exonerated, isn't it? Like Mr. Krishniah [editor of the
        Eastern Sun] you are exonerated.

Replying to questions from the floor, Lee claimed he was "very far from satisfied"
that the *Singapore Herald* had nothing to do with any black operations and professed
extreme perplexity as to why S$1.32 million had to come from a timber company in
Sabah owned by Donald Stephens and some others to start a newspaper in Singapore
"*without them telling us that it was their money.*" [Author's emphasis]

Q: But your suspicions don't go beyond that?
Lee: Well, I think I leave [it] to your imagination. I would be extremely interested
        to know about the investors if any new ones should be found to rescue the
        Herald. The *Herald* had all the hallmarks of a hasty operation. What sane
        person would put money in it? The *Herald* had exhausted some S$2.3 million
        working capital before the end of last year and was running an overdraft.

Interestingly, he did not think that there was a common link between *Nanyang* and
its four detained newspapermen and the *Eastern Sun* or the *Singapore Herald*. There
were, be it noted, he said, several different operations going on "like several elephants
stomping over the same ground."

Q: But when you say "operations" you mean commercial operations or subversive
        operations?
Lee: I think operations for more than just commercial returns. I mean, what I ask
        you—if you would want me to believe as a sane rational fellow, if I were Miss
        Aw Sian—and I never made the money that she has and having got the money
        that she had—I wouldn't part with $500,000, however nice Mr. Hahn looks.
Hahn: She didn't give it to me.
Lee: Nor would I give it to any company managed by Mr. Jimmy Hahn on the basis
        saying "here you are, $100,000, $200,000, $200,000" without knowing what
        was the financial standing of the company and she didn't know until I brought
        Mr. Jimmy Hahn and confronted him.
Kwant: . . . with all the accounts, Mr. Prime Minister. Like I was, you know, a bit
        confused. You don't keep all the . . .
Lee: $500,000 in three months? And you are confused about what it is all about?
Kwant: No. I am not confused about what it is all about. I am confused after meeting
        you.
Lee: You are going to make money or you are going to make other things besides
        money and be prepared to lose it?
Q: Could the Prime Minister suggest where the $500,000 might have come from?
Lee: *I haven't the faintest idea. I wish I had.* I pressed Miss Aw Sian very hard, and
        she was very hard put to say that it was her money and she insisted it was and
        you saw the document. She said she is not going to part with any more money,
        now that she knows what a losing concern it was.
Q: Sir, if the *Herald* should find the money somewhere, what would your view or
        the Singapore government's view to its continued publication?

Lee: We would be interested to know who would be putting what money, and for what purposes?

Q: The major factor in this case is not being editorial criticisms of the government in the *Singapore Herald*?

Lee: I would say the editorial criticism, you know 13,000 circulation, 13,400. But I think they are less long-termed in their planning in the development of the sales and establishment of the companies like, say the *Eastern Sun*. That was a much better "ops" I thought, much better, that lasted five years. And was beginning—yesterday—they reached 20,000.

Kwant: They never audited these figures.

Q: Mr. Prime Minister, do you think the financing of the *Singapore Herald* is just as sinister as that behind the *Eastern Sun*?

Lee: Well, that depends upon what . . .

Q: Communist agents?

Lee: No, no I wouldn't . . . I would find it difficult to find the Communists subsidizing the *Herald*. It has all the hallmarks of a hasty "ops." [Author's emphasis]

Kwant, a banker, could be forgiven for being all at sea after encountering the maestro in action. This was vintage Lee weaving a baffling tangled web of foreign intrigues over Kwant's run-of-the-mill bank customer. He could not, however, point a finger of suspicion at the communists "subsidizing" the *Herald* and, if it was not them, who then could they possibly be, if at all? The funds which had helped to start it up came in large part from Donald Stephens, whom Lee believed did not have the money:

> If I were a Sabah timber merchant with a million dollars to dole out to make money, . . . I would write a nice letter to a colleague whom I know, and say, "My dear Raja,[24] do you know, this is all my money, in fact," [which] would come in really to start a good, fair, critical newspaper presenting the news to the people, adding to the ferment of discussions, and so on. I would have thought that was a very sensible line.

But, hard as he tried, Lee could find no one sinister lurking in the woodpiles of his overwrought imagination. Rajaratnam remarked: "We are not against criticisms, but we want to be quite sure criticisms are not on behalf of somebody else." The ramifications of the *Herald* equity cast doubt, he said, on whether it was on behalf of some purpose other than purely commercial reasons. Lee strongly suspected that Stephens was acting as a front for a foreign country, but neither he nor Rajaratnam publicly or explicitly voiced their inner suspicions that Stephens was acting as a proxy for the Malaysian government. Questioned on the government's attitude if the *Herald* had local finance, Lee replied that if it had "genuine local finance" from people in Singapore, it would be different, because not only would Singaporeans have the right to make money, they would have a right to make politics. "And I think I would acknowledge that right." But, given the momentous events which were soon to engulf the domestic media, it was another PAP pie in the sky.

At a press conference that evening, Hahn, in a poignant understatement, declared the government was exerting "undue influence" on the bankers to foreclose on the *Herald*, whilst Khaw accused the prime minister of using the charge of black operations as a window to look into the *Herald* accounts, and, on seeing it was "seriously in the red," provided the bankers with an opportunity of declaring that its operation was not as sound as it was before, so that they could recommend foreclosure to their head office;

and with touching naïveté warned that they would seek injunctive relief from the High Court if the bank "foreclosed" on its overdraft.

Denying that any member of the *Herald* staff, management or editorial, was in any way involved with black operations, Hahn said that if the prime minister wanted to close the paper, "let him announce it" and reveal the evidence, and he would ask for a White Paper or a commission of inquiry to be set up. Hahn revealed that a sorely disappointed Miss Aw Sian had telephoned from Hongkong, whose conversation was tape-recorded for distribution among the press corps, in which she asserted that her two-day meeting with the prime minister was "a total waste of time." She had tried to clarify for him her position as an investor in the *Herald*, but he seemed to have adopted an attitude of inexplicable hostility towards the *Herald*.[25] He had also cast doubts publicly on her motive. She continued:

> *This is all the more surprising because earlier this year, I took pains to clear these matters personally with Mr. S. Rajaratnam.* As a result of my conversation with Mr. Rajaratnam, I understood that I could go ahead with plans to put the *Herald* on a firm commercial basis. Since then, however, the Singapore government has embarked on a series of actions against newspapers.
>
> It is not for me, in this context, to comment on the cases of the *Eastern Sun* or the *Nanyang Siang Pau*. The point, as far as I am concerned, is that neither the *Singapore Herald* nor I were, or could conceivably be associated with whatever those newspapers or their proprietors are said to have done. Yet the Singapore government has deliberately tried to suggest some associations by insinuations and innuendoes. Such a suggestion, of course, is entirely unfounded.
>
> It was in these circumstances that I received a request from Mr. Lee Kuan Yew to see him in Singapore. I assumed that this would be an opportunity to set his mind at rest regarding my investment.
>
> I had a two-hour meeting with Mr. Lee on Monday, May 17. Again, at his request I stayed for another day and on Tuesday spent six and a half hours with officials again with Mr. Lee.
>
> Although I offered every proof that my interest was purely commercial and that none of the other publishers whom I had hoped to interest had sinister motives, it was to no avail.
>
> Mr. Lee appeared to have a fixed idea that there was something suspicious and the only purpose of our discussions seem to be to make me admit it. Since there was nothing to admit, the meetings despite their length were a total waste of time.
>
> *I have already made it clear that I have reached the original limit to support the Herald. I told Mr. Lee that I would not go beyond that amount in the face of the hostile government attitude.*
>
> I can only observe that from my short connection with the *Herald*, it will be regrettable if the skills, enthusiasm and idealism of the staff of the *Herald*, most of them young and all of them dedicated to the future of their country, is wasted.
>
> As for myself, I have offered Mr. Lee every opportunity to satisfy himself of my good faith. He has neither accepted these opportunities nor has he been able to substantiate or even specify his allegations. They are therefore clearly shown to be without any foundation whatsoever. [Author's emphases]

Compared with the prime minister's own statements at the press conference, Miss Aw's statement had a refreshing scent of truth about it for, among other things, it showed that Lee had not told the whole truth regarding her investment in the *Herald*. In any event, there was a notable lack of response to her statement—an uncharacteristic lapse on Lee's part. Far from succumbing to the pressures put on it, the staff of the *Herald* soldiered on, and the daily circulation of the embattled paper rose steadily from 13,500 to 28,000 copies. Countless Singaporeans came out to support it. When it finally ceased publishing, its circulation had reached 50,000 copies.[26]

A Legal Notice of Demand

On May 20, 1971, the bank's solicitors gave formal notice of demand to the *Singapore Herald*[27] to repay within 48 hours loans totalling S$1.03 million, in the first step towards foreclosure. The loans, the bank stressed, had been made on "purely commercial considerations," which was at that time thought "a good risk." The legal notice of demand came in the afternoon, as employees of the *Herald* rallied round the management by offering to work without pay, seven days a week, to help keep it going despite its being in the red by S$4.5 million. Late that night, the *Herald* announced a "marvellous gesture" by its entire staff, who had signed a pledge to work without pay indefinitely. Khaw announced: "We have emergency plans. We will continue to publish as long as we can. In fact, we have every reason to believe we shall be continuing to publish for a very much longer period than anticipated by some people." They were fighting words, which Lee was unaccustomed to hearing and which, no doubt, raised his hackles.

Meanwhile, in Hongkong, Miss Aw Sian announced that she had not given up her bid to save the *Herald*, and reproached Lee for "totally unethical behaviour."[28] Amplifying on her reproach of his conduct, her spokesman disclosed that, while she was in conference with the prime minister, he actually sent for the bank and demanded from it details of the *Singapore Herald* indebtedness to it. After the bank had given him the requested information, he then asked it to say affirmatively whether or not it would foreclose on the paper. It was an amazing revelation, which did little to burnish the tarnished reputation of the prime minister or of Singapore as a regional banking centre. It revealed the contempt with which he held the laws of the land and the confidentiality of banking transactions. Troubled by repercussions touching its banking integrity, the Chase Manhattan Bank insisted that whatever confidential details it gave to the Singapore government about the *Herald* were obtained under duress. As a pertinent *Review* editorial noted at the time:

> Western and Chinese businessmen are uninterested in the bank's explanations. As businessmen, they want their bankers to fight to the bitter end to ensure their accounts are shrouded in secrecy. Lee's remarks on his suspicions of the motives of certain foreign investors, and his government's readiness to denounce such major sources of new capital as Hongkong, are hardly calculated to advertise Singapore as Asia's most agreeable business climate.[29]

Acknowledging that "our motives almost certainly will be questioned by the government of Singapore, but that is its privilege," Jack Spackman, an Australian journalist and chairman of the Hongkong Journalists' Association, proposed a fund-raising campaign to help the *Herald*. He said it would be worthwhile if the association's effort helped the *Herald* to survive even "for only one extra day."[30]

The opposition United National Party and the University of Singapore Students' Union, in separate statements,[31] called on the government to set up a commission of inquiry into "the entire black operations affair." Like the earlier call by Hahn, this latest call for a commission of inquiry fell upon the tin ears of the administration. Singapore Polytechnic students held "demonstrations" in their campus protesting, amongst other things, the government's action against the press. Public sympathy was slowly but steadily coalescing around the *Herald*.

Interviewed in Canberra in the interim, Stephens denied that there was anything sinister about the *Herald* or his interest in it, underscoring the fact that all shareholders in the *Herald* had signed a declaration upon its launching that they would not interfere in Singapore policies, but would instead report the news fairly and without bias.[32] He was first approached about starting a newspaper in Singapore in 1969 by Jimmy Hahn, an old friend from the Reuters news agency and now managing director of the *Singapore Herald*. Saying he had faith in Singapore as a stable country which could well support another newspaper, he had invested through a Hongkong holding company called Heeda. There was nothing secretive about it. The owner of the *Hongkong Standard*, Miss Sally Aw Sian, put S$1.5 million into it. There were several other backers behind the paper. Stephens discounted Rajaratnam's reported statement that a consortium of financial interests in Hongkong, the United Kingdom, Australia and the Philippines was forming to save the *Herald*. The Hongkong interests would be Heeda and Miss Aw Sian, and others, just friends who already had a financial interest in the paper. There were also Singaporeans with an interest in the paper.[33]

On May 21, 1971, Dr. Ernest Meyer, the director of the International Press Institute (IPI), cabled Lee appealing for a postponement of action against the *Herald* pending the "constitution acceptable to you of a neutral commission to investigate those aspects of the newspaper's finances and operation which have caused you to take action against it and which may involve principles which the IPI is committed to preserve."[34] Meyer sent a copy of his cable to the Chase Manhattan Bank, Singapore, and to David Rockefeller, chairman of the Chase Manhattan Bank in New York, requesting the bank to postpone action in the hope that the appointment of such a commission would result in a situation to which further investment in the paper would be possible. In response, on May 28, Rockefeller asked Lee to defer a final decision on the newspaper until "a bank official could look into the situation more closely."[35]

In a lengthy provocative cable in reply to the IPI—which was sent under the name of the Minister for Culture Jek Yuen Thong, but which bore the unmistakable finishing touches of the maestro—the Singapore government prevaricated that it was "very interested" in the reasons why a Malaysian politician, Stephens, should have invested S$1.5 million in the *Herald* via a holding company in Hongkong, making him the principal and majority shareholder of the *Herald* without anyone being able to know of it, until recent disclosures.[36] The cable asked: "Is it his own money? Or is he in turn a nominee of other persons with a keener interest in the politics of Singapore?" We have earlier seen the innocuous circumstances of Stephens's involvement in the *Herald*, but Lee subscribes to the fervent belief that an allegation, if repeated often enough, will sooner or later be believed.

Ignoring Miss Aw Sian's earlier explanations, the cable persisted: "The government is also interested to know how Miss Aw Sian was made to part with S$500,000—S$300,000 for shares, S$200,000 for loan. What were the rates of interest and time for repayment of the loan? Was it her own money? Why were there no documents for these payments other than receipts? How was she to obtain control of the management of the *Herald* over Donald Stephens's S$1.5 million shares? He who pays the piper calls the tune. This has been the case with the *Herald*."

Jek Yuen Thong—whose peripheral role as minister for culture in this whole sordid saga has already been noted—disclosed the receipt of a letter by the prime minister from Stephens in which Stephens had agreed to the removal of the former editor Francis Wong, after Miss Aw Sian had begun investing in the *Herald*. After referring to the foregoing, the cable inquired: "Who is now the controlling shareholder in the *Herald?* Stephens with $1.5 million or Miss Aw Sian with $500,000 for shares and a loan?" Jek also told Meyer that the government would be very grateful if he could find out the reasons for the two foreigners investing in a nonprofitable newspaper venture in Singapore. The government would like to know, too, whether the Chase Manhattan Bank had extended credit well beyond the assets of the *Herald*, and whether there had been any special guarantor for the S$1.8 million due to them. The cable ended: "You want to find further funds for the *Herald*. There were also recent press reports from Hongkong of an international consortium to invest in the *Herald*. But the principal shareholder, *Tan Sri Datuk* Donald Stephens, yesterday publicly denied that a consortium of financial interests outside Singapore was being formed to save the *Herald*."[37]

The official cable reply was replete with questions, the answers to most of which Lee and the Singapore government already had known from personal interrogations of Miss Aw Sian, Kwant and several others; and, in any event, all of which the constitution of an independent commission of inquiry could investigate or lay to rest; but Lee, being the good advocate, knew fully well that a commission of inquiry was only worthwhile if its conclusions went a predetermined way. No such tribunal on the *Herald* affair was ever set up because it could not be milked for his political advantage. Indeed, if at all, it would work to his political detriment.

Late that same night, the IPI made an unprecedented appeal to its individual members for urgent funds to keep the *Herald* going, for the closure of the paper "would be one more battle lost in the fight for the freedom of the press."[38]

On May 21, 1971, the Singapore National Union of Journalists (SNUJ) launched a "Save the *Herald*" campaign, urging its members and the public to give at least one day's wage each to the *Herald*, and sign up for a year's supply of the newspaper to "keep the paper going during its present financial crisis."[39] Affirming its commitment to Singapore's continued security and stability, the SNUJ declared that it was not convinced by statements made so far by the Singapore government that the *Herald* posed a threat to the security of Singapore, unless the government could substantiate its charges against the newspaper. The SNUJ strongly believed that fair criticism and comment were an integral function of a newspaper, and any attempt to intimidate a newspaper into acting otherwise was repugnant to the profession.[40]

The University of Singapore Democratic Socialist Club called for a public clarification of the "confusion and doubts surrounding the Singapore government–*Singapore Herald* controversy," and urged the parties to answer publicly:

- WHY Mr. Lee Kuan Yew was "far from satisfied" that the *Singapore Herald* had nothing to do with any "black operations?"

- WHAT was the government's allegation against the *Herald*? Is it involvement in "black operations" or "taking on the government?"

It asked the government to define the demarcation between criticisms and "eroding the will of the Singapore people" and what the government meant by the *Herald* "taking on the government." "Until and unless involvement in black operations by the *Singapore Herald* is proved, the issue clearly remains a matter of freedom of the press," the statement said. Among the student organizations involved in the Save the *Herald* campaign was the Student Christian Movement of Singapore (SCMS), which was accused some 16 years later of being a Marxist organization.[41]

The Industrial Workers' Union of Singapore accused the prime minister, in a public statement, of side-tracking the issue in his charges of black operations against the *Herald*. Instead of giving prominence to his charges of black operations, Lee had brought in the newspaper's money crisis. The union said it believed Lee's action "to stop all money from flowing into the *Herald*" was intended to "force the *Herald* to bow down to him."[42]

The opposition political party, Barisan Sosialis, commenting on the *Nanyang* arrests, the *Eastern Sun* closure and the *Herald* affair, accused the government of conducting a "campaign of terror tactics" against the local press. The newly formed opposition political party, the Peoples' Front, called for an independent commission of inquiry "to clear up the black operations affair once and for all."[43]

Meanwhile, the *Herald* was deluged with telephone calls and personal visits by friends and well-wishers pledging money and support, and "endless sources of people who wanted to help the *Herald*" raise money to meet the 48-hour notice of demand by the Chase Manhattan Bank. Eight thousand dollars were received by the *Herald* from the public on that day alone.[44]

At a press conference, Hahn disclosed that in its efforts to forestall closure by its bankers, the *Herald* was planning to apply for listing on the stock exchanges "so that Singapore people who care can be more actively associated with the company." The listing requirements of the stock exchanges of Singapore and Kuala Lumpur—the stock exchanges were then fused—were that a company must have a paid-up capital of at least S$2 million of which S$750,000 or 25 percent, whichever was more, must be in the hands of not fewer than 500 shareholders holding not more than 10,000 shares and not less than 500 shares each. For that reason alone, if not hidden official pressure, it was unlikely that the *Herald* would be able to procure a listing on the stock exchanges.

Deploring Chase Manhattan Bank's capitulation to Lee's "unfair pressure," Hahn noted the bank had not even asked the *Herald* for permission, either verbal or written, to publicly disclose details of its financial position. He had sought legal advice on this and on the bank's notice of demand; and was advised that it was "most unusual" for a commercial bank to recall a loan by giving 48 hours' notice, especially when the company was a going concern and not under any threat of execution by its creditors. It was normal practice that, when a commercial bank was no longer willing to finance a company, it would endeavour to make the company slowly liquidate the overdraft or pressure it to find an alternative banker, threatening legal proceedings only after all efforts by friendly means to recover the loan had failed. It was unprecedented for a commercial bank to appoint a receiver and manager under a debenture immediately on the expiry of a 48 hours' notice of demand.

Considering that its loan was fully secured, and all things being equal, a commercial bank would take such a drastic step only to enforce the debenture on a company's property when its security was endangered by either fraud or threatened execution by other creditors with prior claims. Sometimes, if sufficient securities were given, such as guarantees from directors and other persons of good financial standing, the bank might allow the company to continue for a while to find the money to repay the bank in the future, as what the bank was concerned with most was the recovery of its loans and not the demise of the company. Thus, Hahn asserted that unfair pressure "most certainly" had been brought to bear on Miss Aw Sian to sign the aforesaid note that she would not put any more money in the *Herald*. Miss Aw Sian's note was, therefore, "questionable." Hahn reiterated that if Lee had evidence of black operations "let him bring it out" in a commission of inquiry.[45]

On May 22, 1971, in response to appeals by the IPI and others, Chase Manhattan Bank in New York announced that it would send its senior vice-president for Far East Trading, Francis Stankard, to Singapore to make an on-the-spot assessment of the paper's financial situation, pending further action. The bank's officials indicated privately that the move was aimed at giving the *Herald* newspaper a breather for a few days at least to come up with new money or guarantors. It was a welcome, albeit brief, respite from imminent closure.

In an interview with the London *Sunday Times*, Hahn repeated: "We intend to continue publishing to the very end," and, referring to Jek's recent statement, said:

> Once again a junior minister Mr. Jek Yuen Thong, minister for culture, has resorted to insinuations and innuendos to try to justify the draconian and unjustified action taken by the government against the *Herald*.
>
> Mr. Jek should realize that character assassination is absolutely useless. Instead of hot air, he should urge Mr. Lee Kuan Yew to establish an independent commission of inquiry to investigate publicly the finances of the *Singapore Herald*.
>
> Mr. Jek questioned the reasons for two foreigners investing in a not profitable newspaper in Singapore.
>
> I have also one question to ask Mr. Jek: "How many industries in Singapore, with or without financial support from the government, have been able to make a profit in less than a year in an atmosphere of extreme hostility from Mr. Lee Kuan Yew?
>
> I would urge the minister of culture to do his homework in future before issuing statements against the *Singapore Herald*.[46]

Meanwhile, students, accountants, shop assistants, journalists and many others were making a beeline for the *Herald* office offering their services, free of charge, whilst others were clearing up an accumulation of administrative work, answering telephone calls and receiving cash donations.

In Kuala Lumpur, the *Utusan Melayu* editor-in-chief cabled the IPI protesting Lee's crackdown on the press in Singapore and advising that he would not attend the Helsinki conference the following month if Lee was allowed to speak there. In Manila, the National Press Club of the Philippines, in a cable to the IPI, voiced its concern at the "strong-arm tactics" used on the *Singapore Herald*, and, in a press release, declared:

The National Press Club of the Philippines views with alarm reports that undue pressure is being brought to bear upon the *Herald* of Singapore for its critical posture against the administration of that state's government.

A pattern of notion has become common in governments which are being subjected to severe criticisms by the mass media—the adoption of oppressive methods to stifle legitimate dissent and criticism.

The harassment of the press for performing its bounden duty is not at all new, even in countries where democracy is being preached.

So it is not at all surprising if the government of Singapore would use strong-arm tactics against one of its more perceptive critics like the *Herald.*

But such moves have only toughened the resolve of those in the press, and the people whose interest they are sworn to serve to protect the cherished freedom of expression.

The NPC registers in no uncertain terms its vehement protest to any form of intolerance to the exercise of the freedom of speech and to the press, be they heads of state, governments, government functionaries and their hirelings, or private citizens.[47]

The National Press Club of the Philippines (NPC) cabled David Rockefeller to "use his influence in freezing any move that will lead to a foreclosure of the *Herald*," the demise of which "would be a blow to press freedom." Writing to *The Times* of London, Khaw said:

This newspaper began almost one year ago with one purpose—to provide this state with an English-language newspaper which would reflect the news and aspirations of Singaporeans from their own viewpoint.

Now, because we have done just that, our very existence is in danger because of "black operations" charges laid against us by the government of Singapore.

We do not set ourselves up as champions of press freedom—we only ask for our rights as human beings.

We hope world opinion may help to sway our case—for, no matter where those rights are impinged upon, we believe they affect all men everywhere.

Britain has an enviable record of defending those rights, not only at home, but also abroad. That is why we are moved to ask for your support.

We have the strength and stamina to fight for our own battles, but the support of friends can nevertheless be welcome.[48]

The Jakarta Foreign Correspondents' Club cabled Lee protesting the strong measures taken against the Singapore press. So, also, did the Australian Broadcasting Corporation in a cable protesting "attacks on free and democratic press in Singapore."

On May 23, 1971, the *Straits Times* published a significant NTUC statement that if the *Herald* was to be saved, it should be done by local financiers, "who are not likely to act as Trojan horses for hidden foreign operators," and not by any foreign sources. The case against the *Herald* was taking a subtle turn. The mounting national and international pressure on Lee and his government was having an effect, albeit still slight.

Meanwhile, the Save the *Herald* movement gathered momentum as more people visited the newspaper's offices to offer help in money and in kind. On one day alone, the *Herald* received more than S$40,000 in donations, advance subscriptions and payments by casual advertisers who had joined the movement. Students were still going out on to the streets to canvass subscriptions on the paper's behalf, while the paper's staff continued working long hours to demonstrate their faith in the paper. Right up to the very last day, university and polytechnic students were helping to sell copies of the *Singapore*

Herald. Acknowledging the unparalleled outpourings of public support and assistance offered, the paper said:

> Your help—and more important your determination to help us defend what you believe to be precious—gives us courage to continue.
> We will not buckle under and the picture is not as bleak as it has been made out.
> We shall overcome.[49]

Hahn repeated yet again his call for a commission of inquiry: "If the prime minister has anything against us, why not appoint an independent commission of inquiry? If there are political overtones in our case, let the government say it." Commissions of inquiry are, in fact, an old staple in Lee's political arsenal to which he resorts as often as the opportunity and the end result warrant it; but, given the facts in this case, Hahn and all its protagonists might just as well be baying at the moon. It was not—and could not—possibly be to Lee's political advantage to hold a commission of inquiry into the crackdown on the media, especially the *Herald.*[50]

On May 23, 1971, the SNUJ, *Times* chapel, expressed its support for the *Herald* asking its members to give one day's pay plus one year's subscription to the *Herald* because it could

> not accept the government's accusation that the *Herald* was involved in black operations merely upon the government's bare say-so, without proof of it. That being the case, they could not stand idly by and let the government close down the *Herald* through putting pressure on the bank. . . . The government had made so many allegations but had not or would not substantiate what it had made about the *Herald.* Until the government produced the evidence they could not accept the government's fears on the basis of what it had said so far. The *Herald* had not in any way shown a pattern of being consistently against the government. It might have criticized the government but that did not add up to the black operations pattern that the government was insinuating.[51]

Officialdom was suffering a severe image problem in Singapore and with the international media. It was a situation which had not entered into Lee's calculus of strategy and stratagems. Something had to be done soon before the situation spun irretrievably out of control. It came in the form of the NTUC's timely call that the *Singapore Herald*—a victim of Lee's paranoia—should be saved by Singaporeans themselves. The NTUC enjoys a symbiotic relationship with the PAP, and one of the prime minister's most trusted lieutenants then, C.V. Devan Nair, was its secretary general who was charged with the grave responsibility of keeping an eye on labour. On several occasions, Devan Nair, an eloquent orator, had acted as Lee's troubleshooter.

Meanwhile, the chairman of the Press Foundation of Asia (PFA), Joaquin Roces, and his chief executive, Amitabha Chowdhury, flew into Singapore from Manila to meet with Lee and Rajaratnam, but Lee had little time for them.

In Kuala Lumpur, the National Union of Journalists—Malaysia, *Utusan Melayu* chapel, condemned "Lee Kuan Yew's dictatorial attitude towards the freedom of the press." Planning to raise funds for the *Herald* journalists, it released a statement endorsing the "view of the SNUJ that Mr. Lee's statements that the *Herald* is a threat to Singapore's security is far from convincing." But the *Straits Times* for its part responded in an editorial, thus:[52]

In taking action he has against three Singapore newspapers, Mr. Lee Kuan Yew was aware that his motives might be questioned. He could be quite certain that newspapers, newsmen and their professional associations would respond, as they always do, to any challenge to press freedom. Even so, Mr. Lee cannot have expected quite the storm that has gathered, in particular the emotions aroused in Singapore. . . .

Mr. Lee has accused all three papers, the *Nanyang Siang Pau*, the *Eastern Sun* and the *Singapore Herald* of complicity in "black operations," of adopting editorial policies inimical to Singapore's interests and security.

. . . The case of the *Singapore Herald* has excited much greater interest, is more difficult to unravel, and because of the *Herald's* feud with the Singapore government, raises as neither the *Nanyang* affair nor the *Eastern Sun's* closure does, the question of freedom of the press. Money has been invested in the *Singapore Herald* from outside Singapore. This is clear. But was this a "black operation"? There is no suspicion or taint of Communist money.

Every journalist and every Singapore newspaper will feel some sympathy for the *Herald*. Its plight has a simple economic explanation. The *Herald* was undercapitalized. It is possible that the paper's founders and its original backers saw an opportunity which did not exist. Their published aims were impeccable. The *Herald* announced in its first issue the intention "to involve itself totally in the many-sided efforts of Singaporeans to enrich the content of an independence they did not seek, but of which they are now proud." The money ran out. The *Herald*, as launched, was not a viable proposition without the certainty of a great deal more capital becoming available as the need arose.

It is a little difficult to understand on what basis the additional capital which is the subject of interest was invested. It could not have been contributed with much hope of money making. Our own concern has rested largely on the sternness of the government's attitude. It seems, however, to be the government's contention that the *Herald* has said and done nothing which could bring real official wrath upon its editors. It is a matter again of money. We hope the *Herald* will survive. But generally speaking where there is evidence of "black operations," and where, for purposes of circulation and popularity, there is a concentration on communal causes which can rouse racial emotions, placing in jeopardy the basis of Singapore's unity, the government cannot fail to act.[53]

Replying to the above editorial, Khaw, quite properly, said:

. . . It takes two to quarrel, and we have *not* had a feud with the Singapore government, as alleged. We have only been at the receiving end for months of a relentless battering by the government. Patiently, we held our fire until we were forced to the wall a week ago.

What feud are you talking about? Are you referring to the ban imposed on us secretly by Mr. Lee Kuan Yew on two occasions? Could you possibly also have heard of Mr. Lee's personal vendetta against our first Editor-in-Chief, Mr. Francis Wong?

You say in your editorial that additional equity could not have been contributed with much hope of money making. A firm as reputable as Cooper Brothers completed a project analysis and cash flow which showed that the *Herald* project could be economically viable. In every business, there is an element of risk.

You say our plight has a simple economic explanation—that our project was under-capitalized. Up to yesterday records at the Registrar of Companies showed that the *New Nation*, of which the *Straits Times* Group is a partner, had an authorized capital of two million dollars and paid-up capital of two dollars—made up of the *Straits Times* one dollar and the *Herald Weekly Times* Limited one dollar.

In the last sentence of your editorial, it is implied, without any basis whatsoever, that there has been a concentration on communal causes in our paper. Even the government has not accused us of concentrating on communal causes which can arouse racial emotions. [Author's emphasis]

In a footnote, the *Straits Times* editor rejoined:

Mr. Khaw overlooks the editorial flat statement that in our opinion "the *Herald* has said and done nothing which could bring real official wrath upon its editors." Earlier the editorial questioned whether anything the paper had done could be called a "black operation."

The reference to a concentration on communal causes, which followed our conviction that the *Herald* had said and done nothing to merit real official wrath, quite clearly harked back to the government's accusations against other newspapers. There was no imputation against the *Herald*. Finally, in the matter of newspaper finance, as Mr. Khaw points out, there are circumstances in which two dollars can go a very long way.[54]

On May 25, 1971, under the inspired guidance of Devan Nair, the NTUC secretary general, 26 NTUC-affiliated unions came out with a joint statement approving the NTUC stand that only local financiers, and not foreign investors, should be allowed to keep the *Singapore Herald* going, and took Hahn to task for, amongst other things, "denigrating the credit of the prime minister and the elected government of Singapore, nationally and internationally."[55] Somehow, the allegations of black operations had quietly receded into oblivion.

On May 26, 1971, the Singapore Polytechnic Students' Union issued a statement supporting the *Herald* in its "praiseworthy struggle." Urging the government to exercise "rationality and restraint" in the matter, it said, until the *Herald* was proved to be antinational, it had "every right to live and grow to a viable state." It added that "unless its present actions can be in any way vindicated, the government should refrain immediately from any further harassment of the press."[56]

Also on May 26, 1971, PFA executive Amitabha Chowdhury indicated in Singapore that the PFA would ask the IPI to withdraw the invitation to Lee to speak at Helsinki "to express the disgust of the world press at the way Mr. Lee has been trying to kill the *Singapore Herald*."[57] But, in Zurich, Dr. Ernest Meyer said there was no reason not to have Lee at the conference where he would have to undergo a "confrontation with over 300 editors and publishers, which would be very desirable." In a letter to IPI members, Meyer urged them to consider whether they could offer financial support to the "maintenance of this paper, the closure of which would be one more battle lost in the fight for the freedom of the press."[58]

The "Save the *Herald*" Charade

The timely call of the NTUC—which has a symbiotic relationship with the PAP—provided Lee with a way out of the political morass of his own creation. In spite of the carefully staged press conference, Chase Manhattan Bank had not moved as speedily or as resolutely as Lee had planned. For the weight of universal opinion had influenced the bank's head office in New York and its chairman into giving the *Herald* a period of grace to enable it to come up with new money or with an acceptable proposal for its debt reduction. The longer the *Herald* struggled to remain alive, the greater the public sympathy and the pressure on the government to ease up on the *Herald*. The unforeseen groundswell of support for the *Herald*, encompassing, as it did, a wide spectrum of

Singapore society, including university and polytechnic students, was politically disquieting. The *Herald's* capacity to withstand those relentless body blows from Lee was winning it not only respect and admiration but was rallying all manner of people to its cause, and the freedom of the press.

A Mysterious Financier Appears On Monday, May 24, 1971, the government slyly whipsawed the *Herald* and its supporters by a sudden announcement that (1) it had agreed to a leading Singapore financier's "genuine" offer to "save" the *Herald* "now under foreign control," but deliberately omitted the name of the financier; and (2) it would withdraw the *Herald* printing permit held in the name of former founder-editor Francis Wong by Friday, May 28, 1971, but would issue a temporary licence to the intending buyers pending final agreement, if negotiations between the parties reached a satisfactory stage.[59] Why did it stress the word "genuine"? As the events unfolded, it was easy to see the reason why. The operative word was undoubtedly "genuine"—but was there really a genuine offer? Time was of the essence in the negotiations. The key clause in the fine print was, "if negotiations between the parties reached a satisfactory stage"; but could they really within the time constraint? It presupposed the mysterious financier would have already worked out carefully the pros and cons, as well as the all-important mathematics of acquisition and management of the *Herald*, save perhaps for the finer details which only a direct discussion with its staff and personnel could provide or clarify.

The parties, or rather the *Herald*, were given a mere five days within which to complete a multimillion-dollar commercial deal, a time frame which was as unrealistic as it was absurd, more particularly if Lee's own vaunted investment yardstick was applied. The timed cancellation of the printing permit immediately made the *Herald* a hostage to any serious buyer, let alone the bashful financier, whose identity and situation were well within the ken of Lee and his government. The so-called genuine offer was, in retrospect, a red herring to diffuse the concentration of protests and defuse a politically explosive situation.

The mysterious financier's conditions, pre-approved by the authorities, were:

1. He would take over the enterprise as a going concern, but without encumbrances or liabilities to various and unknown creditors. Without this condition, there was little hope of attracting genuine investment finance. This condition required that a receiver be appointed with whom he could negotiate terms;
2. The paper should continue production during the transitory stage under its present staff and that a temporary licence be issued to him to allow production to continue.
3. Singapore citizens, who had invested money in the *Herald*, should be given rights issue in the new enterprise to enable them to recoup their losses should the new enterprise prove viable,
4. Share participation should be restricted to Singapore citizens; and
5. The government should clearly announce the right of the paper to criticize the government's policy, provided the paper acts in good faith and is satisfied with the bona fides of the critics.

There was strictly no need for an appointment of a receiver to enable the shy financier to negotiate the terms of a takeover of the *Herald* as a going concern. He could just as easily have negotiated with the *Herald* management. The appointment of a receiver ipso facto relegated the *Herald* management to the sidelines, to an observer's role with no real powers of intervention in the negotiations. Upon the receiver's appointment, the *Herald* management would be virtually powerless to say or do anything concerning the disposition of its assets. Therefore, it was usual to appoint a receiver *and* manager, usually in the same person, so that he would have the authority not only to receive but to manage the assets of the enterprise.

Conditions 1 and 2 appeared contradictory, and were calculated to mislead. Taken together, they were the bait concealing the hook within, the lure which was calculated to mislead the *Herald* management, its supporters and well-wishers into a belief that the *Herald* was in fact being saved. But the appointment of a receiver per se gave him no implicit powers of management. Thus the *Herald* could not strictly in law continue production in the circumstances for the reasons mentioned if no manager was appointed.

Conditions 3, 4 and 5 in themselves were unexceptional and were merely the icing on the cake, as it were. They were ingeniously dangled before Singaporeans as the prospects of recovery of investment losses with a tantalizing admixture of narrow nationalism and freedom of speech and expression. In purporting to agree to the financier's proposal, the government claimed that "the real issue is not freedom of the press. It is whether foreigners, including an ex-chief minister [Donald Stephens] of a foreign government, and currently a high-ranking diplomat in its employ, should occupy a commanding position from which they could manipulate public opinion in the republic. No government can allow this." Once again, the Singapore government chose to blatantly ignore the fact that Stephens's investment in the *Herald* was known to it, and had its tacit blessings, and that there was absolutely no evidence whatsoever that Stephens had interfered with the editorial policy of the paper or had attempted to manipulate public opinion. Stephens's involvement and large holding in the *Herald* was purely fortuitous, as explained in his personal letter to Lee and corroborated by Francis Wong himself in his own letter to the *Herald*, to which reference has already been made.

Blissfully unaware of the cruel charade being played on it, the *Singapore Herald*, in all seriousness, agreed to the takeover proposal by the unknown financier—on two conditions. First, all the present shareholders, guarantors and financial supporters should not suffer any losses "for having shown faith in the *Herald* and its commercial potential," and, second, the newspaper be given at least two months to negotiate the transfer with the unnamed financier "in a calm and businesslike manner."[60] It was not an unreasonable request, but the sands of time were running out fast for the *Herald* and its presumptuous management, which did not seem to have realized it was no longer in a position where it could dictate terms. Nonetheless, both Hahn and Khaw boldly stated:

> We are conscious, however, that the threat by Mr. Lee Kuan Yew to close down our paper on Friday by withdrawing our licence has left us at the mercy of the mysterious financier who can then take over at bargain basement terms an enterprise that will obviously be a blue chip, if run honestly.
>
> This is unconscionable devaluation of assets of shareholders whose only fault is that being foreigners, they invested in good faith in a Singapore commercial venture.
>
> Our staff would cooperate loyally with the new owner if they could be satisfied that, in fact, this so-called rescue operation is not a manoeuvre for the take-over of the paper by a political party, and that the *Herald* would be permitted to exist and to serve the public honestly without political pressures in reporting the news or expressing views.

It is most unfortunate that the government has not seen fit to name the financier so that we could have some indication as to the bona fides of his independence from government pressure.

The picture is now clear: The government has decided unfairly to interfere in a commercial enterprise in an unprecedented manner on the excuse of editorial manipulation of the *Herald* by foreign elements although the government has not a shred of evidence that we had at any time acted against the national interests of Singapore.

We have always acted as a loyal and absolutely honest Singapore newspaper free from policy directives from any outsider.

One views with dismay, therefore, that a straightforward commercial venture in the journalistic field has been brought to its knees.

We deeply appreciate the efforts of the prime minister to find local capital for us.

Nevertheless, we are puzzled that Mr. Lee should do this after so many months of intense hostility towards us, which has led to the forced resignation of Mr. Francis Wong, the expulsion of three of our senior journalists, vicious and unproved attacks on Miss Aw Sian, a reputable Hongkong publisher who is chairman of the International Press Institute, and unfounded allegations of "black operations" against *Tan Sri* Donald Stephens, former journalist and publisher and now a Malaysian diplomat.

PFA chairman and publisher of the *Manila Times*, Joaquin P. Roces, saw through the charade, and, on May 25, 1971, issued a strong statement in Singapore, equating the government's plans to save the *Herald* as a means "to cause the murder of an infant newspaper." The Press Foundation, he said, had kept a "self-imposed silence on the growing tension in Singapore in the hope that this would prove to the Singapore government the Foundation's desire was not to aggravate the situation," but that "all this sensitive consideration, and desire to seek durable solutions to the problems of newspaper operation in a multiracial society and in cooperation with Mr. Lee's leadership, is a total waste." He disclosed Lee's arrogant dismissal: that he "could not care less what the world's press thought of his action" and "would not like to discuss this matter with representatives of the region's press."

Commenting on the current plan to finance the *Herald*, Roces said that the Singapore government was "importing a new method of subversion through financing agencies which, if it goes unchallenged or unexposed, may have dangerous implications to the future of the publishing community and journalists everywhere in Asia."[61] To its lasting credit, the PFA was the only organization which saw through the sham negotiations for the acquisition of the *Herald*.

The next day, May 26, deriding the Press Foundation of Asia as the latest of "outsiders" to join in the *Save the Herald* operations, Rajaratnam denounced the "violent comments" and the "long, angry, and fanciful account" of the two top PFA executives, who were "more concerned with the interests of the *Singapore Herald's* original foreign investors than in freedom of the press." It was a statement which was grossly untrue. Alleging that the real purpose of their visit was "not freedom of the press nor of our relations with the *Nanyang*, the *Eastern Sun*, or even of the *Herald's* future as the voice of democracy and progress in Singapore," Rajaratnam tried to read a murky complot into the PFA's statement:

That the chairman of a Foundation should charge the Singapore government with the "murder" of a newspaper and accuse it of "a new method of subversion through financing agencies" and warn the government that "it may not be dealing with only a few helpless journalists" and he would not like "to broaden the perimeter of the conflict" suggests that we are bringing into the open those outsiders with high stakes in the *Herald*.

The chief executive of the PFA, Mr. Chowdhury has gone one step further to reinforce Mr. Roces's threats. According to today's *New Nation* he says that "the PFA executives will mobilize efforts on a regional scale" to save the *Herald* "even with alternative employment when the blow falls on this infant paper."[62]

The Saviour Appeareth   On May 25, 1971, the banker-industrialist, Wee Cho Yaw, emerged from the shadows of his self-imposed reclusivity into the limelight of a press conference, where he disclosed that he headed a group of investors (some of whom were the original *Herald* shareholders) who were interested in buying over the *Herald*, and that there was no mystery surrounding his identity, as Hahn knew of it and had a discussion with him over the weekend.[63] But Hahn clarified that Wee then did *not* make any formal offer at their meeting that he and his group would take over the *Herald*. When the government in its statement came out with an unnamed buyer, he did not know his identity as he knew of another prospective Singapore buyer who had also approached the government.

The Charade Continues   On May 26, 1971—just two days before the imminent expiry date of the printing permit—negotiations on the takeover of the *Singapore Herald* began with a meeting between managing director Jimmy Hahn and the receiver, Jackson Lee, and thereafter between the receiver and Wee Cho Yaw. That same afternoon, before an assembly of eager reporters, the Laodicean banker presaged the depth of his acquisitive interest with this languid announcement:

> I don't know whether or not the negotiations will succeed. It all depends on how much money the receiver wants. The assets of the company are being worked out. We expect to get an offer from the receiver. If it is viable, we will make our own offer and take over the paper. If not, it will just be the end of it. . . . Its chances of survival depend upon the support of the people.[64]

Given the best will in the world, it was difficult to conceive a more dismal setting in which to conduct an unequal parley for the rescue of a corporation than the receiver-Wee-*Herald* negotiations. Within the given time framework, a satisfactory stage in negotiations had to be reached between the parties before the government would condescend to issue a temporary printing permit. It was not therefore difficult to empathize and agree with the PFA's chairman in his candid statement on this uneven method of negotiations, to which Rajaratnam had taken such special exception. Within 24 hours of that fateful meeting with the receiver, Wee, not unexpectedly, declared his disinterest. Thus, on the following morning of May 27, Wee made an epigrammatic announcement: "Following my discussion with the receiver, Mr. Jackson Lee, and my subsequent discussion with a group of local businessmen, it has been decided not to take over the assets of the *Herald*. This was because the value of the assets, which the receiver has in mind is $1.7 million, which is far in excess of our valuation. We have, therefore, decided not to proceed with the proposed takeover."[65]

The swift and sudden announcement stunned Hahn and the staff of the *Herald*, among others, who had pinned their wishful hopes on Wee as the white knight in shining armour. That same afternoon, the receiver, Jackson Lee, commented on Wee's statement: "The amount of S\$1.7 million of the assets of *Singapore Herald* is not my valuation. I do not know what is the valuation placed by Mr. Wee because he did not make an offer to me."[66] This was an astonishing statement—and there was no reason to believe the receiver had any axe to grind.

Hahn confirmed that Jackson Lee indeed had made no offer to Wee nor had Wee made even a bid. To a press question as to his valuation of the assets as a receiver, Jackson Lee said candidly he was still waiting for the financial accounts from the *Herald*, adding, "Mr. Wee has to make an offer. He did not make one." Hahn revealed, at a press conference, that Wee had asked him "yesterday to arrange with Cooper Brothers, a well-known international firm of professional accountants, to do a professional valuation of the *Herald* assets and liabilities" and, that same day, he had instructed Cooper Brothers to do so. But, when he asked Wee if he would foot the accountants' bill, Wee had told him to "hold on." That same day, however, Wee had made this "amazing statement [of not taking over the *Herald*] to the press." Who were playing games when the stakes were so high?

Thus trying to avoid being placed on the spot, Wee called a press conference as "it was his duty to put the matter in perspective," and insisted it was the receiver who had told him "in the presence of my assistant general manager Allan Ng" that "the assets of the *Herald* amounted to S\$1.7 million."[67] But the receiver—when contacted by the *Straits Times* on Wee's statement—maintained that he had never given the figure to Wee and, with the final words, "I have no further comment," brought the charade to an ignominious end. A dispassionate observer could well see that the receiver was swiftly finding himself out of his political depth, and that if he was not careful he, too, might be swept away by the treacherous undertow that had beset the *Herald* and its officers, for this was no comedy of errors.

Unfazed by this abrupt turn of events, Hahn bravely told a press conference: "As far as we are concerned, we will continue publishing until our permit is withdrawn. If the government withdraws the permit, then Mr. Lee Kuan Yew will be guilty of premeditated murder of a newspaper."[68]

The Permit Revoked

On May 28, 1971, the *Herald* printing permit was revoked by the government, as negotiations had "not been successful and consequently the group has not made any approach to the government for the issuing of a temporary printing permit."[69] The charade was successful. It was neat—a dangerous situation had been defused. Lee and his government were off the political hook. Labelling the revocation "brutal, callous and a black day for Singapore," Hahn, with engaging naïveté, believed that there was every chance of the *Herald* resuming publication if the prime minister would "give it that chance," and, in what is one of the many great understatements in this whole sorry affair, said: "It is not possible to conclude negotiations in three days."

A publishing or a printing permit, temporary or otherwise, is not commonly issued to a group or to a person who is not intimately or professionally involved in the publishing of a newspaper. The normal procedure for granting such a permit or licence—as Khaw quite rightly pointed out—was for it to be applied for by and granted to an editor of a newspaper, and not to a financier. When Francis Wong resigned as editor of the *Herald* under Lee's relentless pressure at the end of February that year, Khaw was enjoined by law to apply to the ministry of culture for new publishing and printing permits to be issued in his name, which he promptly did in the first week of March. The ministry did not acknowledge the application until he sent a reminder a week later. Another two months passed before Khaw received the application forms, after which he promptly filled in and sent the completed forms back to the ministry. Several months later, his application still remained unprocessed, pending ministerial decision. The proverbial efficiency of the Singapore bureaucracy unfortunately did not extend to applications for publishing and printing permits by troublesome newspapers and their editors. Its state of studied inertia drove Khaw to reluctantly arrive at the obvious but painful conclusion that his editorial direction of the *Herald* was "not something that the Singapore government cared for."[70]

Notwithstanding this unhappy turn of events, and still confident of receiving financial help from local sources, Hahn requested the government for two months grace to negotiate for new funds. When his request was pointedly ignored, he valiantly protested: "We shall carry on the fight unless we are legally prevented from doing so."

On Friday, May 28—the eve of the dreaded deadline—Khaw told his staff, "I just want to run a good newspaper for this community. We just want to live as a newspaper. We don't want to bash the government or overthrow it." His application for a temporary printing permit so that the company would have "more time to attract an investor" was unsuccessful, as was his request for an appointment with the minister for culture to discuss the application for a new licence.[71] Accordingly, Khaw wrote again to the minister for culture asking for a decision on his "longstanding" application for a publishing permit and a printing licence.[72] The result was equally predictable.

Commenting on the *Herald's* shameful demise, the *Straits Times* said:

> There will be much sympathy for the *Herald*, and stronger feelings yet among those who have actively supported the paper's strident campaign in the past week. And there has been much talk of the death of freedom of the press. It is as well to say again that this is not, and never has been, the issue. Freedom of the press in the classic Western sense does not exist. The foundations of this concept—stable and widely accepted values born of common traditions—these essentials are not present.
>
> . . . the *Herald* was not a viable commercial operation, given the thinness of its resources. A combination of this situation and the Singapore government's conviction that "a black operation" was in the air resulted in the closure.
>
> More has happened in Singapore than the end of a newspaper. Politically, the PAP's leaders are perfectly capable of discerning that, in the public response to the *Herald's* survival campaign, there was not only sympathy but an expression of frustration and resentment despite the material achievements of the last decade.[73]

The editorial betrays the subtle transformation that had taken place in the *Straits Times* since the days when it spoke out loud and clear for freedom of the press. The *Herald* had denied the allegations of black operations and, together with several others, had repeatedly called for an independent commission of inquiry to investigate into them. Lee ignored the many calls. Why? Was it because no evidence of a black operation was uncovered, in spite of the ISD—an awesome apparatus of state security—and

its ubiquitous agents? The *Herald* was, of course, highly critical of Lee and his government, frustratingly contrariwise and intractable to official advice in publication.
Therein lay the nub of the problem. Surely, not the "thinness" of its resources. If the
Herald would not conform, then it had to be nipped in the bud, ripped off, destroyed.
No issue of security, internal or external, was involved, but security, as we have seen, is
always a convenient stalking horse for repressive actions. In the final analysis, the freedom of the press—and not its want of financial resources—was the bedrock on which
the *Herald* finally foundered.

Meanwhile, *Tan Sri* Donald Stephens, in an interview with *The Australian* newspaper
in Sydney, maintained that the *Herald* had indulged in "constructive, but not destructive criticism." And, in an appealing afterthought: "I do not intend to take control of a
newspaper in order to give trouble to Mr. Lee Kuan Yew. If Mr. Lee is not happy, he can
return my money and I will withdraw."

Three years later—in 1974—during the debate on the media, the minister for culture
explained the revocation of the *Herald* permit in parliament: "The *Singapore Herald* . . . was
also financed with funds from foreign sources, conducted a campaign to mislead the people
of Singapore especially the English-educated. The government had, therefore, in 1971, to
withdraw its publication permit."[74] A simplistic but grave distortion of the truth.

Of Overdraft and Guarantors

On May 28, 1971, to bolster its crumbling credibility, the government revealed a confidential overseas telephone conversation which the prime minister had with David
Rockefeller, chairman of Chase Manhattan Bank, who had told him that it was his
bank's standing rule not to lend money to newspapers for "the very reason newspapers
get involved in politics." But, as we have noted, confidentiality was never an obstacle to
disclosure as long as Lee could score a political point. It seemed that Kwant "unfortunately" had not known of this ruling, and had given the overdraft—and that he (Rockefeller) was sending the senior vice-president for the Far East and Oceania Zone, Francis Stankard, out to Singapore to make an on-the-spot assessment. The statement
further stated that Rockefeller had agreed to the prime minister's request that Stankard
should clarify the bank's standing rule and ascertain "there were no secret guarantors or
security for the [*Herald*] overdraft."[75] But, to Lee's intense disappointment and even
greater disbelief, Stankard had reported there were no secret guarantors or security.

At a noon meeting the following day, Stankard, Kwant and Jim Bish, the bank's regional executive for Southeast Asia, met with Lee and Rajaratnam. The relevant minister for culture was conspicuous by his absence in these deliberations—although the
matter was well within his portfolio. According to the official statement released thereafter, Stankard admitted that the assets of the *Herald* "were going to waste," and that
there was going to be a loss to the bank for what was due from the *Herald,* while Bish
acknowledged that "the ball was in his court and that the ball game would begin." The
prime minister had warned them that he would "judge the bank from their actions
whether they were acting as prudent bankers would in the circumstances, or whether
they had other considerations." As to Rockefeller's confirmation to the prime minister
on the bank's standing rule on loans to newspapers, Stankard explained that he did not
believe the rule was universally promulgated throughout the bank, and that he had tried

to tell it to Rockefeller in a long-distance telephone conversation, but the telephone connection was bad.

The aforesaid official statement followed a UPI report datelined Munich, Germany, quoting Rockefeller as saying that the day before he had received reports that Lee had threatened to withdraw the bank's licence unless it foreclosed on the *Herald*, thus exposing the iron fist in the velvet glove.[76]

On June 7, 1971, a Malaysian-born Singapore resident publisher and hotelier Cho Jock Kim, together with a group of local businessmen, suddenly made a momentary appearance to negotiate with the receiver to take over the *Herald*, and just as suddenly faded from the scene.[77] He was apparently unacceptable to the establishment.

The International Press Institute Conference, Helsinki

The official reason for the enforced closure of the two English-language newspapers, the *Eastern Sun* and the *Singapore Herald*, was that "*no* mass media controlled by outside capital should masquerade as the voice of the people of Singapore." The repression of the domestic media created an uproar, which reverberated far beyond the shores of Singapore, exacting a heavy toll on Lee's international reputation and stature, from which he never fully recovered. The rumblings of press outrage preceded the meeting of the General Assembly of the International Press Institute (IPI) to which Lee had earlier been invited to deliver a keynote address. On the eve of the address, the *Manchester Guardian* editorialized:

> In the case of all three newspapers Mr. Lee has raised the bogy of "foreign interests," operating allegedly against Singapore's well-being. With the *Eastern Sun*, the first newspaper he attacked, the charge was that the proprietor had received money secretly from pro-Peking sources although no action has been taken against the proprietor. But with the two other papers the charges were vague in the extreme. The second Chinese-language paper was accused of inciting communalism, while with the *Singapore Herald* Mr. Lee has questioned the motives of outside businessmen in starting an initially loss-making paper. As a general issue, it should be a matter of concern to a country if its main newspapers are foreign-owned or unrepresentative of the political spectrum. But that was not Mr. Lee's point. He raised no queries about the foreign-owned but pro-government *Straits Times*. What concerns him is the expression of any editorial opinion other than his own. For an island which already has no opposition in the National Assembly, and uses detention without trial on political opponents, this new trend is another step backwards.[78]

Breathing defiance—"the Singapore government does not cringe from any face-to-face encounter"—Lee journeyed to Helsinki, with Alex Josey, a crony and sometime golfing partner in tow, to deliver the keynote address, and ride out the gathering storm of protests at the repression of the press in Singapore. The subject of his address, "Statesmen and the Media," had pertinently been changed to "The Mass Media and New Countries."[79]

On June 7, 1971, on arrival in Helsinki, at a brief airport press conference Lee disclaimed any knowledge about the reported issuance of a new printing permit to the *Herald*. And, instead, he announced that he had documentary proof that the *Eastern Sun* had received vast financial backing from communist sources, which he was prepared to place before the assembly. The documents were actually four in number—and were not even remotely indicative of black operations against the *Singapore Herald*. Asked on Finnish Radio and Television as to whether the "war on newspapers has caused changes in his image and the image of Singapore," he replied: "I am interested in realities. Images can be altered and changed with time but realities cannot. I think reality is what eventually must become apparent to everybody if they have honest, objective newspapermen reporting these matters."[80]

He said there had been instances in the past of communists trying to exert influence in Singapore through newspapers via Hongkong, and there had also been "some American intelligence operators and some smaller neighbours interested in manipulating news and opinion in Singapore." This was not a very subtle reference to Malaysia and Indonesia. The Singapore government, he carried on, was unlikely to allow people like a former Malaysian chief minister to continue control of the *Singapore Herald*: "As far as the continued ownership and manipulation by people like the former chief minister, I think it is most unlikely that we shall again open the doors and let him continue control." It was a scandalous reply which ran wholly against the grain of truth, predicated as it was upon the untrue premise that there had been manipulation of the *Herald* by Stephens.

"The danger of outside influence on newspapers through money from outside Singapore depended on whether the money came in openly or from unknown owners who slanted their news, headings and editorials claiming that they were the voice of the people," he said. He described as "dangerous" such investors "masquerading as Singaporeans, and using a Singapore national as a nominal editor to slowly drip acid drops on the soul of the people." It was never ever shown that Francis Wong was a nominal editor, or whose editorials had really dripped those acid drops on the soul of the people.

On June 9, 1971, in a BBC interview from Helsinki, Lee stated that the two *Nanyang* newspaper editors would be tried in court. "I think what I intend to do when things have subsided is to ensure that suitable damages are paid, for having uttered untruths against me and my colleagues."[81] But after the delivery of his keynote address, in an overtly significant change of mind, he refused to answer direct questions on whether he would bring the four *Nanyang* executives to trial, except to say that he was consulting his lawyers "for claiming damages for what they had written about him. Even though he had their so-called confessions in hand, no such legal action was ever commenced against any of them. Why? For Lee Kuan Yew—an egregious litigant—who never allows any perceived defamatory statements of him, especially by the press, to pass unchallenged, without seeking legal retribution from their authors, it was a wonder in itself. His failure to do so in this case provides eloquent testimony to the strength of his—and the government's—case against the *Nanyang*, its owners and its editors.

On June 9, 1971, with an eye on stemming the repercussions from the Singapore media havoc, Lee gave a self-serving address to the IPI assembly:

> What role would men and governments in new countries like the mass media to play? I can answer only for Singapore. The mass media can help to present Singapore's problems simply and clearly and then explain how, if they support certain programmes and policies, these problems can be solved. More important, we want the mass media to reinforce, not to undermine, the cultural values and social attitudes being inculcated in our schools and universities. The mass media can create a mood in which people become keen to acquire the

knowledge, skills and disciplines of advanced countries. Without these, we can never hope to raise the standards of living of our people.

If they are to develop, people in new countries cannot afford to imitate the fads and fetishes of the contemporary West. The strange behaviour of demonstration- and violence-prone young men and women in wealthy America, seen on TV and the newspapers, are not relevant to the social and economic circumstances of new underdeveloped countries. The importance of education, the need for stability and work discipline, the acquisition of skills and expertise, sufficient men trained in the sciences and technology and their ability to adapt this knowledge and techniques to fit the conditions of their country: these are vital factors for progress.

But when the puritan ethics of hard work, thrift and discipline are at a discount in America and, generally, in the West, the mass media reflecting this malaise can, and does, confuse the young in new countries.

We have this problem in a particularly acute form in Singapore. We are an international junction for ships, aircraft and telecommunications by cable and satellite. People from the richer countries of the West, their magazines, newspapers, television and cinema films, all come in. We are very exposed. One consoling thought is Arnold Toynbee's thesis that cross-roads like Lebanon benefit from the stimulation of ideas and inventions from abroad.

. . . Western engineers and managers, and their families . . . live in Singapore, reinforcing by personal contact, the impact of Western mass media. To take in Western science, technology and industry, we find that we cannot completely exclude the undesirable ethos of the contemporary West. This ethos flakes off on Singaporeans. So we must educate Singaporeans not to imitate the more erratic behaviour of the West. . . .

With parts of our population it has been wiser to inoculate them from these maladies. Those who have been brought up in their own traditional life styles and cultural values have greater resistance to Western ills. By all means the pill to keep the birth rate down. But must it lead to promiscuity, venereal diseases, exhibitionism and a breakdown of the family unit? I do not have all the answers. I can only hope the pill plus the traditional importance of the Asian family unit, where paternity is seldom in doubt, can prevent the excesses from imitating contemporary Western sexual mores.

To compound our problems, the population of Singapore is not homogenous. There are several racial, linguistic, cultural and religious groups. For the Singapore Chinese, about 76 percent of the population, there is a wide range between Confucianism and Taoism to Maoist materialism. They can view or read the output of local talent, or that of free-wheeling Hongkong, with its own brand of Westernized life styles, or the archaic values and political styles of Taiwan, by and large still those of Kuomintang Nanking, or films and publications of the People's Republic of China, every product dyed in Maoist red. Censorship can only partially cut off these influences. It is more crucial that local production of films and publication of newspapers should not be surreptitiously captured by their proxies.

The Malays of Singapore, some 14 percent of the population, have the mass media from peninsular Malaya and Indonesia. These irredentist pulls are reinforced by visits of business-men and tourists.

For the Indians of Singapore, some 7 percent, there are Indian publications and films, primarily from South India, carrying the pulls at the heartstrings of cultural and ethnic loyalties. But the second generation are nearly all English-educated, more interested in their future in Singapore, and less in India's destiny.

The rest of the population, 3 percent, are Eurasian, Ceylonese, Pakistanis. They are nearly all English-educated and present no problems of irredentism.

But with nearly all sectors of the population the deleterious influence from the mass media of the West is an increasing problem. Fortunately, we have not gotten to the stage of mod styles, communal living, drugs and escapism.

An interesting question is whether the mass media can affect a people to an extent where over a sustained period they not only determine social behaviour but also spark off political action. I believe every now and again they do. People are affected by the suggestion of the printed word, or the voice on radio, particularly if reinforced by television picture.

Twelve thousand Sikhs from the Punjab form one of the smallest communities in Singapore. They are split into contending factions, reflecting the contest between contending groups in the Punjab, of which they have heard on radio and have read in Punjabi language news-sheets. A recent fast to the death by a Sikh leader in the Punjab to get Chandigarh given to the Sikhs, generated tension among Sikhs in Singapore. True, nearly 60 percent of the adult Sikhs were born and bred in the Punjab and emigrated to Singapore after their cultural values were settled. I believe, and hope, the second generation Sikhs will be different.

In 1950, the publication of a photograph in a Malay newspaper of a Muslim girl in a convent, with the Virgin Mary in the background, caused riots. It was known as the jungle girl case. A Dutch girl, given to a Muslim Malay woman to look after, as the Japanese overran Southeast Asia, was rediscovered by her Dutch mother. She claimed her return. The girl had become a Muslim convert. The court, presided by an English judge, ordered the girl to be sent to a convent, pending the outcome of the trial. There were four days of rioting. Some 50 [*sic*] Europeans were slaughtered and many more maimed by Malay and Indian Muslims.[82] Their sin was to be European Christians, like the judge. The police, then mainly Muslims, just looked on.

And, again, on July 21, 1964, a sustained campaign in a Malay language newspaper, falsely alleging the suppression of the rights of the Malay and Muslim minority by the Chinese majority, led to riots in which 36 people were killed and many more injured, during a Prophet Mohammad's birthday procession.

There have been several outbursts of violence by young Chinese workers and students. They were communist-inspired, though few were themselves communists. These riots and arson were invariably preceded by calculated campaigns in which they staged mass rallies to stoke up enough emotional steam for the explosions the communists required for their "people's uprising."

I used to believe that when Singaporeans become more sophisticated, with higher standards of education, these problems will diminish. But watching Belfast, Brussels and Montreal, rioting over religion and language, I wonder whether such phenomena can ever disappear.

Finally, making for more pressures is the interests in Singapore of our smaller neighbours and that of several great powers. The smaller countries do not have the resources or the stamina to be a threat. But in the growing contest for maritime supremacy of the Indian Ocean and the South China Sea, the great powers are prepared to spend time and money to influence Singaporeans towards policies more to their advantage. They play it long and cool. Radio reception on handy transistors gives Singaporeans a whole variety of programmes, from the Voice of America to Radio Peking, and also the Voice of the Malayan National Liberation League clandestine radio station. The Malayan Communist Party wants to "liberate" not only West Malaysia, but also Singapore. On top of this, foreign agencies from time to time use local proxies to set up or buy into newspapers, not to make money, but to make political gains by shaping opinions and attitudes.

My colleagues and I have the responsibility to neutralize their intentions. In such a situation, freedom of the press, freedom of the news media, must be subordinated to the overriding needs of Singapore, and to the primacy of purpose of an elected government. The government has taken, and will from time to time have to take, firm measures, to ensure that, despite divisive forces of different cultural values and lifestyles, there is enough unity of purpose to carry the people of Singapore forward to higher standards of life, without which the mass media cannot thrive.[83]

Questioned by IPI delegates on the *Herald* affair, Lee said it was *discovered* that the *Herald* was "financed not by Singaporeans but what is said now to be a Malaysian . . . but he's not listed among the shareholders nor does his name appear in the Hongkong company which holds the majority block of shares."[84] Comment has already been made on this so-called discovery elsewhere. Lee accused the *Herald* of trying to persuade the people of Singapore that "it's futile and foolish" to have a defence force. "No one is allowed to use foreign capital to plug that line."

Control of the Chinese press was stricter than that of the English-language press, Lee said, "because the English reading population is more sophisticated." But, in the last throes of its life, the *Herald* printed criticism freely, and "every vicious, puerile attack was allowed. For a riotous fortnight every sort of attack was carried out by the paper. They did not sell it. They gave most of them away."

In spite of all his efforts to sway the delegates to the IPI general assembly to his side, it adopted a resolution "calling for the release of the four detained *Nanyang* executives and a special inquiry into the allegations against the *Singapore Herald*." The resolution read in full:

> The executive board of the International Press Institute, meeting in Helsinki on June 10, 1971, acting on the direction of the General Assembly:
> 1. NOTING that the Singapore government has detained four management and editorial executives of the *Nanyang Siang Pau* without trial and that it has withdrawn the printing licence of the *Singapore Herald* after exerting other pressures which included the cancellation of government advertising and denial of news-gathering facilities, in an attempt to make this newspaper change its editorial policy.
> 2. NOTING also that the Singapore government has sought to justify its actions by alleging that the *Nanyang Siang Pau* and the *Herald* had lent themselves to externally-directed activities detrimental to the security of Singapore.
> 3. NOTING further that both papers have denied the allegations, argued that the real reason the government has acted against them is because they declined to co-operate in attempts to manage the news and because they criticized the policies of the government.
> 4. CALLS on the Singapore government to release the detainees from the *Nanyang Siang Pau* or to bring them to trial in open court, and to accept the *Herald's* call to hold a commission of inquiry into the allegations against it, so that it may be able to regain its licence.
> 5. SHOULD the Singapore government refuse to adopt these measures which are required by elementary justice and the rule of law it must be concluded that freedom of the press has ceased to exist in Singapore.[85]

On June 10, 1971, in a remarkable press conference,[86] Lee repeated his charges against the *Herald* and the *Nanyang Siang Pau*. Many of his press opponents appeared, including Miss Adele Koh and Francis Wong, and the conference degenerated into a free-for-all of charges and denials. Claiming that the CIA chief for Southeast Asia,

William Nelson, had told him that the CIA did not finance the *Herald*, Lee said, "I've got Nelson's word for that. I must find out what agency is pumping money in. Who is playing Father Christmas?" Although the CIA was not directly involved, he believed American intelligence had at least an indirect involvement in the *Singapore Herald*, nevertheless. "Well, there are ramifications of this." Attempts by reporters to clarify what were the "ramifications" were, not surprisingly, unsuccessful.

Allowing that he is "quite a suspicious man by nature," he reiterated that he had asked the manager, Chase Manhattan Bank, for the name of the "secret guarantor" behind the "unsecured" loan of S$1.8 million, banking confidentiality notwithstanding. But David Rockefeller had telephoned from Brussels to assure him that there was no secret guarantor and the bank "makes no loans to newspapers"—and, purporting to underscore the apparent discrepancy, remarked: "But it lent money to the *Herald*." He then added: "If I were an American what I would want would be a weapon to formulate opinion, to act as a pressure point on the government for or against certain policies." It was an intriguing aside. He had unconsciously revealed that he was judging others by his own dark standard of conduct and behaviour, not to mention philosophy.

Lee repeated ad nauseam that the S$500,000, which Miss Aw Sian—the IPI chair—had put into the *Herald*, was not her own money. She had, as already noted, stated that it was her own money. "Either I am lying or—well, I never like to call a lady a liar." Conceding Miss Aw was a "shrewd business woman," he said, amidst laughter from the gathered newsmen: "It would be a very foolish newspaperwoman to pump money into a newspaper that lost money as fast as the *Herald*." He produced several documents which, he claimed, backed up his case against the *Herald*. But what were they? One showed the newspaper's losses. The second was Miss Aw's note, on which she had written, at his request: "I don't intend to put any more of my *own* money in it." Lee drew attention to her use of the word "own." The third was the letter from Stephens, saying he had invested in the *Herald* to "get a living out of my investments" when he retired. "Well, he has lost his old-age pension," Lee quipped. And the fourth and last document listed Stephens's investment in the *Sabah Times*, a North Borneo newspaper. It is difficult to conceive how the sum total of those four documents could possibly add up to a case of a black conspiracy against the *Herald*.

"The question is: who owns the *Herald*?," he posited. He never answered his own question directly but, instead, indicated his suspicions of the strange roles played by the CIA, the Chase Manhattan Bank, Donald Stephens, Miss Aw Sian and others. "We assume the *Herald* is not a communist operation." The *Herald* had an "unsecured overdraft with the Chase Manhattan Bank of S$800,000." Later, the bank loaned the newspaper S$1.8 million. "If we had done nothing, other people's money would have gone in. The question is—whose?" he asked rhetorically, admitting that he had come up against a "blank wall" in his attempt to trace the "ramifications of the *Herald* investments." Miss Aw had only three documents—three receipts—to show him in connection with her two investments in and one loan to the *Herald*—"no interest rate, no date of repayment." "We find the *Herald's* financing to be highly suspicious. My situation [*sic*] in that situation is to oppose it. Now, the banker says there was no secret guarantor. It's a shaggy-dog story."

As for Bob Reece, Lee asserted, he was fired when he tried to "meddle" in local news—the *Nanyang* case. Foreigners were not allowed to handle local news. Whereupon Miss Adele Koh jumped on him saying that her husband had resigned—and was not fired—before the *Nanyang* case arose. Lee ignored her retort, and quoted Khaw, Reece's editor, that Reece "seems to work for a lot of things. He never quite fathomed where Reece's paymasters are." But Khaw, for his part, denied having made such a statement.[87]

Miss Koh retorted that foreigners did write editorials for the *Straits Times*. "Not on local matters," replied Lee. But she persisted that foreigners wrote editorials on local matters. "Quite right," Lee then conceded. "That's a hangover of the past. And every Singapore citizen knows that the *Straits Times* is foreign-owned."

Koh: You have never taken action against them.

Lee: It depends on the impact. I don't know how long you have been in the newspaper business—you just graduated from college?

Koh: No. I've worked for the *Straits Times*.

Lee: Every Singaporean knows that this is run by the British. When they say, "We, the people of Singapore," that means you take it with a grain of salt.[88] But the *Herald* pretends from the very beginning that it is the voice of the people of Singapore. Mr. Francis Wong, who for many years was in Kuala Lumpur . . . Mr. Wong is a politician, in his own right . . .

Wong: You have described me already as half a politician, half a newspaperman.

Lee: That's right.

Wong: I've not been, and am not, a member of a political party.

Lee: Well, that makes it worse, doesn't it?

Wong: How does that make it worse?

Lee: If you are a member of a party I respect you for the credentials you carry, I say, here's my badge.

Lee then accused Wong of having been involved in past political activities.

Wong: That's not true.

Lee: No, no, no, no, . . . Mr. Wong, as far I am concerned, you set out in the *Herald* to pretend this is the voice of Singaporeans . . . I never believed you and I watched you all the time and I asked, who pays? Because he who pays can fire you, and Mr. Donald Stephens says he fired you.

Not to be outdone, Miss Aw Sian called her own press conference at Helsinki to refute Lee's charges against her. She reiterated she had invested her own money in the *Herald*:

I can simply state it's my own money. There is nothing secret behind it and I am not sheltering anyone. I have been a publisher and own a substantial number of publications. No paper only seven months old can be expected to be in the black. It was a simple commercial venture. If it had been making money, they would not have needed more capital. I came in because I thought it was a good long-range investment.[89]

Miss Aw Sian divulged that she had intended to put in an ultimate total of S$1,500,000 so that she and Stephens, the major original backer of the *Herald*, would have equal shares. "There was an understanding that I would have eventual financial control but that it would be editorially independent of me." Thus ended the Helsinki conference.

On June 11, 1971, a *Straits Times* editorial commented on the IPI resolution:

> Up to a point confrontation in Helsinki on the affairs in Singapore was to everyone's good. . . . Can the concepts of the Western press be applied universally? And in particular in Singapore? The Singapore government will reject the Board's ultimatum. And where will this leave us all?
>
> Where will it leave Singapore's newspapers, to begin with? Worse off. Should the Singapore government refuse to adopt the measures which the Board proposes, then "it must be concluded that freedom of the press has ceased to exist in Singapore," the resolution declares. We reached that conclusion years ago, and have often said so. But the press in Singapore is not shackled as the newspapers of many Asian so-called free countries are. We have said that too, often enough. The Singapore government's action, we emphasized at the beginning of the affair (before the *Singapore Herald's* future monopolized the headlines) must be judged not by the canons of the freedom of the press, but the purposes of regulations designed to maintain public security, to prevent subversion and to guard against communal conflict.
>
> We hoped the *Herald* would be saved. It can, of course, be resuscitated. But in its last two weeks of struggle, it added to its wounds. The IPI has insisted in lacerating them. . . .
>
> The government cannot afford, however, report and comment which may encourage division among the major communities. And it is intensely suspicious of hidden capital or ownership which could mask "black operations." Suspicion increases when these interests are deliberately hidden, or do not appear to be commercially justified. Singapore needs, and eventually will have, a truly free press. This will be when Singapore has learned self-discipline, and its people have established the common values of a Singapore identity.

On June 12, 1971, the U.S. State Department announced that no American agency had been involved in the operation of the *Singapore Herald*.[90] Although Lee had reluctantly absolved the CIA of "direct involvement," he had persisted in his belief that other U.S. propaganda agencies were likely financiers, such as the U.S. Information Service and the Voice of America.

A *Singapore Herald* Trust Fund was set up in the interim. Even after the withdrawal of the printing permit, contributions from the public and the staff of other Singapore newspaper companies continued to flow in for the paper and, as at the date of its cessation, the fund stood at over S$70,000 in advertisements and donations.[91]

The *Singapore Herald* Co-operative Rescue Effort

On May 27, 1971—after the Wee Cho Yaw fiasco—a pro-tem committee of "five concerned citizens," namely University of Singapore's economics lecturer Dr. Lee Soo Ann, lawyer Francis Khoo Kah Siang, political scientist Patrick Low, bank officer Mok Kwong Yue, and architect Tay Kheng Soon, stepped forward and issued a statement calling upon the people and the government to "support our efforts to set up a co-operative to purchase the *Singapore Herald* and to turn it into a Citizens' Paper."[92] Its editorial policy would be, amongst other things, to:

- Stand independent of any political party;
- Uphold the principles of a multi-lingual, multi-racial society based on democratic social-ism;
- Provide a forum for the expression of public opinion;
- Keep its readers informed on domestic, regional and international issues, and
- Take a 100 percent pro-Singapore stand.

They proposed a donation of 10 percent of its profits to the National Defence Fund, which Lee, in Helsinki, dismissed as "a gambit, just a gambit."

They engaged a lawyer to register a co-operative, and negotiate the acquisition of the newspaper through public subscription of shares ranging from a minimum of 500 units to a maximum of 5,000 units of one-dollar shares.

Late on the night of May 28, 1971, after meeting with Rajaratnam and Jek Yuen Thong, the Singapore Herald Co-operative Society's pro-tem committee issued a state-ment that both ministers "saw no objection to the group's proposal," and that Rajarat-nam had advised them to begin negotiations with the receiver.[93] They had appealed to the ministers to grant a temporary licence to either the *Herald* editor or the receiver so that the publication could continue, but were told it was not possible. The temporary permit was to ensure the survival of the *Herald* through which they could appeal for public subscriptions to the Trust Fund. The ministers recommended that they set up the co-operative first with a bona fide management which could then apply for the li-cence and buy out the *Herald* assets.

On May 30, the *Sunday Times*, quoting a reliable source, said that, although the gov-ernment had no objection to "proposals to form a cooperative to run the *Herald*," it had reservations as to the time it would take for its formation, amassing an amount of capi-tal and running expenses, and establishing an independent editorial board. The pro-tem committee announced it had received more than S$15,000 for the *Singapore Herald* Trust Fund, in addition to "pledges of substantial contributions." Several physicians had pledged $15,000 each. Encouraged by the initial public response, the pro-tem commit-tee decided to raise the ceiling on the number of shares each citizen could buy to 10,000.

On May 31, an official spokesman said that the government was encouraging a change of ownership in the *Singapore Herald*. Unless and until that problem was settled, no one would be issued with a temporary printing permit to resume publication of the newspaper.[94] On being asked to participate, millionaire banker Wee Cho Yaw reiterated his disinterest in taking over the *Herald*. Meantime, the *Herald* staff were busily out in the streets in downtown Singapore distributing co-operative forms inviting Singapore-ans to subscribe to the *Herald* Trust Fund.

On June 1, Francis Khoo wrote to the prime minister setting out the pro-tem com-mittee's proposal and inquiring whether the society would receive a temporary printing permit.[95] The letter was channelled to the ministry of culture whose assistant secretary, on June 4, gave a boiler-plate noncommittal reply that "any group of Singapore citizens is entitled to form a co-operative for the running of any legitimate co-operative busi-ness, including running a newspaper." The government had no "objections" to the pro-posal for the co-operative; but sounded a note of concern that it did "not get into finan-cial difficulties," and hoped that "they would ensure that local contributors were given a hard-headed and objective business assessment of the venture."[96] Heartened by the overall tone of the reply, the committee set out vigorously to complete the registration of a co-operative society, apply for a licence to print and publish a newspaper, negotiate the purchase of the assets of the *Singapore Herald* as a going concern and solicit pledges and contributions for the co-operative.

On June 7, the committee—following two meetings with the minister for foreign affairs, Rajaratnam—applied again for a temporary licence.[97] According to an official source, as reported in the *Straits Times*, the government was prepared to grant the licence provided the co-operative was properly registered, and the government was satisfied as to the bona fides of the financial supporters. The pro-tem committee confirmed the government had approved in principle its plans to form the co-operative and buy out the assets of the *Herald* and resume publication. In the exhilaration of the moment, one particular person appeared to have been overlooked, without whose imprimatur all the ambitious plans for the *Herald* revival were doomed to failure. But he was not in Singapore. He was en route to Helsinki.

On June 8, Dr. Lee Soo Ann publicly announced his confidence that the final negotiations between the pro-tem committee and the receiver would be successfully concluded by the end of the week. Asked to confirm—upon his arrival in Helsinki for the IPI conference—the announcement of the pro-tem committee spokesman the night before that foreign minister Rajaratnam had promised the *Herald* would get a new permit, Lee replied that he had not "the faintest idea as he had been flying for 20 hours." He did not think that any "radical changes could have taken place during my flight." At the Vaakuna Hotel, Helsinki, at a special briefing for selected journalists, when asked again to comment on the persistent speculation that his government intended to restore the *Herald* licence so as to "take the heat off" him in Helsinki, Lee imperiously dismissed it:

> My cabinet colleagues are not men who melt easily, nor do they expect me to melt because of a little heat in Helsinki. *I will not issue a licence for a new Herald until I am sure it is not backed by unknown foreign investors.*[98] [Author's emphasis]

Lee's peremptory statement made it abundantly clear where the real power lay—and, probably, realizing that he was supposed to be the "captain of a soccer team," and not a singles tennis player, hastened in his next breath to retrieve some face for his cabinet colleagues:

> If and when the government and I are satisfied that this time there will be no unknown foreign investors using proxies to own and control the *Herald*, when we are sure that it is Singapore-owned, then we shall consider issuing a licence, but not before.

On June 11, the receiver agreed in principle to sell the assets to the co-operative society on deferred terms.[99] On June 17, the *Straits Times* reported that, in view of Lee's statement in Helsinki that *he* would not issue a new licence for a new *Singapore Herald*, until he was sure it was not backed by unknown foreign investors, the pro-tem committee would meet with the minister for foreign affairs the next day to seek clarification of the actual situation. Until a licence was granted, potential investors were said to be adopting a "wait and see" attitude. A licence in hand would pave the way for "substantial" investments to flow in.

As if to underline the fact that politics do make strange bedfellows, the Democratic People's Republic of North Korea, on June 18, decided to fish in the troubled waters of Singapore, alleging that the *Singapore Herald* had been acting "in collusion with U.S. imperialists" in Singapore, and praised the Singapore government for closing it. Said the official Communist Party newspaper, *Rodong Shinmun*:

> The measure taken by the Singapore government this time is another blow dealt at the U.S. imperialists engrossed in all kinds of criminal acts against the Singapore government and people. The U.S. imperialists are slandering the measure taken by the Singapore government and pressing it to "re-open" the paper.[100]

On June 18, the pro-tem committee, accompanied by the dean of the law faculty, Professor Tommy T.B. Koh, met with the minister for foreign affairs on the *Herald* "take-over," but no joyous announcement emanated after the visit, save for a promise of a statement the next day.[101] It was a bad augury. One can only surmise the electronic to-ings and fro-ings that must have taken place between Helsinki and Singapore, and vice versa, leading to the inevitable news of gloom and doom. On June 20, the pro-tem committee announced that the registrar of cooperative societies had informed that "it should be run on the lines of a company registered under the Companies Act or a partnership." In view of that reply and following discussions with the foreign minister, S. Rajaratnam, the committee had decided to discontinue its efforts to revive the newspaper. The statement continued: "The committee is not interested in forming a company or a partnership because such institutions would not enable the attainment of the ideals and objectives of the five original convenors."[102] Their ideals and objectives were a paper "responsive to the views of a broad cross-section of the people, and not merely of a small group of major shareholders, a paper whose editorial policy and direction could not be easily manipulated." They had chosen the concept of a co-operative, and not a private or public company, for three reasons:

- A co-operative would enable mass participation in the ownership of the newspaper, which would have enabled the paper to approach the ideal of a paper owned by the people and of the people.
- In a co-operative all members, irrespective of the amounts of their financial contributions, would have an equal voice in determining the policy of the newspaper. This would reinforce the objective of publishing a newspaper responsive to the views of a broad cross-section of the people and not merely to a small clique.
- A co-operative would reduce the inherent risk of outside manipulators seeking to gain control of the paper. To reduce this risk further, it was proposed that a board of trustees be appointed to ensure that the editorial policy of the newspaper did not deviate from the trust deed of the cooperative society.

The government did not want, it was said, to have to deal with an "unwieldy" group of members and preferred a "compact group of four or five financiers." A cynical observer might well have declared that the pro-tem committee had advanced officialdom's reasons against granting a printing permit to a cooperative society, an organization difficult of political oversight.

Justifying the change of the official position, a senior government official lamely said that the government did "not want any more trouble" and it had to be careful to whom it issued a licence. "If the cooperative group could not present a viable scheme to the satisfaction of the government, then there was no point in issuing them with a licence." The group, he said, must also prove that it had the money to buy the assets of the *Herald* from the receiver and pay for recurrent expenditure. Furthermore, the government wanted proof that the money did not come from sources outside Singapore. "If the group cannot fulfill those conditions, what is the point of taking a licence?"

On June 20, a job placement centre was set up to find employment for the 200-odd *Herald* employees, signalling the inevitable collapse of a Singapore dream.

On June 25, the Commonwealth Press Union, meeting in London, unanimously expressed its "concern at the manner of the withdrawal" of the *Singapore Herald* printing permit, and urged the Singapore government to give a favourable hearing to the *Herald* publishers should they ever be in a position to apply for a renewal of the licence.[103] It came too late to make any difference to an unequal struggle, waged on terms and conditions dictated by an unsympathetic and suspicious government.

On July 21, 1971, at the ceremonial opening of the second session of the second parliament, President Benjamin Sheares underscored a warning to the press over sensitive issues:

> No one, and especially any one working in the mass media, has the right to play with the emotional reflexes of our different communities. . . . We cannot allow anyone to work up heat on the gut issues over language, culture and religion, grating the raw nerves of our people.[104]

Although those words were spoken by President Sheares, it had the unmistakable timbre of Prime Minister Harry Lee Kuan Yew.

In September that year, Hahn had the humiliating experience of being summoned by immigration officials to attend them with his passport and, upon so doing, had his passport defaced with the words "prohibited immigrant." He left Singapore that same month.[105]

The Final Curtain Falls

On August 30, 1972, the final curtain dropped on the *Herald* drama when its former bankers, the Chase Manhattan Bank, petitioned the high court for a winding-up order against the Singapore Herald Ltd. on the ground that it was insolvent and was unable to pay its debts.[106] The amount of the debt was said to be S$623,439.00. The sound and fury of its valiant but futile struggle for survival having long subsided as other events overtook it, the *Singapore Herald* went out without a whimper of protest, scarcely noticed by most Singaporeans.

In summary, the thrust of the complaint against the *Herald* was not that it had foreign investors or had received foreign funds, but that it was creating unwelcomed "pressure points on the government" almost right from its first issue to its final demise. It waged a campaign, so it was alleged, to influence the people against such administrative sacred cows as the national service and the Internal Security Act (ISA). Its editorial on the *Nanyang* arrests, as noted, while short of outright condemnation was not really enthusiastic of the administration's action. "Never where it was necessary to take a stand for Singapore was it prepared to. And to that extent, therefore, we said then criticism becomes something else," charged Rajaratnam.

Lee accused the *Herald* of being backed by foreign interests, which, when stripped of its veneer of diplomacy, were in fact Malaysian interests with ties to the Malaysian government, and the *Eastern Sun* financed by the Hongkong-based branch of the Bank of China, a Chinese government communist agency. Granted the in-flow of foreign capital and expertise, which the authorities were trying to attract to Singapore, it was not illegal for foreigners to invest in local companies, including newspaper companies. Indeed, Lee himself admitted to having once invited press czar Lord Thomson of Fleet to invest and start a newspaper in Singapore, but Lord Thomson had declined mainly because the *Straits Times* was too well entrenched, and considerable resources were needed to compete against it. Lee said:

> I think the answer to this problem is not to exclude foreign capital or expertise, which is what New Zealand tried to do when Thomson was about to take over New Zealand newspapers, because if we did that we would have lifeless or unattractive newspapers.
>
> I think if it were possible what we should try to achieve is a division between financial and organizational control of the business side of a newspaper, which may be in the hands of foreign investors, and editorial control over newspapers which should be in a board or group of trustees of people who are eminently loyal to the country because, if they tried to undermine it, they would only be undermining their own future.
>
> If something along those lines could be worked out, then I think foreign capital and enterprise would be useful in giving Singapore newspapers the kind of filling that has been given Singapore industries.[107]

That was precisely the way the British-owned Straits Times had ordered its affairs,[108] which was to inspire the basis of the subsequent press restructure. That the government had no objection to foreign investments even in the newspaper business may be further seen in Lee's own remarks: "You may come in to do business. We encourage them. You can even come in and do newspaper business." But he nonetheless strove hard to cast grave doubts on Stephens's investment in the *Herald* through the Hongkong holding company and, to score a dubious point, alleged that Francis Wong had not told Rajaratnam about the size of Stephens's investment in the *Herald*. "He didn't tell me the figure—I didn't know the figure till very recently."[109] Did it really matter? In the final analysis, the *Herald* paid a heavy price for its ideals, exacted by an intolerant and insecure government.

The Foreign Media Reassured

Because foreign minister Rajaratnam's speech on the *Herald* crisis implied that many foreign newsmen were involved in black operations financed by foreign sources, a concerned Foreign Correspondents Association of Southeast Asia in Singapore—since renamed Foreign Correspondents Association of Singapore—sought clarification and assurance from the prime minister.[110] On June 26, 1971, the association released an exchange of correspondence between itself and the prime minister in which Rajaratnam reassured foreign correspondents in Singapore that they need not fear for their visas if they reported "what they believed to be the truth or their honest opinion." But Rajaratnam reiterated that the government would not stand idly by if a correspondent went beyond the "legitimate function of reporting and interpreting news to his own people" and became involved in domestic disputes affecting the fate of the republic.

In the Aftermath

To the envy, and sometimes great annoyance, of his political opponents on both sides of the causeway, Lee enjoyed a good global press ever since his debut on the political scene; but the savage suppression of the Singapore press, particularly the contrived demise of the *Singapore Herald*, marked a reversal of his international reputation. Until then, the world media often tended to turn a Nelsonian eye to his transgressions on fundamental rights or freedoms as but a small price to pay for political stability and economic progress. Since then, the universal press and influential world leaders began to take a closer look at him and his premiership of Singapore. They did not quite like all that they saw or heard.

Lee had calculated that by delivering a carefully chosen topic, "The Mass Media and New Countries," at the IPI conference, Helsinki, to underline the socioeconomic and political problems endemic in new countries, and the necessity for tight media controls, he could win back sympathy and understanding, and recapture his old mystique with the international media. But he was to be sorely disappointed. He left Helsinki bloodied but still unrepentant. As his second, he had brought along his loyal chronicler, Alex Josey, to help soften the ground of opposition and smooth away any wrinkles with the international media, more particularly, the British press, but to no avail. The press confrontation alienated sections of the British media.[111] Typical among the adverse international reactions was *The Australian*, which editorialized on Singapore's tarnished image:

> Singapore is a one-party State and bears the injuries that all one-party States do to themselves.
> Those who see the power of the Singapore government and the lengths to which Lee Kuan Yew is prepared to go to hang on to it are frightened by what is likely to be the result of it. In Singapore the question is being asked more often these days: what is the point of being one of the best fed, best administered, best educated nations in Asia if that nation is also one of the least free?[112]

The disapproving echoes of his media crackdown at Helsinki continued to rumble and, finally, crescendoed in the Socialist International conference in London, where the Dutch Labour Party—supported by the British Labour Party—moved for the expulsion of the People's Action Party from the organization for, among other things, repression of the press and the arbitrary incarceration of journalists and dissidents, which we shall discuss shortly.

Lee himself was, and is, not unaware of the critical reaction of the Western media, especially of the American press, which he accuses periodically of mounting a campaign against him. On January 19, 1977, in the mountain resort of Baguio in the Philippines, at a joint press conference with President Ferdinand Marcos, he chided the Western media: "The more they exaggerate our warts and moles the less credible they become." He pretended that he really had "little interest in the gratuitous advice that the press lords proffer from time to time as to how I should suck the Singapore banana."[113] At a press interview with Colin Smith of *The Sunday Observer*, he said: "They can paint me as a demon, but, given two or three TV opportunities in the U.S., I can demolish it. I'm prepared to meet them, my accusers, face-to-face on television. Let them show me up as an ogre, a demon, a Honecker."[114]

On May 24, 1990, at a press conference in Paris—while en route to London—Lee was seriously vexed by a question from an Agence France-Presse correspondent on press criticisms of the way he governed Singapore, and answered him "with some vehemence," accused the Western media of "an insidious tendency of living [sic] up to show solidarity," and issued them with a challenge to an open debate on "*my*" television:

> I govern Singapore with the consent and votes of the Singapore people, not the consent and votes of the Western press. . . . Dow Jones was wrong! The *Asian Wall Street Journal* was wrong! So is the *Far Eastern Economic Review*, in interfering in my daily politics and refusing me a right of reply. They lost the argument but the Western press is not interested, they just repeat that I am shutting up the press.
>
> Rubbish! I engaged them in an argument blow for blow and they lost the argument. And it's all documented. . . . I am not afraid of the open debate. . . . But I believe before you ask me any questions, do me the courtesy of getting the facts, and not just repeat what the American press and the British press, in sympathy with the American press, are saying.[115]

As we shall presently see, the seeds of Lee's designs on the mass media germinated at the fateful Helsinki conference. In conclusion, it may be worthwhile to recall the succinct observations of author T.J.S. George on Lee's technique of repression:

> It would have been untypical of Lee if he had merely sent his police to close the *Herald* and jailed its editors. He spun an intricate web of international intrigues, complicated financial conspiracies and mysterious political plots, worked himself into a position of taking the whole world on, brought a cross-section of Singapore papers into the arena and, by the time he was through, left two papers dead and the top men of a third in prison.[116]

Postscript on the *Singapore Herald*

On May 28, 1987, the Ministry of Home Affairs issued a press release on the arrest of 16—subsequently augmented by the arrest of another six—young professionals, Roman Catholic Church and lay workers and social activists, alleging that they were involved in a Marxist conspiracy to overthrow Lee and his government and replace it with a Marxist state. Some of the arrestees were members of the Student Christian Movement of Singapore—an alleged Marxist organization—which was involved in the Save the *Herald* campaign. In recalling the earlier incident, the *Straits Times* depicted the *Singapore Herald* as follows:

> The *Singapore Herald* was a completely foreign-owned English-language newspaper which began publication in July 1970. It closed down in May the next year when it failed to get local financiers to take over the newspaper and the government revoked its printing permit.

The newspaper was ostensibly owned and financed by the late *Tan Sri Datuk* Mohammad Fuad Stephens, a former chief minister of Sabah, Malaysia.

The government accused the paper's foreign owners of having political motives.

The government later required that the paper's ownership be changed to comprise only local investors or its printing permit would be revoked. But the paper was in debt. Bids by its staff to get local financiers to take over the paper proved unsuccessful.

A trust fund set up to raise money for the paper also failed.[117]

Truth sometimes suffers in the re-telling, and, given the above, this instant case proves the axiom! For it graphically illustrates the steep descent of the *Straits Times* into being a propaganda tool of government.

Notes

1. *Hansard*, Malaysian Parliamentary debates, December 18, 1964, cols. 5075–5083.

2. *Straits Times*, June 11, 1971; see also Patrick Smith, "Pressed into Wedlock," *Far Eastern Economic Review*, April 23, 1982; V.G. Kulkarni, "Arts and Society: Newspapers," *Far Eastern Economic Review*, June 21, 1984; Nigel Holloway, "Fall from Grace," *Far Eastern Economic Review*, January 22, 1987.

3. *Straits Times*, May 21, 1971.

4. *Straits Times*, June 11, 1971.

5. A.k.a. Sandrasegeram s/o Woodhull.

6. *Straits Times*, May 20, 1971.

7. Ibid.

8. Jacula Prudentum (1640), *Bartlett's Familiar Quotations*. Boston: Little, Brown Inc., 1980.

9. *Straits Times*, May 21, 1971.

10. A variation on the theme may be seen in the remarks of information minister, Brig. Gen. George Yeo, to visiting Asean journalists that foreign journalists may not get the free access ministries and statutory boards give to the local press "because they are not part of the family." *Straits Times*, Weekly Edition, October 30, 1993.

11. *Straits Times*, May 12, 1971.

12. Ibid.

13 *Straits Times*, August 30, 1972.

14. *Straits Times*, September 11, 1972.

15. *Sunday Times*, May 16, 1971.

16. *Straits Times*, May 18, 1971.

17. *Straits Times*, May 19, 1971.

18. *Straits Times*, May 18, 1971.

19. Letter, Bob Reece, "Why I left the Herald," *Straits Times*, June 19, 1971.

20. *Straits Times*, May 20, 1971.

21. *Straits Times*, May 19, 1971.

22. *Straits Times*, May 18, 1971.

23. *Straits Times*, May 20, 1971.

24. An abbreviation of "Rajaratnam" also evocative of familiarity.

25. See David DeVoss, "Southeast Asia's intimidated press," *Columbia Journalism Review*, March/April 1978.

26. Elliott S. Parker, "Singapore," *World Press Encyclopedia*, ed. George Thomas Kurian. London: Mansell Publishing Limited, 1982.

27 *Straits Times*, May 21, 1971.
28. Ibid.
29. *Far Eastern Economic Review*, May 29, 1971.
30. *Straits Times*, May 21, 1971.
31. Ibid.
32. Ibid.
33. Ibid.
34. *Straits Times*, May 22, 1971.
35. *New York Times*, May 29, 1971.
36. *Straits Times*, May 22, 1971.
37. Ibid.
38. Ibid.
39. Ibid.
40. Ibid.
41. *Straits Times*, May 28, 1987.
42. *Straits Times*, May 22, 1971.
43. Ibid.
44. Ibid.
45. Ibid.
46. *Sunday Times*, London, May 23, 1971.
47. *Straits Times*, May 23, 1971.
48. *Sunday Times*, London, May 23, 1971.
49. *Straits Times*, May 24, 1971.
50. Ibid.
51. *Straits Times*, May 24, 1971.
52. *Straits Times*, May 25, 1971.
53. *Straits Times*, May 24, 1971.
54. *Straits Times*, May 25, 1971.
55. *Straits Times*, May 26, 1971.
56. *Straits Times*, May 27, 1971.
57. *Straits Times*, May 28, 1971.
58. Ibid.
59. *Straits Times*, May 25, 1971.
60. Ibid.
61. *Straits Times*, May 26, 1971.
62. *Straits Times*, May 27, 1971.
63. *Straits Times*, May 26, 1971.
64. *Straits Times*, May 27, 1971.
65. *Straits Times*, May 28, 1971.
66. Ibid.
67. *Straits Times*, May 29, 1971.
68. *Straits Times*, May 28, 1971.
69. *Straits Times*, May 29, 1971.
70. Ibid.
71. *Sunday Times*, May 30, 1971.
72. *Straits Times*, June 3, 1971.
73. *Straits Times*, May 29, 1971.
74. Hansard, Parliamentary debates, March 27, 1974, cols. 913–14.
75. *Straits Times*, May 29, 1971.
76. *Far Eastern Economic Review*, June 5, 1971.

77. *Straits Times*, June 8, 1971.

78. *Manchester Guardian,* June 7, 1971.

79. *Straits Times,* May 20, 21, and June 6, 1971.

80. *Straits Times*, June 10, 1971.

81. *Straits Times*, June 11, 1971.

82. Nine persons were killed by rioters during the Hertogh riots, of whom six were Europeans, two Eurasians and one Indian. One hundred and thirty-one persons comprising Europeans, Eurasians, Chinese, Indians and Malays were injured by the rioters. "Report of the Singapore Riots Inquiry Commission, 1951." Singapore: Government Printing Office, 1951. The figure of 50 Europeans killed is, therefore, sheer hyperbole.

83. Lee's speech, verbatim, delivered at IPI General Assembly, Helsinki, June 9, 1971. Besides IPI's own records, it was reproduced in domestic and foreign newspapers and news publications.

84. *Straits Times*, June 10, 1971.

85. *Straits Times*, June 11, 1971.

86. Ibid.

87. See Reece's letter, *Straits Times*, June 19, 1971.

88. The *Straits Times* was then largely British-owned, and several British editors and leader writers, who were longtime residents, wrote on local matters.

89. *Straits Times*, June 11, 1971.

90. *Sunday Times*, June 13, 1971.

91. *Straits Times*, May 29, 1971.

92. *Straits Times*, May 28, 1971.

93. *Straits Times*, May 29, 1971.

94. *Straits Times*, June 1, 1971.

95. *Sunday Times*, June 20, 1971.

96. *Straits Times*, June 5, 1971.

97. *Straits Times*, June 9, 1971.

98. Ibid.

99. *Straits Times*, June 13, 1971.

100. *Straits Times,* June 19, 1971.

101. Ibid.

102. *Sunday Times*, June 20, 1971.

103. *Straits Times*, June 26, 1971.

104. *Straits Times,* July 22, 1971.

105. Conversation with the author.

106. *Straits Times*, August 30, 1972.

107. Press Conference, International Press Institute, Helsinki. See *Straits Times*, June 11, 1971.

108. See C.M. Turnbull, *Dateline Singapore: 150 years of the Straits Times*. Singapore: Singapore Press Holdings, 1995.

109. *Straits Times,* May 21, 1971.

110. *Sunday Times*, June 27, 1971.

111. James Morgan, "Low profile in UK," *Far Eastern Economic Review*, December 9, 1972.

112. *The Australian*, May 21, 1971.

113. *Times* (London), January 20, 1977.

114. "The PM Who Fines You for Not Flushing the Loo," *Sunday Observer*, December 10, 1989.

115. *Straits Times*, May 25, 1990.

116. T.J.S. George, *Lee Kuan Yew's Singapore*. London: Andre Deutsch, 1973.

117. *Straits Times*, May 28, 1987.

6 The Divestiture of Control

-
-
-
-

The Member [for Seremban Barat][1] says the Straits Times *is a PAP paper—the kiss of Judas for any political party.*

Lee Kuan Yew[2]

-
-
-
-
-

Having carefully set the stage for the forthcoming general election the previous year, Lee predictably played up the hoary scenario of black operations during the 1972 general election, accusing the opposition political parties of acting as proxies for foreign interests, without the slightest attempt to produce evidence to substantiate the accusations. Lesser PAP candidates quickly took up the cue, and insinuated large sums of money, as much as S$600,000, were paid by foreign sources to opposition political parties to act as their proxies,[3] while the prime minister made great play of holding a commission of inquiry after the general election to investigate those allegations of tainted payments, and to introduce legislation to empower the Registrar of Societies to call upon opposition political parties to open up their books for inspection. Needless to say, no commission of inquiry was ever set up, it remained for what it was—an election gimmick.

On November 15, 1972, casting aside the mantle of guest of honour at the Singapore Press Club's annual dinner, Lee read out the riot act to his startled hosts and equally startled gathering of newsmen, local dignitaries and foreign diplomats. Asseverating that he would be the judge of what news was fit to print in Singapore, he declared that the Chinese- and Malay-language media, and, in a more limited way, the Indian media, bore the more careful watching than the English-language press, as they "make much more emotive and powerful appeals in the mother language" that "tugs at the heartstrings." That was why, in the case of the *Nanyang*, "though I did not twist their necks, we took firm measures." And, in an obvious signal of dire things to come, Lee growled aloud, "the business is not over yet."

> Every morning my task begins by reading five—four now—newspapers. And it's a tiresome business. I note the scurrilous, the scandalous. I can live with that. But when any newspaper pours a daily dose of language, cultural or religious poison, I put my knuckle-dusters on as the first stage. If you still continue, then I say here are the stilettos. Choose your weapons.

Stressing the good sense and importance of having controls, he bluntly declared:

> [T]he communist countries are thoroughly consistent. They have decided that the mass media is a very powerful instrument. They do not let anyone use it, other than those who will advance the cause of the communist state, and to advance its current policies.

But in laissez-faire dissemination of views, regardless of whether they are truthful, sound or relevant, when it comes to garnering voters, provided you are allowed to get your point of view across, however hostile the press or the TV commentators, a determined and effective political leadership can beat them.[4]

It was an augury of what was to descend on Singapore and Singaporeans, and the eventual accomplishment of a carefully worked-out plan.

Within three months of that remarkable speech, the government in January 1973 served notice that all newspaper companies had to convert themselves into public companies. Harry Lee Kuan Yew had neither forgotten nor forgiven Lee Eu Seng for spurning his conditional offer to release the Nanyang executives. It was the beginning of the end of large private ownerships of newspapers, but, as in the game of chess to which he was fond of alluding, Lee delivered the coup de main in two moves, the second move timed a year after the disgraceful arrest and detention of Lee Eu Seng.

Unctuously professing no intention of interfering with newspapers "as an economic activity" but only of "safeguarding public interest by ensuring that undesirable foreign elements do not gain control of our newspapers, and use them against the welfare of our society,"[5] the government repealed the Printing Presses Act, Cap. 258,[6] and re-enacted, with significant amendments, the Newspaper and Printing Presses Act (NPPA) 1974, effective from January 1, 1975. The minister for culture introduced the bill in these grandiose terms:

> [W]hile it is necessary to ensure that control of our newspapers remains in the hands of our citizens, the government also does not wish to upset the commercial operations of newspaper companies, or intervene in the market forces determining the value of their shares. We certainly do not want to get involved in the day-to-day running of newspapers. Management will be free to operate the newspapers as commercial enterprises, provided they ensure that there is no manipulation by foreign elements and that no attempt is made by them, or through their proxies, to glorify undesirable viewpoints and philosophies.[7]

Left largely unsaid was the underlying motivation for the action, that the two Chinese-language dailies were comparatively more fiercely independent than the newspapers in the Straits Times group, and, therefore, needed the closer monitoring. But the pretext used was foreign manipulation, funds and influence. In the final analysis, all newspapers were caught in the throw of the net. The NPPA directed privately owned newspaper companies to convert themselves into public companies and create two classes of shares, i.e., ordinary shares and management shares which would constitute 1 percent of the paid-up ordinary shares of the company. In editorial policy and matters, including the appointment or dismissal of directors or of editorial staff and so on, however, a management share carried a voting power 200 times greater than that carried by an ordinary share. But, in dealing with financial matters and the day-to-day running of the newspaper, the voting powers were equal. Financial control of the paper would continue to remain in the hands of the owners, but control of editorial policy would be transferred to the majority of management shareholders.

Management shares could only be issued to citizens of Singapore and corporations approved by government, whose approval to hold such shares may be revoked by the minister at any time, and which were not transferable except with his approval. The government assured members of the newspaper-owning families, senior editorial staff, and senior management staff that approval would be given to them to hold and own management shares. The effect of the NPPA was to dilute and disperse the shares of the owners in their own newspaper companies among a wider number of shareholders, thus paving the way for government to seize management control of them. No newspaper company could receive foreign funds without the approval of the minister for culture.

However, the thin end of the wedge was that a percentage of the share-holdings had to be allotted to wholly owned government companies, such as Temasek Holdings Limited and MND Holdings. By a legislative sleight of hand, the government held substantive management shares through nominees not only in the two Chinese newspaper companies but also in the *Straits Times*, the largest English-language newspaper in Singapore, whose parent company owns Malay-language and other newspapers and publications. The prime minister placed his own press secretary, the irrepressible James Fu Chiao Sian,[8] on the editorial board of the *Nanyang Siang Pau* and, also, had him appointed a director of its management board as a nominee of Temasek Holdings.[9] Similar steps were also taken to ensure a strong government voice on the *Sin Chew Jit Poh* editorial board.

Several PAP cadre members were already serving on the editorial boards; and, pursuant to the NPPA, government nominees now openly sat on the board of directors of these newspaper companies. With the amendments, news dispensation and manipulation was effectively in the hands of government. "The Act therefore cleared up all ambiguities by legitimizing the PAP leadership's direct control over the press, through its nominees."[10] The two independent mouthpieces of Chinese news, language and culture were silenced. This sweeping action, however, was only a preliminary step in an exercise in absolute government control.

The Press Council

In January 1973—at the time of Lee Eu Seng's arrest—the government suddenly announced its intention of establishing a Press Council "as soon as possible before the end of the year," which would include a tripartite representation of newspaper management, journalists and the government. It would "lay down guidelines for all newspapers." The idea was first mooted in a conversation between the prime minister and A.C. Simmons, chairman and managing director of the *Straits Times*, whose reaction to the concept was reportedly guarded.[11] At a subsequent press conference, Rajaratnam, the foreign minister, sketched out further the other purposes and functions of the Press Council: it would scrutinize appointments of key personnel on the editorial staff—those with the authority and responsibility for deciding what, where and how any article or report was published in the paper. It would not be an advisory body but one with powers to deal with newspapers which took the subversive line to endanger the republic's security. It would act as a buffer between ownership and management, as well as to restrict the exercise of management in a way which would be detrimental to the interests of Singapore. Rajaratnam said that "some people" might say the government was running the newspapers through the Press Council, but he assured them that "it was not our objective."

He underlined the fact that the establishment of the Press Council was "a better alternative in a democratic society to a government takeover of newspapers."[12] No Press Council, however, was ever set up—and the reasons therefore are apparent from the narrative herein for, in a massive change of governmental heart, the minister for culture said:

> It is not practicable under our present conditions. First of all, who is to be chairman? Who gives the order? Who lays down policies? These are all very complicated matters and, I think, it would be better that the press be allowed to manage themselves. *Therefore, we have introduced these management shares to ensure that only the right people are allowed to exercise the powers of management of newspapers.*[13] [Author's emphasis]

There was no one around to call the government into account for that sudden change of course or challenge those dubious assertions. Parliament was wholly controlled by the PAP. However, in 1991, the acting information minister, Brig. Gen. George Yeo, adverted to the matter again but with a different stress: "Press Councils in countries like Britain and the Philippines are independent, non-profit, volunteer organizations set up by the media" and it was up to the Singapore media, and not the government, to consider the setting up of a Press Council to look into complaints against the media.[14]

The Socialist International Entr'acte

On May 28–29, 1976, the Dutch Labour Party tabled a memorandum at the bureau meeting of the Socialist International in London proposing the expulsion of the People's Action Party from the Socialist International, which it supported with a detailed record of violations of human rights and civil liberties, including the suppression of the media and the incarceration of newspaper owners and their practitioners. It, however, bore signs of a hastily prepared presentation. The works of Malcolm Caldwell, *Lee Kuan Yew—The Man, His Mayoralty and His Mafia*,[15] among others, were used in support of the proposal. But what was particularly hurtful to Lee was that the Dutch proposal was supported by the British Labour Party, with which he had friendly party ties and many of whose senior members, like Harold Wilson, were close personal friends. It was not without significance that at the time James Callaghan had succeeded Harold Wilson as Labour prime minister. Reading the signs of the times at the 1974 Jamaican meeting of Commonwealth prime ministers, Lee, pointedly quoting Sun Tzu, the famous Chinese military strategist, had remarked: "I know myself. And I know my enemy. What I did not bargain for was the weakness and soft-headedness of my friends."

However that may be, the British Labour Party tabled an article at the meeting entitled: "Lee Kuan Yew & the Singapore Media" containing two commentaries—(1) "Purging the Press" by Simon Casady, an American journalist; and (2) "Protecting the People," by Dr. John A. Lent, an American academic—as evidence of serious infringements of press freedom.[16] Casady's otherwise admirably succinct article on the *Nanyang Siang Pau* and the arbitrary detentions of its owners and senior executives, and the enforced closures of the *Eastern Sun* and the *Singapore Herald* was, however, marred by some inaccuracies, viz., "Foreign magazines are regularly censored. The *Far Eastern Economic Review*, . . . is now banned in Singapore . . . When *Time* contains an offensive (to Lee) article, it is scissored out of every copy by government censors."

Although the *Far Eastern Economic Review* was never banned, several *Review* correspondents—whose circumstances are dealt with later in this narrative—were, however, personas non grata with the government, and the steady deterioration of the magazine's own relationship with Lee spurred its editor-in-chief, Derek Davies, to seek an amicable resolution with Lee in March 1976. Lent's article was, in truth, unexceptional; its interpretation of the facts and the laws accorded with the rendition of many other responsible commentators then or since. The events leading up to the enforced closure of the *Eastern Sun* are well discussed in the Casady article, and elsewhere in this book. Apprised of the Dutch move long before it came on to the floor, Lee had written a defensive open letter to the Socialist International accusing it of "becoming a vehicle to further the communist cause in Singapore."[17]

Charging that the Dutch Labour Party's memorandum had "originated from a communist front group in Singapore to back the release of their collaborators and to win support for their candidates in the anticipated general parliamentary election," Lee began to ferret out persons in Singapore whom he suspected to have been responsible for the Dutch Labour Party's action, labelling them communists. Meanwhile, he dispatched his trusty knight-errant, Devan Nair—NTUC secretary general and PAP MP—to London to join issue with the Dutch Labour Party, and to dissuade the bureau meeting from going through with the expulsion. There, the starry-eyed loyal disciple, who had been well primed by Lee himself before his departure, assailed the Dutch memorandum, arguing, inter alia, that the articles on "Lee Kuan Yew and the Singapore Media" were "not distinguished for their accuracy, and even less for profundity of insight," and that Casady's article "Purging the Press," in particular, contained "downright falsehoods." Nair's valiant disquisition on the gospel according to Lee before an increasingly disbelieving audience proved a dismal failure, and, observing the mood and temper of the conferees, he tried to preempt the ignominy of expulsion by tendering a PAP letter of resignation from the Socialist International, which the PAP had joined some 10 years earlier, to proud acclamation. Nair was at his "most eloquent as an evangelist" whose evangelism apparently had a "profound effect on the German and the Israeli delegates," but, save for them, he did not make any serious converts to his cause. No decision, however, was taken as the bureau decided to let the letter of resignation "lie on the table."

Meanwhile, anxious negotiations went on behind the scenes to prevail upon the Dutch Labour Party to withdraw its divisive proposal, but the Singapore government—as if to underline that "Socialism that works" is "the Singapore way"[18]—arrested in June 1976 several persons whom it labelled pro-communist, among whom was a well-known political dissident and former detainee, Dr. Poh Soo Kai, whose release became an inflexible article of demand by the Dutch Labour Party for the withdrawal of its memorandum.

On September 7—just four days before the meeting of the full Congress of the Socialist International—the government publicly disclosed for the first time that it had arrested several other persons, including Goh Lay Kuan, the so-called Red Ballerina, and released their bespoke "confessions." Those "confessions" had been extracted from them between July 30 and August 8, 1976—some six weeks earlier, with the public being kept wholly in the dark, except for those whose lives had been touched by the arrests. Where does the right of the government to withhold such information end, and the public right to know begin? If the spate of arrests was intended to demonstrate the pernicious influence of the so-called communist adherents and their supporters and to influence the deliberations of the Congress of the Socialist International, it certainly failed. Instead, it was construed as wilful defiance of or contempt for the congress. For the Dutch Labour Party circulated a letter dated June 25 among member parties stating that the arrests only served to reinforce the allegations in its memorandum, and underscore the cynicism of the PAP, and dismiss the allegation of a "red plot" as having been "trumped up by the PAP to preserve their image at home and abroad." The arrests of those persons with their confessions-to-order had proven counterproductive to the PAP's cause.

On September 11, 1976, the Congress of the Socialist International met and considered the Dutch Labour Party's proposal to expel the People's Action Party, but not before the PAP's robust reply to the Dutch memorandum was further augmented by a potpourri of supportive articles, essays, speeches, commentaries and exchanges of correspondences, hurriedly compiled and edited by C.V. Devan Nair, and rushed into print as a book called *Socialism That Works: The Singapore Way,* too late to make any difference in the consideration. The congress magnanimously accepted the resignation of the PAP from the Socialist International, instead of expelling it.

The arrests of Singaporeans conveniently labelled as communists continued spasmodically in Singapore well into the new year. Lee exacted a terrible political vengeance against those whom he held or believed responsible for the PAP's mortifying withdrawal from the Socialist International. More than fifty persons, including several journalists, were arrested in Singapore in 1976 alone. The search for so-called communist subversives extended across the Straits of Johor to the woodpiles of Malaysia—many knowledgeable persons suspected the long arm of Lee in this awesome exercise—to A. Samad Ismail, the managing editor of the *New Straits Times* and his alleged cutout, Samani Mohamad Amin, the Singapore-born news editor of the *Berita Harian* (Malaysia), embroiling the UMNO leadership, among several others, which is discussed elsewhere in this book.

The 1976 General Election

Although the general election was not due to be held until September 1977, Lee had quietly planned a December 23 election—just two days before Christmas, at a time when the people were more preoccupied with celebrations and festivities. Furthermore, the political ground had already been softened by the arrests of many Singaporeans, who were alleged to be communists. The general election ran its course and ended in predictable fashion—a stunning PAP victory! But after the general election, an unsuccessful opposition Workers' Party candidate, Ho Juan Thai, was sought by the police and accused of playing up "gut issues" to incite "violent chauvinistic reaction among the Chinese-speaking population in Singapore." He fled to England, where he remains in exile. Another unsuccessful opposition candidate and former *Nanyang* editor, Shamsuddin Tung Tao Chang, was detained under the ISA accused of stirring up "communal and chauvinistic emotions." Yet another unsuccessful opposition candidate, Leong Mun Kwai, secretary general of the People's Front and consultant-editor of his party organ, the *Barisan Rakyat,* was jailed for 18 months by the ambitious senior district court judge, T. S. Sinnathuray, for criminally defaming Lee in two speeches at election rallies.

On October 17, 1972, he was sentenced to one month's imprisonment and fined S$3,000 "for inciting violence at a political rally against the prime minister and his wife, PAP ministers and MPs." On October 30, he was jailed by the same district court judge for six months for libelling the head of state, President B.H. Sheares, in an article in the July 1972 issue of the *Barisan Rakyat* by calling him a "puppet" and being "slavish." His appeal against sentence was dismissed.[19]

During the election campaign, the PAP candidates reiterated vague allegations against opposition political parties of having received large sums of money from foreign powers to act as their proxies. As before, no evidence was ever produced to substantiate the allegations. Then, on February 25, 1976, the Singapore government shook pan-Malaysian ties by charging the Malaysian Special Branch with trying to use a "discredited" politician, Leong Mun Kwai, while he was in Malaysia, to undermine Lee and his PAP government in a black operation. Leong claimed that a journalist from the *Shin Min Daily News* and the former editor of *Nanyang Siang Pau*, Shamsuddin Tung Tao Chang, were used by the Malaysian Special Branch to "condition" him. A televised press conference was staged in the Radio and Television Singapore studios, at which foreign correspondents from the *Daily Telegraph* (London), the *Melbourne Herald*, *The Age* (Melbourne), the BBC, UPI and CBS were invited to interrogate Leong; but they declined as they felt it was "a staged production." They refused to be made use of and to lend legitimacy to the political pantomime, which greatly annoyed the government.

On January 4, 1977, the *Far Eastern Economic Review* local correspondent, Ho Kwon Ping, was arrested and charged with disseminating protected information in an article, "Washington Aids ASEAN Build-Up," in the *Review*—to wit,

> Singapore's Chartered Industries, manufacturers of M-16s, is also exporting shipments of the semi-automatic weapons to its neighbours. Singapore's own cash purchases were not explained, but the government recently purchased two old mine-sweepers and six landing craft from the U.S. . . . without the consent of the competent authority under Regulation 4 of the Essential (Control of Publications and Safeguarding of Information) Regulations, 1966.[20]

Ho had previously worked for the government-owned Radio and Television Singapura, and the *Straits Times*. Four additional charges were preferred against him on January 21, 1977, based on handwritten notes found in a search of his home, alleging unlawful possession of protected information regarding absenteeism in the 4th and 5th Singapore Infantry Regiments; extortion and secret society activity in the army; the setting up of sniper platoons and wings in the army; and the establishment of a scout platoon in the army, without having previously obtained the consent of the competent authority for possession of the information. The prosecution proceeded only on the fifth charge relating to the setting up of the scout platoon. Ho pleaded guilty to it. The four other charges were taken into consideration. His counsel pleaded in mitigation that he did not "steal" the protected information, but had merely recorded information, which he could not help knowing as a full-time national serviceman, and that he honestly believed that no consent was required as some of the facts had been published "here and everywhere." The "protected information" in the *Review* article had previously been widely published outside Singapore, and later in Singapore itself. He was fined S$7,500 (US$3,061) by the ever-reliable senior district judge, T. S. Sinnathuray. After the case ended, Ho tendered his resignation to the *Review*, which was accepted "with equal regret."

On February 10, 1977, lawyer Gopalan Krishnan Raman—known professionally as G. Raman—was arrested for alleged involvement "with a group of Euro-communists to exert pressure through the Socialist International on Singapore to release hard-core communist detainees." Two days into his interrogation, he admitted in a 26-page "handwritten confession, signed and dated on every page" that "I was then a full-fledged communist and I am still a communist now," and implicated some 10 others—including Arun Senkuttuvan, a former *Review* Singapore correspondent and at the time correspondent of the *Financial Times* and *The Economist*, and Brian Maurice, a United World College British school teacher—for passing him letters from a "British publicist" described by the Singapore government as a radical. Maurice was promptly expelled from the country.[21]

On February 15, Arun Senkuttuvan was arrested; and on March 12, appeared, together with G. Raman, at a carefully staged televised conference of foreign newsmen, presided over by the prime minister's gadding scrivener, who prodded his reluctant audience in vain to ask questions of them. In the result, it was a theatrical flop. A visibly riled foreign affairs minister subsequently characterized their "studied silence" as "deafening."[22] Notwithstanding, in an incredible "confession," Arun implicated his former *Review* editor-in-chief, Derek Davies—in what was described as an "intricate plot" involving confidential tape recordings, and an intention to damage diplomatic relations between Singapore and Malaysia. Although Arun was not a communist himself, the implied purpose of the plot was apparently to assist communist attempts to undermine the Singapore government. No formal charges were brought against either of them and, therefore, none of the evidence could be openly tested in a court of law. The *Times* of London, in its editorial: "Singapore's Denial of Dissent," described their televised statements as "hollow-sounding recitals with a dictated air—by whatever means they were extracted."[23]

The tape in question related to a confidential Davies-Lee meeting at the *Istana* (Palace) Annex on March 22, 1976, on the role of the press in general and the *Review* in particular, which then turned to a general discussion on Asian affairs. After the meeting, Davies recorded on tape at his hotel an account of the interview with the prime minister on matters of "direct interest to the *Review*" in the presence of Arun, to whom he gave it before leaving for London, stressing its confidential nature, with instructions to send it by registered airmail to Russell Spurr, then acting editor in Hongkong "for his eyes and ears only," and with the injunction that "Spurr could communicate those portions which were immediately relevant to the *Review* to the three other responsible editors on the *Review* staff."

Arun, however, made a copy of it for himself without Davies's knowledge or authority, which he played to other people, including Raman, who gave it to Dominic Puthucheary, a Malaysian lawyer, whose brother, James, was said to be interested in hearing it, and who might have passed it on to *Datuk* Hussein Onn, the Malaysian prime minister. James Puthucheary, however, denied ever seeing or hearing the tape.

A ministry of home affairs (MHA) statement charged that Davies's tape was "a tendentious and selective recollection of a lengthy private conversation . . . a mixture of truths, half-truths, and some serious omissions, such as the prime minister's high regard for Malaysian prime minister, *Datuk* Hussein Onn." In a non sequitur, it said that "Mr. Davies may not have intended to promote the communist cause, but there is little doubt he knew the tape must cause mischief between the leaders of Malaysia and Singapore."[24] It accused Davies of deliberately violating the ethics of his own profession by selectively recounting on tape "for a wide and indeterminate audience, what he admitted was a private conversation." Davies termed the MHA charge as "positively breathtaking on a par with the Goebbels philosophy that any lie will be believed if it is big enough."[25] The MHA knew full well it was made for the *Review*'s own record and for a "strictly limited editorial staff directly interested in Lee's comments," he added.

The *Review* countered that its lawyers had advised that the statements of the MHA and the two detainees, including Arun Senkuttuvan, contained "several gross libels," and while not precluding legal action, the *Review* considered its readers "the best judges of the credibility of the various parties involved. On the one hand, was the evidence of persons detained without trial, on the other, numerous organizations and individuals who are free." With compelling logic and reason, Davies demolished the dissembling nature of the MHA statement: "The only provable friction and suspicion has been deliberately created by Singapore. Singapore has imprisoned Arun and seized his copy of the tape. If it wished to minimize misunderstanding it could all too easily have suppressed any revelation about the tape. Instead it chose to blow it up into a major issue and create large question marks around its contents."[26]

Rejoining that the MHA itself was guilty of its own "tendentious" misrepresentation in its claim that he had omitted to record Lee's expression of high regard for *Datuk* Hussein Onn, Davies said that Lee had not made "any such positive tribute," but a statement from which could be drawn an "implied but obvious expression of confidence in Hussein's leadership." There was nothing on the tape, in his view, which could embarrass relations between Singapore and Malaysia. (Lee had discussed some possible future leaders of Malaysia and their qualities—not defects—"in seven, eight, nine years' time.") To clinch his assertion that there was nothing on it which could be construed to harm relations between Singapore and its neighbours, and to correct the misrepresentations regarding its contents, Davies asked for official permission to publish the tape in its entirety. No reply, significantly, was received from the Singapore government, whose obstreperous defence of perceived hurts or inaccuracies was proverbial. Davies had called the prime minister's political bluff. The tape-recording event only came to light, be it noted, one year after it was made.

A decade or so later, Lee alluded again to the aforesaid event, and—forgetting what his ministry had earlier alleged against Davies—by way of a backhanded compliment, admitted that it was recorded "with such detailed excerpts that [Davies] must have been a person with a 100 percent total recall, or he [must] have been assisted with a tape recorder smuggled into the interview."[27] It will be recalled the MHA had claimed at the time that the tape was tendentious in that it was, among other things, "a mixture of truths, half-truths and some serious omissions"!

On March 12, 1977, Ho Kwon Ping was arrested again, this time under the ISA, accused of "anti-government activities." Within a month of his arrest, Ho made a remarkable mea culpa on public television, confessing that he "saw the *Review* as a vehicle through which he could create issues and propagate his 'pro-communist ideas,' and thus 'maneuvered himself' onto [the *Review*] staff," so that he could "systematically use his articles to discredit the Singapore government internationally, to portray it as an 'elitist, racist, fascist, oppressive and dictatorial' regime." It was denied by the *Review*, which took the view that the "confession" had been coerced out of him. The government rejoined that if the confessions of the detainees were not true and had been extracted "through torture and coercion," it would be known to their friends, "and soon most of Singapore would know. Singapore is a compact society. No such allegations have been made." The logic ex facie was irresistible. Compare, however, with the notorious case of the twenty-two alleged Marxists, nine of whom after their release foolishly took the government at its word. In 1987, complying with the tantalizing rejoinder, they rudely shocked the government by publicly protesting their innocence in writing, and denouncing the coercive methods employed by the ISD to obtain their "confessions," resulting in their re-arrest, including their lawyer, on the grotesque pretext that they had "not been sufficiently rehabilitated yet."

The MHA cited two specific examples of Ho's allegedly slanted reporting, an article entitled "Union Chief Sides with the State"[28] (which was a summary of the rejoinder by NTUC's head, C.V. Devan Nair, to the "ignoramuses" who were agitating for the expulsion of the PAP from the Socialist International) and an article captioned, "Countering the Communist Sinister Conspiracy"[29] (an exposition of the alleged conspiracy together with the prime minister's analysis). Citing chapter and verse, the *Review* showed that the allegations could not possibly be true.

Arun Senkuttuvan, a Singapore citizen of Indian origin, was deprived of his Singapore citizenship while in detention. Ho Kwon Ping was released on April 29, 1977.

The Divestiture Continues

With the passage of time, one's memory of events tends to fade. It is also true of legislative or administrative acts and actions, especially where their effects touch only a small segment of society, or only an individual or individuals. Few remembered that the *Nanyang Siang Pau* owner-publisher, Lee Eu Seng, was still languishing in prison because of his uncompromising stand on the freedom of the press. With the 1976 general election now a distant memory, the time was opportune for further amendments to the Newspaper and Printing Presses Act. The penultimate phase of Lee's grand design was accomplished with minimum fanfare and even less debate. Important amendments, however, were still in the offing. With the issues of the original owners and their rights to ownership now lying half-buried in the sands of time, Lee moved to break up the long-established, family-controlled newspaper companies, beginning with the charge that privately owned Chinese newspapers were being run by their owners "according to their whims and fancies." But those "whims and fancies" were never spelt out. In any event, there was very little Lee Eu Seng could do from the fastness of Lee Kuan Yew's prison, deprived as he was of access to his newspaper and to the world.[30]

In 1977, Lee made his next move against the media. Further amendments to the NPPA were said to be necessary, as "the situation is still far from satisfactory because the ownership of some major newspapers remains in the hands of a small group of people." Without mentioning names, the *Straits Times* group was equally snared. Thus, on June 29, the minister for culture Jek Yuen Thong, in moving the amendments to the NPPA, declared:

It is undesirable to allow any person or family to have monopolistic control of any major newspaper. . . .

In seeking to break the monopolistic hold of newspapers by a few families and a small group of people, we are trying to spread the ownership of newspapers to as wide a public as possible. . . . If everything goes on well there is a real hope that a free, healthy and responsible press will gradually be institutionalized in Singapore. Newspaper editors and reporters need not be afraid of newspaper owners breathing down their necks. There will be no interference from the owners. The journalists will be able to carry out their duties according to their best professional judgment and with the interest of the nation at heart.[31]

No person was allowed to hold more than 3 percent of the ordinary shares issued by a newspaper company. And any person holding such shares in excess of the permitted limit had up to December 1, 1977, to dispose of them, but the minister was empowered to extend the time on such conditions as he might impose to enable a shareholder to dispose of his surplus shares. As for newspaper companies whose paid-up share capital did not exceed four million dollars as of February 22, 1977—the date those proposals were announced in parliament—the bill made different provisions.

The right to transfer the surplus shares was vested in the public trustee whose duty it would be to sell them by ballot to the public at a price sufficient to cover his fees, expenses and the net asset value of such shares and then to pay to the person whose shares he had sold the proceeds of sale less his fees and expenses. In determining the net asset value of the shares to be sold by the public trustee, no account was to be taken of any value attaching to the grant of a licence and permit to the newspaper company and its chief editor under the NPPA, 1974.

On February 1, 1978—five years and three days later—Lee Eu Seng was released from prison, by which time he had been, to quote the terse MHA statement, "divested of his control over the *Nanyang Siang Pau*" under the NPPA, as amended. By spreading the ownership as widely as possible, newspaper editors and reporters "need not fear direction from the owners to embark on agitational journalism. Mr. Lee can no longer make use of the *Nanyang Siang Pau* against the public interest."[32] This statement was not only tendentious but begged many questions. In any event, there were none to raise them.

On March 26, 1981, the NPPA, 1974, was further amended to prohibit a person from "owning either directly or indirectly through his nominees more than 3 percent of the ordinary shares issued by a newspaper company without having obtained the prior approval of the minister, who may grant approval on conditions."[33] The approval, however, could be revoked at any time. Writing on the effects of the amendments, Peter Lim, editor-in-chief of the *Straits Times* group of newspapers, said:

We all work under the Newspaper and Printing Presses Act, which exercises control by requiring newspapers, publishers, printers and chief editors to be licensed.

There is an additional, reserve power. Newspaper companies must issue management shares but only to those with government permission to hold them. These shares have 100 [*sic*] times the voting power of ordinary shares in any resolution to appoint or dismiss any director or staffer.

The effect is that the government can put anyone into or remove anyone from any position in a newspaper company. The reality is that the reserve power has never been exercised;

the reality is that there is probably no need to, because of the influence and record of the government.

Whatever the Singapore journalist's dreams, he cannot afford to forget this reality.[34]

In 1987, Peter Lim himself was to feel the sharp cutting edge of those amendments. He was eased out of his powerful position as editor-in-chief of the *Straits Times* group of newspapers, the genesis of which began, innocuously enough, in his report on the relative marksmanship in the sultanate of Brunei of the prime minister and his son, Brigadier General Lee Hsien Loong, to which the latter took umbrage. There, at an army firing range, the much-touted Singapore-made weapons were being demonstrated for accuracy, reliability and versatility, at some stage of which both the father and the son participated. Peter Lim reported the prime minister had scored direct hits with the weapons whereas his soldier-son had "washouts." The embarrassed general disputed the report claiming that he had tried for a more difficult target behind the target in question. In any other milieu, it would have been dismissed as absolute trivia but not by a self-conscious young Singapore army general with overweening ambitions. It resulted in the most servile apology ever published by an editor of the *Straits Times* in his own newspaper. It was, also, a sign of the times.

When time had healed the wound and dulled the painful severance from the *Straits Times* group, Peter Lim, choosing his words with care, told *Asiaweek*:

> I know it's said that I was acceptable politically and then I wasn't acceptable any more, so either the government engineered my removal or the board decided to remove me. What actually happened was that I was told by the board, "Look, you've been editor-in-chief for eight years, your deputy Cheong Yip Seng is ready, we feel you should hand over to him." I agreed. For two reasons. First I agreed that Cheong was ready. And, secondly, when your bosses tell you they think your number two is ready to take over from you, what do you say? If by saying I was eased out people mean that kind of situation, I guess they're right.[35]

The handwriting was on the wall, and, in the circumstances, it was decidedly the best face Peter Lim could put on it.

The Anson By-Election

On October 31, 1981, the opposition Workers' Party secretary general, Joshua Benjamin Jeyaretnam, won the Anson constituency by-election caused by the ill-starred elevation of NTUC secretary general and PAP MP, C.V. Devan Nair, to the presidency of the republic of Singapore, thereby breaking the PAP's monopoly on political power. Besides the sudden trauma of defeat for the PAP, long used to absolute electoral returns, Jeyaretnam's victory marked an important crossroad in the political history of Singapore. In an incredible display of questionable political sportsmanship, Lee raved and ranted at a press conference and threatened the Anson electorate with dire political consequences for the defeat; a scapegoat had to be found—and he beheld it in the configuration of the media, which was blamed for the loss of the Anson constituency for having given support to the opposition by creating a negative feeling towards the government. Its perceived role in the lone opposition member's electoral victory provided the catalyst for the change in direction in Lee's media plans, for if the press was not reeled in soon enough, more such political upsets were likely to occur. Consequent upon the Anson defeat, newspaper editors were harshly criticized by Lee and his cadres and "persuaded" to stop news coverage of the political opposition; but, unlike the 1971 crackdown on the press, when they were accused of subversive writings, the government said the news coverage was "inaccurate" mainly because of untrained and inexperienced journalists.[36]

Nevertheless, the mood of the government was still so dark that it threatened to put two senior civil servants, a permanent secretary, Cheng Tong Fatt, on to the *Straits Times* board of directors, and one Lim Siew Mei, to the managing director's staff "to monitor the internal workings of the company, in particular the operations of the editorial department." The *Straits Times* group top management, fearing "a real possibility of disintegration of its editorial team and of a government team of officials taking charge of the newspapers," demurred, and compromised by accepting a former director of the Security and Intelligence Division, S.R. Nathan, as director and the executive group chairman.[37]

The powers of the PAP government had grown so prodigiously since 1959 that it could now appoint at will onto the board of directors of the once-almighty *Straits Times* "digits," who—to paraphrase the words of former senior minister S. Rajaratnam—could now not only pass through "the gates of heaven" but also presume to speak with the voice of divinity. The appointment of S.R. Nathan as a "watchdog" had a demoralizing effect on the newsroom staff of the *Straits Times* group, and precipitated the severance of its joint venture with the Herald and Weekly Times Ltd., Australia's largest newspaper group and publisher of the *Melbourne Herald*. It originally had a 50 percent share in the group's afternoon newspaper, *New Nation*—which was launched in January 1971—but had scaled it down to 3 percent in line with the amended law. Sir Keith MacPherson, chairman of the Herald and Weekly Times Ltd., in resigning from the board of directors of the *New Nation*, wrote to the prime minister informing him of the severance and the reasons for it, adding that the appointment of a Singapore government representative as executive chairman of the *Straits Times* group was "incompatible with press freedom." "Quite obviously," he wrote, "it is not possible for us to continue an association with a newspaper which is now clearly government dominated."[38]

S.R. Nathan was subsequently appointed high commissioner to Malaysia,[39] and was succeeded by Frank Yung, who, on June 17, 1988, abruptly "resigned to pursue his career elsewhere" with "six months pay in lieu of notice."[40] In September 1988, he was succeeded in turn by Lim Kim San, a former senior cabinet minister and trusted political confidante of the prime minister—and, whenever the occasion arises, acting president of the republic of Singapore. At the time of this writing, he still holds the appointment.

This may be a convenient point to digress to note that the Herald and Weekly Times Ltd. was a foreign enterprise, which had a seat on the board of a *Straits Times* group subsidiary. Lee's destructive observations on the *Singapore Herald* investors did not affect the *New Nation* or the *Straits Times* group's investment activities overseas. Be that as it may, while investments by foreigners in a Singapore newspaper company were vociferously discouraged and looked upon with dark suspicion, it was, however, perfectly in order for Singaporean investors and companies to venture overseas and take up substantial stakes in foreign companies, newspaper and related companies included. The *Straits*

Times group had through the years acquired substantial interests in newspaper and related companies in countries spanning the entire globe, one prize acquisition of which is their substantial stake in the *South China Morning Post*, a prestigious Hongkong newspaper; and in 1994 the Singapore Press Holdings Ltd.—on which more will follow later—was reported to have taken "a 35 percent stake" in a venture to launch a daily English-language regional business newspaper, *Business Day*, in Bangkok early 1995.[41] Wherefore, there is one rule for foreign investors in Singapore newspaper companies and another rule for Singapore investors in foreign newspaper companies overseas.

The Restructure

As already noted, the NPPA initially mandated newspaper companies to convert themselves into public companies with two classes of shares, which was followed by the prohibition of large shareholdings by any one person. Any misgivings concerning the government's motives and intentions on those amendments had since been dissipated when, on April 22, 1982, Lee dropped another bombshell on an already stunned media, which had "failed to see the coming of the storm."

Armed with its new powers under the NPPA, the government delivered the coup de maître by ordering a wholesale restructure of the print media which—in the words of John A. Lent, professor of communications, Temple University—was "even more sweeping [than Malaysia], encompassing the folding of three newspapers, and the establishment of a new company of three dailies, among other radical changes."[42] The SNUJ expressed its concern, at an emergency meeting over the "impact of the restructuring," pledging to safeguard the rights and interests of its members, and advising its members to remain "united and calm in the difficult weeks ahead."

A statement issued by the prime minister's office proclaimed the "need to restructure the ownership of the English and Chinese newspapers," and decreed an "arranged marriage" between the *Nanyang Siang Pau* and the *Sin Chew Jit Poh*, the two leading Chinese newspapers.[43] The two long-established Chinese news arch-rivals were compulsorily merged into a single holding company called the Singapore News and Publications Limited (SNPL), in which they became wholly owned subsidiaries functioning under a unified management and financial structure "to pool their financial and manpower resources to achieve economies of scale essential for viability which also will help to raise journalistic standards." To provide "strong management backing," the government permitted 30 percent of its shares to be held by the United Overseas Bank group (UOB)—whose chairman was none other than Wee Cho Yaw of *Singapore Herald* fame. The Overseas Union Bank (OUB) and the Development Bank of Singapore (DBS) were invited to subscribe to 3 percent of SNPL's enlarged capital when the merger took place. Senior government officials were seconded to manage the new company.

The government had sponsored in 1980 the formation of the Singapore Monitor (Private) Limited for the purpose of publishing an English-language newspaper, the *Singapore Monitor*, as a daily morning competitor of the *Straits Times;* but, for a variety of reasons, its debut was delayed. The SNPL held 52 percent of the shares in the Singapore Monitor (Private) Limited, and the remaining 48 percent of the shares were held equally by the three leading local banks, UOB, OUB and DBS—which were prodded by the government to prop up the Singapore Monitor (Private) Limited in its publication of the *Singapore Monitor*, in addition to the Chinese dailies.

Confronted with a "Hobson's choice" in the media restructure, the *Straits Times* group agreed, albeit reluctantly, to cease publication of its profitable afternoon tabloid, the *New Nation* (circulation 44,205) and its Sunday edition (circulation 88,700) and to give its competitor, the *Singapore Monitor*, "a helping hand" by "lending" its successful mastheads for one year from May 1, 1982, for a nominal consideration, in the first instance. But, from November 16, 1982, the Singapore Monitor (Private) Limited dropped the *New Nation* masthead, and officially launched it as the *Singapore Monitor*: "Nowhere else and never before, as far as we know, has any newspaper been asked to lend a helping hand to a potential rival."[44]

Nowhere else in the whole world but in Singapore could this have happened. It could only be conceived and executed in a country whose paramount leader speaks of the use of "knuckle-dusters" and "stilettos" with spirited skill and easy familiarity. In the circumstances, was it any wonder that no one, not even the persons most affected by the restructure—the shareholders, the editors and the journalists—dared to raise any objection? But Peter Lim described the grotesque situation in more sophisticated Asian metaphor: ". . . the arrangement is so unusual, this plan to help a rival paper to launch, with the pay-off from a third party, that one was reminded of a Chinese saying about being in the same bed and dreaming different dreams."

In an interesting aside, Singapore official propaganda put it out that the *Straits Times* group had wanted to cease publishing the *New Nation* because of a shortage of available English-language journalists, which had prompted the government to request the *Straits Times* group to kindly lend its masthead to the *Singapore Monitor*. That bland assertion presented a far too simplistic picture, and defies basic commercial sense. In any event, the *Singapore Monitor*, when it commenced, would also be drawing from the same reservoir of available journalists, whose level of journalistic talents the *New Nation* had allegedly found low and wanting. Every which way it was, the *New Nation* was a successful and profitable afternoon paper, notwithstanding. Although there was avowedly a scarcity of good, trained English-language journalists available in Singapore, the talent situation could easily be alleviated by temporary recruitment from abroad, even though the government considered it "not desirable to have too many expatriate journalists running Singapore English newspapers."[45] Turnbull, however, mentioned that the government initially had wanted the *Straits Times* group to hand over the *Business Times*, together with their companies and staff, but a compromise was reached whereby only the *New Nation* was given up, without its staff.[46]

As a sop to the *Straits Times* group, it was guaranteed a monopoly of the English-language newspaper morning market for three years, and, as a further sop, permitted to acquire and publish an afternoon Chinese-language newspaper, which it did via the purchase of a 45 percent controlling interest in a Chinese afternoon tabloid, the *Shin Min Daily News*. On the other hand, to sweeten the bitterness of the enforced merger, the government dangled before the SNPL shareholders the prospect of access, transitory as it turned out, to the "growing English newspaper readership through the Singapore Monitor (Private) Limited taking over the readership of the *New Nation* as an afternoon paper and the *Sunday Nation* as a Sunday paper."[47]

Asked to comment on the charge that the restructure was really a means of asserting governmental press control, a senior official callously replied: "They can interpret it whichever way they want. We have our own ideas and we are carrying them out." The government's stand had long been that press freedom takes second place to national development, and a cabinet minister was later to remind reporters that they were "Singaporeans first, journalists second."

The aforesaid statement from the prime minister's office on the restructure portrayed the Chinese-language press as being under siege, whose long-term viability was threatened by the prospect of more Chinese Singaporeans turning to English-language newspapers, as a result of more parents sending their children to English-stream schools. Therefore, the reorganization of the media was devised to meet the challenges arising from a changing trend in newspaper readership: a growing readership of English newspapers and the prospect of a stagnant and ultimately declining readership of Chinese newspapers. The official statement was taken as gospel. No one appeared to have questioned it at the time. But the figures given below do not necessarily support the assertion of the administration.

According to the *Singapore Yearbook*—an official publication of the Ministry of Culture—for the relevant years, the total daily circulation of newspapers in Singapore for 1980 was 615,600 copies, out of which Chinese newspaper daily circulation was 307,800 copies as against 268,600 copies for English newspapers. For the year 1981, it was 644,300 copies, out of which Chinese newspaper circulation was 320,400 and English newspaper circulation 283,700 copies. For the year 1982, it was 653,300 copies, out of which Chinese newspaper circulation was 326,600 copies and English newspaper circulation was 285,500 copies. In 1983, the total daily circulation of newspapers was 676,000 copies, out of which Chinese newspaper circulation was 332,700 copies as against 301,700 copies for English newspapers.[48]

Chinese newspaper circulation per se did not, therefore, appear to be stagnating or declining. The prognosis of a "stagnant and ultimately declining Chinese readership" was an excuse spiked with a little good old-fashioned Han chauvinism to soothe, if not lull, the Chinese ego. If this visage is stripped away, the underlying motive for the reorganization may be better seen in perspective. The restructure envisioned, cosmetically, "two economically viable and eventually competitive publishing houses, each capable of producing a Chinese and an English newspaper" in free competition with one another. Despite these awe-inspiring reorganizational moves in the infrastructure of the media, Lee had yet to play his final card.

Meanwhile, on March 16, 1983, the *Nanyang Siang Pau* and the *Sin Chew Jit Poh* ceased their separate publication and, with their cessation, their proud and time-honoured names became a part of media trivia. In their stead, there sprang up the pedestrian names of *Lianhe Zaobao—United Morning News*—and the *Lianhe Wanbao— United Evening News*—the latter degraded to the status of a tabloid like the *Shin Min Daily*, both of which reportedly enjoy large circulation: about 113,000 and 107,000 copies per issue respectively.[49]

The *Kuai Bao*, a Chinese daily afternoon newspaper, owned by the publishers of the *Nanyang Siang Pau*, who had started it in 1980, was absorbed into SNPL. It, however, discontinued publication in October 1983, and its resources were transferred to the

Lianhe Wanbao. Before leaving the two Chinese newspapers to history, Elliott S. Parker's shrewd observation might be noted here:

> Singapore's most influential paper remains the *Straits Times* since, as an English-language daily, it is the one read by people from all linguistic groups, although it does not carry the ethnic or cultural flavour of the vernacular papers. On the other hand, the Chinese papers do a better job of covering local news and analyzing contemporary issues.[50]

A similar point was made by the prime minister, albeit in a different way, when he warned his English-educated listeners during the 1976 general election at a Fullerton Square rally: "If you read, and you understand only the English language, then you are at a very grave disadvantage because you really don't know what is going on in a large part of Singapore. If you believe that the *Straits Times* and the *New Nation* is what Singapore is about, then you are living in a dream world."[51]

Consequent upon the revamping of the media, the two rival media groups, the *Straits Times* and the SNPL, were quietly girding themselves for the circulation battle. Each had planned to change the form and contents of its papers, and recruit high-powered expatriate editorial and journalist staff. The tabloid *Singapore Monitor*, on the other hand, had planned to go broadsheet. Various strategies were worked out by the rivals to win readers' favours. In anticipation of keen competition ahead, the *Straits Times* group had "pre-empted the market by buying up syndicated rights to all the major publications in the English-speaking world," "the best cartoons," and "hired the best or better journalists."[52] Wherefore, there were considerable obstacles to the *Singapore Monitor* breaking into the market. But, unknown to the editors and journalists, the shareholders and the public alike, Lee was about to administer the coup de grace on the print media.

Suddenly, there was an about-face. In a joint press statement, the managements of the *Straits Times* group and the SNPL announced a shock merger between them, astounding the public and shaking the print media to its very foundation. In the statement, they attempted to explain the reasons for the merger:

- To immediately avoid the costs of a "long and hard" circulation struggle and duplicated capital expenditure, and thereafter to realize long-term economies of scale;
- To create a major publishing base which will have both the financial and human resources to not only strive for excellence in its own home products but also to seize new opportunities in the growth areas of communications and information technology; and
- To develop common ideals for newspapers in the different languages and to continue the upgrading of editorial content. In this way, the divisive effects of a newspaper battle can be avoided and the opportunity is created to further unify the main language streams.

As to the loss of competitive spirit, they believed that the merger could be organized in a manner which provided for that competitive element to be preserved by each newspaper remaining different "by retaining its own style and formula, and continue to compete for readership and stories." The status quo in all businesses would be maintained; but in the longer term there would be reorganization which would permit the exposure and interchangeability of key executives and staff between the three groups so that in time "they will gain a new identity to which all will subscribe, a new philosophy with which all can identify, and one common corporate loyalty."

In a craftily worded statement, the government denied that the initiative for this final phase of restructure had emanated from the government or from Lee himself. Given the Singapore context, is it really possible? In any event, Lee's fingerprints could be seen all over the merger agreement. It transpired that, sometime in May/June, 1984, the prime minister had met separately with the representatives of the *Straits Times* group and the SNPL who, be it noted, "*knew*" of the government policy. In the event, with his tacit agreement quiet negotiations began in early June between the *Straits Times* group and the SNPL to merge the companies within their respective groups into one entity. The merger agreement was reached on June 18, and made public on Wednesday, July 11, 1984, on the 6:30 evening news bulletin.

Prior to the fateful announcement, in the afternoon of July 11, 1984, Lyndley Holloway, representing the *Straits Times* group,[53] and Lee Hee Seng, representing the SNPL, allegedly at their own respective requests met with the prime minister on the merger agreement apparently to obtain his benediction on it, before its announcement. At this meeting, Lee made it clear to them that, the merger notwithstanding:

> The rules would allow for fair competition, that there could be no pre-emption by over-booking of syndicated articles or cartoons, and that there would be free bidding for the services of journalists, and that it was our intention to gradually allow a temporary inflow of foreign journalists to make up for the shortage of local ones.
>
> . . . that with free rules of competition, it was unlikely that the *Monitor* could ever be crushed as so many other newspapers had been crushed in the past. . . . there were three banks on the side of the *Monitor*—the Overseas Union Bank, the United Overseas Bank, and the Singapore Development Bank. There were also the resources of the daily revenues of the Chinese newspapers to back it.
>
> . . . But some members of the *Straits Times* group were under the impression that they could go for broke, and, therefore, I was asked to confirm that was the government's position. I did so and, as far as I know, I needed no other words of persuasion to let them come to the conclusion that they could either take up the cudgels and slog it out for five, seven or more years, and then share the market, or come to terms as best they can. . . . We have enough powers to make sure that both play according to the rules of the game. I make no apologies for these powers. They are necessary.[54]

The news of the sudden merger surprised and shocked the editors, the journalists and the employees of the rival groups alike, who resented what they perceived was a reversal of a solemn promise that there would be two major publishing houses in competition with one another.

However, Lee's long-cherished ambition and *real* plans became an actual reality when the SNPL merged with the *Straits Times* group to form an umbrella company, Singapore Press Holdings (SPH), the largest industrial group and sixth-largest listed company on the Singapore Stock Exchange, with a capital base of S$1.4 billion (US$660 million). It was also the only monopoly listed on the Stock Exchange of Singapore. Under the 3 percent holdings rule, companies that were exempted from the ruling in the past had to divest excess SPH shares over a period of two years, commencing January 1994, to the stock market, Temasek Holdings and MND Holdings, the two wholly owned government companies, which the minister for finance promised would be split into affordable odd lots and offered to Singaporeans eventually.[55]

The political opposition denounced the "shotgun merger" as being politically motivated because the government feared a free competition would mean a "livelier" and "more dangerous" journalism. Over 100 placard-carrying journalists demonstrated outside the premises of the *Straits Times* over fears for their jobs and over principles of press freedom, watched and photographed by labour ministry officials, the police and the ubiquitous plainclothes ISD officers. Supporting the theory that the merger would eliminate wasteful competition, the ever-dependable second deputy prime minister, S. Rajaratnam, with typical PAP logic, pontificated:

> The trouble with us is we always think as though we are Europeans.
>
> You try and study prospects of the newspaper in terms of Singapore, with two-and-a-half million people.
>
> What is competition? It means one paper tries [to] kill the other. It will cost $40 million to $50 million—some tell me it's $80 million—for the *Straits Times* to kill the *Monitor* and vice-versa. So you spend the money and, at the end of it, you have two corpses. What for?
>
> So why not use the money saved to train and pay journalists better, get the best men possible, raise standards as well as new publications. Because of competition, many newspapers have died—and that is bad.[56]

But Dr. Toh Chin Chye, a former deputy prime minister turned critic, disapproved of the merger, warning that Singapore could lock its press into the role of an obeisant official mouthpiece along the lines of the Soviet Union's *Pravda* or China's *People's Daily*. He later ascribed public perception that "the merger . . . was seen to be government-inspired" as one of the causes for the swing against the PAP in the 1984 general election, and was one of several "weird" PAP policy changes in the 1980s.[57] Others called it "a step backwards, not only for journalists but also for the people of Singapore."

On October 19, 1984, in a written answer to opposition MP Jeyaretnam's parliamentary question, the minister for culture, S. Dhanabalan, denied that the merger of the newspaper publishing companies in Singapore was directed or initiated by the government. When the idea was mooted by the publishing companies themselves, the government had no objections.[58] "The merger made sense because it avoided vast capital expenditure in acquiring plant and equipment," he asserted. As a financial exercise, he boasted, it was an accomplishment worthy of the best of Wall Street mergers and acquisitions—an exquisite non sequitur which had absolutely nothing whatsoever to do with the subject under discussion.[59] The government tried to assuage fears amongst newsmen and the public that the merger would lead to greater control over or muzzling of the press. Given the situation, a *Straits Times* reader prophesied the rise of popularity of the foreign media: "I dread the day when our thinking public resorts to international radio broadcasts and foreign newspapers to find out what is happening in the country."[60]

Meanwhile, the government continued to reiterate that the amalgamation was necessary because of "the prospect of a stagnant and ultimately declining readership of Chinese papers," and a shortage of journalists made it impractical for the *Straits Times* and the *Monitor* to compete in the morning market. The total daily circulation, however, continued to show a pattern of rising sales in Chinese newspapers, and the year 1983 proved no exception. According to the official figures, the total daily newspaper circulation in 1983 was 676,000 copies, out of which the Chinese daily newspaper circulation was 332,681 copies while the English newspaper circulation was only 301,205 copies.[61] The statistics indicated the Chinese newspaper readership was in reasonably robust health; and the official claim of "stagnation or ultimately declining Chinese readership" was unsupported by its own official figures. (See Appendix A for a chart of the daily newspaper circulation of the Chinese- and English-language newspapers from 1984–1989 which, save for the year 1984, shows the state of robustness of Chinese newspaper readership.) One swallow in the year 1984 does not make a summer of stagnating Chinese newspaper readership. Or, in the more vivid metaphor of the government-linked periodical *Singapore*: "The prophets of doom could not have been more wrong." *Singapore* reported that since the amalgamation in 1983, the combined daily circulation of Chinese newspapers had gone up to 450,000, an increase of 130,000 over 10 years.[62] And its report in the March-April 1994 issue only served to reinforce the aforementioned observation:

> Recent figures released by the Singapore Press Holdings reveal that in the past 10 years, readership of Chinese newspapers rose from 836,000 to 1,117,000, an increase of 40 percent. . . .
>
> Today, 39 percent of the 1,117,000 readers of Chinese newspapers in Singapore are educated in the English stream, compared to 1983 when the English-educated made up 29 percent of the 836,000 Chinese newspapers readers in Singapore.[63]

The 1984 General Election

In the 1984 general election, the government lost another seat to the opposition, which increased its number from one to two members in parliament, an event momentous enough for a furious prime minister to publicly utter all sorts of dire threats against the people of Singapore, including changing the electoral system. In spite of the prime minister's bold, reassuring words, on July 14, 1985, the *Singapore Monitor* closed down, citing mounting losses. It had exhausted its capital of S$20 million (US$9.1 million) and owed S$6 million to its parent company, SNPL. With the loss of the Anson constituency, Lee's attitude on the benefits of a competitive press had also undergone a fundamental metamorphosis. It was the consensus among the cognoscenti that the *Singapore Monitor* might have survived, if Lee had not lost interest in seeing competition between the newspapers as a result of the Anson defeat.

Stephen Taylor, writing from Singapore in the aftermath of the poll shock, put his finger right on the problem of defeat:

> Soon thereafter, a spate of letters began to appear in the papers offering explanations for the significant swing to the opposition. Although couched in restrained language, they reflected a common theme: the ruling People's Action Party had been overtaken by arrogance and had failed to read the signs.
>
> Further correspondence took issue with Mr. Lee's threat to review the one-man-one-vote system and his views on genetic breeding: rare, if only implicit, criticism of the prime minister. The *Straits Times*, the main English-language newspaper, described the threat as disturbing.

But the most outspoken comment was a column in the *Sunday Monitor* which openly admitted the press had failed in its responsibility to reflect voter frustration before the election. With a candour unprecedented in recent years, the columnist, Margaret Thomas, wrote: "Why didn't we? Let's not be coy about it: because we toe the government line."

Local journalists readily acknowledge that the [loosening of] controls referred to by Mr. Goh amount to a fear of offending the authorities than any overt censorship.

Rather than being detained or disappearing, the Singapore reporter who is too forthright risks demotion or a public tongue-lashing from an irate minister, and consequent loss of face.

The ultimate sanction in Singapore is usually economic and the press is no exception. Most local publishers are prevented from going out on a limb by the possibility that their annual licences will not be renewed.[64]

Denying opposition SDP MP Chiam See Tong's charge during the 1993 budget debate that the monolithic Singapore Press Holdings was "pro-PAP and anti-opposition," information minister, Brig. Gen. George Yeo, said that local newspapers are "neither pro-PAP nor pro-opposition—but pro-Singapore. They are an important factor in Singapore's success as they explain complicated social and other policies"—an assertion which runs contrary to popular perceptions, and notwithstanding the protestations of the *Straits Times* editor, Leslie Fong, that he was unashamedly pro-government.[65]

The year 1994 ended—as in previous years—with only one gigantic publishing monolith in Singapore, the Singapore Press Holdings Limited, a conglomerate comprising the Singapore News and Publications Ltd. (SNPL), the *Straits Times* Press (1975) Limited and the Times Publishing Company. The Singapore Press Holdings Limited owns, publishes and prints three local English-language newspapers, the *Straits Times* and its Sunday edition, the *Sunday Times*, the *Business Times* and the *New Paper;* a Malay-language newspaper, the *Berita Harian* and its Sunday edition, the *Berita Minggu*; and three Chinese-language newspapers, the *Lianhe Zaobao*, the *Lianhe Wanbao* and the *Shin Min Daily News* and their Sunday editions, among other publications. There are no competitors.

Towards the end of 1995, Singapore Press Holdings announced its acquisition of the Tamil-language daily newspaper, *Tamil Murasu*, for $500,000. A memorandum of understanding was signed with Hipro Printing Pte Limited, the owner and publisher of the newspaper. The newspaper was founded by G. Sarangapany in 1935, and was a family-run sole proprietorship until 1994, when it was converted into a private limited company. With the acquisition of this independently owned newspaper, the government-run SPH will have a monopoly of all daily newspapers published in Singapore in the four official languages—save for the *Navijiwan*, a small vernacular newspaper of limited importance and indifferent quality catering to the ethnic Punjabi minority.

Other Domestic Publications

We have hitherto been discussing the mainstream newspaper publications vis-à-vis their problems with Singapore's officialdom. Needless to say, other domestic publications were equally affected by the same laws and policies. To give a more comprehensive picture, it is proposed to deal briefly with the trials and tribulations of some of these publications.

The *Business Times*   In September, 1976, the business section of the *Straits Times* evolved into a newspaper in its own right under the name of *Business Times* with Tan Sai Siong—who also writes under the pen name of Tsai Tan—as the first and "only woman editor to head a financial daily in the Commonwealth." Sometime in the 1980s, Roy MacKee joined as editor. The paper dared official displeasure when it editorialized in October 1986 that the decision of the government in restricting the circulation of *Time* weekly magazine was "regrettable," and expressed surprise that it appeared to have been taken on the evidence of one article, "while other publications, particularly from Hongkong, had been more regularly critical of Singapore's policies." This editorial comment was considered unacceptable to the government, whose information ministry rebuked it for giving "succour to foreign publications at Singapore's expense" by editorially criticizing the government's decision to restrict the sale of *Time* magazine.[66] Mano Sabnani took over from Roy Mackee as editor, but, in early 1992, was himself moved over to the *Straits Times* as one of several executive editors and replaced by Patrick Daniel, a Cambridge graduate and a senior official in the ministry of trade and industry, whose minister was the young prime-minister-aspirant Brig. Gen. Lee Hsien Loong, and for whom he reportedly acted as occasional ghostwriter. Daniel's transfer to the *Business Times* was regarded in media circles as a prelude to the ultimate post of editor-in-chief of the *Straits Times* group, after Brig. Gen. Lee assumes the premiership mantle. But the sudden illness of his mentor and the 1994 investigation of the *BT* under the Official Secrets Act by ISD officers—which is dealt with later—appears to have cast a shadow over his future. It also underscores the pitfalls which beset even favourite journalists in their quest for information for their papers.

The *Berita Harian*   The *Berita Harian*, an influential Malay-language daily in the *Straits Times* stable of newspapers, gave generous space in its columns to Malay disagreement over the state visit of the president of Israel, Chaim Herzog, to Singapore on November 18–20, 1986—which did not please the government. The state visit was vociferously opposed by the Muslim populations in both Singapore and Malaysia, whose opposition soon translated itself into demonstrations, which severely embarrassed the government—and of whose state visit Lee, incredibly, albeit characteristically, disclaimed any knowledge. He was not informed of the president's visit, he claimed. The Philippine government, on the other hand, taking note of aroused regional sensitivity, cancelled that leg of the visit by the Israeli president to the Republic of the Philippines. In December 1986, Lee singled out three *Berita Harian* stories quoting criticisms by Malay groups of the Israeli president's state visit to Singapore. The sum total of Lee's displeasure led to the eventual lateral transfer of the *Straits Times* editor-in-chief to organize and head a new afternoon newspaper with the uninspiring name—the *New Paper*.

The *New Paper*   On July 26, 1988, the rather inconsequential afternoon tabloid appeared on the streets, whose "main selling point was not independent, critical and up-to-the-minute news coverage, but bright and breezy reports with its screaming suggestive headlines that are supposedly 'fun' to read." Or, as the *Asiaweek* magazine called it, "*risqué* reading." Published by the *Straits Times* group, the paper is aimed at providing "fast-and-easy-to-digest" news and targeted at English-educated blue-collar readers.[67]

On February 21, 1990, Peter Lim, the editor, suddenly announced his resignation from the *New Paper* and the *Straits Times* group "to try his hand at writing a novel." It was rumoured abroad that he was sometime afterwards asked to take a cut in his salary— a not too subtle way of conveying the suggestion to him to begin looking for greener pastures. Given its "sexy stories, the weirdest punchlines, and heart-wrenching tales," sales topped 86,000 copies in 1992. No doubt pleased with the sales statistics and the handsome profits therefrom, SPH's executive chairman, Lim Kim San, reportedly enthused: "The paper has the right formula. It presents news in a time-saving and racy style."[68]

By most accounts the *New Paper* is doing well, given its virtual monopoly of afternoon tabloid papers. At the end of 1994, the daily readership of the paper was estimated at 443,000.

Another New Paper? During a surprise April visit by Senior Minister Lee Kuan Yew to Singapore Press Holdings, he told senior SPH managers that a new paper should be published outside the group to provide competition which he believed would help improve the quality of the domestic print media.[69] Subsequently, it was reported that the Singapore government had granted a licence for a new English-language newspaper daily that would compete with the SPH, whose publisher was expected to be the National Trade Union Congress, a government-controlled labour organization with vast business interests.[70] So far it has not made its debut.

Political Organs, Newsletters, Etcetera

There are no limits placed on the number of political newspapers in Singapore, which are ostensibly subject to the same laws as other newspapers. No news organ of a political party has been banned or suspended, but over the years many have ceased to exist through officialdom's machinations, attrition or the demise of the party itself. But the printers who do printing work for the political opposition or oppositionists often face harassment from the authorities, as may be seen by this random example:

On February 5, 1963—during the notorious security exercise Operation Cold Store—10 publications of opposition political parties, trade unions and student associations were proscribed under the Undesirable Publications Ordinance. Six of the publications, including the Chinese edition of *Wartawan*—the organ of the Singapore National Union of Journalists—were printed by the Boon Hua Printing Press, which was called upon to show cause why its application for the renewal of its licence should not be refused, in view of the "many undesirable publications it had printed in the past." The firm's printing press, in addition, was ordered to cease operating pending a final decision on the application. Boon Hua Printing Press was also a printer for the PAP's organ, *Petir* ("lightning"), and other PAP propaganda and literature, as well as a booklet, *Battle for Merger*, a compilation of a series of radio talks by Lee Kuan Yew. But, when the breakaway opposition party *Barisan Sosialis* also used its services, the PAP switched to another printer, Chip Bee Press. Another firm, which had printed some of the proscribed publications, was apparently not affected because it was printing "a lot of pro-PAP material."[71] After Boon Hua Printing Press regained its licence, it predictably announced that it would no longer print for the *Barisan Sosialis*, which protested the government's action as an "indirect attempt to ban its party journals." No other printing firm would undertake work for the *Barisan Sosialis*, which had perforce to resort to a stencilled edition of its party organ, and, finally, to a purchase of its own offset press. (See "The Plebeian," below.)

The harassment of political parties has not ceased by any means as may be seen in this recent incident: Singapore Democratic Party (SDP) secretary general, Chee Soon Juan, in his current book, *Singapore, My Home Too*, detailed the SDP printers' experience at the hands of the police for a minor infringement of the printing laws—an omission of the printers' name in the party's political flyers.[72]

The notable past and present organs of political parties are discussed below:

The *Plebeian* The experience of the *Plebeian*, the official organ of the former opposition political party, the Barisan Sosialis, with the authorities—which became increasingly contumacious—is an object lesson in Lee's repressive techniques. It was launched after the seminal split from the PAP in August-September 1962, as a fortnightly broadsheet in English. An initial bureaucratic delay in approving the necessary permits was swiftly rectified when the delay was noisily and publicly ventilated by the dissidents, thus testifying in some small way to the efficacy of a sturdy political opposition. The first editor was Dr. Lim Hock Siew who, together with several other Barisan leaders, was later arrested under a mammoth security operation, code-named Cold Store, in February 1963, resulting in the temporary disruption of the publication. Dr. Lim was incarcerated without trial for almost 20 years. Meanwhile, the party chairman, Dr. Lee Siew Choh, stepped into the breach in editorial responsibilities.

Difficulties with the printers arose soon after Operation Cold Store. The government pressured the Barisan Sosialis's commercial printers not to print for the party and, to augment the pressure, the printer's permit was suspended for two weeks for some vague legal infractions. The permit was restored after the printers agreed to stop printing the Barisan Sosialis organ. News of the suspension became known to other printers who shied away from doing any printing work for the party. It became virtually impossible for the party to obtain the services of professional printers even though it was prepared to pay higher than the usual commercial rates as added incentive. In the final result, the party had to resort to self-reliance. It initially purchased a cyclostyle machine for its printing needs. The broadsheet was replaced by a stencilled version of the paper called the *Plebeian Express*, whose printing and visual results were mediocre. A year or two later, the party bought an offset printer, which gave much improved and better results. The *Plebeian Express* was retained for publication of "extras" during elections and campaigns, and for the dissemination of urgent news. A Malay version of the *Plebeian*, edited by Said Zahari, ceased publication altogether after his arrest and detention in the same round-up.

Its Chinese version, *Chern Sien Pao*, had a more chequered career than its English counterpart, and was involved as defendant in several defamation proceedings, initiated by either Lee or his PAP government. In 1964, it was prosecuted for publishing a seditious article by some left-wing trade unions and, in 1965, it was sued for libel, but the case was settled out of court upon payment of token damages. An early editor was Barisan Sosialis MP, Chia Thye Poh, who was arrested in May 1966, tried and fined for publishing a "seditious" article in the *Chern Sien Pau*—criticizing the government's treatment of another Barisan MP, who was then held in detention under the ISA.[73] In October that same year, Chia was arrested for planning public demonstrations against American involvement in Vietnam on the eve of President Lyndon B. Johnson's official visit to Singapore. Since then, he has been detained for 23 long years, one of the longest-held political prisoners in the world. No formal charge was ever preferred against him. He was released in May 1989, on restrictive conditions, and exiled by cynical officialdom to Pulau Sentosa—Isle of Tranquillity—a Disneyesque resort island, opposite the main island of Singapore. Since then and, as a result of adverse international reports, he has been permitted to move back to the main island of Singapore, where he now lives with his parents, but still restricted in his speech, movement, and association.

In 1972, one Yeo Ah Ngoh, as publisher of the *Chern Sien Pao*, was committed to one month's jail for contempt of court. He had published an article in which the high court was described as a "puppet high court," and the senior district judge, T.S. Sinnathuray, as a "reactionary authority."[74] In 1973, the prime minister was awarded damages against the paper, Yeo Ah Ngoh as editor, the Barisan Sosialis as publisher, and Dr. Lee Siew Choh as party chairman, for publishing slanderous remarks made by lawyer Harban Singh, a Barisan Sosialis electoral candidate in the 1972 general election (who was himself jailed for one month for criminal defamation of the prime minister), who remarked that, "if left unchallenged, [the prime minister's] effectiveness in governing Singapore and maintaining law and order would be that much reduced."[75] Interestingly, the defendants were ordered to place the advertisement of apology in the *Nanyang Siang Pau* because it "would be read by more of the people," but *Nanyang*, however, refused to carry it. *Nanyang*—it will be remembered—was having its own problems with the prime minister. Meanwhile, Dr. Lee, ill-counselled, allowed his name to remain as a defendant in the proceedings without challenging its inclusion. Upon the inevitable judgment, he was left to foot the entire bill of about S$60,000—a princely sum in those days—in damages and costs as the other defendants were virtually men of straw.

Given his initial hollow victories in those defamatory suits against his political opponents after the 1972 general election, Harry Lee Kuan Yew introduced new rules and regulations, which required a political party, when applying for or renewing publishing or printing permits, or both, to furnish the names and personal particulars of not only the editor and the publisher but also the names of all its central executive committee members and their assets, including movable and immovable properties and their respective values. Implicit in the new rules was the threat that, in any successful defamation suit against a publication, it would not be just the editor and the publisher, but all the named persons who would have to assume liability for the defamation.[76] As no Barisan member was willing to put forward his name in the application form, no application to the licencing authority was submitted for renewing the publication permits. Eventually, the papers ceased publication altogether. Lee could, with some justification, claim that he had never really banned the *Plebeian*, intractable and incorrigible though it was, but that it was the party itself which had not submitted its application for renewal in accordance with the law—a law carefully crafted to achieve the same effect. (See *The Hammer,* below.) In addition to cowing the political opposition, Lee's string of striking forensic victories has had the effect of impoverishing many of his political opponents, as well as jeopardizing their electoral prospects at the polls.

Before leaving the Barisan Sosialis and its feisty organ, The *Plebeian,* it may be germane to mention here a fact, not generally well known: consequent upon his accidental discovery in 1968 that his home had been electronically bugged by the Special Branch—as it was then still known—Dr. Lee Siew Choh called a press conference at his party's Victoria Street headquarters—which, paradoxically, was unbeknown to him also bugged—to announce the sordid facts of discovery and display the listening devices recovered from strategic sites hidden in the ceiling of his home. It appeared that his residence was not the only place which had been bugged by the Special Branch. At the conference, he released a press statement that was scathing in its reproach of the government for its rampant use of such stratagems. Scenting blood in the air, the eager local newshounds scribbled excitedly on their note pads and poked around those devices while their equally fascinated photographer-colleagues took "innumerable" photographs of them "from every conceivable angle." This unexpected discovery, without a doubt, was grist for the news mills, as an irate Dr. Lee grimly thought, for the morning papers the next day would surely carry, in his words, "some appetizing news to rivet the attention of Singaporeans, who would have plenty of material for their morning coffee-shop chatter for some time to come." But, the next day dawned without a single word or photograph of the devices published in any newspaper. It was a sudden media non-event. The incident was a custom-made political cudgel against the government. What deus ex machina had intervened to resolve the awkward moment of truth? It required no quantum leap of imagination to fathom the answer. The *Plebeian,* subsequently, reported it in its characteristic prose, which guaranteed against it being read by a wide public.[77]

***The Hammer,* and the Workers' Party Newsletters** *The Hammer*—the tabloid-size official organ of the Workers' Party—is published bimonthly in English, Malay, Tamil, and Chinese sections. It is not a specifically inspiring or lively paper, whose sales depend on a loyal band of party stalwarts. Notwithstanding, *The Hammer's* circulation is reported to "exceed 35,000 copies" per issue, completely devoid of commercial advertisements. It does not sell or distribute its paper through traditional channels for the reasons hereinafter mentioned. The Housing & Development Board (HDB), a division of the ministry of national development, is the largest landlord in Singapore of apartment blocks, including shops and newsstands. And because of their real fear of the authorities, few newsstand owners would willingly accept copies of opposition newspapers for sale to the public. A newsstand owner, who did was warned in no uncertain fashion that he would lose his newsstand licence if he persisted in selling them—a microcosm of the myriad problems facing the political opposition in Singapore. Workers' Party members, including their secretary general, are, therefore, driven to vending them personally, usually on Sundays and public holidays at public places. Members of the public often pay more than the published price of 50 cents per copy as a gesture of sympathy or empathy. *The Hammer* has not only to pay its way but is also an invaluable source of party revenue. So far as is known, none of the members, including the secretary general, has been prosecuted for hawking in public without a licence.

Thus, to help level Singapore's uneven political field a little, several young professionals in the mid-eighties voluntarily offered their assistance and ideas to opposition MP Jeyaretnam on the publication and distribution of *The Hammer*. As the paper improved in quality and tone, as well as in contents and standard of printing, these bright young men and women were arrested by the government under the ISA, accused of "manoeuver[ing] themselves into positions of influence in the Workers' Party," and "captur[ing] control of *The Hammer*, which they saw as a useful medium to disseminate anti-government propaganda and influence public opinion against the government."[78] Among those arrested were Kenneth Tsang, who was accused of being the de facto editor, and his journalist wife, Jenny Chin, and Tan Tee Seng, who was accused of being a de facto member of *The Hammer* editorial board. Paradoxically, the Workers' Party organization and its appurtenances, including *The Hammer*, had always been run by the imperious Jeyaretnam as his own personal fief—and over his futile protestations, the government publicly accused them of being members of a "conspiracy to overthrow the government and replace it with a Marxist state," an accusation which was as unjust as it was ridiculous, and which is now generally conceded to have been a knee-jerk reaction. For, astonishingly, Lee had—in the privacy of an Istana meeting—conceded that they were "do-gooders"—thus contradicting his own government's public statements.[79]

On October 27, 1986, the Speaker of Parliament announced receipt of a complaint from the leader of the house, S. Dhanabalan, against the member for Anson, J.B. Jeyaretnam, for alleged breach of parliamentary privilege in sending five signed newsletters to his Anson constituents purporting to report on the daily disciplinary proceedings of the committee of privileges meetings into Jeyaretnam's conduct as a parliamentarian. The complaint was referred to the committee of privileges.[80]

On March 18, 1987, the Speaker of Parliament announced that he had received another complaint from the leader of the house, this time, against Jeyaretnam as editor, publisher and printer of the Workers' Party publication, *The Hammer*, for contempt in an article, "Committee of Privileges Hearing/Jeya Denied Fair Hearing," in its January/February 1987 issue. It was referred to the committee of privileges, as "the matter complained of prima facie affects the privileges of parliament."[81] Jeyaretnam was predictably found guilty on all charges and fined.

During the 1993 budget debate, Information Minister Brig. Gen. George Yeo, professed to be "saddened" that a recent issue of *The Hammer* had "extracted articles written by foreigners against Singapore." *The Hammer* had reproduced two thought-provoking articles from *The Economist* issue of August 22, 1992, which was inspired by an esoteric essay, "A Tale of Two Cities: Factor Accumulation and Technical Change in Hongkong and Singapore," written by Professor Alwyn Young of the Sloan School of Management, Massachusetts Institute of Technology, who had compared the methods used by Singapore with Hongkong in pursuit of economic growth, and concluded that Singapore had only a few more years left for economic growth unless it changed its policies:

> To put it crudely, Hongkong got richer by becoming a lot more efficient in the way it used people, capital and technology. Singapore became richer by thrusting its hands ever deeper

into its citizens' pockets—through taxes, forced savings and subsidies to multinationals—and throwing the money at the problem. . . . For Singapore, however, Mr. Young's analysis has a gruesome and more or less immediate practical implication. If he is right, Singapore has very few years of growth left along the old lines: it simply cannot extract much more savings from its people—already the biggest savers in the world—to support its growing craving for capital.[82]

Disgracefully employing a racist remark reminiscent of his mentor Lee, Yeo interpolated: "Is there such a poverty of ideas, paucity of writers that you have to use others to be your surrogate? Or do we still have this servile mentality, that what the white man says must be right?"[83] In the process, *The Hammer*—in quoting *The Economist*—had unwittingly sown the seeds for the latter's circulation restriction. However that may be, Young's article was criticized by the minister for trade and industry, Brig. Gen Lee Hsien Loong, whose criticisms were duly reported by the *Straits Times*, but not the article in its entirety—as it was wont to do, if it was flattering of the prime minister and his governance of Singapore or of other ministers, sometimes serialized over days.

In November 1995, *The Hammer* ran into another misfortune. It published an article, "The Tamil Language Week—A Drama Enacted to the Written Ruling," in the Tamil language in its Tamil section, alleging the government was "merely paying lip service to the Tamil language, and that the Indian PAP MPs had used the 'Tamil Language Week,' then in progress, to advance their own political agenda." Alleging that it was defamatory of them, the Indian PAP members of parliament, including the minister for law, threatened legal proceedings. Given its dismal history of forensic failures, the Workers' Party, as publisher, including all members of its executive council, thought it more politic to immediately and publicly apologize for those "false and baseless allegations" against them in the forlorn hope of lessening the damages and legal costs.[84] Intriguingly enough, some of those council members were not Indians and totally ignorant of the Tamil language, but, as we have noted, the prime minister cast a wide net. Notwithstanding, the paper continued to be sold but with the offending parts voided in black ink emblematic of the woeful state to which the party and its publication had been reduced.

The *New Democrat*   The *Democrat*, the organ of the Singapore Democratic Party, was said to be "in a derelict state." Planned as a quarterly, its appearance had, however, been disappointingly irregular and, when it did appear, its editorial contents, news and views left much to be desired. Having regard to the total governmental control over the print and voice media, it was remarkable that the party had not attempted to make a more serious effort to utilize its news organ to better effect.

However, since Dr. Chee Soon Juan took over as secretary general of the party, the tabloid-size paper of about 20 pages has not only reappeared with a promise of regularity, but its contents, too, are interestingly informative, better laid-out, sometimes with colour photographs. It, too, is devoid of advertisers, for reasons which do not require much explanation. The paper has been renamed the *New Democrat*, and priced at 80 cents per copy. But it has still a long way to go. Like the Workers' Party political organ, *The Hammer*, its members have to make an especial effort to distribute it, given the culture of fear in Singapore.

Fajar   *Fajar* ("dawn") was the organ of the University of Singapore Socialist Club, one of the oldest and most outspoken student bodies on the university campus, whose first chairman of the editorial board was James Puthucheary, now a retired lawyer in Malaysia. He was twice detained in Singapore under the provisions of the ISA. In May 1954, it published an article, "Aggression in Asia"—which was considered seditious by the colonial government for condemning the formation of the American-inspired SEATO (Southeast Asia Treaty Organization) against the communist threat in the region, and calling Malaya "a police state" in its war against the communist terrorists. All the members of the editorial board were arrested and charged with sedition. Lee Kuan Yew, legal adviser to the Socialist Club, featured prominently then as a freedom fighter and, at the trial, acted as junior defence counsel to an English silk, D.N. Pritt. The case was subsequently dismissed for want of proof. A contemporary photograph in the *Straits Times* showed a beaming Lee and the acquitted students happily drinking a toast to the Queen's Counsel and to "freedom of speech." Given what has befallen the present-day media through his stratagems, it is ironic—if not Rabelaisian—to behold that this self-same man had once lustily saluted freedom of speech and expression. This sedition case, and his subsequent legal representation of the postal strikers in the 1950s, were given wide coverage by the print media, which first started the young Lee in his climb to political power.

Paradoxically, the *Fajar* magazine became an early casualty in the running war which Lee later had with the print media. In early February 1963, it was banned by the government. About eight years later on May 28, 1971, the club itself was declared by the registrar of societies to have officially ceased to exist after it had failed to furnish "proof of its existence."[85] Until its demise, the club was often at the centre of political storms in the campus, and beyond.

The *Singapore Undergrad*   The *Singapore Undergrad*, a weekly organ of the University of Singapore Students' Union (USSU), like many university students' organ, was a mélange of news and entertainment, and tended at times towards irreverence and provocation. It was freely available to the public. In 1969, it was suspended for publishing accounts of a noisy confrontation between Lee and the dissident faculty staff and the students, after ignoring repeated official warnings not to do so. The local media was at the time "advised" not to give any publicity to news on the USSU, the faculty staff and other campus activities. Several newspapers complied; but the *Nanyang Siang Pau* and the *Singapore Herald* ignored or refused to comply with the advice, the consequences of which we have already seen. Foreign journalists, however, were able to recount the messy confrontation in their publications. As a condition for the restoration of the permit, the *Singapore Undergrad* was prohibited from being sold to or distributed among members of the public, except among the students.[86] Subsequently, when the student-editor wrote a series of brilliant but biting articles, he was quietly summoned to the office of the vice-chancellor, and there pointedly reminded that he was attending the university on a scholarship.[87] The articles ceased.

In the maelstrom swirling around the *Nanyang*, the *Eastern Sun* and the *Singapore Herald* newspapers over black operations, little notice was paid to a news report that the *Singapore Undergrad*—which was critical of the government's action over the *Singapore Herald* affair—had been asked to get a new printer due to "pressure of work" by its longtime printers, Eurasia Press.[88]

The *Singapore Technocrat*   The *Singapore Technocrat*, an organ of the Singapore Polytechnic Students' Union, was accused of "wilfully publishing distorted social issues in such a way as to provoke students' opposition to government policies." According to the government, this came about because the Malayan New Democratic Youth League (MNDYL)—a Communist Party of Malaya satellite organization—had gained control of its editorial board so as to "indoctrinate the student body with communist ideology."[89] The MNDYL's plans, it claimed, were disrupted with the arrests of the student leaders in September 1976. In a public television appearance, the president of the Singapore Polytechnic Students' Union, Foo Chin Yen—one of the student leaders arrested—abjectly "confessed" that "to arouse political consciousness and anti-government feelings among the students, he "ensured" that the *Singapore Technocrat* reported "topics of interest," and that published articles were "always distorted [so as] to put the government in an unfavourable light."[90]

The *Catholic News*   This fortnightly newspaper, with a circulation of about 12,000 copies per issue, is published by and for the Roman Catholic archdiocese of Singapore, and distributed among its adherents. Father Edgar Kenneth D'souza was—at the time of the arrest of the so-called Marxist conspirators—one of the two editors. Besides church and parish news, it published editorial comments and opinions of socioeconomic importance and other matters of the moment. The paper's critiques on such topical matters, however, incurred the displeasure of the Lee government. On December 20, 1985, Archbishop Gregory Yong, as the named publisher of the *Catholic News*, was summoned by officials of the ministry of communications and information—which had been renamed from the ministry of culture—and warned that the *Catholic News* was publishing and commenting on political issues. The archbishop was bluntly told that the government took especial exception to articles written by a group of writers from the Justice and Peace Commission—an organization under the aegis of the archdiocese—under the pseudonym Justus, which had suggested that the government was not necessarily "right all the time," and cited examples—one of which was the "insidious clampdown" on the freedom of the press. One contributor was Vincent Cheng— later accused of using the *Catholic News* "to purvey his radical ideas"—whose comments on the existing labour system "as repressive and exploitative" were said to be "false," as were his "allegations about oppression and wrongful beating up of workers by the police."[91] In May/June 1987, Vincent Cheng was arrested—together with 21 other Roman Catholic church and lay workers, professionals and social activists—for allegedly being the local mastermind of a dangerous Marxist conspiracy. The *Catholic News* was also accused of publishing critical "news reports and editorials, dwelling on issues outside diocesan matters and which put the government in a bad light."

On July 9, 1986, the permanent secretary to the ministry of home affairs, Brig. Gen. Tan Chin Tiong, reminded the archbishop of the prime minister's earlier warnings of the government's concern over the involvement of Catholic activists in political issues. Voicing fears that he might be "muzzling" the *Catholic News* if he curtailed its freedom of expression or disallowed the editorial board from publishing comments on widely-talked-about issues, the archbishop was, however, sharply rebuked, and firmly told that members of the Church establishment could air their views on public issues in their personal capacities, but they could not use the Church newspaper as a cover to vent their criticisms because it would give the impression that their criticisms had the tacit support, if not the official approval, of the Church. Stressing the difficulty of drawing a clear line between political issues on the one hand and social and religious issues on the other, the archbishop felt that certain issues should be reported on for the information of parishioners. But he was sternly reminded that the permit issued to the *Catholic News* was only to publish news and articles concerning the Catholic faith, and that it might not venture into the domain of public policy, which had nothing to do with the Church. It was not the responsibility of the *Catholic News* to inform the parishioners on public issues—that was the job of the newspapers!

At that meeting, the archbishop was shown samples of articles with the so-called offensive sections "highlighted," on which the government was unhappy. Among them was an editorial endorsing the Law Society's position regarding some proposed legislative bills, including the controversial Newspaper and Printing Presses (Amendment) bill. The archbishop was brusquely told that the *Catholic News* had "stepped out of line, and was publishing articles commenting on non-religious and controversial issues. . . . [B]y advocating changes to government policies, the *Catholic News* was exerting political pressure on the government and embroiling itself in policy formulation, an area which was the concern of government and political parties."[92]

The archbishop was instructed to send copies of each issue of the *Catholic News* to the monitoring unit of the ministry of information and the arts (MITA) for scrutiny for political correctness by an ISD officer, who would submit regular evaluation reports to the ministry, including the prime minister. This is an important unit—whose main responsibility is to monitor, prepare and despatch daily synopses of media output, including all foreign publications on Singapore, its leaders and government, to the press secretary to the prime minister for onward transmission to Lee himself. Even though Lee is no longer prime minister, the daily synopses are still being sent to him.

Because of the increasing volume of news, articles, essays, etc., on or written about Singapore, it has become a virtually impossible chore for a single individual to read them all. Hence, the creation of the special monitoring unit in the ministry of information and the arts. Although its embassies abroad keep the government informed of the media coverage on Singapore in their respective jurisdictions, it is believed the government also retains the service of an international news-clipping service for such information.

Within three weeks after the July 1986 meeting, the "Justus" column—authored by Father Edgar D'souza—was discontinued; and the *Catholic News* initiated self-censorship of its publications to appease the authorities.

The authorities put on hold the archdiocese's application for a permit to publish parish news in a Chinese-language edition—the *Zhonglian*—pending a change in the editorial stance of the *Catholic News*, as was its proposal to turn the *Catholic News* into a weekly. When the permit was finally approved, the archdiocese's request to amplify the description of its contents in its application for renewal to include "articles on Christian and family values and the social teachings of the Church," were pointedly omitted in the approval.[93]

The simmering dissension boiled over in May/June 1987, with the aforesaid arrests of several Roman Catholics accused of being Marxists. Prominent among the Roman Catholic priests who protested the arrests was Father Edgar D'souza, who stoutly defended them in and out of the columns of the *Catholic News*. It provoked the government into a scurrilous and vicious campaign to discredit him; and, fearing for his safety, he wisely fled to Australia where he now lives in exile.

The *Singapore* A bimonthly magazine named *Singapore*—whose editor-in-chief is Chan Heng Chee, an NUS professor of political science—is published by the Singapore International Foundation (SIF), an organization established on August 1, 1991, ostensibly to complement Singapore's globalization agenda with an endowment of S$25 million from the government and another S$25 million from the private sector. The magazine is distributed free among Singaporeans overseas and friends of Singapore to keep them "informed of events and life in Singapore." Apart from the publication of this magazine, SIF is involved in other activities. It is also the sponsor of SITV—a regional satellite broadcast service.

As of March 1993, publishing permits were issued to ten political parties and to four student bodies involved in politics.

Notes

1. Enche' Siow Loong Hin.
2. Replying to Alliance MP Enche' Siow Loong Hin's allegation that the *Straits Times* is a PAP tool: *Hansard,* Malaysian Parliamentary debates, December 18, 1964, col. 5076.
3. *Straits Times,* August 29, 1972.
4. A sanitized version of the speech appears in the *Straits Times,* November 20, 1972.
5. *Hansard,* Parliamentary debates, June 29, 1977, col. 66.
6. *Statutes of Singapore,* 1970 edition.
7. *Hansard,* Parliamentary debates, March 27, 1974, col. 914.
8. A.k.a. James Fu alias Andrew Fu.
9. C. V. Devan Nair, ed., *Socialism That Works: The Singapore Way,* Annexure XIII, Appendix A.
10. Tan Teng Lang, *The Singapore Press: Freedom, Responsibility and Credibility.* Singapore: Times Academic Press for the Institute of Policy Studies, 1990.
11. C.M. Turnbull, *Dateline Singapore: 150 years of the Straits Times.* Singapore: Singapore Press Holdings, 1995.
12. *Straits Times,* January 29, 1973. See also "Editorial: Vital Questions," ibid.
13. *Hansard,* Parliamentary debates, March 27, 1974, col. 932.
14. *Straits Times,* May 8, 1991.
15. Federation of United Kingdom, Eire, Malaysia and Singapore Student Organizations. London: Spider Web, 1979.
16. *Index on Censorship,* vol. 4, no. 3, 1975.
17. *Far Eastern Economic Review* (hereafter, *Review*), June 11, 1976.
18. A title of a book of essays, compiled and edited by C.V. Devan Nair.
19. *Straits Times,* October 31, 1972.
20. See generally *Far Eastern Economic Review,* Jauuary 14, 1977.
21. *Sunday Times,* February 13, 1977.
22. *Hansard,* March 23, 1977, col. 1524.
23. *Times* (London), March 18, 1977.
24. *Sunday Times,* February 13, 1977.

25. In the interest of historical accuracy, it was Adolf Hitler, not Goebbels, in *Mein Kampf* (1924).

26. For a fuller account, see "Putting the Record Straight," *Review*, March 25, 1977.

27. *Lee Kuan Yew v Derek Davies & Ors* (1990) 1 *Malayan Law Journal* 390.

28. *Review*, May 7, 1976.

29. *Review*, May 14, 1976.

30. *Hansard*, June 29, 1977, col. 67.

31. *Hansard*, Parliamentary debates, June 29, 1977, col. 67.

32. *Straits Times*, February 2, 1978.

33. *Hansard*, Parliamentary debates, March 26, 1981, col. 1284.

34. *Straits Times*, April 23, 1982. See also "Shake Up & Merger in Singapore," *Asiaweek*, May 7, 1982.

35. April 6, 1990. See also *Asiaweek*, September 25, 1992.

36. John A. Lent, "Testimony," House of Representatives, Committee on Foreign Affairs, Subcommittee on Human Rights and International Organizations, July 7, 1988.

37. *Straits Times*, April 23, 1982.

38. "Shake-Up & Merger in Singapore," *Asiaweek*, May 7, 1982.

39. His overzealous extracurricular activities, while high commissioner, upset the Malaysian authorities, leading to his transfer as ambassador to the United States.

40. *Far Eastern Economic Review.* July 6, 1989.

41. *Asian Wall Street Journal*, May 26, 1994; *Review*, November 9, 1995.

42. Lent, "Testimony."

43. *Straits Times*, April 21, 1982.

44. *New Nation*, April 21, 1982.

45. *Straits Times*, April 21, 1982.

46. Turnbull, *Dateline Singapore: 150 years of the Straits Times.*

47. *Straits Times*, April 21, 1982.

48. *Singapore Facts and Figures 1984*, Singapore: Ministry of Communications and Information, 1983.

49. *Singapore*, March 1993.

50. Elliott S. Parker "Singapore," *World Press Encyclopedia.*

51. *Straits Times*, December 20, 1976.

52. *Hansard*, July 23, 1985, cols. 226-227.

53. Lyndley Holloway left the *Straits Times* group abruptly in November 1985, ostensibly for "health reasons." *Review*, July 6, 1989.

54. *Hansard*, Parliamentary debates, July 23, 1985, cols. 226–228.

55. *Straits Times*, Weekly Edition, October 16 and December 11, 1993. *Straits Times*, February 14, 1994.

56. *Straits Times*, July 18, 1984.

57. Interview, *Petir*, August, 1990.

58. See Letters, "Unconvinced," who found it hard to imagine that the boards of the two newspaper groups could have come to an agreement to merge on their own. *Review*, August 8, 1984.

59. *Hansard*, October 19, 1984, col. 2105.

60. *Straits Times*, July 17, 1984.

61. "Mass Media," *Singapore Yearbook 1984*, Singapore: Ministry of Communications and Information, 1983.

62. *Singapore*, September 1992.

63. *Singapore*, March-April 1994.

64. "Liberalizing wind stirs in Singapore press," *Times* (London) January 24, 1985.

65. *Straits Times,* Weekly Edition, March 20, 1993.

66. *Far Eastern Economic Review,* October 30, 1986 and January 22, 1987.

67. *Far Eastern Economic Review,* August 11, 1988. See also *Asiaweek,* April 6, 1990.

68. *Singapore*, March 1993.

69. Intelligence, *Review,* May 7, 1992.

70. May 21, 1992.

71. *Straits Times*, February 7, 1963.

72. Chee Soon Juan, *Singapore, My Home Too.* Singapore: Melodies Press Co, 1995.

73. *Fijar,* no. 24, April-June, 1983.

74. *Straits Times*, November 25, 1972.

75. *Straits Times*, July 11, 1973.

76. *Straits Times*, August 31, 1990.

77. *Plebeian,* vol. 63, May 28, 1968. For further details of the episode, see Francis T. Seow, *To Catch a Tartar: A Dissident in Lee Kuan Yew's Prison,* Monograph 42. New Haven: Yale Southeast Asia Studies, 1994.

78. *Straits Times,* May 27 and May 30, 1987.

79. *Lee Kuan Yew v Derek Davies & ors* (1990).

80. *Hansard*, Parliamentary debates, October 27, 1986, col. 751.

81. *Hansard*, Parliamentary debates, March 18, 1987, col. 451.

82. *Straits Times,* Weekly Edition, March 20, 1993.

83. Ibid.

84. *Straits Times,* Weekly Edition, November 25, 1995.

85. *Straits Times*, May 31, 1971.

86. *Singapore Undergrad*, vol. 3 no. 16, September 8, 1969.

87. *Singapore Undergrad*, vol 3 no. 19, October 22, 1969.

88. *Straits Times*, June 3, 1971.

89. *Straits Times,* September 7, 1976.

90. *Straits Times,* September 8, 1976.

91. *Catholic News*, September 15, 1985.

92. Minutes of meeting between Archbishop Gregory Yong and Ministry of Home Affairs (MHA) dated July 9, 1986.

93. Ibid.

7 The Foreign Media

-
-
-
-
- *It is not a crime nor even a tort to be critical of the prime minister of Singapore.*
- *Before one could accept that, one would have to accept the proposition that Mr.*
- *Lee Kuan Yew is never as a matter of law in the wrong or open to criticism.*
- Geoffrey Robertson, Q.C.[1]
-
-
-
-

Very early on in his political career, Lee depended on former journalist, S. Rajaratnam and, more specifically, on the late British journalist, Alex Josey—whose controversial role in and expulsion from Malaysia is discussed elsewhere in this book—for international media contacts and the inevitable public relations legwork. The foreign mass media's initial romance with the erudite Lee was due in no small way to exertions on his behalf by Alex Josey. But, as Lee became better known internationally and his political fortune waxed, he tended to rely decreasingly on Josey's services. He basked in the agreeable weather of wide international press support and approval. The media lionized him. He was articulate, rational and methodical. He was firm, yet not autocratic, and considerate of other viewpoints. He was understandable. It was not uncommon to encounter media reports in virtually every country, which he visited during those balmy years, where he was not being hailed as "a conquering hero," the problem solver of his nation's ills and who, if only he could trade places with his host counterpart, would heal that country's many ills. Whence cometh such another? All this adulation was like strong potent wine. It went to the head. His attitude towards the foreign mass media, however, underwent a perceptible change—notably after his 1971 crackdown on the domestic media—when they became increasingly critical of him, and whose publications became a vital outlet for frustrated Singaporeans to freely express their thoughts and feelings.

Tallying Foreign Media Vexations

Thus it is difficult to envisage that there was a time in the not so distant past when the Western media was enamoured with Lee, and vice versa, given the present respectful distance maintained by them.

The Singapore government is probably the only government in the entire universe whose captious and sometimes petty reaction to unfavourable comments and critiques by the foreign media has become an emotive byword in the news-gathering world. Nowhere else on earth, not even in pre-Yeltsin Russia, Maoist China, or other totalitarian states, has there been so much outpouring of correspondence by a prime minister and his cabinet ministers, their press secretaries or officials seeking to set right or correct perceived inaccuracies or misreporting in the media, whether domestic or foreign. In 1986 alone, Dow Jones noted, with understandable chagrin, that its publication, the *Asian Wall Street Journal* (AWSJ) had published "14 letters from Singapore government officials, occupying 13 column inches in the newspaper, only 14 fewer inches than the space devoted to letters from officials of *all* other governments combined."[2] But, in case the *AWSJ* or, indeed, any other media publications, misconstrued the purpose or intent of the inundation of official letters upon them, James Fu Chiao Sian, then press secretary to the prime minister, explained in what the *Far Eastern Economic Review* editor-in-chief Derek Davies described as language "worthy of a Dickensian teacher":

> When you receive letters to correct errors and misrepresentation, it means we believe you can and will learn how your paper can report without distortion and be de-gazetted. When you no longer receive any letters—whatever your misrepresentations—it means we have given you up.[3]

The indefatigable James Fu Chiao Sian, it will be recalled, was one of several journalists, including the then secretary general of the Singapore National Union of Journalists, who were apprehended during the infamous 1963 security dragnet, Cold Store. Employed then at the sports desk of the *Nanyang Siang Pau*, Lee's subsequent appointment of him, a former political detainee, to the highly sensitive position of press secretary to the prime minister testifies to political astuteness of a high order, as well as to the thoroughness of Fu's political rehabilitation, considering that Lee makes no secret of the fact that he is "quite a suspicious man by nature,"[4] some would even say, paranoically so. Be that as it may, Fu's letters to editors of myriad publications has made him a household name among the international media.

Newsweek   On November 30, 1974, the international *Newsweek* magazine's local part-time correspondent was found guilty of contempt of court and fined S$1,500, following the appearance of a "scandalizing" article entitled "Singapore—Selective Justice," in the magazine earlier that month. The article had stated that the high court, by its decision in a defamation case, "did little to dispel the notion long charged by critics that the courts of this country are little more than extensions of the one-party system," that "it chose to turn a blind eye to all precedents," and that "the court added insult to injury by also decreeing that the Workers' Party must pay the costs of the action immediately despite the fact that its lawyers had already filed an appeal against the decision," and concluded "with a shocking allegation" that "in the courts in Singapore it makes a vital difference whether it is the government or the opposition that is in the dock."[5] The article had commented on the verdict in a failed slander suit brought by the opposition Workers' Party against a PAP member of parliament. *Newsweek* magazine's Singapore circulation manager and retail sales agent were fined, too. The prosecution had sought jail terms for them.

The *Far Eastern Economic Review*   The *Review*, a highly regarded weekly magazine based in Hongkong, circulates mainly in Asia and, more specifically, in Southeast Asia, wherein Singapore constitutes one of its most lucrative markets because of its economic vitality and growth, and its large English-speaking population. Its independent and lively news coverage and articles on Singapore attracted a growing number of Singapore readers weary of their own tame and tedious newspapers and periodicals to the increasing irritation of Lee and his government, and whose letters column at one stage became "the principal means of finding out about events in Singapore."[6] Its front-line correspondents in Singapore came under constant attack from Lee and his government resulting in many casualties, who had to be transferred to other theatres of assignment.

On June 3, 1971, the government accused Anthony Polsky, a free-lance journalist, who was working part-time for the *Review* and the *New York Times*, and other publications, as well as the National Broadcasting Corporation (NBC), of "interfering in the internal affairs of Singapore," and declared that his continued presence in Singapore was "undesirable." A ministry of home affairs statement accused him of having "collaborated" with a worker from Amnesty International to "compile a report about alleged ill-treatment of political prisoners in Singapore." "Such activities were outside his duties as a journalist," the statement said.[7] It is pertinent to note the government's narrow definition of a journalist, and the limitations on his permissible activities, be he foreign or domestic. It was a recurring theme of contention between the government and the journalists and their editors. Polsky insisted that his relationship with Amnesty International was "purely professional." But the government made it clear that Amnesty International was not welcome to inquire about political prisoners in Singapore, notwithstanding its high reputation and profile, and, resorting to its usual smear tactics, insinuated: "It was not clear where Amnesty International was obtaining its money to finance its activities in Singapore." American journalist Simon Casady recorded an incident which shed some further light on Polsky's disfavour with the government and, more importantly, on Lee's attitude towards journalists:

> What was even worse, a year earlier while Lee was on one of his annual junkets abroad, Polsky had inadvertently precipitated an embarrassing social snub of the prime minister in New York City. Lee had let it be known that he would relish a dinner meeting with the editorial board of the *New York Times*. Lee fancies himself a master of political and sociological repartee and loves to demonstrate this talent in erudite company. Polsky, thinking to win a few Brownie points with Lee, suggested such a meeting to the *Times* editors. They liked the idea and issued an invitation, which was duly delivered to the prime minister, together with a guest list. Polsky's name was on the list. When Lee saw the list, he sent word to the *Times* that he did not care to dine with Polsky. The *Times* responded by cancelling the dinner.
>
> So, Polsky wasn't too surprised when the Singapore controller of immigration, Ho Chee Onn, ordered him to leave the country on 9 July.[8]

The deteriorating relationship between the *Review* and Lee over its news coverage on Singapore culminated in an off-the-record meeting on March 22, 1976, in Singapore, when Lee agreed to meet with Derek Davies at the latter's request to resolve the difficulties, to which reference has been made earlier. As related, a copy of a tape-recording of their private conversation made by Davies for his own magazine's use after the meeting found its unauthorized way across the Straits of Johor to some Malaysian leaders. Although there did not seem to have been any damage done—let alone lasting—to diplomatic relations between the two countries, it nevertheless contributed to an atmosphere of distrust between Lee and the *Review* which was never quite fully erased. Instead of improving relations between them, the meeting only helped to sour them further.

In January 1982, the *Review* carried a report by its resident correspondent, Patrick Smith, on the government's usage of the ISA against its political opponents, which "its apologists said were coincidentally used against some political opponents." This report was known to have irked the government, and Lee, in particular; it was a determinant in the subsequent refusal of Smith's application for a renewal of his work permit. An anonymous writer calling himself Hou Bide—whose penmanship, however, was evocative of the mode and style of S. Rajaratnam, the foreign minister, with his known penchant for anonymity—explained in a letter to the *Review* that, "although Smith did not conduct a deliberate campaign of misinformation against the government, he did base his articles on a misunderstanding of the way Singapore works."[9] Huo Bide gave three reasons for the nonrenewal of Smith's permit, the third reason being of particular interest, as Huo Bide joined issue with Smith in his

> continual reference to the *Straits Times* as a government-controlled newspaper. The *Straits Times* does employ an ex-member of the ISD[10] as a senior member of its staff. The tone of the newspaper and the news it carries have not altered since his appointment, however, which shows that the government does not control the newspaper through him. The *Straits Times* also often supports the government's views, but how can this be described as government control?

They were, indeed, weighty observations, especially in the light of what subsequently befell the media. Be that as it may, its worsening relations with the Singapore government climaxed in another Davies-Lee meeting in Singapore on September 10, 1985, where Lee delivered to Davies an "ultimatum" to "stick to reporting events in Singapore as an outsider and to stay out of local debates and not get involved in domestic politics," or face restrictive sales of its publication—the legislation for which was being drafted, a process that would come to be known as "gazetting."[11]

The strained relationship was further exacerbated by Davies' cutting remarks on the "illogicality" of Singapore-based correspondents "being discouraged from using the columns of the international or regional media, which circulate locally for criticism of Singapore's leadership," while it, however, did "not prevent those same leaders, asking the same journalists why they did not turn their guns on corrupt neighbours, and help end the rule of, for example, the Marcos family in the Philippines. What is sauce for the Manila goose evidently cannot be sauce for the Singapore gander?"[12] The prime minister protested, through his amanuensis James Fu, that he had met with Davies on only three occasions, excluding the interviews in March 1976, April 1977 and September 1985, at which he had "never asked Davies to expose and bring about the fall of neighbouring regimes . . . one must therefore assume that Davies intended to sow doubts and suspicions between Asean leaders and Lee."[13] Davies had not mentioned that it was specifically Lee, who had asked it, nor did Lee deny on behalf of his government or his colleagues the accuracy of those remarks.

The *Asian Wall Street Journal* Dow Jones Inc., which owns the *Asian Wall Street Journal* and the *Review*, explained the deterioration of relations with the government thus:

The motivation for Lee's outburst to Davies is not particularly clear, but two events in 1984 may have played a role. First was Lee's campaign to improve Singapore's genetic pool by encouraging University-educated women to have more children, and by giving the children of better-educated parents privileged access to Singapore's better schools. The suggestion was met with substantial ridicule in the foreign press, including a June 5, 1984, *Asian Journal* article: "Singapore Intensifies Efforts to Obtain More Educated Babies," which is said to have greatly angered the prime minister. (Although Lee told Davies in September 1985 that the *Asian Journal* was a model foreign newspaper, the prime minister was also reportedly disturbed about the *Asian Journal*'s coverage of his ouster of President Devan Nair in early 1985, ostensibly on charges of alcoholism. Nair, a prominent labour leader and close associate of Lee's in the building of Singapore as a nation, has since become a de facto leader in exile of those Singaporeans who oppose Lee.) Possibly of greater significance, the PAP suffered a stinging rebuke in December 22, 1984, Singapore elections. In that tally, the party's share of the vote sank from 75.5 percent (in 1980) to 62.7 percent; for the first time, two opposition MP's (including J.B. "Ben" Jeyaretnam) were elected to Parliament. Lee was so furious that he took to the airwaves to threaten to revamp the entire "one-man, one-vote" system in order to curb what he considered symbolic protest voting. In all, 1985 was probably the year in which Lee's eventual ouster by democratic means seemed most possible. Whether or not there was a causal connection, it was also the year his recent foreign press crackdown began.[14]

Just five weeks after Lee's "ultimatum" to Davies, on October 17, 1985, the *AWSJ* published an editorial headlined: "Jeyaretnam's Challenge." Describing the prosecution of Jeyaretnam—leading to his eventual ouster from parliament, and from the bar—the *AWSJ* said:

> [Mr. Jeyaretnam] has recently suffered what many Singaporeans believe is official harassment . . . The problem here is government credibility. We don't know if Mr. Jeyaretnam is guilty. But even if he were, many Singaporeans wouldn't believe it because court actions, and especially libel suits, have long been used in Singapore against opposition politicians.

This was apparently too much for Lee, who instructed his attorney general to prosecute the offending parties and who, on October 30, 1985, dutifully moved the high court to have the owners, Dow Jones Publishing Company (Asia) Inc., the editor and publisher, Fred Zimmermann, the Singapore correspondent, the *AWSJ* printer and the distributor all held in criminal contempt for publishing the editorial, which contained "irresponsible and offensive statements . . . that [Singapore] courts are not independent, that they do not decide on the evidence, the law and the arguments openly placed before them, and they are influenced by outside considerations," which were "calculated to bring the judiciary of Singapore into contempt or to lower its authority."[15] Upon legal advice, the *AWSJ* apologized and pleaded guilty, a point which the Singapore government subsequently made much issue of in its campaign to discredit the foreign media. However it may be, the presiding judge fined Dow Jones Publishing Company (Asia) Inc. S$6,000 (US$2,822), the editor and publisher S$3,000 (US$1,411), the Singapore printer and the distributor S$500 (US$235) each. In an outburst of judicial exuberance, he also fined the *AWSJ* editorial-page editor and writer a total of S$6,000 despite the fact that neither of them had been named a defendant in the proceedings. It was the *AWSJ*'s first brush with Lee Kuan Yew and his government. Any reportage, coverage or comment which may be considered supportive of the opposition and oppositionists is looked upon askance by Lee.

Lee followed up this forensic victory with a personal attack in parliament on Jeyaretnam who, he insinuated, was responsible for the *AWSJ* editorial.[16] At a parliamentary committee of privileges set up at the instance of the government to examine Jeyaretnam's allegations of executive interference in the subordinate judiciary, Lee vehemently accused him of misinforming the *AWSJ* that the transfer of senior district judge Michael Khoo to the attorney general's chambers was a "demotion."[17] Lee further accused him of "setting the circumstances and whispering the right ideas to the right people that were gathered together into that article which, unless challenged head-on, item by item, would lead to more such foreign journals assuming that we are another Marcos-like regime—that we fix our judges, that we can switch decisions at will, when an accused person, a convicted person, becomes a hot political potato."[18] To save his face and that of the *AWSJ*, Lee charged that Jeyaretnam had made the allegation of executive interference in parliament to give it wider coverage and dignify it with parliamentary privilege. Jeyaretnam, predictably, was found guilty and fined S$1,000 (US$467).

Reuters News Agency   In March 1986, Reuters correspondent Marilyn Odchimar was expelled from Singapore for "irresponsible reporting" in connection with a story on the total collapse of the six-storey New World Hotel in Singapore that trapped many people amidst the rubble, in which she had quoted a survivor who said that he had heard a rescue worker demanding money to assist a dying woman. The government alleged that the reporter had given a false impression of the rescue operation by "interviewing [the survivor] while he was delirious in hospital," and faulted her for not seeking to verify his allegations. According to a *New York Times* article, the prime minister said the story "had blemished Singapore's image overseas."[19]

The *Times*, London   The foreign media's next brush with the Singapore government was over a trenchant article, "The Law Grossly Misused," by well-known columnist Bernard Levin of the *Times*, who recounted therein the legal hounding of lone opposition MP J.B. Jeyaretnam, and who saw in it a portent of the destruction of democracy in Singapore.[20] Offended at the tone and tenor of the article, the Singapore government, through its high commissioner in London, sent a letter to the editor, who deleted a paragraph and edited another before it was published. The Singapore government insisted that the *Times* should print the letter in full. But it refused, citing its defamatory implications, whereupon the government offered to buy advertisement space in the newspaper for its publication and undertook to indemnify it fully against any such legal action. the *Times*, however, still refused. The government then bought space in the *Financial Times* and the *Guardian* to advertise its dispute with the *Times*. Levin responded to the "weird" paid advertisements—which assailed the *Times* for "refusing to print in its entirety a letter complaining about Levin's article about the corruption of justice in Singapore"—with another mordacious article entitled, "A Lively Trade in Vilification."[21]

Significantly, Lee did not issue a writ for defamation against Levin or the *Times*. Instead, he offered to debate with Levin his article on British television, which Levin declined to extend beyond the pages of his newspaper. This seemingly odd twist to Lee's swift and familiar recourse to the law courts was not lost on informed observers. Many wondered: Could it be that the Royal Courts of Justice on the Strand were not as politically conscientious or as correct as the Supreme Court of Singapore?

In a somewhat similar vein, the *Review*, consequent upon a legal dispute with the prime minister, refused to publish part of a letter from the obdurate James Fu touching on the matter in dispute as it was under judgement. But, ignoring such legal niceties, the Singapore government had the full text of his letter widely published in the Singapore media. After persistent threats from James Fu, the *Review* reluctantly allowed the government to take out a paid advertisement in its magazine captioned, "Telling It Like It Is?"[22] One is driven to wonder at the lopsided observance or efficacy of the laws of contempt in Singapore in disputes involving the government or its leaders, and whether all men are, indeed, equal under the law. In this connexion, one is once again forcefully reminded of the intrepid Soviet deputy Vladimir I. Denisov who—before the cataclysmic crackup of the Soviet empire—said of President Mikhail S. Gorbachev and the Soviet judiciary: "No supreme court judge in this country would dream of judging against him in his worst nightmare."[23]

The *Star* In 1987, the *Star*, then a feisty Malaysian English-language tabloid became the first-ever subject of a libel action instituted by Lee in Malaysian courts. The tabloid is largely owned by the Malayan Chinese Association (MCA), a partner in the Malaysian Alliance coalition government. In February 1987, it ran a series of two patently defamatory articles on Lee and his PAP government in Singapore, entitled "Graft in the Squeaky Clean Republic," and "Second Shock in Graft Affair," on the suicide of Lee's protégé, Teh Cheang Wan, the minister of national development, in December 1986. On May 13, 1991, the suit was settled out of court with the *Star* newspaper agreeing to, amongst other things, apologize to Lee, withdraw unreservedly its allegations, pay M\$200,000 (US\$72,500) in damages, and the full costs of the libel proceedings estimated at M\$70,000 (US\$30,000), and publish an apology in a prominent position on the newspaper's front page. American constitutional rights lawyer Floyd Abrams attended the court proceedings on behalf of the New York-based Committee to Protect Journalists, but was refused the status of amicus curiae. It was the first time Lee had ventured to sue outside his island bailiwick. But the case is more notable for the fact that the two offending articles were written under the byline of one Anton Xavier, said to be "a research officer familiar with Singapore politics," but whose name did not appear in the blacklist of foreign journalists maintained by the Singapore authorities in its morgue, and against whom the government ran a computer check only to discover that it was a pseudonym.

To conclude this particular sector on foreign vexations, on May 31, 1988, the first deputy prime minister, Goh Chok Tong, in a puerile attempt to justify before a tamed parliament the expulsion of a U.S. diplomat from Singapore and this author's arbitrary arrest under the ISA, purported to express "outrage" at the Western media—singling out the *Bangkok Post*, the *Far Eastern Economic Review*, the *Asian Wall Street Journal* and *Asiaweek*, in particular—for "building up" this author by identifying him as "a leading dissident," "a sharp critic," "a prominent lawyer," among other laudatory names and expressions—and threatened that "if the offshore press continue to actively engage in our domestic politics and try to sway the ground before the next general election against the government, we shall counter them. We see little reason to accord them the privilege of stationing correspondents here to interfere in Singapore's domestic politics."[24] Therefore, presumably, the offshore media should have given this author negative news coverage.

The Foreign Media's Turn: The Circulation Restriction

By 1986, Lee had achieved total and absolute control over the local newspapers. It was a media enthralled. They became, in effect, propaganda tools of the PAP government regurgitating long, dreary and uncritical screeds of official press releases and ministerial statements and speeches—including maps, charts and graphs—sometimes serialized over successive days, which soon bored a sophisticated reading public and drove them to seek more critical and reflective news coverage and reportage on Singapore from regional news sources, and an alternative independent outlet for venting their feelings and views on domestic matters. Longtime resident journalist and writer Dennis Bloodworth found two aspects of local media coverage irksome, the incessant charts and the "absolutely ridiculous" lengthy reporting of speeches of politicians, which "bored stiff" the reading public.[25] It needs to be mentioned here that the *Straits Times* coverage of international news and events is reasonably good, and ranks in excellence with the best of the regional press. Its domestic coverage and patently partisan reportage bordering on obsequiousness, however, leaves much to be desired, and is a pale shadow of its former greatness.

In 1986—the year the crucial amendments to the Newspaper and Printing Press Act were legislated—one copy out of seven of the total sales of the *Asiaweek* magazine, the *Far Eastern Economic Review* magazine and the *Asian Wall Street Journal* was sold in Singapore.[26] According to Lee, "Singapore is the largest single-country market for the *Far Eastern Economic Review* and the second largest for the *Asian Wall Street Journal.*" As of May 1986, the *Review* circulation in Singapore was 7,927 out of a global circulation of 64,138 copies. Singapore was its third-largest market and its share of total circulation had been steady at around 12.5 percent for the past several years.[27] Given their popularity and rising circulation, "they [were] almost like a local newspaper."[28] But what Lee and his ministers pointedly omitted to say was that these foreign publications had become a useful vehicle for the articulation of grievances and comments of official policies by Singaporeans who had been denied a window of opportunity by their own domestic media. The *Review* was the most popular foreign weekly then. Most Singapore correspondents in their letters to the editor tended to protect themselves from vengeful authority with the cloak of anonymity, as may be seen from these random examples.[29] Thus, foreign journalists were repeatedly warned by cabinet ministers and government officials to report on Singapore "as outsiders for outsiders,"[30] an injunction more honoured in its breach than in its observance.

Concerned at this new trend in the reading habits of Singaporeans,[31] the government sought hard to make the foreign media walk the chalk of self-censorship, but as these publications are foreign-owned and mostly published outside Singapore, it was difficult to muzzle them. Besides, it would be politically awkward to ban outright the importation of offending foreign publications into Singapore, which were not really communist or subversive so as to give them, to borrow Lee's words, the satisfaction of "the moral high horse [*sic*] of being banned." Furthermore, adverse international repercussions could damage the government's efforts to promote Singapore as a regional marketplace for a free flow of ideas and information—not to mention the vast financial stakes involved in the investment of large sums of money in telecommunication installations of machinery and equipment to make Singapore the communications centre of Southeast Asia.

Wherefore, to restrain, if not to deter, such media coverage on Singapore by regional publications, save through official press releases or handouts, the government on May 5, 1986, introduced a bill to amend the Newspaper and Printing Presses Act, whereby the sale or distribution in Singapore of a foreign publication published outside Singapore would be restricted, if the relevant minister declares it in the *Government Gazette* "to be engaging in the domestic politics of Singapore"—a clause which was capable, to quote the attorney general, "of a wide construction [but] incapable of legal definition," a point of view not shared, however, by the court of appeal.[32] (For a discussion of the amendment's legal implications, see Nancy Batterman's essay: "Singapore's Newspaper and Printing Presses (Amendment) Act 1986: A Bad News Bear?"[33])

The Law Society of Singapore's critique on the proposed amendments as "ambiguous" and "superfluous," amongst others, received wide coverage in the domestic and regional media, engendering lively discussion thereon. Angered by what he considered to be an unwarranted intervention, Lee accused the Law Society of wilfully placing itself "on a collision course" with the government, and perceived in it a pocket of opposition, which had to be swiftly neutralized. Using its massive parliamentary force, the government steam-rollered amendments to the Legal Profession Act, Cap. 161, to prohibit the Law Society from, inter alia, commenting on existing or proposed legislation unless the government specifically invited it for its views. The absurdity of the latter amendment was explained away by a curious statement that, unless the government sought the Law Society's views, any voluntary expression of collective opinion on legislation would be tantamount to the Law Society acting as a political pressure group—which was undesirable for the nation.

As of July 31, 1986—the date of the passage of the amendments to the Newspaper and Printing Presses Act—there were 82 foreign correspondents and representatives working and living in Singapore, who represented 65 news agencies, news magazines, newspapers and broadcasting stations.[34]

The foreign publications, which fell victim to the new law, included *Time* magazine, the *Asian Wall Street Journal, Asiaweek* magazine, the *Far Eastern Economic Review* and *The Economist.*

Time

Time, the American international weekly magazine, became the first casualty of this diktat. It had published a sensitive article on an opposition member of parliament, J.B. Jeyaretnam, entitled: "Silencing the Dissenters." It was gazetted on October 15, 1986. *Time* magazine's circulation of 18,000 copies a week was reduced to 9,000 copies as from October 19, 1986, and then to 2,000 copies as from January 1, 1987, after it refused the press secretary to the prime minister James Fu's demand that his letter to the editor responding to the article be published unedited. Negotiations on this demand ensued, but eventually broke down. Fu warned the magazine to publish his letter in full: "Not to do so will lead the government to draw certain conclusions." By refusing the press secretary to the prime minister the "right of reply," the minister deemed that *Time* magazine had "engaged in the domestic politics of Singapore." On the same day the restriction was announced, the chairman of *Time* Inc. Magazine Group telexed the prime minister claiming it was "standard practice to edit all letters published for reasons of space." About a fortnight later, *Time* magazine capitulated to the Singapore government, and printed the reply in full, adding that it did "not agree with all the corrections cited . . . but prints this letter in the spirit of full discussion of issues."[35] Some nine months later, its circulation was restored.

The Asian Wall Street Journal

On September 23, 1986, at the PSA Building, Singapore, the rising son and political heir, Brig. Gen. Lee Hsien Loong (who held two ministerial portfolios of trade and industry and of defence), met with senior Dow Jones executives, and warned them of officialdom's displeasure at the *AWSJ*'s "slanted reporting against the Singapore government" over the past few years, which might cause it to apply the NPPA provisions to the *AWSJ* and restrict its circulation in Singapore.[36] Present at the meeting was Wong Kan Seng, the minister of state for communications and information.

There the matter rested until December 12–13, 1986, when the *AWSJ* published an article headlined "Singapore Exchange Puzzles Financiers," by its resident Singapore correspondent, Stephen Duthie, on a proposed second securities market, SESDAQ—Stock Exchange of Singapore Dealing and Automated Quotation Market System—wherein some critics were quoted as saying the government would use it to "unload state-controlled and government-backed companies." On the same day, Koh Beng Seng, a director of MAS—the Monetary Authority of Singapore—wrote to the *AWSJ* editor asserting that Duthie had exhibited "bias" and "prejudice," and set out a list of "errors and omissions" in the article. After an investigation, *AWSJ* editor-publisher Fred Zimmermann responded by letter that he had determined the article complained of was "fair and accurate," and the personal attacks on its author were "unwarranted." Because of these personal attacks, he declined to publish the MAS letter, but concluded, "We are willing to publish a letter from you, if you care to write it, stating your point of view on the subjects dealt with in the article." On January 17, 1987, the MAS director wrote again, repeating many of the same allegations of personal irresponsibility against Duthie, and concluded ominously: "If you persist in refusing to publish my letters, my chairman will have no alternative but to draw his own conclusions."[37] On January 23, 1987, Zimmermann replied: "We don't believe it serves our readers to print personal attacks or allegations of errors that we're confident don't exist."

On February 9, 1987, the *AWSJ* was gazetted, effective one week later. Its domestic circulation was restricted from 5,100 copies a day to 400 copies a day. The information ministry issued the *AWSJ* distributor with a list of 143 libraries in Singapore, which would have priority in the receipt of the 400 copies, "thus continuing public access to the newspaper." But, according to *AWSJ*: "In fact, however, only a few libraries permitted to receive the *Asian Journal* are routinely open to the public—many are in government or quasi-government offices, or in those of private companies."[38] Meanwhile, the gazetting of the *AWSJ* aroused universal media criticism from the American Society of Newspaper Editors, representing 974 newspapers in the United States, who criticized the restriction in circulation.

On February 10, 1987, the American Business Council in Singapore (ABC) issued a statement (which was published in the *AWSJ*) that executives in the United States considering investment in the republic would now "carefully consider the disadvantages of limited coverage of news affecting their operations," which drew a sharp rebuke from the Singapore government that it was "not for foreign companies operating in Singapore to decide what the Singapore government can or cannot do in its relations with the foreign press."[39] On February 13, 1987, the ABC clarified its position:

> The sole intent of the ABC statement was to express our concern that potential foreign investors could react negatively to what could be viewed as a reduction in the flow of business and economic information. . . .
>
> . . . the ABC was in no way attempting "to decide what the Singapore government can or cannot do in its relations with the foreign press."
>
> . . . the ABC has taken no "stand on the *AWSJ* issue" because we are not in a position to judge either the article or the exchange of correspondence. Our stand has to do with the perception of potential foreign investors with regard to the flow of information in Singapore.

U.S. State Department   On February 11, 1987, the U.S. State Department expressed regret over the restriction of the *AWSJ*. On February 12, 1987, the Singapore government protested at this "unprecedented interference in its internal affairs":

> No foreign newspaper has an automatic, let alone an inalienable right to circulate in Singapore. Circulation is a privilege extended by the Singapore government. Foreign newspapers are sold here on terms and conditions set by the government. They must publish government letters correcting grave errors of reporting.
>
> . . . The restriction on the *AWSJ* circulation would not have been necessary, had the *AWSJ* accorded the Singapore government the same freedom that it arrogates to itself. It is the Singapore government which has been denied the right to have its views heard by the *AWSJ's* unjustifiable refusal to publish a rebuttal to an inaccurate and malicious article.
>
> MFA would appreciate if the State Department first ascertains who is the aggrieved party before making knee-jerk reflex comments on domestic Singapore matters.

The State Department confirmed the aforementioned remarks had been made by its spokesman, but maintained that it did "not take sides in the particulars of . . . the case of the *Asian Wall Street Journal*." But, dissatisfied with the reply, the Singapore government, on February 21, 1987, asked the State Department to clarify "several unresolved issues":

> How is this impartiality consistent with the regret expressed by the State Department spokesman at the restriction on the *AWSJ*, and the hope expressed in the aide memoire that a way can be found to end the restrictions quickly?
>
> If indeed the U.S. government does not support the claims of any party to the dispute, on what basis has it concluded that the action of the Singapore government is regrettable?
>
> Does the U.S. government believe that the *AWSJ's* refusal to publish letters from the Singapore government setting out the Singapore government's view of an unbalanced story is entirely consistent with internationally recognized principles of freedom of speech?
>
> If not, does the U.S. government intend, on the same grounds of impartiality and press freedom, to express regret over the refusal of the *AWSJ* to publish these letters?

How is Singapore's action inconsistent with the principle of a free and unrestricted press, when the information in the restricted publications has not been restricted, but on the contrary the newspaper is freely available in public places and libraries in Singapore, to be read or photocopied by any Singaporean for his private use?

Does the U.S. government concede that the Singapore government has acted completely within its rights on a purely domestic issue?

On March 10, 1987, the State Department replied that "it does not support the specific claims of any party to this dispute," and stressed its "fundamental and longstanding commitment to the principles of a free and unrestricted press." It continued:

One aspect of those principles is our recognition that while freedom of expression includes a right to voice publicly one's view in response to media reports or commentary, there is no obligation for a privately owned newspaper to print those views, however unfair that may seem. The U.S. government claims no right to publication of its response to media comment, fair or unfair. "Free and unrestricted" in American usage, means that within broad limits, set at the boundaries of other individual liberties (e.g. criminal libel), the press is free to publish or not publish what it chooses, however irresponsible or biased its actions may seem to be. Where the media are free, the marketplace of ideas sorts the irresponsible from the responsible and rewards the latter.

Considering the explanation inadequate, S. Dhanabalan, the foreign minister, tried to underscore the government's case by exaggerating an old refrain: "In Singapore, when reporting has been left to the marketplace of ideas, it has from time to time led to civil commotion, riots and mayhem."[40] Anyway, to place Singapore's position beyond doubt, the MFA, on March 13, 1987, delivered a third note to the State Department, stating:

Singapore is not America, and we have no "free and unrestricted" press in American usage, meaning that "the press is free to publish or not publish what it chooses, however, irresponsible or biased its action may seem to be." . . .

The Singapore government has never undertaken any obligation to uphold a "free and unrestricted press," let alone to accept the American definition of this term. No foreign publication has the right of sale or circulation in Singapore.

The *AWSJ* is not an issue which has arisen between the two countries; it is a Singapore matter which the State Department has made into a public issue. If the State Department feels a continual obligation to do so, the problem can be pre-empted by keeping U.S. journalists and newspapers out of Singapore. Then no dispute can possibly arise.[41]

International Federation of Newspaper Publishers On February 17, 1987, the information ministry sent a letter to the president of the International Federation of Newspaper Publishers, Paris, justifying its action against the *Asian Wall Street Journal*:

This action was taken because the *AWSJ* has persistently refused to print letters from the Monetary Authority of Singapore (MAS), refuting *AWSJ's* unfounded and baseless allegations against the Singapore government in its 12–13 December 1986 issue . . .

You will note that it is the *AWSJ*, and not the Singapore government, that has censored information by refusing its readers access to the other side of a malicious story. Freedom of expression surely cannot mean giving the media the licence to publish irresponsible and baseless allegations, and then refusing to print corrections.

The *AWSJ* is not banned, contrary to *AWSJ's* misrepresentations. It is still circulating in Singapore and is available in some 140 public and listed libraries. Restricting its sale to 400 copies does not deprive Singaporeans of information. It deprives the *AWSJ* of sales and advertisements from the other 90 percent of its previous circulation. Anyone can photocopy them from the 400 copies for their private use.

In the interest of freedom of expression and more importantly, in the interest of truth, you may wish to make available copies of the attached documents to your members so that they too can judge for themselves who is censoring and restricting the flow of information.[42]

The Voice of America   On February 11, 1987, the Voice of America (VOA) made an editorial broadcast on the *AWSJ* restriction which, on February 19, 1987, prompted a written response from Tommy T. B. Koh, formerly Singapore's ambassador to the United States, to the VOA director, the nature and contents of which are dealt with later.

To return to the *Asian Wall Street Journal* itself. On February 12, 1987, in an editorial captioned "Singapore's Trouble," it compared the decision of the Singapore government to a "banana-republic action beneath Singapore's stature in the world," and continued:

The immediate offense is refusal to publish a letter to the editor from a Singapore official, which editors of the paper felt was inaccurate and unfair to its reporter. The paper has already published a series of letters from officials, but in the end editors bear some responsibility for the accuracy and fairness of even letters to the editor. Singapore officials seem to be using their new press law to claim unlimited access for whatever they choose to allege, and self-respecting editors must somewhere draw a line. All the more so if they expect that in Singapore's present mood they will sooner or later be banned anyway. . . .

These actions [of the Singapore government] are a warning not only to the press, but to any business that wants to risk locating in Singapore. . . . If the prime minister and his government prefer policies that will put an end to all criticism, it may end up largely uncriticized. Not because an interested world will remain silent, but because in the end, no one will care. The citizens of Singapore deserve better.

The Singapore government replied through ambassador Koh, requesting the *AWSJ* editor to publish the letter—and it was, in all three editions of the newspaper, "in the interest of your readers who need to know the full story." The letter stated:

The editorial ridiculed the Singapore government's "banana-republic action" in "suppressing" the *AWSJ*. . . . But the government is not suppressing the information contained in the *AWSJ*. It is restricting *AWSJ* circulation in Singapore. Singapore's 2.6 million citizens lose nothing. In the age of the photo-copier, reducing *AWSJ's* circulation from 5,000 to 400 does not deprive 4,600 readers of information. It does deprive the *AWSJ* of 4,600 copies worth of sales and advertising, as it is intended to do.

The editorial stated that the *AWSJ* "has already published a series of letters from officials," but "self-respecting editors must somewhere draw a line." These earlier letters had nothing to do with SESDAQ, the proposed second stock exchange in Singapore, and the subject of Mr. Stephen Duthie's article in the *AWSJ*. As for SESDAQ itself, publication of a letter from the private sector does not justify refusal to publish the views of the monetary authority of Singapore.

The editorial studiously avoided any mention of the substance of the dispute. . . .

The editorial said: "These actions are a warning not only to the press, but to any business that wants to risk locating in Singapore." No foreign firm will commit its investment purely based on information provided in the media. Foreign investors in Singapore know that for nearly 29 years the Singapore government has never flinched from an open argument, but has always insisted on its right of rejoinder.

. . . The editorial made much of the right to freedom of information, and the right of the press to criticize. Freedom of the press must always be a two-way street. It is only fair that a party which has been attacked by a paper be given a right of reply. The *AWSJ* is entitled to write about us as it pleases, and has done so. Surely we too are entitled to put our points of view as we please. To deny this is to assert double standards. Must we be told how we may write our letters of correction?[43]

In an editorial footnote to the letter, the editor stated: "Rather than making allegations of his own, Mr. Duthie reported concerns held by members of the Singapore financial community," whereupon the Association of Banks in Singapore, the Stock Exchange of Singapore Ltd., and the Singapore Merchant Bankers' Association, in a rare display of coordination and purposeful action, wrote in within days of each other to say that they did not hold the concerns reported. *Wall Street Journal* editor Robert L. Bartley might well be forgiven for thinking that this spate of letters was inspired, if not actually directed, by the Singapore authorities, as evidenced by his letter. On March 11, 1987, Bartley wrote to the prime minister, carbon copied to ambassador Koh and two of the associations, that it was not publishing those letters, as "the details of the SESDAQ dispute have already been covered extensively in the *Asian Wall Street Journal,* and in our judgment are of marginal interest to the readers of our other editions." He continued:

I am writing to you directly so that I can add one thought: If a government directs vituperation at the American Business Council and its own Law Society, and for that matter jails and expells [*sic*] members of parliament, it also cheapens public comments by officials of organizations like the Stock Exchange of Singapore and the Association of Banks. The climate of intimidation makes such quasi-official statements less credible and less newsworthy.

I am quite sure that neither you nor Tommy Koh believes that the brevity of our editorial note means we accept every point he raised. We simply felt that readers could make their own judgments without further instruction from us.

We are always willing to consider letters from officials and citizens of Singapore or any other nation, but we have the responsibility of making our own editorial judgments in trying to best serve our readers. Their continued world-wide interest and support is ongoing testimony to the wisdom of this practice.

On April 14, 1987, the prime minister, through his press secretary, entered the fray:

Whether you publish any letters you receive is your prerogative. One would have thought, however, that since you had publicly defended your original article on SESDAQ on grounds that Mr. Duthie merely "reported concerns held by members of the Singapore financial community," the fact that neither the stock exchange, the banks nor the merchant banks in Singapore shared these concerns would interest your readers. Your statement had been printed in all your editions. Since you feel that "your readers could make their own judgments without further instruction from us," would not this information be relevant to their judgment?

... The Singapore government is always ready to justify and defend all its actions, ... But none of this is relevant to the fundamental issue in dispute: namely that the *Journal* is suppressing views it happens to disagree with, and facts which demolish errors it has maliciously published. When the editor of the *Wall Street Journal* resorts to vituperation, it is a fair conclusion that he is running out of arguments.

The Stock Exchange of Singapore bought advertising space in the *Asian Wall Street Journal* "in order to inform ... readers that the Stock Exchange of Singapore has been actively involved in the development of SESDAQ and our members do not hold the concerns reported in Mr. Duthie's article."[44] But, significantly, unlike the Stock Exchange of Singapore, the other two associations—whose membership is composed of expatriates—did not do so. Concurrent with the continuing drama, and "exploring ways to continue reaching its readers," Zimmermann, on February 20, 1987, wrote to the ministry of communication and information, offering to supply the *AWSJ* newspaper

> free of charge to all paying subscribers and hotel purchasers that were on our rolls as of February 13, immediately prior to the ban. If you allow us to do this, we would agree that an independent accounting firm would periodically examine our records and certify to you that we are indeed providing the newspapers free of charge and are not receiving any circulation revenue from these free copies. We are willing to incur the expense of free distribution so that business people in Singapore can once again have access to the newspaper ...
>
> I have noted the suggestions of government officials that people will simply obtain photocopies of the newspaper if they feel a need for it. Aside from the questionable legality of that under copyright laws, it obviously would be much more convenient for them if we could deliver it to them at our expense. ...

AWSJ subscribers were informed on the same day of the offer he had made to the government. On February 25, the information ministry gave a scoffing reply:

> The minister notes your concern for the convenience of your subscribers in Singapore. He regrets that this concern for your readers did not extend to publishing *in toto* the correspondence between yourself and Mr. Koh Beng Seng of the Monetary Authority of Singapore. Had you done so, all this consequential anxiety would not have been necessary.
>
> You have proposed to distribute the *Asian Wall Street Journal* free of charge to subscribers in Singapore. Under your proposal the *Journal* would forgo its sales revenue, but not the advertising revenue from its circulation in Singapore. To pretend that advertising rates have nothing to do with circulation figures would be less than honest. Indeed, there are many newspapers which operate solely on the basis of their advertising revenues, and which are distributed free of charge to their readers as a matter of course.
>
> Contrary to your statement, it is perfectly legal for anyone to photocopy articles from the *Journal* for his private use. Notwithstanding this, the minister has agreed to meet your concerns for subscribers and hotel purchasers by allowing you to distribute the *Journal* free to subscribers in Singapore, provided all advertisement spaces are left blank. This can be easily arranged by your printers. Indeed the minister would have no objection should you wish to extend this service to an unlimited number of other readers in Singapore as well.

The conditional offer was rejected. Zimmermann replied that "news and advertisements are integral parts of the newspaper," and "any suggestion to create and print a special edition each day for Singapore and then distribute it free is unreasonable—in terms of additional mechanical costs as well as daily scheduling problems."[45] Zimmerman, in a statement made in Hongkong, said his offer was "sincere" and not motivated by "advertising considerations. . . . Our advertising revenue and circulation are continuing to grow, and we don't foresee any measurable loss of advertising because of the ban. The *Asian Journal* did not have a guaranteed circulation base in particular countries on which rates were calculated. The Singapore ban did not, therefore, affect the paper's ad rates. As for circulation, it is higher today than a year ago. Financially, the main result of the ban was that it had significantly reduced their costs for printing and distribution in Singapore, at the expense of some Singaporeans and local companies."

The information ministry offered to share any additional cost of producing a special edition without advertisements, as it reckoned the total incremental cost would be US$0.07 cents a copy. Rejecting it, the *AWSJ* said it did not "take financial assistance from governments. Our readers therefore . . . know that nothing appearing in the paper (even a letter to the editor) is there as a result of any government's pressure, and they know that nothing is left out (even advertising) because of any government's pressure."[46] On February 28, 1987, the ministry replied to the rejection:

> . . . You claim total independence in running the *AWSJ*. You want freedom not only to write what you like, but also to determine what opposing views may be heard in the *AWSJ*. You have not conceded to the Singapore government the right to reply as it chooses, to a malicious and erroneous article. This is your prerogative.
>
> The Singapore government has the duty to govern Singapore. This includes deciding which foreign newspapers can be sold here, and under what conditions. We do not allow *Izvestia* or *Renminribao* to circulate freely in Singapore. But we have given the *AWSJ* this right to circulate, on condition that we can rebut your errors and misreporting in the manner of our choosing. If you choose to reject these terms, so be it.
>
> As for being bemused by our offer to share your additional expenses, we do not want to leave any of your supporters befuddled with the idea that you were defending the freedom of information. You want the freedom to make money selling advertisements. If our offer helps to dispel this myth, it has served its purpose.[47]

The government claimed its action against the *AWSJ* was taken on its "right of reply to correct snide and malicious misreporting" in a foreign newspaper,[48] but the official reason given for gazetting the magazine, *Far Eastern Economic Review*, was far removed from this pious claim. Indeed, as will be seen, the latter gave Singapore officialdom so much column space to the "right of reply," to the utter annoyance of its other readers.

On March 20, 1987, the information minister, Dr. Yeo Ning Hong, stated in parliament that none of the "business executives, including foreign bankers whom he had met on different occasions, had complained to him that they had been hampered by the restriction, although the *AWSJ* had repeatedly claimed that they had been. The government had made an offer of unlimited circulation in Singapore, conditional upon all the advertising spaces being left blank and the newspaper distributed free of charge, but the *AWSJ* had rejected the offer. That offer was still open."[49]

On May 8, 1987, the *AWSJ*, through its lawyers, filed a motion in the high court for leave to issue an order of *certiorari* to quash the ministerial orders and, on May 11, 1987, the motion papers were served on the attorney general. Pending the hearing of the motion, on April 14, 1988, the prime minister defended the press restrictions before the American Society of Newspaper Editors, Washington, D.C., proclaiming, inter alia, that "the American concept of the 'market place of ideas' instead of producing harmonious enlightenment has from time to time led to riots and bloodshed," and that publications such as the *AWSJ*

> are no longer the foreign press. They have become, in fact, the domestic Singapore press based offshore. Their correspondents act like journalists do in America, and they take sides to determine the outcome of issues under debate.
>
> . . . We allow American journalists in Singapore in order to report Singapore to their fellow countrymen. We allow their papers to sell in Singapore so that we can know what foreigners are reading about us. But we cannot allow them to assume a role in Singapore that the American media plays in America, that of invigilator, adversary, and inquisitor of the administration. If allowed to do so, they will radically change the nature of Singapore society, and I doubt if our social glue is strong enough to withstand such treatment.[50]

Reacting to Lee's remarks in Washington, D.C., the *Wall Street Journal*, on April 20, 1988, in an editorial "The Press and Mr. Lee," set the record straight by reminding its readers of the reasons first given by the Singapore government for the restriction of the two publications:

> When we refused to print a tedious government letter to the editor on this racially charged matter [on the establishment of a second financial securities exchange], the government restricted our circulation to 400 copies a day. . . . the *Far Eastern Economic Review* was restricted over a story on an alleged "Marxist conspiracy," but whatever racial tensions the *Review* might stir also will be stirred by the pirated copies now circulating under the imprimatur of Mr. Lee's government. Or perhaps the racial tensions are stirred by advertisements, which are the only things excised from the pirated copies.

Dow Jones Publishing Company (Asia) Inc. Application On August 12, 1987, counsel for Dow Jones Publishing Company (Asia) moved the high court for orders of *certiorari* to quash the order made by the minister for communications and information on February 9, 1987, declaring the *AWSJ* to be a newspaper engaging in the domestic politics of Singapore, and the decision restricting the sale or distribution of the *AWSJ* in Singapore to 400 copies per issue until further notice under the Newspaper and Printing Presses Act, Cap. 206.[51] The NPPA, as amended, was of immense importance to the universal news media, but the lot fell to Dow Jones Publishing Company (Asia), as owners of the *AWSJ*, to challenge the ministerial orders under the press laws, and, more specifically, test the limits of this unique edict. At the hearing, the attorney general expanded the government's complaint against the *AWSJ* to include 10 previous articles in the year leading up to the publication of the offending article, "Singapore Exchange Puzzles Financiers" which, he said, also constituted "engagements" in Singapore's domestic politics. Those articles, he submitted, were "not only critical of the actions of the Singapore government and the public institutions of Singapore but also contain errors, omissions and misrepresentations and . . . designed to portray these bodies and Singapore generally in a negative light to the *Asian Journal* readers."

On May 16, 1988, within three days after the conclusion of legal arguments, T.S. Sinnathuray—now elevated to the high court—in a 42-page prepared judgment dismissed the application, and came up with what Dow Jones described as "a breathtaking definition" of a key phrase, "domestic politics," to include "all the multifarious and multifaceted activities with which a government is concerned."[52] But of the word "engagement," Sinnathuray said:

Whether the conduct of a foreign newspaper amounts to "engaging in the domestic politics of Singapore" is a matter solely for the minister, and not for this court to decide, unless it can be shown on the facts that the minister has exercised his power in bad faith or has acted irrationally or unreasonably in the Wednesbury sense.[53]

Dow Jones thought a Singapore government propaganda brochure, *The Right to Be Heard* (detailing its dispute with *Time* magazine and the *Asian Wall Street Journal*) provided "more helpful" examples of "engaging in domestic politics" as "publishing material intended to generate political, ethnic and religious unrest; indulging in slanted, distorted or partisan reporting; or persistently refusing to publish government's replies to refute misreporting and baseless accusations."[54]

Dow Jones (Asia) Inc. appealed to the court of appeal which, after hearing legal arguments, reserved its judgment.

Last Avenue of Appeal Closed   Pending delivery of judgment by the court of appeal, the PAP-dominated parliament, on April 21, 1989, passed a momentous bill into law restricting the right of appeal of litigants from the court of appeal in Singapore to the much-lauded Judicial Committee of the Privy Council in London, where—to recall the pearls of wisdom spoken by the prime minister on an earlier occasion—"undue influence cannot be brought to bear."[55] But what had brought about this transilient change? Just some months earlier—on November 21, 1988—the Privy Council—in a landmark judgment allowing the appeal of lawyer J.B. Jeyaretnam, the prime minister's political bête noire, against his disbarment—had rebuked the chief justice and the Singapore courts for their convoluted legal reasoning in trying to sustain a criminal conviction against him, and recorded their

> deep disquiet that by a series of misjudgments the solicitor [Jeyaretnam] and his co-defendant Wong have suffered a grievous injustice. *They have been fined, imprisoned and publicly disgraced for offences of which they were not guilty.* Their Lordships' order restores him to the roll of advocates and solicitors of the Supreme Court of Singapore, but, because of the course taken by the criminal proceedings, *their Lordships have no right to right the other wrongs which the solicitor and Wong have suffered.* Their only prospect of redress, their Lordships understand, will be by way of petition for pardon to the President of the Republic of Singapore.[56] [Author's emphasis]

Notwithstanding his manifest admiration for the Privy Council, the ever-pragmatic prime minister suddenly realized he could no longer afford the hard political currency of an unfettered appellate court in London—even though it consists of judges with the finest legal brains and intellect—which his supine law minister had once proudly touted as the "litmus test of Singapore's judicial independence." The amendments had serious repercussions for persons reluctantly involved in litigation with the prime minister or the Singapore government.

Appeals to the Privy Council in civil matters were limited only to cases where the parties had entered into a prior contractual agreement in writing stipulating that the Privy Council would be the final court of appeal. There was no such agreement in the case of Dow Jones Publishing Company (Asia) "since no one had imagined any such requirement when the case started."[57] As a transitional measure, however, the law would not apply to cases in which the court of appeal had already ruled, but the Dow Jones ruling was still pending. So, unless the court of appeal delivered its judgment before the bill became law, Dow Jones would be seriously disadvantaged in any further appeal. Its dire plea, through its counsel, Louis Blom-Cooper, Q.C. (who specially flew out from London to Singapore) to the court of appeal to render judgment before the law took effect, and give its written opinion later, if necessary, so as to preserve their last tier of appeal to the Privy Council, fell on unreceptive ears. The court of appeal would not be hastened. It saw no reason for judicial accommodation—judgment would be delivered "in due course." In the predictable event, Dow Jones lost its last avenue of appeal to the Privy Council, Singapore's ultimate court of appeal in London.

Six weeks later—on June 1, 1989—the court of appeal delivered its judgment upholding the gazetting order. It held that section 16 of the Newspaper and Printing Presses Act, as amended, does not

> expressly require [the minister] to be personally satisfied, whether subjectively or objectively, of the existence of any precedent fact or condition before he can make the order. Nor does it require him to hear the foreign newspaper before or to give reasons after the making of his decision thereunder. No authority directly in point has been cited to us which has decided or discussed a discretionary power in such statutory form. In our view, since the minister has no formal, procedural or other requirements to be satisfied before he can make the order, it must follow that any declaration that he makes under section 16 must be deemed to be valid until it is proved otherwise by any foreign newspaper aggrieved by his decision. The maxim *omnia praesumuntur rite esse acta* would apply to the making of such an order upon its being gazetted. The gazetting of the minister's order *ipso facto* presumes its legality. It has the effect of placing the burden of proving that the order is unlawful on any aggrieved foreign newspaper which challenges it.[58]

As to the issue of right of reply, the court of appeal said:

> If the contents of that article amount to engaging in domestic politics, then a refusal to publish a reply from the authorities to correct the erroneous image portrayed would be tantamount to a decision to perpetuate the erroneous image that had been portrayed. In our judgment that would be to continue engaging in domestic politics.[59]

As to whether or not the reporting of those articles, including the SESDAQ article, amounted to be "engaging in the domestic politics of Singapore," it said it depended on the meaning of that expression:

> In the context of Singapore, domestic politics would, in our view, include the political system of Singapore and the political ideology underpinning it, the public institutions that are a manifestation of the system and the policies of the government of the day that give life to the political system. In other words, the domestic politics of Singapore relate to the multitude of issues concerning how Singapore should be governed in the interest and for the welfare of its people. In this broad sense, the political, social and economic policies of the government of the day are part and parcel of the domestic politics of Singapore.[60]

As to the meaning of the words "engaging in," the court of appeal disagreed with Sinnathuray's view that the court could not interfere with the minister's decision, unless it was made mala fide or he had acted irrationally or unreasonably in the *Wednesbury* sense. It said:

With respect, if parliament has left it to the minister to decide what is "engaging in the domestic politics of Singapore," then whatever he decides as such cannot *ex hypothesi* be *ultra vires* or irrational or unreasonable nor can it be a decision made in bad faith. It seems to us that the judge's finding on this point amounts to saying that the meaning of the expression "engaging in," in the context of section 16, is as wide or as narrow as the *ipse dixit* of the minister. We do not agree with this conclusion.

The ordinary meaning of the phrase "engage in" [an activity] is to do it or be involved in doing it. . . . we also do not agree . . . that the expression "engaging in the domestic politics of Singapore" does not cover reportage or editorial comment on such matters in Singapore. In our view, it depends on the content and purpose of the reportage or editorial comment.

Factual reporting of "domestic politics" can be said to be not engaging in it. But there is no reason why reporting or editorial comment which goes beyond what is factual may not amount to engaging in domestic politics if it is made with a view to espouse political ideas or causes or seeks to influence public opinion in any direction in respect of such politics. The espousal need not be confined to political parties; it can extend to non-political pressure groups or indeed any group which has an interest in the matter that is being espoused, be it the party in government or the party in opposition.

Mr. Blom-Cooper has submitted that the word "meddling" which has been used by the *AWSJ* in the report published on 8 August 1986 is a perfectly good word to describe "engaging in." We agree with him in this respect.

In section 16, the words "engaging in" have the connotation of "interfering in" or "meddling"; in other words, involving oneself in affairs with which one has no right to be concerned with [*sic*]. Translated into the domestic politics of Singapore, the meddling need not be for or against the policies of any political party, or the interests of any non-political group in Singapore. It is simply involving oneself in some matter, in this case the domestic politics of Singapore where such involvement is neither solicited nor welcomed by those who are concerned with or affected by such matters, i.e. the people of Singapore. As an illustration, if the *AWSJ* were to publish an article or an editorial comment advising or exhorting the people of Singapore on the moral or ethical principles or cultural values that should be accepted or rejected as part of the national ideology of Singapore, it would be wholly appropriate in this regard to describe such activity as engaging in the domestic politics of Singapore.

In our view, the fact that the advice is intended to be constructive or otherwise is not relevant. What the expression imports is that the domestic politics of Singapore is for Singaporeans and any attempt by non-Singaporeans to take part in it in any form or manner directly or indirectly is engaging in such politics.[61]

Dow Jones Publishing Company (Asia) made one last desperate attempt to pursue its appeal to the Privy Council, the amendments notwithstanding, by moving the Privy Council itself in London. However, on July 20, 1989, the petition for special leave to appeal to the Privy Council was, on the motion of the attorney general of Singapore, dismissed for want of jurisdiction, but their Lordships noted in their brief judgment:

Their Lordships understand the petitioner's sense of grievance that, after the appeal from the judgment of Sinnathuray, J., had been argued and at a time when it was known that the Act of 1989 would shortly come into operation, the court of appeal in Singapore did not accede to an invitation to give their decision promptly, if necessary giving their reasons later, which would have enabled the petitioner to take advantage of the transitional provisions in the Act of 1989.[62]

Thus ended the unequal battle fought on uneven ground with the rules governing the battle changed even as the battle was being fought to the detriment of the aggrieved party.

In answer to the government brochure: *The Right to Be Heard: Singapore's Dispute with Time Magazine and the Asian Wall Street Journal,* Dow Jones & Company issued its own brochure, *Lee Kuan Yew vs the News: A History,* outlining the "deep-seated philosophical disagreement" and travails of foreign publications with Lee and the Singapore government, and Dow Jones & Company in particular, in the light of the Newspaper and Printing Presses (Amendment) Act, 1987.

The Asian-Pacific Economic Cooperation Conference   With the consequential Asian-Pacific Economic Cooperation (APEC) conference scheduled to begin on July 30, 1990, in Singapore, and its journalists declared persona non grata, Dow Jones decided to enlist the aid of the U.S. government to persuade the Singapore government to allow *AWSJ* and *Review* correspondents to enter Singapore to cover the APEC conference. But the Singapore government turned the U.S. government's request down flatly. On July 19, 1990, the Singapore government—in a 28-page press release—declared that it would not allow them into Singapore to cover the APEC forum, "even though it was a matter admittedly unrelated to the 'domestics politics' of Singapore or anywhere else." On the same day, Dow Jones Vice-President for International Affairs Karen Elliot House voiced Dow Jones's concern to First Deputy Prime Minister Goh Chok Tong:

Up to now, your government's position has been that it has the right to control foreign publications' coverage of Singapore's internal affairs when that coverage will be read by Singaporeans.

This event is an international meeting and has nothing to do with Singapore's internal affairs or its people. Unless we are to believe that the government's planned refusal is purely coercive or punitive, we are at a loss to understand the reasons for it.

Indeed, it appears that the Government of Singapore is now asserting its right to control what other Asians are permitted to read about major international meetings that happen to occur in your country. . . .

The questions you raise about the defenses that our attorneys have asserted on our behalf in the prime minister's personal libel case against the *Review* are more difficult. . . . But our lawyers have advised us that whether or not they will be successful, the defenses are well grounded under the law of Singapore.

You seem to be saying that we may not, nonetheless, assert them in Singapore's courts on pain of continued restriction of the circulation of our publications.

. . . We do not understand why those hauled before Singapore's courts should not be permitted to defend themselves fully under Singapore's laws.

Legal arguments aside, it seems to me that each time we try to reach areas of understanding on issues at hand, the government responds by raising new problems.

. . . It's rather difficult to play a game in which an adversary constantly moves the goal post.

. . . We concede . . . that the Government of Singapore has the sovereign power to restrict circulation of publications and news gathering by reporters within its borders for any reason, or, indeed, for no reason at all.

But we regret that you are now extending this power over other governments and other peoples.[63]

On July 23, 1990, Goh replied:

. . . You are mistaken that I have shifted my position. It is still as expressed in the note I handed to you in Washington. To use your metaphor, the problem with the game is not that Singapore's goal posts are moving, but regrettably that Dow Jones seems to be using two balls at the same time—one played by you, the other by your lawyers. . . .

The note . . . explicitly stated that foreign correspondents do not have the right to be stationed in Singapore. This, like circulation of foreign newspapers here, is a privilege.

The government sees no reason to grant it to foreign publications which have repeatedly tried to engage in domestic politics and take on the Government. . . .

I therefore cannot see how excluding journalists from the [*Review*] and the *AWSJ* will restrict what other Asians are permitted to read about major international meetings that happened to occur in Singapore.

. . . Since you had maintained that Dow Jones did not seek to engage in domestic politics, I wanted to understand whether you meant that Dow Jones was entitled to the rights which your lawyers are claiming. As I pointed out in my last letter, these included claims to:

* comment on matters of public importance;
* provide information which the Singapore public were entitled to receive and which the *Review* was under a corresponding duty to provide;
* exercise the freedom of expression guaranteed by the Constitution for citizens;
* inform the public to what extent the government allowed freedom of religion; and
* afford persons who have been attacked publicly by the Government the right of reply.

To the Singapore government, these "rights," when exercised, constitute engagement in domestic politics.[64]

Meanwhile, the *Wall Street Journal* responded with an editorial captioned "Singapore Scheme":

It now turns out that the Singapore hosts also have their own private scheme, using the visiting dignitaries to wave a mantle of international legitimacy over their ongoing efforts to intimidate the press. . . . bragging that it had turned down applications to cover the conference from the *Asian Wall Street Journal* and the *Far Eastern Economic Review*, and complaining about affronts to the dignity of Singapore by those publications and various officers of their publisher, Dow Jones & Co. We urge officials of the other 11 governments to peruse the extraordinary assertions in this document—for example that it is illicit for attorneys for defendants to raise certain arguments in Singapore courtrooms. The ministers attending the conference ought to know why they will not be allowed to explain their actions first-hand to correspondents of the two publications most relevant to their collective enterprise.

They may also want to ponder the issue of consultation about matters so obviously pertinent to the organization they are trying to launch. Singapore's action was taken against the advice offered by several of the other governments, which cannot bode well for the future of APEC. In the case of the U.S. government, Singapore's treatment of Dow Jones publications was raised by President Bush during the recent Washington visit of Goh Chok Tong, Singapore's first deputy prime minister, and by Vice-President Quayle, Secretary of State Baker and other U.S. officials. We thank them for their efforts, which may have contributed to Singapore's permission for a correspondent for the U.S. edition of the *Wall Street Journal* to enter Singapore on Secretary Baker's plane. But most governments do not, as Singapore did, require advance clearance for press accompanying the Secretary of State. . . . It has restricted *Time* and *Asiaweek* as well as the Dow Jones publications, but its battles with the press are merely one facet in the broader picture. The various frictions are those bound to arise in an interdependent world from heavy-handed efforts to stifle local dissent and criticism.[65]

On July 27, 1990, the *Bangkok Post*, a premier English-language newspaper in Thailand, referring to the restriction and the barring of *AWSJ* and *Review* journalists, editorialized:

> The Asian Pacific Economic Cooperation Conference is a major international meeting. Current practice in almost every country, and quite correctly so, is to allow the press to cover such meetings. Singapore neither helps its own case nor, in the end, the publications it seeks to punish. By barring serious economic reporters from a serious conference, the Singapore government succeeds only in appearing oppressive, hardly the judgment it seeks. That the outside world cares little about the specific reasons for such action only further hurts Singapore's image.
>
> Mr. Lee and Mr. Goh, both statesmen of world class, can perform better than this. Most governments in the world have come to a truce, however uneasy, with foreign newsmen without either giving up their own rights, or forcing reporters to give up their claims to cover news as they and their publications see fit. The Singapore press dispute has dragged on for years. Instead of seeking impossible redress for events in a past long forgotten by the public, Singapore might well consider calling a truce and looking to the future in this matter.

What the *Bangkok Post* had overlooked in its statesmanlike commentary was that it was dealing with a prime minister who, in his own words, not only has a long memory, but who does not forgive slights easily.[66] On July 30, taking a leaf out of the government's book, the *AWSJ* took out a full-page advertisement in the *Straits Times* reproducing the *WSJ* editorial, a sore point with the Singapore government, which saw it as an attempt to influence the Singapore electorate. On same day, Karen Elliot House returned to the controversy:

> You are correct that the note . . . makes clear that stationing a correspondent in Singapore is a privilege granted by the Singapore government—as it is in most other countries in the world—and we understand this to be your long-stated position. But banning correspondents from covering international meetings in Singapore, in our view, represents an extension of Singapore's policy of controlling the foreign press. This is the point we sought to explain in our recent editorial.
>
> The more significant issue raised by your letter, however, is the question of how the legal process and attendant legal arguments in the courts of Singapore ought to affect our dialogue. From our first meeting in Washington in April . . . I assured you then we would accept service of any legal documents and, in my first letter, repeated that Peter Kann[67] was personally willing to accept service. Yet no one attempted to serve him until two weeks ago when we accepted service. . . .
>
> . . . we accept we have no general "right" to station correspondents in Singapore or to publish and circulate there. You can and have restricted both. But, at the same time, we believe that when and while we are in Singapore we are—or at least should be—fully protected by Singapore's own laws, no matter who our adversary is or what his cause is.
>
> Thus, our lawyers are not asserting, in contradiction of my comments to you, that we have the affirmative right to circulate in Singapore. They claim only that, once in Singapore, we have the rights under its laws, for example, to publish comments on matters of public importance, and afford persons who have been attacked publicly by the government

of Singapore the right of reply, . . . that we enjoy full protection under Singapore's own law of libel.

. . . Fundamentally, our dispute is over what constitutes interference in Singapore's internal affairs. You have said Singapore does not mind critical articles, only interference in its domestic politics. I have said, and sincerely repeat, that we have no intent to interfere in any nation's domestic politics but simply to report and interpret news events as accurately and honestly as we can for an Asian and global business audience. Respectfully, this seems a philosophical issue, not of necessity a legal one.

On July 31, the Singapore government, in a lengthy reply, accused Dow Jones of using "the [APEC] conference and the presence of foreign dignitaries to pressurize Singapore into lifting the restrictions." This letter, albeit a reiteration of the Singapore government's vexation with foreign publications, is useful as it crystallizes the points at issue with the *AWSJ* and the *Review*:

> Their circulation in Singapore is a privilege, and not a right; they should not interfere in Singapore's domestic politics; and they should be subject to the jurisdiction of the Singapore courts. . . . It follows from this policy that foreign correspondents have no right to be stationed in Singapore. That an APEC meeting is taking place does not entitle *AWSJ* and [*Review*] correspondents to enter Singapore. The government sees no reason to grant this privilege to *AWSJ* and [*Review*] because they have repeatedly engaged in domestic politics and taken on the government.
>
> The government restricted *AWSJ*'s circulation for refusing to publish official replies to a hostile article. . . . The editorial itself clearly shows Dow Jones's intent to interfere. It criticizes the government for "being embroiled not only with its natural political opponents, but also with longtime associates," because it "engaged in a tiff with the Catholic Church and exchanged unpleasantries with the Privy Council," and for "heavy-handed efforts to stifle local dissent and criticism." These are all internal actions and policies. Foreign publications can report on them, but they have no business taking sides for or against them. If Dow Jones does not seek to interfere in Singapore politics, why did it take advertising space in a Singapore newspaper on July 30 to print in full this editorial, attacking the Singapore government?
>
> Until Dow Jones understands that its promise not to engage in Singapore's domestic politics means not taking sides for or against the government on Singapore's internal actions and policies, the restrictions on *AWSJ*, [*Review*] and their correspondents will stay.[68]

However, under increasing international pressure, particularly from the United States—its largest trading partner—and a growing awareness that its pigheaded obstinacy might damage the attraction of Singapore as a convention centre, among others, the government finally relented, but only to the extent that it would permit a New York-based Dow Jones journalist from the *Wall Street Journal* and the A.P.-Dow Jones News Service, but not its Asian-based journalists, to enter into Singapore to cover the conference. A distinction without a difference—but, more importantly, the Singapore government's brittle honour remained seemingly intact and face was given to the U.S. government and its leaders. Notwithstanding, the regional media dispute, however, continued to smoulder. On August 3, 1990, Goh agreed in a letter to Karen Elliot House that "fundamentally, our dispute is over what constitutes interference in Singapore's internal affairs," and proceeded to detail them all over again.[69]

Following the cessation of litigation in the Singapore courts between Lee and Dow Jones, the *AWSJ* in September 1991 was rewarded with a partial restoration of its circulation—as many as 2,500 copies a day—from October 1, 1991. Its daily circulation at the time it was restricted was 5,000 copies a day. Meanwhile, it was allowed to circulate at a banking conference.[70] It was a positive step forward. As a well-known Chinese proverb says: A journey of a 1,000 *li* must begin with a single step. Since then, the steps have not only quickened but lengthened. In November 1991, in a speech to the Foreign Correspondents Association of Singapore, on "Singapore and the Foreign Press: The Next Lap," the information minister, Brig. Gen. George Yeo, alluding to the improved climate between the government and the foreign media, pronounced the *AWSJ* had been "fair and balanced in its reporting over the last two years."[71] On July 1, 1992, its circulation was allowed to be increased to 3,500 copies a day. Pleased at the increment, the new *AWSJ* editor Urban Lehner evinced the hope that "some day in the future, the Singapore government will eventually let the market determine the proper circulation." On May 7, 1993, a MITA spokesman announced that the *AWSJ* would be allowed to increase its present circulation of 3,500 copies by another 1,500 copies to 5,000 a day (which restored its circulation to its pre-restriction level) and to have a correspondent based in Singapore as of July 1, 1993; but that it would still remain a gazetted publication—like a menacing Damoclean sword, in case the paper steps out of line again. On May 2, 1994, the *AWSJ* reported that it had been allowed to sell as many as 7,000 copies a day, effective immediately.

Asiaweek

Next to fall in swift succession under the NPPA, as amended, was *Asiaweek*, a regional weekly magazine owned by *Time* Inc. It was already drawing official ire for its fine and comprehensive coverage by Lisa Beyer, its resident correspondent, of the May/June 1987 ISA arrests of the 22 Roman Catholic church and lay workers, young professionals and social activists, accused of being engaged in a clandestine Marxist conspiracy to overthrow the Singapore government through violence, and their subsequent allegations of abuse, ill-treatment and torture by ISD officers to extract confessions to order. The magazine, however, came a cropper when the editor inexplicably blue-pencilled an official letter in reply disputing an article on the alleged Marxist conspiracy, and annotated it to form the basis of another article entitled "A Distortion of Facts, You Say?"[72] The indefatigable press official wrote again demanding that both his letters should be published in toto and, when they were not, *Asiaweek* was gazetted, and its circulation ordered reduced from 10,000 copies to 500 copies per issue. *Asiaweek* repented, and published them one month later. Meanwhile, the magazine was as anxious for a restoration of its circulation to the pre-gazette level as the government was desirous of being rid of a correspondent, whose finger on the body politic of the nation was as firm as it was sure. For Lisa Beyer was able to relate to the people of Singapore. Hard-line governments regard reporters of her genre as not conducive to their long-term interests.

On June 4, 1988, James Fu—now information director in the ministry of communications and information—was seen at lunch with *Asiaweek* editor-in-chief Michael O'Neill at the Singapore Cricket Club, Singapore's historic downtown watering hole. Two days later, able *Asiaweek* resident correspondent Lisa Beyer received a sudden notice to relocate to Hongkong within 30 days. O'Neill denied any horse trading with Fu, and disputed Beyer's claim that she was removed from Singapore in exchange for a rescission of the restriction.[73] On June 14, Lisa Beyer resigned. But, as the saying goes, the proof of the pudding lies in the eating. On October 10, *Asiaweek* circulation was partially restored from 500 copies to 5,000 copies per issue. In September, 1990, the *Asiaweek* circulation restriction was further relaxed up to 7,500 copies per issue. Lisa Beyer was succeeded by other journalists in residence—who, after finding the atmosphere inhospitable for independent and balanced reporting, left or were transferred—and, finally, by Alejandro Reyes, a Filipino-Canadian journalist.

In March 1995, *Asiaweek* published a review of a book, *Dictionary of the Modern Politics of Southeast Asia*, by Professor Michael Leifer, in which the reviewer commented on "some odd omissions and biases: Singapore's exiled former solicitor general Francis Seow doesn't rate an entry . . . Not all foreign ministers are represented, yet his colourless compatriot, the current foreign minister S. Jayakumar, is."[74] The government took offence at the reference to the foreign minister as "colourless." It did not make note of the mention of this author's name. In an intriguing twist to an old tale, the magazine was quietly informed that its circulation was being restricted by a reduction of 3,000 copies. No formal gazetting was published. It is not unlikely that the government has begun to realize that its noisy disagreements with the media was making it the butt of international comments and was counterproductive of its efforts to turn Singapore into the information hub of Southeast Asia.

Far Eastern Economic Review

The next foreign publication to fall foul of the law was the *Far Eastern Economic Review*, a wholly owned Dow Jones publication. The delicate thread of its relationship with the prime minister was already badly frayed and it needed very little for it to snap. As with the case of the *Asiaweek* magazine, it came about over the *Review*'s spirited coverage of the alleged Marxist conspiracy and the arrests of the so-called conspirators to which Lee and his government took strong exception. Considering an article, "New Light on Detentions," by its correspondent Michael Malik, as "false" and "defamatory," Lee personally sued it for libel, which is discussed below. The government, for its part, drastically restricted the *Review* circulation from 9,000 to 500 copies per issue on December 26, 1987, effective three days later, alleging:

> [The *Review*] has attempted to pit the Catholic Church against the prime minister and the government, and sow suspicion among Catholics in Singapore against them. In a multiracial, multireligious society, where freedom of worship is vital for national cohesion, such allegations that the prime minister and the government are attacking a major religious group cannot be taken lightly.[75]

In an editorial captioned "A Ban by Any Other Name," Derek Davies declared the gazetting "invidious" and "unacceptable" and, as the reduced size of its circulation would "in effect place the distribution of the publication into the hands of the Singapore authorities, allowing them to pick and choose the institutions or readers which the *Review* reaches," he had "reluctantly" decided to cease circulation altogether in Singapore on December 30, 1987. Furthermore, the act of gazetting would enable the government to claim that the publication had not been banned.[76]

To counter the *Review* cessation of circulation in Singapore, the information minister, Dr. Yeo Ning Hong, on January 27, 1988, moved another amendment to the NPPA "to provide for the reproduction of gazetted publications for sale or distribution in Singapore."[77] In an extraordinary display of PAP logic, the government, with its tongue firmly in cheek, accused the *Review* of impeding the free flow of information into Singapore for ceasing distribution of its publication, and thus inconveniencing Singaporeans making the further amendment necessary. The amendment would empower the minister to approve the reproduction of a gazetted foreign newspaper by any person, without the publisher's permission, for sale and distribution, subject to the conditions that the advertisements therein were blanked out in the photocopies, and no profits were made from their sale or distribution, save for the cost of production and services connected therewith. Copies of such a gazetted foreign newspaper would not be an infringement of copyright, as it was "in the spirit of the Copyright Act,[78] which allowed photocopies to be made not for profit, but for personal use and research."[79] The amendment to the law would, it was argued, give all readers in Singapore "easy" access to gazetted publications.

Accordingly, the cessation of sale by the *Review* would do "no harm to Singapore or its economy and, more particularly, to its function as a communications and information centre, as businessmen could obtain photocopies of the material they needed in the *Review* or the *AWSJ*, without contradicting international agreements on such matters as copyright and the transfer of intellectual property."[80] The minister stressed that the amendment did not affect other publications at all. Nor did it "dilute" in any way Singapore's commitment to bilateral arrangements with other countries on copyright protection. As astonishing as it was, the minister adverted that, after the passage of the amendment into law, Singaporeans and news agents could "pop over easily to Johor Bahru (a capital town on the opposite side of the Singapore-Johor causeway) to collect their free copies from the *Review* and, with approval, bring them back to Singapore and make reproductions, make copies, for sale."[81] All this was allegedly in keeping with the spirit of the Copyright Act, which the government lauded at the time of its passage as providing "comprehensive copyright protection to all forms of intellectual property."[82]

The *Review* protested the government's immoral barefaced piracy of its intellectual property to no avail.[83] As of March 31, 1988, 17 persons and organizations had applied for, and had been granted, approval "to import, reproduce and distribute" counterfeit copies of the *Review*, among which the Singapore Manual and Mercantile Workers' Union, a subsidiary of the NTUC—National Trade Union Congress—was the only one making copies for sale, whose weekly replication of the *Review* is so perfect that it was difficult to tell the counterfeit from the genuine copy save for the denudation of advertisements.[84] The counterfeit copy is sold to the public allegedly "at cost."[85] In a money-oriented Singapore society, where a venture or enterprise is invariably measured by dollars and cents, it strained the bounds of credulity to suggest that those counterfeit copies were being printed and disseminated by the NTUC subsidiary essentially as a labour of love.

According to the minister, the *AWSJ* and the *Review* had claimed that the government, in restricting their sales in Singapore, was preventing a free flow of information. The government had agreed to the *AWSJ* offer to distribute its newspaper free of charge to its subscribers, subject however to the exclusion of advertisements; but the *AWSJ* had "turned tail," pleading "added cost," although the government had offered to meet part of the marginal cost. The government was prepared and ready to make the *Review* the same offer as it did to the *AWSJ*—circulate in Singapore freely, for free, but without advertisements. As those gazetted publications had insisted the government was fearful of their criticisms, the latest amendment to the NPPA would "nail those lies, once and for all" that it was not "fearful of their different points of view."

Consequent upon the passage of the bill, the *Review* managing director, Charles Stolbach, wrote to the information minister proposing to provide copies of the *Review*, totally devoid of advertisements, for Singapore distribution with the editorial content intact. The *Review* would not profit from the exercise but sought only to recover production and distribution costs as was permitted under the new law. The faithful James Fu, as director of information,[86] replied to Stolbach saying the offer to "circulate for free with advertisements blanked out" was still open, but "instead of distributing for free you have asked to recover costs," and sarcastically remarked that the *Review* had "descended to bargaining for approval to collect more money." The government "will approve your request, subject to standard conditions applicable to everyone reproducing copies of *Review* in this way." His ambiguous phraseology created confusion momentarily. The *Review* application, however, was rejected as it allegedly did not fulfil two conditions: (1) the original copy or copies of the gazetted foreign newspaper must be sent to the ministry "for marking," and (2) the "reproduced copies shall only be made from the copy or copies so marked." The *Review* had proposed providing the ministry with the "original bromides" of its editorial, and pages from which copies would be made by the Times Printers of Singapore.[87]

The loss of its Singapore market affected its 1988 profit and loss sheets. But it gallantly described its loss in advertisement revenues, as "money we happily give up for freedom of the press."[88]

While all this media furor was going on, the London-based *Economist* decided to move its correspondents from Singapore, while *US News and World Report* closed its office in Singapore. We pause now to consider the legal action brought by the prime minister against Derek Davies, the *Review* and others.

Lee Kuan Yew v Derek Davies & Ors   In January 1988, the prime minister commenced a legal action against Derek Davies and Michael Malik, editor-in-chief and journalist respectively of the *Review*, its publishers and printers, claiming damages for alleged libel in an article, "New Light on the Detentions," in the December 17, 1987, issue of the magazine, legal costs and interest, and an injunction restraining the defendants from "further publishing the said or any similar words defamatory of the plaintiff."[89] On September 26, 1989, the libel suit began in the high court before Justice L.P. Thean, who, after hearing the evidence and counsels' submissions, reserved judgment. On November 30, 1989, Justice Thean—in a 114-page judgment—rejected all the proffered defences, and "to no one's surprise," found that the *Review* had libelled the prime minister, and awarded S$230,000 in aggravated damages because of defence counsel's conduct in cross-examining the prime minister on "irrelevant issues," and putting "offensive questions designed to hurt his feelings," plus interest at 6 percent per annum from December 31, 1987, as well as the plaintiff's costs in full, and an order restraining the magazine from repeating the libel. Lee had demanded an apology, but no apology was forthcoming.

As the prospects for success of litigation in the Singapore courts did not appear too promising, before the trial the *Review* sought the prior consent of the prime minister, as the other litigating party, to agree to the Privy Council in London being the ultimate court of appeal, but the prime minister's lawyers parried the approach as premature. When the *Review* appealed against the high court's judgment, Lee cross-appealed, seeking to increase the damages. The *Review* disclosed that it had planned to seek an agreement from the prime minister so that either party could appeal to the Privy Council against the decision of the court of appeal. For under the new law, appeals to the Privy Council in civil cases could only be made with the consent of both parties—a diabolically clever move that was designed to prevent an easy appeal to the Privy Council—for which successful litigant in the court of first instance was ever going to agree to the other's request?

At the Foreign Correspondents' Club, Hongkong, on October 26, 1990, during a question-and-answer assembly of newsmen, it was put to the prime minister that if he was so confident of his case against the *Review*, he would agree to the appeal to be heard by the Privy Council, but Lee characteristically tergiversated in his reply that he did not need the Privy Council to decide on his libel suit because he had proven his case both in the Singapore court and to Singaporeans at large. And—no doubt recalling the Privy Council's judgment on the Jeyaretnam case—somewhat defensively said: "My case does not depend on whether the Privy Council likes or does not like the findings of fact by the judge in Singapore." But Nury Vittachi, then with the *South China Morning Post*, pointed out that his win against the *Review* was like a home team winning on home ground. "If it had been won in the Privy Council, the Western press would have nothing else to say."[90] Vittachi should have added not only that it was won on home ground but that the umpire, the referee and the linesmen were all members of the home team, too!

Meanwhile, in New York, Dow Jones's president-publisher Peter Kann, criticized the Thean judgment:

> A Singapore court has entered a libel judgment in favour of Singapore's prime minister, based on an article the prime minister found personally offensive. The article contained an essentially accurate portrayal of highly newsworthy events relating to the detention without trial of Catholic social workers by the Lee government, and relations between the Catholic Church and Mr. Lee. Solely because it was read to be critical of Mr. Lee, however, it has resulted in this unwarranted determination against the *Review*. We can only hope that in the long term the *Review's* punishment will not, as doubtlessly intended, still honest and independent voices in Singapore.
>
> Mr. Lee has insisted that members of the foreign press are in no position to judge the actions of the government of Singapore. It is nonetheless indisputable that no people are free so long as their rulers forbid criticism and their press can report only that which the government finds acceptable.[91]

The critique was published in the *Wall Street Journal* and, with minor variations, in the *Asian Wall Street Journal* and the *Review*. Acting on Lee's instructions, the attorney general charged that Kann had committed wilful contempt of court, and, on December 19, 1989, before the high court in Singapore, claimed that the Kann statement would inevitably lead citizens and others who have recourse to our courts to question the integrity and impartiality of the judiciary in Singapore. These imputations and allegations are clearly calculated to undermine confidence in our judiciary and to lower their authority. They could excite in the minds of the people a general disaffection with all judicial decisions.[92]

The *Review*, however, was not charged with contempt probably because it was no longer circulating in Singapore, except for the government-pirated, advertisement-free version, against which no legal action was taken. On December 29, 1989, Lee stepped up the pressure by announcing his intention to commence libel suits in Singapore and Malaysia (where the *AWSJ* circulates without let or hindrance) against Peter Kann for his critique of the Thean judgment, as well as against the editors, publishers, printers and distributors of the *AWSJ* and the *Review* respectively. In January 1990, Lee made good his threat. Significantly, no action was commenced against the *AWSJ* in the courts in Hongkong. It is equally exceptional that no libel or any other legal actions whatsoever were commenced in the U.S. courts against Dow Jones, Peter Kann or the *Wall Street Journal*. Like the wily Chinese strategist Sun Tzu, Lee knows the cardinal importance of choosing his battleground with care.

On January 11, 1991, the ever-dependable Justice Sinnathuray did not disappoint in a 43-page judgment, when he ruled that the *AWSJ*, its editor and publisher were guilty of contempt over the Kann statement on the Thean judgment. Sinnathuray had no doubt whatsoever that an ordinary reader would find the article contemptuous of the trial judge and of the high court: "Clearly, the reader would conclude that the plaintiff won the libel action against the defendants because he was the prime minister and not on the merits of his case." He fined them a total of S$9,000 (US$5,266), and ordered them to pay the costs of the legal proceedings. He also found the *AWSJ* printer and the Singapore distributor guilty of contempt, but imposed no penalty on them other than their share of the costs of the proceedings. The company decided not to appeal the finding, although a Dow Jones spokesman announced in New York that it "continues to believe that the court's contempt judgment against the paper wasn't warranted by the facts. But, under the circumstances, and particularly considering the small size of the fines imposed, we have concluded that the expenditure of time and money necessary to appeal is not called for."[93]

The first break in the clouds over the darkening relationship between Dow Jones and the prime minister appeared when Reuters reported, in an interview with information minister, Brig. Gen. George Yeo, that Singapore would allow the *AWSJ* and the *Review* to circulate freely again if they avoid domestic politics: "There must be some assurance of good faith and goodwill but, basically, if those conditions are met we will relax their circulation in Singapore."[94]

Encouraged presumably by the new political climate and information minister Yeo's remarks, Dow Jones Vice-President Karen Elliot House wrote to Lee that Dow Jones was willing to withdraw the appeal of the *Review* against the Thean judgment in his favour but for the fact that he had cross-appealed. On February 20, Lee replied that if the *Review* withdrew its appeal, he would drop his cross-appeal, on Dow Jones agreeing to pay his full legal costs in all those cases. Pursuant to the agreement, on March 27, 1991, the *Wall Street Journal* announced, "Dow Jones Withdraws Appeal in Singapore; Lee Kuan Yew Drops All Related Cases": "Our 1989 statement expressed our view that the judgment in the *Review* libel case was unwarranted, but we never intended to defame Mr. Lee in any way or imply that Mr. Lee had improperly influenced the trial judge." In an accompanying editorial, it said:

> We have agreed to pay Mr. Lee's court costs in all of the cases, and he is entitled to cite this traditional symbol of victory in Commonwealth jurisdictions. . . .
>
> The settlement . . . does not . . . restore the circulation of the *Asian Wall Street Journal* or the *Far Eastern Economic Review*. Nor are there any back-channel deals to that effect. Our publications will continue to practice honest and accurate journalism.
>
> . . . our point has been that there are limits to what we can accept without compromising the integrity and credibility of our world-wide operation. We need to assure readers around the world that any mistakes are our own, not the result of a self-censorship imposed by someone else's agenda. We have not compromised this fundamental principle in Singapore, and will not there or elsewhere.[95]

As part of the global settlement, Lee discontinued his libel suits against the *AWSJ* and the *Review* in Malaysia (which he had begun at about the same time as his legal suits in Singapore). While flinty commercial interests undoubtedly influenced Dow Jones of the futility of pursuing the forensic battle, especially in Singapore, it was seen by many, however, as a victory for Lee. Hard-headed business considerations had prevailed, and, in this respect, Lee was proven right. The *New York Times* headed the settlement: "Dow Jones Threw in the Towel"—which speaks it all.[96] Before the year ended, the *AWSJ* was rewarded by a partial restoration of its circulation, and the *Review* with 110 copies per issue distributed free at the transit airline lounges of Singapore's famed Changi International Airport.[97]

As we have already noted, a threat by the prime minister to his perceived traducers to see them in court has proven remarkably efficacious in dampening editorial exuberance, especially with regard to his unbroken record of forensic victories in Singapore over newspaper owners, editors, journalists, publishers, printers and distributors.

Although most foreign publications with circulation in Singapore have decided to walk the chalk of self-restraint, the *Review* still continued to publish letters from readers critical of Singapore and its leadership. Seriously irked with the *Review* for being allegedly the forum of "inaccurate or unfounded stories on Singapore," which, regardless of official corrections, "continues to publish letters that repeat earlier inaccuracies or misstatements already disposed of," the press secretary to the information minister threatened: "Henceforth, we shall not reply to each hostile letter or article in the *Review*, but will take them into account when the *Review* seeks a review of the restriction on its circulation in Singapore."[98] That threat seemed to have had the desired effect.

Since then, a perceptible change has overtaken the *Review* coverage of Singapore, whose pages have noticeably been sparse, bland or noncontroversial almost to the point of disinterest in Singapore and its affairs. Save for the 100-odd copies—referred to above—distributed free at Changi International Airport, the circulation of the *Review* was not restored either partially or otherwise as yet—and it is not for want of trying. However, on April 15, 1994, the government announced that, beginning on May 1, the *Review* may distribute 2,000 copies in Singapore.[99] And, according to an official spokesman, the restriction was further relaxed by another 2,000 copies per issue from May 1, 1995, although it still falls far short of its pre-gazetted level. Until its partial circulation restoration, the *Review* continued to suffer its publication being officially counterfeited weekly—a virtually unheard-of phenomenon in a civil society.

The Economist: A Missing Key Sentence?

Just when it was thought that the dust of media conflict had settled, the government re-engaged the foreign media in another skirmish, on this occasion, with the prestigious London-based *The Economist* over an article, entitled "Psst—Wanna See a Statistic?" on the prosecution of *Business Times* editor Patrick Daniel and others under the Official Secrets Act for publishing "flash" GDP estimates—early calculations of the most recent economic growth—before they were officially released. The article said: "Singaporeans are wondering why there is so much fuss over GDP figures," amongst other things:

> Some defenders of the government claim that the prosecution is an "aberration" and that the administration of Goh Chok Tong, the prime minister for the past two years, is more liberal than its predecessors. But other actions taken during Mr. Goh's tenure suggest that little has changed.[100]

The article mentioned the case of Dr. Chee Soon Juan, a neuropsychologist, and his dismissal by his PAP head of department for alleged dishonesty from the National University of Singapore, after he had stood as an opposition candidate in a by-election against the prime minister, Goh Chok Tong, and the defamation actions brought against him after he had questioned the motives for his dismissal. The prospects of "court-ordered" financial ruin also faced him as it did J.B. Jeyaretnam. Offended at what it described as the "mocking" tone of the article, the Singapore government sent a letter in reply to the article through its high commissioner in London, but a sentence which the government considered "important" was edited out of it before publication, giving rise to what the *New York Times* called an extraordinary exchange of correspondence between them.[101] The expurgated sentence read:

> The government will not acquiesce in breaches of the Official Secrets Act, nor allow anyone to flout, challenge, and gradually change the law, as has happened in Britain with Clive Ponting's case[102] and Peter Wright's book, "Spycatcher."

The dispute revolved around the government's insistence on its right of an unedited reply, which became increasingly shrill and arrogantly menacing in its tone:

> *The Economist* had no right to remove from the High Commissioner's letter, without his consent, a sentence which he and his government considered crucial, especially after he had informed *The Economist* that this was an official reply from his government and had offered to shorten it himself if *The Economist* was under pressure of space. It is for the Singapore government to decide how it wishes to present its case, and for your reader to judge who is right and who is wrong. . . .
>
> *The Economist* had its say in its article in the 26th June–2nd July issue, which mocked the old-fashioned attitudes of the Singapore government. The government is entitled to return the compliment and remind *The Economist* of the maladies which its attitudes have brought Britain.[103]

On July 24, the editor responded:

> I understand that you wish to have the right to choose how to present your case, and I sympathize with that. In return, I hope you understand that I have a responsibility to defend my readers against arbitrary and high-handed behaviour by entities of any sort, be they governments, companies or powerful individuals.
>
> . . . My duty is to my readers, in Singapore and elsewhere, and I must ensure that they are not subject to distortions demanded by outside organizations who are not only on their own high horses but are also waving threats. That is the principle that guides my dealings with all other governments, companies and individuals, and must, for reasons of consistency, guide my dealings with you, now and in the future.
>
> I am fully prepared to allow opposing points of view to be published in our letters page, but I cannot knowingly allow those points to be obscure, misleading or distorting. While you may not have intended your July 12th letter to suffer from these sins, my judgment is that its purpose and point were both obscure.[104]

Notwithstanding, the editor yielded to the government's demand promising to publish it in its next issue. However, it refused initially to publish another official reply to a published letter from opposition lawyer Jeyaretnam, who had explained that he could not appeal his criminal convictions to the Judicial Committee of the Privy Council in London, but, with regard to the order of disbarment, the Privy Council had judged that "the convictions upon which [he] had been disbarred were all wrong in law and that [he] had suffered a grievous injustice."[105] Jeyaretnam's letter had merely set out the facts. On August 2, 1993, the government gazetted *The Economist* "with effect from today," and "*hoped*" that the official letter in reply would be published, making it "unnecessary for the government to reduce your circulation in Singapore." When the magazine agreed to publish it, the government lifted its threat to reduce its circulation, but capped it at its present level of 7,500, and required the magazine to post a bond of US$125,000 with it, and appoint a local representative to accept legal documents in any future legal actions.[106]

Bill Emmott, editor of *The Economist*, whose loss of its Singapore readership of about 8,000 copies per issue would hardly make a dent in its worldwide weekly circulation of more than 520,000, boldly told the high commissioner: "I am quite prepared to have our circulation restricted if that circumstance arose, and indeed to transfer our substantial printing contract out of Singapore to our other regional site in Hongkong." To which the government offhandedly replied: "It is the prerogative of *The Economist* to decide whether to transfer its substantial printing contract from Singapore to Hongkong. *The Economist* is printed by Times Printers Pte Ltd., which is not owned by the government." It, however, is a subsidiary of Singapore Press Holdings, in which the government of Singapore, as already noted, holds—through its two wholly owned subsidiaries, Temasek Holdings and MND Holdings—substantial shares well in excess of the 3 percent limit.

In an explanation to its readers, *The Economist* stated:

> Some readers will ask why we have "capitulated"; others will be bemused at all the fuss. Our policy comes in two parts. First, we try to obey the laws of countries in which we wish to publish, whether they concern official replies, libel or whatever. The only alternative is not to

publish there, which would deprive readers in that country of the chance to buy *The Economist* and would, yes, deprive us of those sales. Such a choice can be taken, but only *in extremis*.

Second, in adhering to those laws we seek to ensure that our readers are not misled or somehow abused. So when, in this Singapore case, a right of reply in local law was implemented through a request to publish two letters from the same person in the same issue, we did not accept it. Similarly, we would not allow our columns to be used as a propaganda sheet; in such circumstances, not yet reached in Singapore, we would choose to cease circulating in that jurisdiction, if there were no other recourse available.

None of this tangled affair will affect, be assured, our own coverage of Singapore—which will remain critical or complimentary, whichever is appropriate.[107]

However that may be, and notwithstanding those words of reassurance, to Singapore-watchers, another foreign publication was perceived as having bitten the dust. A "thinking and cosmopolitan" Singaporean urged *The Economist*

not to give in to the arrogant bully-boy tactics of the Singapore government in "gazetting" your publication.

The Singapore government has absolutely no right in demanding a say over your editorial policy. They have no right to determine what should or should not be published in your letters page. It is interesting to note that the *Straits Times* (which is well known for its pro-government views) states clearly and explicitly in its Forum (letters) page that ". . . we reserve the right to edit any letters selected." Does the editor of the *Straits Times* tell the Singapore government that he reserves the right to edit its letters before publication?

It is ironic that the government has brought up the Official Secrets Act, the Ponting case and the "Spycatcher" episode in Britain. . . . As it stands now, abuses of power, bureaucratic bungles and ministerial misdeeds can all be treated in Singapore as "classified information" and quietly suppressed in the national interest. What a load of self-serving hypocrisy?[108]

On January 15, 1994, *The Economist* was de-gazetted and its ceiling of 7,500 copies was lifted. The weekly magazine was no longer required to appoint an authorized distributor or mark its copies with stickers. But it is still required to obtain a permit to operate as an offshore newspaper, and post a bond of S$200,000 under section 16 of the act. While pleased at the lifting of those curbs, its editor Bill Emmott stressed that the "episode would not change the way the magazine reports on Singapore, or affect the way future replies from the Singapore government are regarded." But *The Economist* made it known that it will continue to circulate in Singapore as long as the government acts "in a reasonable manner in implementing these [NPPA] provisions."[109]

The *International Herald Tribune*

The *International Herald Tribune,* which is based in Paris, is jointly owned by the prestigious *New York Times* and the *Washington Post*. It circulates world wide. Out of a universal daily circulation of 190,000 copies per issue, about 40,000 copies are distributed in Asia, out of which 7,000 copies circulate in Singapore. A subsidiary company of the Singapore Press Holdings (SPH) prints some 17,000 copies of its Asian edition daily.[110] Singapore is, therefore, an important market to it.

On October 7, 1994, the Singapore edition of the *International Herald Tribune* (*IHT*) carried in its opinion page a commentary, "The Smoke over Parts of Asia Obscures Some Profound Concerns," as a rejoinder to an earlier op-ed article, "You May

Not Like It, Europe, but This Asian Medicine Could Help," by Kishore Mahbubani, permanent secretary to the ministry of foreign affairs, in the same newspaper. The writer was Atlanta-born Christopher Lingle, a political economist, who was then 13 months into a two-year contract as a senior fellow with the National University of Singapore. The commentary contained a statement:

> Intolerant regimes in the region reveal considerable ingenuity in suppressing dissent. Some techniques lack finesse: crushing unarmed students with tanks or imprisoning dissidents. Others are more subtle: relying upon a compliant judiciary to bankrupt opposition politicians, or buying out enough of the opposition to take control "democratically."

Although Singapore was not mentioned specifically, the government, nonetheless, contended that the article and, in particular this last sentence, had scandalized the Singapore judiciary and impugned its integrity and reputation.

The Singapore police seized "some magazines and documents" from Lingle's office and home, and interrogated him on two separate occasions to "intimidate" him into an admission that Singapore was in the forefront of his mind. Midway through his interrogation, Lingle was allowed to leave Singapore to visit his ailing father in the United States, and did not return for reasons which were not too difficult to empathize with. For Prime Minister Goh Chok Tong was reported to have said, among other things, that the courts would "throw the whole book" at him if he was found guilty, an unfortunate remark and one not calculated to inspire confidence in any defendant in a pending legal matter in which the government was prosecutor, given that the Singapore courts are egregious for their pro-establishment proclivity.[111] It would have been much better if he had heeded his own ministry of foreign affairs' shrill advice to the U.S. State Department to withhold comment until the matter was heard in open court instead of repeatedly characterizing the issue as the right to freedom of opinion and expression. For Goh's gratuitous comment could well be construed as wilful contempt of court as it tended to influence the true course of justice and its consequences.

Meanwhile, upon being informed of senior minister Lee Kuan Yew's displeasure, the newspaper made swift and "unreserved" apologies to him and the judiciary;[112] but, notwithstanding, the government commenced contempt of court proceedings against all persons concerned with the publication, followed by Lee himself with a personal action for libel alleging that the offending passage "could . . . be understood as suggesting that he had sought to suppress political activity in Singapore by bankrupting opposition politicians through court actions in which he relied on a compliant judiciary to find in his favour without regard to the merits of the case."[113] Curiously, no other Asian government or leader has commenced legal proceedings against the newspaper over the article.

IHT Asia editor, Michael Richardson, sought to show that in editing the article he believed that the passage complained of referred to other Asian countries, such as China, Burma or North Korea, and not to Singapore, which the prosecution, quite rightly in the circumstances, described as the stuff of "Alice in Wonderland." To prove that the article referred to the Singapore judiciary, the government had perforce to acknowledge an unsavoury aspect of Singapore political life that many opposition members had been sued in court by the prime minister and other government politicians, some of whom were driven to financial ruin as a result; but it stressed that those cases had been decided solely on their merits, not because of undue pressure or influence on the judiciary.

In a trial whose outcome was never really in contention, the judge found there could not be any doubt that the offending passage was intended by Lingle to refer to the Singapore judiciary. If the criticism impugned the integrity and impartiality of the court, this amounted to contempt of court, even if it was not so intended. None of the defendants' counsel, the judge noted, disputed that an allegation that a judiciary was compliant amounted to contempt of court because it scandalized the court. Therefore, the only issue before him was whether the offending passage referred to Singapore, and the fact that a defendant had not heard of the plaintiff or had intended to refer to someone else did not of itself absolve him of liability for defamation. The sole question before him was whether an ordinarily reasonable reader would reasonably conclude that the words referred to Singapore. In the particular circumstances of the case, he held that they did. In this connexion, the *Australian Financial Times* reported the observations of Justice Michael Kirby, president of the New South Wales court of appeal:

In its treatment of human rights such as free speech, Singapore was in a sort of time capsule of colonial attitudes to law, which have been captured and caught as they were when the British retreated. In this regard, Singapore has not kept up with the developments of the common law in other countries. . . . punishment for scandalizing the courts hasn't been used in England for 60 years.

And the *IHT's* defence plea:

To reinforce his *bona fides* on free speech, [Kirby] took a swipe at the hapless *International Herald Tribune* for running a timid defence. Instead of stating that the article was indeed about Singapore, the judge said the paper "somewhat undermined" international efforts to help by adopting the "pusillanimous" argument that it had really been referring to China. . . . As chairman of the executive committee of the International Commission of Jurists, Justice Kirby played a part in generating those efforts. . . . But the "China" defence blurred the issue. . . .

If you are in the business of upholding free expression, you should do so courageously and boldly and if you are the *International Herald Tribune*, you should do so with confidence in your cause. Right or wrong, you should say that this is our position. As Martin Luther said, "Here is where I stand."

But the *International Herald Tribune* did not do that. Oh no, no, no, this was China! Well, I think the court rightly dismissed that suggested defence with contempt—the contempt that it deserved, one might say.[114]

Richardson, who had been living in Singapore since 1971, a privilege denied most foreign journalists, was until recently in good standing with Lee Kuan Yew and the PAP government. He was fined S$5,000 as Asia editor of the *International Herald Tribune*, while publisher and chief executive Richard McClean was fined S$2,500, the International Herald Tribune (Singapore) Pte Ltd., which distributes the newspaper, and the Singapore Press Holdings Ltd., which prints it, were each fined S$1,500. Christopher Lingle, however, was fined the stiffest sum ever of S$10,000 because he had showed "a total lack of contrition." All five were ordered to pay the fines and the costs of prosecution within two weeks of judgment. Save for Lingle, all the defendants were represented by counsel.[115] Since then, the Singapore government has obtained an order of court calling upon the National University of Singapore (NUS)—Christopher Lingle's former employers—to disclose the amount of money which it holds by way of compulsory savings and salary owing to him, and why it should not be used to pay the fine and the costs of the prosecution. The savings and salary due to him were duly paid into court, notwithstanding that compulsory savings are ordinarily protected from seizure.

Intoning that freedom of expression and speech is not absolute, the judge said, "No one is entitled under the guise of freedom of speech and expression to make irresponsible accusations against, inter alia, the judiciary, otherwise public confidence in the administration of justice will be undermined."[116]

Confronted with the aforesaid judgment, the *IHT* had no other alternatives before it, save to seek a settlement with Lee, to whom it offered to pay S$300,000 in damages and costs, which did not, however, include Lingle, against whom Lee reserved his right of action.

As a random contributor of rather critical articles to the *IHT*, Lingle had unwittingly irked a sensitive government. As a foreigner he had greater licence than a Singaporean academician who would have had no choice but to be circumspect in his writings. Lingle had left a paper trail of tendentious articles and commentaries. Another article, "Don't Trust the Reports of Supercharged Growth," was also published in the *IHT*,[117] for which he was hauled over the coals by the NUS authorities. Although Singapore was not the subject of his scrutiny, the article, however, had referred unfavourably to China, which had become a special ward of Lee, as it were, and whose cause he was loudly championing in world forums. No one crosses Lee with impunity.

The *IHT*, too, was becoming troublesome to the authorities in its publication of commentaries and articles critical of Singapore and its leaders. Besides this latest run-in, it had earlier published an article by Philip Bowring, a former *Review* editor, entitled "The Claims About 'Asian' Values Don't Usually Bear Scrutiny,"[118] alleging that "dynastic politics is evident in 'Communist China' already, as in Singapore, despite official commitments to bureaucratic meritocracy." The article also referred to a "battle between the corporatist needs of the state and the interests of the families who operate it." The prime minister, the senior minister and his son, the deputy prime minister, claimed that the article was defamatory. The *IHT*'s quick and abject apologies "accepting that the implication of nepotism in the article was unfounded" did not save it from the ignominy of a libel suit on the quantum of damages.[119] It was eventually ordered to pay record damages of S$350,000 to the prime minister and S$300,000 each to the senior minister and his son, in addition to the legal costs.[120] The *IHT* decided not to appeal the landmark amount of libel damages awarded.[121]

To many observers, the *IHT* had rather hastily conceded to Lee's interpretation that the offending passages meant that the appointment of his son, Hsien Loong, to the position of deputy prime minister by Goh Chok Tong—and his own earlier appointments as minister of named ministries—were *not* on his own merits but purely because he was his son.[122] It was a case of apologizing in haste to repent at leisure. Once again, significantly, no other Asian country or leaders were offended at this article. Reporting on Singapore and its thin-skinned leaders is not—to borrow an American colloquialism—like shooting fish in a barrel. It requires a mastery of the subject, nimbleness and dexterity, all of which may best be summed up in the German expression *fingerspitzengefühl*: that "combination of sure-footedness on slippery slopes and sensitivity to nuance familiar to mountain goats, safe-crackers and statesmen."

Notwithstanding the foregoing encounters, the *IHT* was not gazetted under the NPPA for alleged "interference" in the domestic debate of Singapore whereby its circulation in

Singapore was restricted or capped. As in the case of *Asiaweek* magazine, it must have dawned on the government that its intensive plans to make Singapore an information hub of Southeast Asia, if not of Asia, and its desire to make Singapore "an ineffable perch" for foreign journalists "to observe" the region, would be severely compromised if it were to continually rely on loud or noisy gazetting of foreign publications which displease it—now that it has a reliable judiciary on which it could count to punish errant foreign publications with substantial damages and costs.

Returning to the police interrogation of Lingle, it might not be generally appreciated that it was also directed towards establishing the complicity of SDP secretary general Dr. Chee Soon Juan—a rising political opposition leader—in the offence. He was a recent target of aborted bankruptcy proceedings by a PAP member of parliament. If it could be shown that Dr. Chee had in some way abetted the writing of that article, he would in all probability have been charged in court for the same offence as well, and neutralized as an electoral candidate in the forthcoming general election with an appropriate sentence of imprisonment or fine, as occurred with opposition MP, J.B. Jeyaretnam.

To Restrict Is Not to Ban   In the age of the information superhighway, it is becoming increasingly difficult, if not impossible, to keep any news or information beyond the determined reach of the people. To restrict the circulation of a publication is not to ban the publication, so runs Lee's argument. But political science professor Michael Haas queried this line of argument: "Aside from the government's advocacy of practices contrary to international copyright laws, would Singapore accept a Malaysian argument that a cut in the water supply to Singapore was not a restriction of water, as used bath-water can be boiled and drunk?"[123] Be that as it may, in thus restricting the circulation of offending newspapers, magazines or periodicals in Singapore, Lee had out-Machiavellied Machiavelli, for universal experience has shown time and again that, when a publication is banned it invariably stimulates circulation and growth by whetting the curiosity of the reading public. For nothing promotes demand better than the lure of forbidden publications!

News publishing being a highly competitive business, its life-blood is decidedly circulation, and the wider its circulation the greater its advertisement rates and revenues. The same may be said of most publications which depend upon media advertising for revenue. Conversely, any significant drop in circulation, even for a short period, affects revenue and, ultimately, profits. In the Asian advertising media market, Singapore is undoubtedly a most-sought-after plum, and an important market to foreign publications in Southeast Asia, because of its affluent, sophisticated and highly English-literate population.

On February 26, 1988, at the Mandarin Hotel, Singapore, Brig. Gen. Lee Hsien Loong told the Singapore Press Club:

> All the gazetted foreign publications have steadfastly denied engaging in the domestic politics of Singapore. All insist that they are only reporting events and analyzing developments. But to the Singapore government, which has the responsibility to decide, there is no doubt that the gazetted publications are not just reporting or analyzing developments but trying to influence them. They have taken sides on domestic issues.
>
> These publications sought the right to play a role in Singapore played by American newspapers in the U.S.—to be a major political force, setting the agenda, sitting in inquisition and in judgment.

. . . the U.S. model does not prevail in all Western countries. The European press, particularly the British, stick much more to the traditional function of reporting news. But even if it did, trying to impose the U.S. model on Singapore would still be illegitimate.[124]

Speaking to the American Society of Newspaper Editors in Washington, D.C., on April 14, 1988, the prime minister disclosed his raison d'être for circulation restriction instead of banning:

> The government could simply have banned these [gazetted] journals. But to ban them would have been an overreaction. Since sales is one of the principal motivations of these journals, it was sufficient to restrict their circulation. . . . By not allowing these journals to increase their sales, the government has achieved some concessions. Both *Time* and *Asiaweek*, after they had been gazetted, published the disputed letters intact.

Thus, Lee's cunningly conceived scheme to hit at foreign newspapers where it hurts most, namely at their pocketbooks, was based on a cynical conviction that foreign newspapers are more interested in profits than in abstract principles of freedom of speech and expression. And that, once they have suffered the hunger pangs of a dwindling breadbasket, they would refrain from writing or publishing anything anathema to his administration. Professor Michael Haas puts it this way:

> The prime minister is ostensibly an atheist, and clearly his ethical views are not those of "secular humanism," which stresses human rights and an intellectual understanding of the world. Instead, his god is Mammon: he begins his speeches on Singapore National Day with a report on the Singapore economy, and even the battle with the foreign press demonstrates an ability to derive economic explanations for nearly all events, when other explanations are more plausible.[125]

However that may be, there are indications that Lee may have momentarily prevailed over the foreign media. Foreign reports and articles on Singapore and its leaders are scarcer and noticeably more bland than before the media crackdown. Foreign news agency and publications media are known in several instances to have sent their commentaries, critiques and articles to him for his prior approval and changes in text and substance before publication. In short, the foreign media in spite of themselves have perforce to practise self-censorship or restraint.

"Singapore needs to co-opt the foreign media in managing its internationalization. We should encourage them and make their work easier—help them to help us," said the information minister, Brig. Gen. George Yeo, at the Singapore Press Club.[126] It gave rise to wishful thinking that the speech could herald a possible change in official attitude of "a kinder, gentler" Singapore towards the foreign media. It was not a "whimsical objective" as Singapore could only succeed economically if it had the widest access to information.[127] In another speech before the Foreign Correspondents Association of Singapore in November 1991, the minister signalled the theme that the "government's policy had always been to encourage the foreign press to operate from Singapore." But the latest skirmishes with *The Economist* and the *International Herald Tribune* are setbacks in media relations, as we have already seen.

The Expulsion of Foreign Correspondents

In July 1965, when Singapore was still a constituent state within the federation of Malaysia, the federal government expelled a British journalist, Alex Josey—an unabashed Lee Kuan Yew partisan—for "interfering in the internal politics of Malaysia while not being a citizen of the country."[128] The expulsion created an uproar in Singapore. Elaborating on the reasons for the expulsion, the acting Malaysian prime minister, Tun Abdul Razak, said that Josey had indulged in activities which were not conducive to the racial harmony of the nation and had repeatedly abused the privilege he enjoyed in Malaysia as a foreign correspondent.[129] Left-leaning Josey came out to Malaya in 1948 at the invitation of the British high commissioner, Sir Henry Gurney, to conduct psychological warfare against the Communist Party of Malaya (CPM), and became adviser on psychological warfare to the director of operations, General Sir Harold Briggs. His contract of employment was not renewed following complaints about the socialist leaven of his radio talks and propaganda. He remained in Malaya, however, working as a free-lance journalist for the left-wing British weekly the *New Statesman*, among other publications. But of greater significance was the well-known fact that Lee employed him periodically to assist him in press relations work whenever he travelled abroad in Europe, Asia, Africa and Australasia. Lee's angry response—as well as that of his PAP colleagues—to Josey's expulsion is tellingly Pecksniffian, when viewed against his own subsequent actions against the foreign media:

> What does this mean? Is this just to make foreign correspondents more amenable to reporting favourably of the central government? Besides being a hint at foreign correspondents, is this at the same time a hint to those who are friendly to these correspondents?[130]

Addressing a large crowd at a by-election rally in Singapore at the time, he expressed regret at the federal government's expulsion order, and extolled Josey as "a very experienced journalist, who had the courage to report factually what happened in the last parliamentary session, quoting Razak, me and other speakers."[131]

On July 8, 1965, Singapore's deputy prime minister, Dr. Toh Chin Chye, called a press conference, at which three other senior cabinet ministers were also present in a public show of solidarity, to explain the Singapore government's stand on the expulsion, and the attempts by extremists in the Alliance coalition, particularly the United Malays National Organization (UMNO), to have Lee arrested. Stressing that the entire Singapore cabinet was "solidly united" on this matter, Dr. Toh charged that the Josey expulsion was only the first step towards the suppression of liberalism in Malaysia's political field. By acceding to the extremists' demand overnight, he declared the federal government leaders had damaged their image abroad as tolerant and liberal men:

> The world press will now find it hard to depict Malaysia to their readers as a growing democracy. In countries which are committed to the defence of Malaysia the question will inevitably be asked: What is that is being defended in Malaysia—democratic freedom or a repressive ruling group? . . . The expulsion of Josey must be interpreted as a threat to the PAP.

Lee called the expulsion order "the mailed fist" of the federal government, which it was displaying to the people in the midst of the Hong Lim by-election "to show how strong they are." And added, "I can get along without Josey. . . . He was just my channel. I speak for myself." An opposition Malaysian politician, Lim Kean Siew, asked, "Why this big fuss over Josey?" and noted that "it is indeed strange to hear this loud protest now, considering that the arrest and detention of previous newsmen, such as the former editor of the *Utusan Melayu*, Said Zahari, and a *Straits Times* reporter, A. Mahadeva,[132] went unchallenged by the PAP. Is it because Josey is a supporter of the PAP?"[133]

Dr. Toh's fervid rhetoric warning the federal government on the injury to liberalism and democracy could be applied with even greater force and justification today to the Singapore government, which booted foreign correspondents out of Singapore for much less cause. Among the many who were expelled or did not have their professional permit renewed or working pass rescinded, were the following.

Anthony Polsky, former *Review* staffer and part-time correspondent for the *New York Times* and other publications, on June 9, 1971, departed Singapore, after his professional visit pass was not renewed. He was accused of colluding with Amnesty International to prepare statistics of political detainees in Singapore to embarrass the government.

Nanyang Siang Pau's Malaysian-born public relations officer and manager, Kerk Loong Seng—who was married to a Singapore citizen—was suddenly informed on August 6, 1972, by the immigration authorities that his employment pass had been cancelled "with immediate effect," that he had been declared a "prohibited immigrant," and been given less than 24 hours' notice to leave Singapore. He was one of the four *Nanyang* senior executives, who were detained under the ISA in May 1971. He was released on December 8 the previous year, and had resumed work until August 6. His professional visit pass was not due to expire until January 25, 1973. No reasons were given for its sudden cancellation.

Malcolm Caldwell, a controversial British Labourite and weekly columnist for the *New Nation* newspaper, who confined his journalistic interests to "local and restricted issues, such as the water supply, the tourist industry, and birth control," was denied re-entry into Singapore in 1972 after returning from an Australian trip.[134] He was later accused of collaborating with lawyer G. Raman to put pressure on the Singapore government through Socialist International to release the political detainees, who were alleged to be communists. At the time, Caldwell was an editor of a London-based quarterly periodical, *Journal of Contemporary Asia*, which was banned in Singapore in 1977 "for publishing leftist commentaries and consistently portraying Singapore in a bad light." In 1978, Caldwell was killed in mysterious circumstances in Phnom Penh, Cambodia, where he and two other American journalists were guests of the Khmer Rouge, when three Cambodian gunmen attacked the guest-house.

Review correspondent Patrick Smith's employment pass was not renewed in 1983. Commenting on the nonrenewal, the minister for culture, S. Dhanabalan, said "most foreign correspondents know what reporting was all about; but Smith during his stay had written articles on "sensitive" issues of which he knew nothing." "Singapore was not prepared to allow the kind of free expression of ideas similar to that in other countries," he added.[135]

Another *Review* correspondent, V. G. Kulkarni, an expatriate Indian temporarily residing in Singapore, whose allegedly "insensitive" coverage on Singapore, particularly on the Malay issue, so offended Lee and his government that his continued presence in

Singapore was made so extremely unpleasant that he requested a transfer. Professor Haas interpreted the Kulkarni harassment as "partly to negate the impolitic remark of his son [Brig. Gen. Lee Hsien Loong] in February 1987, that Malay soldiers in the Singapore armed forces would never be placed in front-line positions against Moslem countries, a statement assumed to question the loyalty and integrity of Singapore's Malays far more seriously than the facts assembled by the *Review* reporter."[136] In the result, *Review* editor Derek Davies posted Kulkarni out to a more congenial station: "Like several of the other correspondents, he simply could not stand being in Singapore" any longer. In September 1985, Davies requested permission to replace him with reporter Nick Seaward but was refused by Lee personally because as Lee's press secretary "incredibly" explained: "Seaward was married to a Singaporean." Instead, Lee advised Davies to send a correspondent who had no ties to Singapore, and who would "report Singapore as an outsider for outsiders," failing which: "Send me a clerk; send me an amanuensis."[137] At first blush, it might seem absurd but, as we will see shortly, there is much method in this madness. Other *Review* correspondents, Anthony Rowley and Susumu Awanohara, too, appeared to have offended the government by their so-called insensitive writings on Singapore, and consequently became non grata.

Reuters correspondent Marilyn Odchimar was expelled in March, 1986, for "irresponsible reporting" in connexion with a story on the total building collapse of the New World Hotel in Singapore.

Another *Review* resident-correspondent, Nigel Holloway's application for extension of his employment pass was refused on April 2, 1987, by the controller of immigration. Davies flew into Singapore specially to make an appeal to the authorities. No reason was given for the refusal, except for a hint by the controller of immigration: "Where the government may not wish a foreign resident to strike roots in Singapore, it does not renew his employment pass indefinitely." Holloway had lived in Singapore for four years, reporting for *The Economist* before joining the *Review*. Davies indicated his readiness to give an assurance to move Holloway to another posting after a further year, and within a fortnight, if he should "in the meantime deepen his roots or publicly demonstrated his very real affection for the place." But the pugnacious minister for community development, Wong Kan Seng, to whom he made his appeals and protests, was "not interested in his assurances, even in black and white. Nothing I could say—and indeed nothing he could say to his cabinet colleagues—could alter the decision. Holloway must go, for reasons unstated."[138] The intractable James Fu cryptically replied: "Nigel Holloway, like Patrick Smith in 1983, ended up with his employment pass unextended. He will not be the last. It was not because of his reporting."[139] Holloway was then engaged to a Singaporean whom he has since married. By the same token, the Singapore government frowns upon Singaporeans working for foreign publications.[140] Information minister George Yeo told the German-language newspaper, *Handelsblatt:*

> [I]f you are a foreign newspaper, you should not employ a Singaporean as your chief correspondent because we don't want foreign newspapers to interfere in our domestic politics.
>
> And if you are a Singaporean writing for a foreign newspaper which circulates in Singapore, this may then become a way by which you use a foreign newspaper to meddle in Singaporean politics, please start a Singaporean newspaper. They are regulated differently. We give different access and we expect different responsibilities from local newspapers.[141]

The application for press accreditation of *Review* Sydney correspondent, Hamish McDonald, who was to have replaced Nigel Holloway, was also refused, with no reasons given. While the brouhaha over the gazetting was going on, the press accreditation of Michael Westlake, the *Review* transport correspondent, was suddenly withdrawn by the immigration authorities. Westlake was then in Singapore for the Asia Aerospace '88 exhibition. An invitation from the civil aviation department to him was abruptly cancelled. Because of the gazetting, delegates to the exhibition were unable to obtain copies of the January 28 *Review* special issue featuring "Focus on Aviation," written mostly by Westlake, and published to coincide with the exhibition.[142]

Jenny Chin Lai Ching, a Malaysian permanent resident in Singapore and *New Straits Times* journalist, living in Singapore, was arrested in May/June 1987, together with her Singaporean husband, Kenneth Tsang, in Operation Spectrum, the notorious security exercise, accused of being involved in a Marxist conspiracy. She was released shortly afterwards without conditions after the National Union of Journalists, among others, protested the arrest.

AWSJ resident correspondent John Berthelsen's employment pass was refused renewal on its expiration in July, 1988. Since then, neither the *AWSJ* nor the *Review* has been permitted to station a resident correspondent in Singapore. Worse still, several correspondents from these two publications were denied entry, even for short visits, into Singapore. The malice runs deep into irrationality. On August 24, 1988, *AWSJ* correspondent Raphael Pura was ordered to leave after he had entered Singapore on the usual 14-day social visit pass to cover the pending general election. Pura was visited at his hotel by immigration officials, who took away his passport, and ordered him to report to the immigration office the next day, saying that he required a professional visit pass, notwithstanding the usual practice of permitting brief visits by journalists on social visit passes. Upon visiting the immigration office the next day, he was ordered to leave Singapore by midnight that very day. *Review* chief reporter Rodney Tasker and assistant editor David Porter were similarly turned away at Changi International Airport when they flew in for the same purpose. Unaware that her professional colleagues had been sent packing back, *Review* staff writer Mary Lee, a Singapore citizen, flew in from Bali shortly thereafter, and was puzzled at being held up at the airport while immigration officials dithered over whether it was in order to let her into the country.

In early 1989, immigration authorities, without betraying the slightest compunction or compassion for the auspicious occasion, turned back *Review* Indian-born journalist N. Balakrishnan at Changi International Airport, when he and his Singaporean Chinese wife flew into Singapore for the all-important Chinese New Year's Eve family reunion gathering, even though he had been granted an entry visa by the Singapore Trade Mission in Hongkong. It seemed a rather strange way to promote in the national psyche Confucian virtues and values with its accent on family, which Lee and his government were fostering as part of their political agenda.

In May 1989, *AWSJ* and *Review* correspondents were prevented from entering Singapore to cover the official visit of U.S. Vice President J. Danforth Quayle to Singapore. First deputy prime minister Goh Chok Tong snubbed his visitor, Vice President Quayle, when the latter queried the exclusion, with the reply that the United States government had no right to question the Singapore government's decision since the *AWSJ* and the *Review* "are not even U.S. publications [but] which happen to be owned by American companies." A bizarre but typical PAP sophistry! In mid-1989, two other *Review* correspondents, Carl Goldstein and Jonathan Friedland, applied for temporary employment passes to visit Singapore to write on business topics, and were refused entry.[143] On October 20, 1989, AP-Dow Jones correspondent Simon Elegant's request for a two-month extension to his employment pass to cover the period between his scheduled departure and the arrival of his replacement was disapproved. No reason was given, except that it was noted that AP-Dow Jones is a joint venture between Associated Press and Dow Jones.[144] On November 18, 1989, AP-Dow Jones's request for a work permit for Matthew Geiger as its new resident correspondent in Singapore was also denied. No reason was given.

Free-lance journalist Jonathan Sikes reportedly had his agenda of appointments with government officials in Singapore cancelled *instanter* when they discovered a Dow Jones connection, notwithstanding that he had left Dow Jones's employ several years before. This was probably the nearest thing to guilt by media association. Explaining its fatuous hostility towards the *AWSJ* and the *Review*, the ministry of home affairs said these journalists had "repeatedly violated Singapore's immigration laws by carrying out journalistic work while here on social visit passes," and "because of this flagrant abuse, the government had decided not to allow any correspondent from the *Review* and her sister publication, the *AWSJ*, to visit Singapore on social visit passes." In so doing, the ministry deliberately chose to overlook the glaring fact that this was the conventional way foreign reporters on short-term assignments enter Singapore—by obtaining a 14-day social-visit pass on entry. Philip Bowring,[145] who had succeeded Davies as the *Review* editor, accused the Singapore government of double standards: "This is the same entry stamp given to bankers, traders, engineers and others employed outside Singapore and visiting Singapore for short-term business purposes."

Ignoring the trenchant comparison, the ministry persisted that reporters from the two publications would henceforth have to obtain temporary employment passes. To test the waters, Raphael Pura promptly applied for such a pass but was pointedly rejected.

Given the foregoing, S. Rajaratnam's earlier response in parliament to British press criticisms about the arrests of local journalists by the Singapore government is particularly apt:

> We have never arrested or deported any [foreign pressmen] or banned their publications merely for critical and even ill-informed articles about Singapore. . . .
>
> Admittedly, Sir, the reputation of the Singapore government has sunk rapidly in the eyes of a handful of British publications, like the *Sunday Times*, *The Times*, the *Far Eastern Economic Review* and *The Economist*.[146]

Equally noteworthy was the explicit statement of the information minister of state, Wong Kan Seng: "we allow journalists to come and stay, and live and work [in Singapore]."[147] And the exclamation of former journalist and PAP MP, Yatiman Yusof, was well in tune with the boastful rhetoric of the times:

> *Is the opposition not aware that anyone can come to Singapore on a social visit pass, write about Singapore, and fly out of the country without any restriction?* Tell me the instances where every journalist who comes into Singapore has got to give the reason for coming and give an undertaking not to write stories about Singapore?[148] [Author's emphasis]

In his speech to the American Society of Newspaper Editors, Washington, D.C., Lee was not free from the same hyperbole: "We allow American journalists into Singapore in order to report Singapore to their fellow countrymen."[149]

These statements were out of sync with reality and were made for the consumption of different audiences, most of whom were ignorant or uninformed of the situation. At last, shedding the mantle of hypocrisy aside, the government stated that it had "decided not to allow any correspondent from the *Review* and her sister publication, the *AWSJ*, to visit Singapore on social visit passes." Period. Some foreign correspondents, the minister for culture S. Dhanabalan was moved to say, "think they are a special group who can demand an employment pass as a right."[150] The official mantra chanted was that it is a correspondent's privilege but the government's prerogative whether or not to grant him an employment pass.

Asiaweek correspondent Roger Mitton was refused a further extension of his employment pass after three years. Another recent addition to this growing list is that of Alejandro Reyes, another enterprising *Asiaweek* correspondent, whose application for a further year's extension of his employment pass was refused. No reasons were given. But the ministry of information purported to clarify the situation: "News organizations which send their correspondents to Singapore know that the employment pass is not automatically renewed. In some cases, they are aware that the employment pass is for a fixed duration and not renewable."[151] The prescient Kyodo News Service,[152] however, noted that Reyes had "reported on several politically sensitive issues such as Singapore's decision to cane U.S. teenager Michael Fay. . . . [and] wrote a piece on his exclusive interview in the United States with Singapore political exile Francis Seow, who was detained in 1988 for allegedly colluding with U.S. diplomats to build opposition in Singapore."[153] This observation was confirmed sometime later by the minister himself to a visiting *Asiaweek* senior executive that "he [Reyes] was getting too close to the opposition."

Ian Stewart, who worked for the Hongkong-based *South China Morning Post* in Singapore—as well as stringed for *The Australian*—had his visa revoked in March 1995. The authorities claimed that the *South China Morning Post* was posting its regional business correspondent to Singapore.[154] This was followed by the rejection of an application by Charles Wallace of the *Los Angeles Times* for an extension of his employment pass in the same month. He was told that he could no longer use Singapore as his base for his journalist activities because several of his articles about Singapore "were not balanced or accurate."[155] Bangkok-based journalist Philip Shenon, of the *New York Times*, was told that he would need to apply for a visa to enter Singapore in the future. Previously, he had been allowed entry without getting an advance visa in another country.[156]

Rationalizing the government's reluctance to allow foreign correspondents to overstay the period of their work passes, Deputy Prime Minister Goh Chok Tong, in a 1989 Agence France-Press interview, said: "If you are here too long, you suffer from what they called *local-itis*. You get to know Singaporeans, you get to know how they feel, and you see certain things get in the way of a foreigner in Singapore and they try to affect the course of politics in Singapore."[157] By using the word *local-itis*—a vernacular variant of localism, meaning to sink roots in Singapore—Goh was effectively saying that the PAP government does not wish foreign journalists to develop an affection for or become too familiar with Singaporeans and Singapore so that they could make value judgments on the politics of Singapore in all its diverse facets. Journalists who stay for a year or so are considered birds of passage, who cannot claim any real expertise on the country and its politics, and whose reports are thereby necessarily limited by that condition. Notwithstanding this so-called policy, there are, however, notable exceptions, such as Dennis Bloodworth, a free-lance journalist and writer, and Michael Richardson, Asia editor of the *International Herald Tribune*, who are regarded as generally sympathetic to the regime.

Not content with its own backyard squabbles with the foreign media, the Singapore government tried to widen them by sounding out other Asean governments to agree on applying a common ban on foreign journalists that offend one member country, but the idea met with resistance in Jakarta official circles.[158] The Indonesian authorities were apparently unimpressed that a Radio Australia correspondent, whose visa to work in Indonesia was not renewed, was also denied a visa for Singapore.[159] Save for Singapore, other Asian countries generally appear to have a higher threshold of tolerance and understanding.

Since then, using a more subtle ploy, information minister Brig. Gen. George Yeo, in Jakarta, called on Southeast Asian nations to rely on their own media to cover developments in the area rather than depend too much on what was provided in foreign agency reports. The "problem" with "reporting each other through foreign news agencies" was that "we see each other through Western lenses. . . . We are in the region and it is best, I think, that we report each other directly rather than through the intermediation of the Western news agency." He said this call was not because he was "offended" by Western news coverage of developments in Singapore, but rather their "lack of understanding."[160] Malaysian premier Dr. Mahathir Mohamad echoed a somewhat similar call: "Some form of an Asian media network is necessary to counter Western dominance in the industry and its misreporting of the region. There is no Asian newspaper for Asians, only Western newspapers published in the name of Asian countries." Citing the *Far Eastern Economic Review* as an example, he said it was printed in Asia but "controlled" from outside Asia, by New York-based Dow Jones. "Their main idea is how to create friction and instability, so that if we are unstable they can compete with us. . . . Unfortunately, Western people tend to read their own media and conclude wrongly about our countries. They miss out on investments because their newspapers are always telling them that we are unstable."[161]

Requirement for Bond, Etcetera

On July 18, 1990, the Newspaper and Printing Presses Act was amended again, this time to require "offshore" newspapers with a circulation of 300 or more copies in Singapore, which contain "news, intelligence, reports of occurrences, or any remarks, observations or comments pertaining to the politics and current affairs of any country in Southeast Asia," to have a permit for its sale and distribution in Singapore. The amendment extended the definition of offshore newspapers to include news coverage *beyond* Singapore to the rest of the region. It was the latest gambit in the government's relentless campaign against foreign publications in general, and the *AWSJ* and its sister publications, the *Review* in particular, to discourage what it considers negative reportage.

An application for the permit may be refused or revoked without reasons being given for the refusal or revocation. The permit, valid for one year, is issued subject to conditions. The minister may—

- specify the maximum number of copies which the newspaper is allowed to sell or distribute in Singapore;
- require the newspaper proprietor to appoint a person in Singapore who is authorized to accept service of any notice or legal process on his behalf or on behalf of the publisher; and
- require the newspaper proprietor to furnish a specified deposit or some form of security to meet any liability or costs of any legal proceedings arising in connection with the newspaper's publication.[162]

Moving the second reading of the bill on August 30, 1990, the minister of state said that the amendments were not intended to curb the circulation of any publication or prevent the free flow of information in Singapore. The Singapore government was not blanketing out criticisms, but it wanted to ensure fair, responsible and objective reporting. Foreign publications were free to criticize the government, but, if they were out of order, it had to have the right of reply. These amendments were intended to drive home the government's demand of a right of reply and underline the "verity that foreign publications circulate in Singapore as a privilege and not as a right." And the requirement that regional publications should submit themselves to Singapore jurisdiction, so as to obviate the repetition of "difficulties" encountered in serving legal notices on the *AWSJ* over a contempt of court action and the prime minister's defamation suit. Twenty foreign publications, including the *International Herald Tribune, Time, Newsweek* and *USA Today*, were affected by the new law.

On October 15, 1990, the *AWSJ* announced that it would stop circulating in Singapore rather than meet the new requirements, saying in its editorial, "Matter of Regret," that "trying to meet the conditions being imposed by the government of Singapore would degrade the integrity of the publication." It stated further:

> The government of Singapore has now chosen to codify and augment its press practices in a new licensing law, requiring a license to circulate and providing a government minister with a range of peremptory powers, including the restriction of circulation, an apparently unlimited power to impose conditions on licensing, a requirement for a bond against legal judgments and so on. Its first deputy prime minister has announced that offshore publications may be required to sign a statement agreeing not to claim rights under the Singapore constitution in lawsuits, apparently to spare authorities the embarrassment of defending their actions in public court hearings. . . .
>
> What the government of Singapore wants is for the foreign press to practice self-censorship. A facade of factual reporting will be allowed, but any statement by authorities must be taken at face value, lest it disturb either the political monopoly of the People's Action Party or the pretense of democracy, the press shall not report the opinions of critics within Singapore, let alone the defenses of those in disputes with the government. Those publications that cooperate will be rewarded with larger circulations, as Time-Warner Inc.'s *Asiaweek* was after its recent cover story on retiring Prime Minister Lee Kuan Yew. Those that insist on independence will be hauled into court, handcuffed in defending themselves, forfeit bonds held by the minister of communication, then post new bonds and sign new waivers for their next license.
>
> . . . we cannot accept the Singapore government's implicit bargain and practice self-censorship. Our aim is to offer our readers around the world one thing: an independence of judgment, the assurance that whatever mistakes we make are our own, not the result of

being bent to someone else's agenda. If we start to censor ourselves over 400 copies in Singapore, readers the world around will have reason to doubt our credibility. . . .

We will continue to report on Singapore as best we can from afar, . . . But we are determined that when we circulate in Singapore it will be with our credibility intact.[163]

On October 19, Gus Yatron, senior U.S. congressman and chairman of the House Foreign Affairs Subcommittee on Human Rights and International Organizations, wrote a letter to Lee expressing his concern at the *AWSJ* decision to halt its circulation in Singapore "in response to press restrictions." Reiterating that foreign publications circulate as a privilege in Singapore, ambassador S.R. Nathan stated in a letter to the *AWSJ* that its cessation of circulation would not affect the flow of information in Singapore.[164]

Asked in Hongkong during a stopover that same day, while en route to China about the *AWSJ* cessation of circulation in Singapore, Lee sniggered: "I sympathize with the *AWSJ* in wanting to use this occasion to gain added publicity . . . It's their prerogative. They are entitled to sell 400 copies. They've now chosen to sell nothing. . . . I don't understand what the purpose is."[165] Employing the same logic that the cessation by the paper was to "inconvenience Singapore readers," Lee dismissively replied, "The decision would not create any problems because Singapore readers could always get any important information of interest faxed to them immediately."[166]

Lee's stopover in Hongkong was to deliver a keynote address at the biennial Commonwealth Press Union (CPU) conference—an association of about 500 newspapers, news agencies and periodicals in 30 Commonwealth countries. An anonymous correspondent observed in the *South China Morning Post*, the incongruity of Lee as the CPU's guest of honour "considering that he had done more to inhibit press freedom in Asia than any other so-called 'democratic' leader."[167] On October 15, 1990, Lee spoke, inter alia, on the role of the Western media in Hongkong politics and its interference in Singapore's domestic politics:

> New technology has made it difficult if not impossible to censor or shut out news carried in the world press. The photocopier, fax machines, computers and satellites make it increasingly difficult to block out news from any literate society connected electronically to this modern world.
>
> But this does not entitle the regional newspapers based in Hongkong and owned by American news corporations to intrude into the domestic debate of small countries and settle their agenda. To remove any doubt over this, the Singapore government has enacted laws which enable us to gazette any foreign newspaper which has interfered in Singapore's domestic politics. The papers concerned are American-owned, based in Hongkong reporting on Singapore to Singaporeans and to others in the region. Gazetting does not mean a ban, but only a limit on their sales of papers with advertisements. If they do not carry advertisements, there is no restriction to the number they may sell. In retaliation, the American press mounted a strong campaign. The European press gave them sympathetic support. But Singapore voters were unmoved. In the last elections in Singapore in September 1988, they gave the Singapore government a solid majority in parliament with over 61 percent of the votes. The American press discovered that whilst they could move mountains in Washington, they were not an irresistible force in a foreign Third World country like Singapore.
>
> The Singapore position is straightforward. It will not allow interference by foreigners in its domestic debate. Singapore's voters are English-educated unlike voters in other countries

in Asia. Singapore is a totally urban society with state-of-art telecommunications and no government can effectively censor what the people read. But the government can and will insist on no foreign interference in the domestic politics of Singapore. We do this by insisting on our right of reply, or if it persists in its partisan reporting of Singaporean issues in order to influence political developments in Singapore, we will restrict the number of copies they can sell.

You may ask what does Singapore gain by this. Well, amongst other things, it brings home to Singaporeans that regardless of the pontifications of foreign correspondents and commentators, it is the values of the elected government of Singapore that must and will prevail. Ministers in Singapore are rational and logical people. They do understand the Western world and the changes which Western technology has brought about. They welcome, indeed they embrace, these changes. Singapore has found its niche in the world as a centre for trade, finance, banking, transportation and telecommunications because its ministers have recognized and embraced these innovations. But the Singapore government cannot change its stand that the political process of Singapore is reserved only for Singaporeans.[168]

During the question-and-answer session, Lee said that the influence of the Western media in Hongkong could be discerned from the style of some of its newspapers. In journalism, as in tennis or golf, there was a certain pace about it, and this was set by the most successful countries. And, so far, the most successful was the United States whose media thus set the pace and style. Many Hongkong newspapers over a period of time followed it. This involved, among other things, taking a certain position. "I have noticed over the years . . . they have tried to clothe themselves with certain of the salient characteristics of an independent, fiercely original and fearless purveyor of views and opinions. And the tide had swept over a large number of Hongkong newspapers," he said. But, when he met Hongkong Chinese journalists "one-to-one," he found that their position was not quite the same.

Foreign correspondents in Singapore had also been influencing local journalists, including those in the *Straits Times*. "That made it necessary for us to offer foreign correspondents TV time, one-to-one, so that we can show that such profound truths which they assume for granted cannot be so easily proved to be profound. This shifted the thinking of the Singapore journalist. It was part of the education process."

Within a fortnight, on October 26, 1990, addressing the Foreign Correspondents' Club, Hongkong, Lee declared:

Amongst the predictable changes is the change in the climate for Western correspondents who use Hongkong to cover the region. Hongkong has provided them with a perch from which to watch events in Asia and to comment on them with that ineffable air of sublime confidence. It is the only place in Asia where the white man still rules. Such a place is not replaceable. All the alternatives, Tokyo, Seoul, Taipei, Manila, Bangkok, Kuala Lumpur or Jakarta do not offer the same congenial ambience for expatriates. If I am right about this, then you should not rule out Singapore. For come 1997, Singapore will look somewhat different from the orderly but sterile, efficient but dull and authoritarian place it has been made out to be. . . .

There has been an unofficial network of mutual editorial support linking the Hongkong foreign publications with regional English-language newspapers and weeklies. Expatriate Americans, British, Australians and New Zealanders editing the English-language papers in Asian capitals share common interests with expatriate journalists in Hongkong. This mutual network support will break up as indigenous Asians take charge of their papers. The mood in Asia is changing. There is self-confidence in their capacity to modernize and compete. There are new models to emulate.

An obvious one is Japan. Japan's successful economy is based on her political and social stability, her orderliness, low crime rates, negligible drug-taking, and strong communitarian values.

Asians are in little doubt that a society with communitarian values where the interests of society take precedence over that of the individual suits them better than the individualism of America. Asians see Japanese achievement standards as higher. And the Japanese are not pushy proselytizers, at least not yet.[169]

During the question-and-answer session, *AWSJ's* Claudia Rosett asked Lee whether he thought intelligent and sophisticated Singaporeans would ever become politically mature enough to allow the marketplace of ideas to help them decide what they should read rather than depend on his rules. Annoyed at the exposure of his underbelly, Lee retorted that while he had agreed to play by the rules of GATT—General Agreement on Tariffs and Trade—in the marketplace of products, he did not extend that to the marketplace of ideas and, tangentially, perorated:

> You quote me a U.N. declaration or a bilateral treaty I have with the Americans that you can enter my marketplace of ideas.
>
> The Singaporean is intelligent, sophisticated and knowledgeable. That was why he voted for the same government time and again and gave me 61 percent of the votes in 1988, after I had had a row with the *AWSJ* and the *Review* and the *Asiaweek* and the *Time* magazine.[170]

And added, impertinently, that a Singaporean "can read it for much less," alluding to the officially connived, pirated *Review*, which was being sold weekly in Singapore at about half the usual cost.

Dismissing the suggestion that he was practising a double standard when he did not allow the foreign press to "meddle" in Singapore politics while he himself often commented on politics in other countries, he airily replied that his comments had to be seen in perspective: "If it's a passing comment on a casual basis, no stone will be worn out by a drip of opinion. . . . But when a weekly or daily newspaper writes about Singaporeans for Singaporeans in order to influence the kind of decisions that Singaporeans must make . . . then it is—if you don't like the phrase "interference in Singapore politics"—participating in the Singapore decision-making process." He did not exclude the foreign press from participating in Singapore politics, but what he insisted on was that if they wanted to meddle in Singapore politics, they had to play by his rules. "And my rules require that I will have the right to reply to what you have said, whether you like it or not."

Commenting on Lee's criticism of the role of the Western media in Hongkong politics, Hongkong barrister Gladys Li, Q.C., wrote:

> The leaders of nations sometimes lose touch with the views and feelings of the people they govern, even in a democratic society. When they do, it is one of the functions of a free press to report on and reflect those unheard views and feelings. The press can then become a convenient scapegoat when the leaders continue to ignore these views and feelings, and public protests ensue. If the message is unpalatable, it's the messenger's fault!
>
> Underlying the whole of Lee's speech is the theme that ordinary mortals cannot be trusted to interpret for themselves what they see and what they read. This is a sad reflection on himself.[171]

On November 9, 1990, major foreign publications circulating in Singapore were ordered to post a security bond of S$500,000 (US$294,000) as a new legal requirement, effective on December 1.[172] But, on November 13, 1990, 14 foreign publications were exempted from its provisions on the ground that they did not report on Singapore, or had not "interfered" in Singapore's domestic affairs. They included *Time, Newsweek,* and *The Economist* magazines, the Thai-language newspaper *Thai Rath,* the *International Herald Tribune,* the *Asahi Shimbun* satellite edition, the *Nihon Keizai Shimbun* Asian edition, and the *Financial Times.* The exemption, however, did not include the three Hongkong-based publications—the *Asian Wall Street Journal,* the *Far Eastern Economic Review,* and the *Asiaweek* magazine, its Chinese edition *Yazhou Zhoukan,* as well as the advertising and marketing trade publication, *Media.* "The pirate advertisement-free edition of the *Far Eastern Economic Review,* printed in Singapore with government approval but without the consent of the copyright owners, is believed to be exempt from the need to apply for a permit."[173]

In conclusion, the control over the foreign media varies only in scope and emphasis from the control over the local media, which has already been touched upon; but, in summary, it is exercised through one or more of these means: (1) the issuance, denial or nonrenewal of a foreign correspondent's employment pass; (2) the expulsion of a foreign journalist or the denial of admission at points of entry into Singapore; (3) the threat of legal proceedings such as committal proceedings, criminal defamation prosecutions or libel actions; (4) the restriction in circulation of a foreign publication in Singapore; and (5) the declaration that a publication is an "offshore newspaper," whereupon it is required to, amongst other conditions, provide a bond deposit of a stipulated amount with the government.

As at end of 1991, there were 119 accredited correspondents or cameramen based in Singapore, representing 63 foreign news agencies, news magazines, newspapers and broadcasting stations. Among the agencies were: Reuters, United Press International, Associated Press, Agence France-Presse, Kyodo News Service, Bernama, Tass News Agency, AP-Dow Jones Economic Report, ANSA News Agency, Jiji Press, Allegemeiner Deutscher Nachrichtendiest, United News of India, Central News Agency, Novosti Press Agency, Xinhua News Agency, Press Trust of India and Knight-Ridder Financial News.

Some well-known daily newspapers and news magazines have established bureaus in Singapore, such as the *Asahi Shimbun, Sankei Shimbun, Yomiuri Shimbun, Nihon Keizai Shimbun,* the *Melbourne Age, Neue Zuercher Zeitung,* Netherland Press Association and the *International Herald Tribune.*[174] Among the notable absentees are the *Far Eastern Economic Review* and the *Asian Wall Street Journal.*

Singapore: A Salubrious Perch?

At the Foreign Correspondents' Club, Hongkong, Lee panegyrized that, after 1997 following Hongkong's return to China, Singapore would be the most attractive possible alternative to their loss of the Hongkong "perch." It may be wishful thinking, if not rather premature, on Lee's part, in the light of a subsequent Malaysian government announcement of its intention to turn Kuala Lumpur—the capital city of Malaysia—into "a media and information centre for the region." The Malaysian government is sparing no efforts to actively woo the regional and international publications presently based in Hongkong with tax breaks and perks, liberalization of rules and regulations to make it not only attractive but easier for foreign newsmen to set up their operations, obtain work permits, office space and accommodation, etc. Towards this end, Malaysia is "upgrading its communications infrastructure" and put its own communications satellite known as "Measat" in orbit in early 1996.[175] It will pose a direct and serious challenge to Singapore's own attempts to make the island republic the regional media and information hub. The Singapore government cannot hope to accomplish its objective without loosening up its own rigid media command and relaxing its attitudinal aggression towards foreign publications if it wants to lure them over to set up or indeed even remain in Singapore. Competition may yet refine and smooth the sharp and ugly features of Singapore authoritarianism.

The Right of Reply Revisited

Almost every major Singapore ministry, statutory board and important department of government, as already noted, has its own public relations officer or ad hoc press secretary, whose duty is to screen daily the media for any perceived press misdemeanours and, whenever necessary, prepare draft letters in reply for approval by the respective minister, before dispatch. It is, however, more often than not the minister himself, who drafts or "fine-tunes" the letters in reply for signature by the relevant officer or press secretary. In any event, the letters are vetted by him before signature and dispatch. Lee no longer drafts the letters himself but leaves it to his press secretary who, if necessary, liaises with the other relevant ministers and departments. But they are usually approved by him before the press secretary signs, seals and dispatches them. Letters emanating under the signature of his amanuensis, James Fu, often bear the unmistakable language and style of Lee himself.

The Singapore government is often miffed, as we have noted elsewhere, whenever its letter in rebuttal is edited or not published in full, or at all. It invariably demands as of right a reproduction of its letter in reply, unexpurgated. After all, a lot of thought and effort had gone into crafting the reply even though it may at times appear petty, repetitious or stereotypical to the editor or readers of the publication concerned. The foreign, or, more specifically, the American media's attitude towards the vexed question of the right of reply is best exemplified in the statement of Fred Zimmermann in Dow Jones Publishing (Asia) Inc. application to quash the ministerial orders restricting the circulation of the *AWSJ*:

> It is a fundamental condition of a free press that newspapers should be free to decide what they will print without fear of or favour from any external source, and that it is the judgment of the editor and not the dictates of any government which should determine what appears in the newspaper.[176]

This attitude was amplified by a U.S. State Department communiqué, on March 10, 1987, to the ministry of foreign affairs that the refusal of the *AWSJ* to publish an allegedly "inaccurate report" was consistent with its "commitment to the principles of a free and unrestricted press in American usage." Americans believe that "the press should be free to publish or not publish what it chooses, however irresponsible or biased its actions may seem to be. The logic is that where the media are free, the marketplace of ideas sorts out the irresponsible from the responsible and rewards the latter." It is, indeed, a position at the other end of the spectrum, which the Singapore government rejected outright as "unacceptable."

The Singapore government's stand on the right of reply was repeated by its ambassador to the United States, Tommy T. B. Koh, on February 19, 1987, to Voice of America's director, in response to an editorial broadcast on the *AWSJ* restriction a week earlier:

> All that the Singapore government is asking is that where it disputes the facts, it should have the right to have its views published and published in the way it chooses to present them. Surely competition in the marketplace of ideas does not mean that only the press has the right to publish what it pleases and the aggrieved party, the Singapore government, has no right to respond? Exchange of ideas must be a two-way process.[177]

Ambassador Koh restated the same sentiments in a letter in response to *New York Times* columnist Anthony Lewis's column, "Respectful Press?"[178]

Couched in those terms, it is an argument which could find support among many sectors of opinion, but what follows when the right of reply itself is abused, such as nit-picking, tedious repetition, official propaganda or a reply which annoys other readers of the publication or defames the subject of the original report or its author, or where a matter is sub judice. Who is the arbiter of it? "There is nothing in my letter which prejudices the case [against the magazine, &c.] before the courts," saith the persistent James Fu; but the reluctant editor-in-chief Derek Davies thinks otherwise: "We still feel that it is inappropriate. It is not for Fu to decide whether or not there is anything in his letter which would prejudice the case before the courts: that is a matter for the judge."[179] Would the government's undertaking to indemnify the publication from any legal action alone be sufficient? Aside from the legal niceties, there is also the moral aspect. When and where does an editor begin to draw the line and use his blue pencil? As *The Economist* noted, the government replies are "usually in excruciatingly long-winded and boring letters to the editor."[180] The *Asiaweek* magazine letter-page editor's overzealous use of his blue pencil, distorting the Singapore government's reply to its coverage on the so-called Marxist conspiracy, sparked off official anger, and provided the catalyst for its restriction in circulation. Apart from *Asiaweek*, three other international publications, *Time*, the *Asian Wall Street Journal*, and *The Economist*, were gazetted after disputes over their failure to print letters or for printing them in a manner unacceptable to Singapore officialdom.

On May 26, 1987, at the 40th World Congress of Newspaper Publishers, Helsinki, Brig. Gen. Lee Hsien Loong said that the government's dispute with *Time* magazine and the *Asian Wall Street Journal* revolved around the right of reply, and not around the concept of press freedom:

> My point is simply that the right of newspapers not to publish a reply can hardly be deemed a fundamental one. It is this right of reply which is in contention in the Singapore government's disputes with *Time* magazine and the *Asian Wall Street Journal*. . . . Circulation [of foreign publications in Singapore] is a privilege we grant on terms. One term is that they will publish our corrections and rebuttals. Foreign publications may naturally refuse these terms, in which case they can either not circulate here, or have their circulations restricted. . . .

. . . to describe the influence of the press in Singapore as innocuously contributing to the marketplace of ideas is simplistic. Any elected government of Singapore which adopted a laissez-faire attitude to the foreign press would be in grave dereliction of its duty.

And he proceeded to define the boundary for "foreign publications with significant sales" in Singapore, thus:

Foreign correspondents are free to report about Singapore in any way they choose to foreign audiences, provided they get their facts right. . . . Their ideological biases or political slants do not matter to us. . . .

But when foreign journals with significant circulations in Singapore start to report on Singapore for a Singaporean audience, the government has to take care. We do not want such foreign journals to take sides on domestic political issues, whether to increase their circulation in Singapore, or to campaign for a particular outcome they prefer. The foreign press has no part to play in what should be a purely domestic political process.

. . . But if a foreign newspaper publishes biased one-sided reports and distorts its facts, and the government is unable to compel it to acknowledge errors in its coverage, it can build up unchallenged, a skewed view of reality which will sway opinions and shape events in Singapore. That is why the government considers refusal to publish corrections and rebuttals to be an interference in Singapore's domestic politics. And when a newspaper becomes involved in domestic politics, the government will move to curb it. [181]

A former *AWSJ* editor, Robert Keatley, said of the speech that ". . . the basic problem was that our stories were too accurate—not that they were false or distorted," while Ken Morgan, director of U.K.'s Press Council, called it "the most chilling piece of political language I have heard for a long time," leading him to conclude that "my fellow speaker's government does not understand press freedom, and it leaves me in great doubt as to whether it understands democracy either."[182]

Spelling out the "operative principle" underlying the right of reply, the redoubtable James Fu posited: "When in doubt, ask: Is this meddling in Singaporean domestic politics? As long as Western foreign correspondents report Singapore to their domestic foreign audience, we are not concerned either with their ideological biases, or political slants. When important facts and conclusions are wrong, we write to correct them."[183] It became not uncommon to see not only the name of "James Fu Chiao Sian" appearing as a regular feature, but as many as three other official correspondents nit-picking in the letters columns of the *Review* every week, so much so that many readers were moved to complain.[184] One such correspondent, Lei Ren He, writing from Vancouver, Canada, pleaded: "Is there no respite to be had from the ramblings of various hacks employed by the Singapore government to abuse the patience of the *Review's* subscribers through your correspondence columns. . . . Can we not be spared such infliction in the future?"[185] Explaining his publication of the continuous stream of letters from Singapore officials in the *Review* to the annoyance and boredom of its readers, Davies replied:

We did this only partly because we believe the government has a right of reply; we printed them partly also because their content and tone revealed more about the mentality of Singapore officialdom than could the most gifted journalist.

In 1987 alone, the *Review* published no less than 30 letters from the Singapore government. Notwithstanding, the *Review* was gazetted, moving it to reply:

> For many months now the *Review* has tried the patience of many of its readers by taking the Singapore government at its word. Lee Kuan Yew's son, Brig. Gen. Lee Hsien Loong, recently reconfirmed that international publications would be allowed to circulate freely provided they allowed the government the right to reply to articles it felt were biased or inaccurate. That pledge has been broken with the banning of the *Review* by Singapore on the grounds that the magazine has been "engaging in the domestic politics of Singapore."

But the versatile James Fu denied on behalf of Brig. Gen. Lee Hsien Loong that he had ever given such an assurance, and lapsed into a familiar liturgy:

> Foreign publications are allowed to circulate freely provided they do not engage in Singapore's domestic politics. They should report Singapore as outsiders for outsiders. Refusing the government the right to reply constitutes engagement in Singapore politics.[186]

Asked by the German financial daily *Handelsblatt*, in an interview, why the government was constantly writing letters to newspapers, information minister Brig. Gen. George Yeo replied: "The question to us is: Is it important or not? If it is not important, we don't care. But if it is important, we get the facts right. If we do not get the records straight, then the inaccuracies mount. Then there'll be an erosion of trust and institution's integrity."[187]

But, as Professor Michael Haas noted, the government's claim of a right of reply appears to be a one-way street, for when the government issued clearly defamatory statements about a Catholic priest and a woman in December 1987, neither the priest nor the woman was invited to exercise a right of reply, and the effort of the *Review* to print their side of the story led to restrictions.[188]

Interviews with the Prime Minister

A press interview with the prime minister is not—to use an American metaphor—a cakewalk. He rarely gives walk-in press interviews. A reporter has first to write in for an appointment, spelling out the newspaper he represents, its circulation and other publishing trivia, and reasons for the interview. Depending upon his humour and other obligations, it may be days, weeks and even months before the reporter is deigned with an appointment, if at all. In addition, he has to submit his curriculum vitae and samples of previous journalistic efforts. Before Lee condescends to the request, a list of questions has to be submitted before the date of the interview—which gives him an opportunity to assemble the information requested, as well as other facts and figures. It also provides Lee with an insight into the level of the reporter's approach, competence and expertise.

No deviation from the questionnaire is generally allowed at the interview, as a *Baltimore Sun* Beijing correspondent discovered to his acute embarrassment. He had submitted a list of questions. After the submission but before the appointment date, the Michael Fay case erupted onto the pages of the world's media. When he raised it at the interview, he had his ears bashed—metaphorically speaking—by an irate and defensive Lee for going out of his text. But had the reporter failed to do so, it might have been construed as a reflection on his journalistic expertise and experience. Notwithstanding, Lee is known to terminate interviews abruptly if he considers them a waste of his time. As one journalist said: "You sometimes get the feeling that you are not interviewing him but that he is interviewing you." One common flaw among eager foreign journalists who seek to interview him is that they often neglect to do their homework, thus enabling Lee to run rings round them. There is no way they could ask intelligent, critical and challenging questions save for the template variety. Consider *New Yorker* reporter Stan Sesser's remarks:

> Lee granted me two interviews totalling almost three hours, and instead of evading tough questions in the manner of leaders around the world, he responded to everything directly and frankly. Since Lee possesses an awesome intellect, the interviews turned into an exciting verbal sparring match.
>
> At the end of the second interview, I talked to Lee about his reputation for shouting down reporters and cutting interviews short. Since I had experienced none of this, I asked him whether he was mellowing with age. Lee's reply revealed another interesting facet of this remarkable man. In an era when political leaders are usually no deeper than a sound bite, Lee had taken the time to read a twenty-thousand-word article merely to check out a visiting journalist. "If I know someone is out to get me, I'll get them first." Lee told me. "But I read your article on Laos, and I knew you couldn't have written that unless you had entered the country with an open mind. So I assumed you were open-minded about Singapore, too."[189]

Aping the master, the lesser minions also tend to invest themselves with the same aura of arrogance regarding requests for interviews by foreign correspondents. These foreign correspondents—who eventually are assigned to other places in the region, for example, Malaysia or Thailand—are usually startled to find refreshingly easy access to prime ministers and ministers for press interviews, which are conducted in warm, friendly ambiences. No daunting rigmarole, including the correspondent's curriculum vitae, is requested or demanded prior to an interview. No formal appointments need be made.

I conclude this chapter with an official report on the state of foreign media representation in Singapore as at the end of 1993: There were 178 accredited correspondents representing 73 foreign news agencies, news magazines, newspapers and broadcasting stations.

Among the agencies based here were: Reuters, Associated Press, Agence France-Presse, Kyodo News Service, Jiji Press, Bernama, Itar-Tass News Agency, AP–Dow Jones News Service, Dow-Jones Equity Report, ANSA News Agency, United News of India, Press Trust of India, Central News Agency, Novosti Press Agency, Xinhua News Agency, Knight-Ridder Financial News and VWD Financial News. Among the daily newspapers and news magazines, which established bureaus here, were: *Asahi Shimbun, Disnis Indonesia, Borneo Bulletin, Daily Telegraph, International Herald Tribune, L'Express, Los Angeles Times, Neue Zuercher Zeitung, Nihon Keizai Shimbun, The Age* (Melbourne), *Sankei Shimbun, United Daily News* and *Yomiuri Shimbun*. Among the notable absentees were: the *Asian Wall Street Journal*, the *Far Eastern Economic Review* and *Asiaweek* magazines. Among television and broadcasting organizations based in Singapore were: the All India Radio, BBC, German Radio and Television, Kansai Telecasting Corporation, Nagoya Broadcasting Network, Nippon Hoso Kyokai, Asian Business News, Televisa SA (Mexico) and ZDF German Television.[190]

Notes

1. Closing submission, *Lee Kuan Yew v Derek Davies & ors* (1990). 1 *Malayan Law Journal* 390.

2. Dow Jones, *Lee Kuan Yew vs The News: A History*. New York: Dow Jones Co., 1990.

3. Letters, *Far Eastern Economic Review* (hereafter *Review*), February 4, 1988.

4. Interview, International Press Institute, Helsinki, Finland, June 10, 1971.

5. *Attorney General v Pang Cheng Lian & ors* (1975) 1 *Malayan Law Journal* 69.

6. Michael Haas, "The Politics of Singapore in the 1980s," *Journal of Contemporary Asia*, vol. 19, no. 1 (1989).

7. *Straits Times*, June 4, 1971.

8. Simon Casady, "Lee Kuan Yew & the Singapore Media: Purging the Press," *Index on Censorship*, vol. 4, no. 4 (1975).

9. *Review*, February 24, 1983.

10. S.R. Nathan, who was appointed executive chairman of the *Straits Times* group.

11. Dow Jones, *Lee Kuan Yew vs The News: A History*.

12. "Traveller's Tales," *Review*, May 14, 1987.

13. Letters, *Review*, June 18, 1987.

14. Dow Jones, *Lee Kuan Yew vs The News: A History*.

15. *Attorney General v Fred Zimmermann & ors* (1986), 1 *Malayan Law Journal* 89.

16. October 17, 1985.

17. First Report of the Committee of Privileges, Complaints of Allegations of Executive Interference in the Judiciary, Parliamentary No. 3 of 1987, January 21, 1987, D483 et seq.

18. Ibid.

19. *New York Times*, April 6, 1986.

20. *Times* (London), June 14, 1989.

21. *Times* (London), August 24, 1989.

22. For full text of Fu's letter, see *Review*, January 18, 1988.

23. *New York Times*, February 2, 1990.

24. *Hansard*, Parliamentary debates, May 31, 1988, cols. 299–300.

25. *Straits Times*, Weekly Edition, July 25, 1992. See, also, Tan Teng Lang, *The Singapore Press: Freedom, Responsibility and Credibility*. Singapore: Times Academic Press for the Institute of Policy Studies, 1990.

26. *Hansard*, Parliamentary debates, August 1, 1986, col. 430.

27. *Review*, September 4, 1986.

28. *Hansard*, Parliamentary debates, July 31, 1986, col. 370.

29. *Review*, Letters, Unconvinced, "Pressured press," August 9, 1984; My Pseudonym: Concerned Citizen, "Readers' Rights?," June 18, 1987; Another Apprehensive Singaporean, August 13, 1987; Ho Juan Thai, "Defining an exile," October 15, 1987; Free Spirit, "Weapon backfires," February 18, 1988; and Janamitra Devan, "Singapore Debate," June 2, 1988.

30. "The PM who fines you £50 for not flushing the loo," *Sunday Observer*, December 10, 1989.

31. Minister of State Wong Kan Seng, ministry of communications and information: "Since 1974, the sales in Singapore of foreign publications have increased. The total circulation of some of the major dailies and weeklies like *Asiaweek*, *Review*, *International Herald Tribune*, *Time*, *Asian Wall Street Journal* and *Newsweek*, is about 59,000." *Hansard*, Parliamentary debates, July 31, 1986, col. 370.

32. *Dow Jones Publishing Company (Asia) Inc. v Attorney General* (1989). 2 *Malayan Law Journal* 385. See, also, *Straits Times*, March 15, 1989.

33. In *Lawasia: Journal of the Law Association for Asia and the Pacific*. University of Technology, Sydney, 1987.

34. *Hansard*, Parliamentary debates, July 31, 1986, col. 374.

35. *The Right to Be Heard: Singapore's Dispute with TIME Magazine & the Asian Wall Street Journal: The Facts.* Singapore: Ministry of Communications & Information, May 1987.

36. Dow Jones, *Lee Kuan Yew vs the News: A History.*

37. Ibid. See also, *The Right to Be Heard.*

38. Dow Jones, *Lee Kuan Yew vs the News: A History.*

39. *The Right to Be Heard,* op. cit.

40. Ibid.

41. *Hansard*, Parliamentary debates, March 20, 1987, col. 672.

42. *Dow Jones Publishing Company (Asia) Inc. v Attorney General.*

43. *Asian Wall Street Journal*, February 24, 1987.

44. *Asian Wall Street Journal*, April 13, 1987.

45. *Asian Wall Street Journal*, February 26, 1987.

46. *Dow Jones Publishing Company (Asia) Inc. v Attorney General.*

47. *The Right to Be Heard,* op. cit.

48. *Hansard*, Parliamentary debates, March 20, 1987, col. 672.

49. *Straits Times,* March 21, 1987.

50. *Straits Times,* April 15, 1987. See also Dow Jones, *Lee Kuan Yew vs. The News: A History.*

51. *Statutes of Singapore,* 1985 edition.

52. *Dow Jones Publishing Company (Asia) Inc. v Attorney General* (1988) 2 *Malayan Law Journal* 416, 417.

53. *Associated Provincial Picture Houses Ltd. v Wednesbury Corporation* (1947) 2 All E.R. 680; Dow Jones, *Lee Kuan Yew vs the News: A History.*

54. Published by the ministry of communications and information, and distributed at the 40th World Congress of Newspaper Publishers, Helsinki, in May 1987.

55. *Hansard*, Parliamentary debates, March 15, 1967, cols. 1294–1295.

56. *J.B. Jeyaretnam v Law Society of Singapore* (1988). 3 *Malayan Law Journal* 425.

57. *Dow Jones Publishing Company (Asia) Inc. v Attorney General* (1989) 2 *Malayan Law Journal* 385.

58. Ibid., pp. 385 and 391.

59. Ibid., p. 395.

60. Ibid., p. 396. See *The Economist*, "No Love Lost in Singapore," August 11, 1990.

61. Ibid., p. 396.

62. Ibid., pp. 321 and 322–323.

63. *Straits Times,* July 24, 1990.

64. Ibid.

65. *Wall Street Journal*, July 23, 1990; *Lee Kuan Yew vs the News: A History.*

66. Speech, Chinese Chamber of Commerce, Singapore, October 3, 1965.

67. *Wall Street Journal*'s publisher and editor.

68. *Asian Wall Street Journal*, July 31, 1990.

69. For exchange of correspondence between Karen Elliot House and Goh Chok Tong, see *Asian Wall Street Journal*, August 13, 1990.

70. *Straits Times,* June 18, 1991.

71. *Straits Times,* Weekly Edition, November 23, 1991.

72. *Asiaweek,* September 27, 1987.

73. Margaret Scott, "A Meeting of Minds," *Review*, October 27, 1988.

74. *Asiaweek,* March 24, 1995.

75. *Straits Times,* December 27, 1987 and *Far Eastern Economic Review,* January 7, 1988.

76. *Asiaweek,* January 7, 1988.

77. *Hansard*, Parliamentary debates, January 27, 1988, col. 446.

78. Chapter 63, Statutes of Singapore, 1985 ed.

79. *Hansard*, Parliamentary debates, January 27, 1988, col. 448.

80. Singapore is not a signatory to the International Copyright Convention or the Berne Convention on Copyright, but has its own law which prohibits reproduction without copyright unless the material is for study or research; *Review*, January 21, 1988.

81. *Hansard*, Parliamentary debates, January 27, 1988, col. 448.

82. *Singapore Yearbook 1989*, Singapore: Ministry of Communications and Information, 1988, p. 157.

83. In February, 1988, the U.S. government publicly criticized the officially sanctioned theft of the *Review*'s copyrighted materials.

84. Letters, Ashleigh Seow, "Separate Activities," *Review*, April 14, 1988.

85. *Hansard*, Parliamentary debates, May 29, 1989, col. 58.

86. In September 1993, the durable James Fu retired as director, and joined Hongkong's Sing Tao publishing group as group general manager, on a three-year contract, whose head is none other than Sally Aw Sian. He was succeeded by Mdm. Yeong Yoon Ying, a senior official in the ministry of information and the arts: *Straits Times*, Weekly Edition, September 25 and December 4, 1993.

87. *Far Eastern Economic Review*, February 11, 1988.

88. *Straits Times*, July 8, 1989.

89. *Lee Kuan Yew v Derek Davies & ors* (1990) 1 *Malayan Law Journal* 390.

90. *Straits Times*, October 27, 1990.

91. *Wall Street Journal*, December 1-2, 1989.

92. *Straits Times,* December 20, 1989.

93. *Wall Street Journal*, February 11 and March 27, 1991.

94. *Straits Times*, January 7, 1991.

95. The accompanying editorial was entitled "Settlement in Singapore," *Wall Street Journal,* March 27, 1991.

96. *New York Times*, March 31, 1991.

97. *Straits Times*, June 18, 1991.

98. Letters, Goh Yew Heng, "Detainee Teo still a threat," *Review*, March 22, 1990.

99. *Review*, April 28, 1994.

100. *The Economist,* June 26, 1993.

101. Philip Shenon, "2 Faces of Singapore: Lofty Aims, Press Curbs," *New York Times* August 5, 1993.

102. Ponting, a civil servant, was charged with but acquitted of leaking information under the Official Secrets Act during the Falklands War.

103. *Straits Times,* August 3, 1993.

104. See ibid. for the full exchange of correspondence between *The Economist* and the Singapore government.

105. Letters, J.B. Jeyaretnam, "Singapore prosecutions," *The Economist*, July 16, 1993.

106. For the exchange of letters, see *Straits Times*, August 3, 1993.

107. "A Singapore saga," *The Economist*, August 7, 1993.

108. Letters, Terence Chou, "Singapore Saga," *The Economist*, August 14, 1993; Suzanne Hill and Michael Jennings respectively, "Sick of Singapore," *The Economist*, August 26, 1995.

109. *The Economist*, August 26, 1995.

110. *New York Times*, August 6, 1995; *Straits Times*, August 7, 1995.

111. *Straits Times,* October 21, 1994.

112. *International Herald Tribune*, December 10–11, 1994.

113. *Straits Times,* Weekly Edition, December 12, 1994.

114. Chris Merritt, "Singapore law in time capsule, says Kirby," *Australian Financial Times* February 9, 1995.

115. *Straits Times,* Weekly Edition, February 11, 1995.

116. *Straits Times,* February 8, 1995.

117. *International Herald Tribune,* January 19, 1994.

118. *International Herald Tribune,* August 2, 1994.

119. *International Herald Tribune,* August 31, 1994.

120. *Straits Times,* August 7, 1995.

121. Ibid.

122. *International Herald Tribune,* August 31, 1994. See, generally, Garry Rodan, "Symbolic Clash with International Press in Singapore," *Asiaview,* vol. 5 no 1, April 1995.

123. Haas, "The Politics of Singapore in the 1980s." See, also, *Review,* "The 5th Column," March 10, 1988; and *Review,* Letters, "The enemy within," March 24, 1988.

124. *Straits Times,* February 27, 1988.

125. Hass, "The Politics of Singapore in the 1980s."

126. *Straits Times,* April 27, 1991.

127. *Straits Times,* Weekly Edition, November 23, 1991.

128. *Straits Times,* July 8, 1965.

129. Ibid.

130. Ibid.

131. *Tun* Abdul Razak, acting prime minister of Malaysia.

132. Both were detained in Operation Cold Store. A. Mahadeva was editor of the SNUJ organ, *Wartawan,* which was also proscribed at the same time.

133. Alex Josey returned to Singapore after it was no longer in Malaysia, and resumed work as a free-lance journalist.

134. *Straits Times,* March 1, 1977.

135. *Straits Times,* March 19, 1983.

136. Haas, "The Politics of Singapore in the 1980s."

137. Dow Jones, *Lee Kuan Yew vs the News: A History,* p. 34.

138. *Review,* May 14, 1987.

139. *Review,* May 28, 1987.

140. "Foreign newsmen can expect a welcome mat, not an open door," *Straits Times,* Weekly Edition, October 10, 1992.

141. *Straits Times,* Weekly Edition, August 14, 1993.

142. *Review,* February 11, 1988.

143. *Silencing All Critics: Human Right Violations in Singapore.* New York: Asia Watch 1989.

144. *Review,* November 9, 1989.

145. Philip Bowring was later replaced by L. Gordon Crovitz, and reports had it at the time that it was to please the prime minister.

146. *Hansard,* Parliamentary debates, March 23, 1977, cols. 1522–1523.

147. *Hansard,* Parliamentary debates, August 1, 1986, col. 428.

148. Ibid., col. 432.

149. Dow Jones, *Lee Kuan Yew vs. The News: A History.*

150. *Straits Times,* April 19, 1983.

151. Roger Mitton, *Straits Times,* Weekly Edition, October 10, 1992.

152. *Straits Times,* June 1, 1994.

153. Reyes's interview at the Harvard Law School, Cambridge, Massachusetts, in January 1994 entitled "Outside Looking In: An Exile Talks About Himself—and Lee Kuan Yew," appeared in *Asiaweek*, February 9, 1994.

154. *The Sydney Morning Herald*, March 23, 1995.

155. Editorial footnote to Charles Wallace, "Singapore's grip," *Columbia Journalism Review*, November-December 1995.

156. *The Sydney Morning Herald*, March 23, 1995.

157. *Straits Times*, Weekly Edition, October 10, 1992.

158. *Review*, March 9, 1989.

159. Elliott S. Parker, "Singapore," *World Press Encyclopedia*.

160. *Straits Times*, April 30, 1992. See also "Go for BBC ideal, BG Lee tells press," *Straits Times*, February 27, 1988.

161. *Straits Times*, August 4, 1993.

162. *Straits Times*, August 31, 1990.

163. A similar editorial appeared in the *Wall Street Journal*.

164. *Wall Street Journal*, October 30, 1990.

165. Singapore Press Holdings prints 12,000 to 13,000 copies daily for regional distribution.

166. *Straits Times*, October 16, 1990.

167. *South China Morning Post*, October 17, 1990.

168. "The Singapore Raj," *South China Morning Post Asian Wall Street Journal*, October 18, 1990.

169. *Straits Times*, October 27, 1990. See Editorial, "White man's Plot?," *Asian Wall Street Journal*, October 29, 1990.

170. *Straits Times*, October 27, 1990.

171. *Review*, November 1, 1990. See, also, Editorial, "Spontaneous reaction," *South China Morning Post*, October 16, 1990.

172. *Asian Wall Street Journal*, November 9, 1990.

173. *Review*, November 22, 1990.

174. *Singapore 1992*. Singapore: Ministry of Information and the Arts, 1993.

175. *Straits Times*, June 19, 1993.

176. *Dow Jones Publishing Company (Asia) Inc. v Attorney General* (1989) 2 *Malayan Law Journal* 385, 389.

177. Ibid., p. 388.

178. *New York Times*, March 14, 1987.

179. Letters, "Singapore's side of the story," *Review*, January 21, 1988.

180. "No love lost in Singapore," *The Economist*, August 11, 1990.

181. Speech, "When the Press Misinforms," Brig. Gen. Lee Hsien Loong.

182. Derek Davies, "Traveller's Tales," *Review*, June 25, 1987; Letters, James Fu, "Replying to reply," *Review*, July 9, 1987.

183. Letters, "Rule No. 1: No playing games," *Review*, May 28, 1987.

184. See, also, Letters, "Sick of Singapore," *The Economist*, August 24, 1995.

185. Letters, "The rambling voices of officialdom," *Review*, August 24, 1989.

186. *Review*, January 14, 1988. See, also, *Dow Jones Publishing Company (Asia) Inc. v Attorney General* (1989) 2 *Malayan Law Journal* 385.

187. As reported in *Straits Times*, August 4, 1993.

188. Michael Malik, "New Light on Detentions," *Review*, December 17, 1987.

189. Stan Sesser, *The Lands of Charm and Cruelty: Travels in Southeast Asia*. New York: Alfred A. Knopf, 1993.

190. *Singapore 1994*. Singapore: Ministry of Information and the Arts, 1995.

8 Inside the Web

-
-
-
-
  If your ideas, your views cannot stand the challenge of criticism, then they are too fragile, and not sturdy to last.

  Lee Kuan Yew[1]
-
-
-
-

During the 1956 public security debate in the Legislative Assembly, Assemblyman Lee Kuan Yew vociferously assailed the chief minister, David Saul Marshall, and his Labour Front government for prolonging the 1948 Emergency Regulations under the new guise of the Preservation of Public Security Ordinance, which was itself later replaced by the Internal Security Act (ISA). Lee was then speaking as an opposition PAP assemblyman. Notwithstanding, his stirring, earthy words, spoken more than three decades ago, still bear repetition, and are more than relevant today:

> Repression, Sir, is a habit that grows. I am told it is like making love—it is always easier the second time! The first time there may be pangs of conscience, a sense of guilt. But once embarked on this course with constant repetition you get more and more brazen in the attack. All you have to do is to dissolve organizations and societies and banish or detain the key political workers in these societies. Then miraculously everything is tranquil on the surface. *Then an intimidated press and the government-controlled radio together can regularly sing your praises, and slowly and steadily the people are made to forget the evil things that have already been done, or if these things are referred to again they're conveniently distorted and distorted with impunity, because there will be no opposition to contradict.*[2] [Author's emphasis]

Although, strictly speaking, there is no direct censorship of the print media in Singapore, censorship is nevertheless visible in many forms and disguises.[3] The hand of the censor is more often felt rather than seen. For Lee and his government dominate or influence the press in their own inimitable way. Apart from the Newspaper and Printing Presses Act, as repeatedly amended, which provides for certain regulatory offences and penalties thereunder, the government exercises control on the print media through a variety of ways and means, some of which we have already seen, and some specific instances of which are addressed below.

In the days when newspaper companies were independently owned, the annual publishing and printing permits were powerful Damoclean swords, which the government wielded with devilish skill to "persuade" newspaper owners and editors to comply with its orders or directions. Needless to say, a delay in the approval or, worse, the nonapproval of the annual publishing or printing licence presented dreadful economic consequences for a newspaper-owning company, and was to be avoided assiduously.

We have seen earlier the use of the order of suspension or cancellation of the permit as a means of control, which could in either case paralyse the operation of a newspaper or a printing press. In January 1980, the afternoon Chinese tabloids, the *Shin Min Daily News* and the *Min Pao Daily*, were denied a publishing permit for eight days, and, after the papers had pledged not to continue to play up "crime, sex and violence," their permits were renewed but only for three months, instead of the normal one year.

The summary expulsion of key foreign media personnel or journalists employed in local newspaper companies from Singapore is a means of control, which has been dealt with earlier.

Official Advertisements

Newspapers rely on commercial and business advertisements and on legal and official notices for their bread and butter. Official advertisements can be employed, and are used, as an indirect means of control over the media. A signal that a local newspaper may not be in the good books of the government is perceived when there is a deliberate denial of valuable official advertisements and notices, which may represent a substantial portion of its revenue, a loss of which could have serious financial consequences. When the former City Council was under the administration of its erratic PAP mayor, Ong Eng Guan, he ordered the City Council administration to stop giving official advertisements to the pro-establishment newspaper, *Straits Times*, and for one year the Council's works, tenders and legal notices were publicized in improvised news-sheets in English.[4]

Where the *Eastern Sun* and the *Singapore Herald*, however, were concerned, it was the prime minister's office—which expressly instructed heads of government departments, statutory boards and government-controlled companies, which had business or official dealings with the public—not to give any official advertisements and legal notices to them. They were also denied press facilities.[5] Moreover, no "government replies" were extended to correspondents' letters to the editors of those newspapers as a further mark of official disfavour.

In the early years, when the PAP's political fortune was less predictable, the press and pressmen were carefully nurtured for their support. Lee assiduously courted or cajoled them to write agreeable news accounts of him, his party and his government. Many did, but there were others whose commitment was not as constant or as consistent as he would have liked, and who had to be tiresomely nurtured. Francis Wong, editor of the defunct *Sunday Mail*, and subsequently of the star-crossed *Singapore Herald*, was one such journalist, who emerged a political casualty from the PAP's battle for the hearts and minds of the people in the sixties and seventies. *Straits Times* editor-in-chief L.C. Hoffman, who was engaged in a running media war with Lee, did not hesitate but swiftly removed himself from Singapore even before Lee and his noisy PAP colleagues were installed as government du jour. Setting media bête noire aside, Lee appreciates, more than any other Singapore politician, the importance of a good press and the importance of control, not necessarily through actual ownership of the news media, for the advancement of a political party's agenda. In this respect, Lee and the PAP differ markedly from the ruling party across the causeway, where UMNO owns and controls a newspaper empire. An uninformed or disagreeable press could work untold damage to the political prospects of a party or a government. Thus, Lee made it a daily practice to comb through the newspapers, especially the vernacular papers, to ensure whether they had correctly reported the news and events about him, his party and his government. Unversed himself in the *Jawi* script,[6] Lee relied upon his precocious young son, Hsien Loong, for translation: "My son learns Jawi. Every day he reads the newspapers and tells me what they scold me [for]."[7] There is no Malay press today in Singapore which prints in *Jawi*, save in Malaysia.

Some years ago, the government announced its intention to acquire a vast and valuable cemetery for public development in uptown Singapore over the vigorous protests of the Hakka Chinese community which owned the graveyard. All appeals, including to Lee, who is himself a Hakka, were turned down. At about that time, as fate would have it, a distinguished Hakka Chinese leader died in a tragic plane crash overseas, and his earthly remains were brought back to Singapore for burial, the press reported, in the very same cemetery, for which the relevant government department had issued a burial permit. No one, save for Lee, spotted the serious bureaucratic blunder or appreciated the possible repercussions of the ethnic or spiritual sensitivities of an outraged community if, soon after solemn interment, the patriarch's grave was exhumed for reinterment elsewhere. An order was swiftly given to cancel the burial permit for another cemetery unaffected by public development.

Apart from bureaucratic blunders and perceived media misreporting, Lee is sensitive to nuances of words and phrases used by the press and of their double entendre which could advance or cast doubt on his government's policy. On occasion, he is known to have instructed newspaper editors on the word or words to be omitted or used, and even lectured them on their meanings in a given article. For example, the impersonal reference to him as "the prime minister *of Singapore*" in the Singapore newspapers, during the period when Singapore was a part of Malaysia, irked him, as well as the indiscriminate usage of the word "image" in writings about Singapore and its achievements, with its ephemeral undertone, instead of "reputation" with its more lasting connotation.

His interest also ran well beyond news gathering and news presentation to encompass even commercial and business advertisements, and in such mundane matters as "What the Stars Foretell"—then a regular feature of the *Sunday Times*—and its astrological variants in other Sunday newspapers, until the daily appearance in newspapers of advertisements promising, for a consideration, the efficacious service of computerized fortune-telling. While he was prepared to tolerate the former as an innocuous pastime or diversion of Singaporeans, the advent of the latter prompted him to disapprove of it wholly as an admixture of charlatanry and superstition. In deference to his views, newspapers dropped all such lucrative advertisements, and the *Sunday Times* even ceased publishing its own staple feature. Perhaps Lee was right after all, because none of them could foretell the fate that was to befall their host publications! Former political detainee C.V. Devan Nair, who later ascended astral heights in the PAP firmament, used to relate a lighter moment during his incarceration in the fifties by the colonial government for anti-British activities, of a compassionate British prison officer, who proffered him a copy of the *Sunday Times* newspaper to read, in which he wryly noted that his stars had foretold that he would "do a great deal of travelling this week." But history records that he was firmly locked up in the steadfastness of notorious Changi Prison until he was released in June 1959. Advertisements for certain patent medicines with extravagant healing or health-restorative claims were also stopped. Similarly, when Lee—who was never seen without the then fashionable tin of 50 cigarettes in his hand—developed allergic reactions to tobacco fumes, thus causing him to stop smoking, Singaporeans, too, were advised to do likewise, but, when advice and cajolery were not taken too seriously, it soon transmogrified into a diktat. Newspapers, among others, were instructed, nay ordered, to eschew the lucrative tobacco advertisements. And, bowing to the early PAP puritanical campaign against "yellow culture," newspapers ceased publishing weird, salty or spicy stories or news or photographs of scantily clad females, as well as activities of high society or social trivia and events concerning the rich and famous. But with the establishment of the risqué *New Paper*, the wheel has turned almost full cycle.[8] The information minister said: "We need some pruriency in the tabloids because people need an outlet. I tell the editors, 'We can't stop the public having a prurient interest in scandals and in sensational events, and in the weird and the far-fetched, but please have an overall sense of proportion.'"[9]

In April 1986, government officials were reportedly "furious" with the *Straits Times* for irresponsibly describing the premature arrest of one Peter Tham, a fraud suspect connected to the collapse of Pan-Electric Industries Ltd., a major public company listed on Singapore Stock Exchange. The reporter was dismissed. They claimed the hasty report might have prejudiced Tham's arrest.[10]

In November 1991, the monthly lifestyle local magazine, *Woman's Affair*, was suspended from publication for three months for going "beyond its scope of featuring women's lifestyles, fashion and careers to make a statement about our women MPs." It had published a candid article, "Do Women MPs Measure Up?" which the government considered "negative and biased," although it was based essentially on interviews with women, whose views, however, were critical of women MPs.[11] Lawyer-politician Wee Han Kim wrote to the *Straits Times* querying the suspension:

> This is an example of the PAP government's technique of control by depoliticization. It also implies that the government has power to define the "scope" of the magazine and limit it to women's lifestyles, fashions and careers. It is as if the licence given the *Woman's Affair* specified that it should not run articles on the role of women in politics. After all, is not being a woman MP an acceptable role model for career women?
>
> The real point is that the only women MPs are from the PAP and the statement was negative. If it had been positive, would the authorities have complained? . . .
>
> By the way, am I going beyond my scope, by commenting on women's affairs?[12]

Needless to say, his letter was not published. Columnist Raymond Lim, writing in *Viewpoint* captioned, "Will the Next Lap Be a New Era of Intolerance?," questioned the suspension, and asked whether a "rap on the knuckles" and a "warning" would not have sufficed in the circumstances. "Was it necessary to tie the writing hand altogether?"[13]

As the PAP entrenched itself deeper into the body politic, it became commonplace for newspaper owners and editors to receive calls from government officials, usually the press secretary to the prime minister, regarding the publication of specific news items, or their disappointment at the way an article, news item or policy had been presented, or for certain news items to be ignored or muted. Recalcitrant owners and editors, on occasion, were firmly told that they had strayed beyond the pale of nation-building and national security. Turnbull's *Dateline Singapore*, replete with instances of official interventions, related that the prime minister "on occasion summoned and harangued editors." Lee Siew Yee, deputy editor-in-chief of the *Straits Times,* recalled two "extremely unpleasant meetings in 1960 and 1967, when Lee made clear, in brutal language, that the *Straits Times* was 'on sufferance.'"[14] Former *Herald* editor Francis Wong put it: "The Singapore press has been docile for a long time. When the prime minister's office calls up and tells a paper not to print a story, they don't do it. *But we refused to go along and Lee was probably afraid this would spread.*"[15] [Author's emphasis]

When the *Singapore Herald* refused to comply with ministerial directives or injunctions on publication, it faced, as we have seen, Lee's full wrath with its inevitable consequences. Despite official warnings not to publish the expulsion from Singapore of Shirle Gordon, an American woman, whom Lee alleged was a failed CIA agent, the *Herald* nevertheless gave it press coverage.[16] Former *Nanyang Siang Pau* general manager Lee Mau Seng was "advised many times" by foreign minister S. Rajaratnam and culture minister Jek Yuen Thong to refrain from pursuing policies which the government considered inimical to national interests,[17] or, as already noted, the *Utusan Melayu* managing director was pointedly told by Lee himself of the consequences of taking a wrong step. Implicit in all such advice was the veiled threat that if a newspaper did not toe the official line, it would meet with prime ministerial displeasure, which could be unleashed, as noted, in myriad ways. Writing in 1982, Peter Lim claimed that the situation had become better than previously: "At one time there were almost daily calls from ministers telling us what or what not to print, and scolding us for something that had been said. That practice started to taper off about two years ago and now it hardly happens at all."

If, indeed, it had tapered off "and now hardly happens at all," it is probably attributable to the total government control over the media. Journalistic intransigence to official advice today would probably result in lateral shunting or dismissal from service. And with the editorial board and corporate board of newspaper companies now bristling with a cadre of PAP members and government nominees, persuasion is passé. The problem is no longer that of an obstreperous but rather of an obsequious media with a credibility problem. Even Lee was embarrassed by its sycophancy: "I don't want obsequious, inert, dull and stupid newspapers. I want lively and sensible newspapers."[18]

The present political leadership is aware of the necessity for a change in attitude towards the media, but is uncertain of the nature of direction or the limits of that change. The appointment, therefore, of Brig. Gen. George Yeo as information minister may not be entirely accidental, as he appears to be a person after Lee's own heart. He echoes not only the senior minister's thoughts, but apes his turn of phrases with such exactitude that he is spoken of in media circles and elsewhere as the "surrogate son." He is often included in Lee's entourage in his incessant overseas junkets, a sure sign of favour. Like Lee before him, Yeo also appears genuinely desirous of wanting the Singapore media "to blossom and be more analytical, outward-looking and sophisticated," but yet fully cognizant of the injunction that the government would "still have the final say on what they can do."[19] It is a fine but difficult line to walk.

A Special Relationship?

While decrying the media as a fourth estate for Asia, particularly Singapore, MITA minister Brig. Gen. George Yeo nonetheless makes this intriguing observation:

> The media as a group are part of the establishment. And to that extent, they would share many of the values of the PAP government. On core principles, I think we are generally agreed. It doesn't mean we agree on the details. Reporters [and] editors don't take instructions from civil servants or ministers. We discuss, we complain, we exchange views. That we do, because we're all part of the establishment.[20]

He contends that the PAP government does "not send directives to the newspapers that they have to conform" and ministers or MPs, even opposition MPs, can suggest to editors how they should handle a story, or give advice, and herein lies the rub—it does not mean that the editor or the reporter should oblige or take the advice. But it would be different if the suggestion or advice was made by senior minister Lee Kuan Yew, whose "certain remarks about the journalists at *Business Times*, . . . [will be] listen[ed] to very carefully."[21] *Straits Times* editor-in-chief Cheong Yip Seng revealed that Singapore's papers accede "most times, but not always" when government asks for certain stories to be carried, which as a senior editorial staffer explains "means they are carried out 99.9 percent of the time." Beleaguered *BT* editor Patrick Daniel explained the uneasy Singapore government-press relationship thus:

> If a journalist writes a column arguing a different line to that of the government, he can expect a swift response either in a form of a written reply, meant for publication, attacking his line and pointing out all its errors, or he may be asked to have a discussion where he is persuaded from the wisdom of pursuing their line. In some instances, the journalist may be suspended from attending ministry briefings; and, in more serious cases, when the authorities are concerned about an official leak, he may be questioned by the ISD.[22]

After having recently emerged from the bubbling cauldron of ISD experience, Daniel should know. *Straits Times* editor Leslie Fong, however, put it more starkly:

> [W]here the issue in question is one over which the government has taken a determined stand, there is no doubt whose view will prevail. Should any journalist feel that he cannot accept such an outcome, then resignation is the only honourable course open to him. This is just one of the harsh realities which the press here faces.[23]

In the final analysis, the entire Singapore Press Holdings (SPH) board of directors consists of PAP cadres, government-nominees and sympathizers. As an anonymous reporter succinctly puts it: "They appoint the editors, and that gives them all the control they need." Control is exerted at all levels. For instance, as part of a media *entente cordiale*, information minister Brig. Gen. George Yeo meets with editors and senior journalists virtually every month over lunch while Lim Kim San, SPH's executive chairman and Lee's alter ego, meets with editors and other senior staffers "every third Wednesday of the month." Although social in character, these are serious meetings where issues of pitch and moment are discussed and direction laid down, which wayward editors, columnists and journalists ignore at their peril.

Ministers and PAP MPs are encouraged to visit Times House—the administrative seat of the SPH—and meet with journalists "so that there's mutual understanding." Everything considered, governmental control of the media is total and absolute. In the circumstances, it is hardly surprising to note the almost trite observation: "In fact, the editorial directions of all domestic dailies manifest a distinctly pro-government bias."[24]

The Asian Mass Communications Research and Information Centre (AMIC) commissioned a survey on the media role in the 1991 general election. The researchers could not but come to the inevitable conclusion that newspapers, radio and television coverage on the election was "skewed heavily towards the ruling party, the PAP. In both newspapers and television, the PAP received twice the amount of coverage as that given to all the opposition parties combined."[25] It was not an epiphany. It was a confirmation of what Singaporeans of all political hues, including other scholars, had known all along. And it did not take into account the superfluous but pertinent fact that throughout the years leading up to the general election the government had virtual monopoly of the mass media—print, voice and visual—to the almost total exclusion of the political opposition.

Hence, it is drolly apposite when one recalls the somewhat provocative remarks of the former minister without portfolio and now president of Singapore, Ong Teng Cheong, who reproached the opposition SDP MP, Chiam See Tong, for barring a news reporter from the SDP fortnightly fora for his consistently biased coverage of those proceedings: "Imagine what would happen to newspapers if he [Chiam] gets into power. I would not be surprised if he revokes their news printing licences, unless they put him in good light all the time."[26] In pointing a disapproving finger at the opposition leader, Ong had overlooked three fingers pointing accusingly back at him.

Media Blackout?

1988 was election year for the seventh parliament of Singapore. On January 12, 1988, opposition Singapore Democratic Party MP Chiam See Tong ventilated in parliament a complaint by former opposition MP J.B. Jeyaretnam of a news blackout on the Worker's Party by the state-controlled television and radio, and asked for the reasons. The information minister deflected the question with a rather impertinent reply: the newsworthiness of the Workers' Party internal "quarrels, dissensions and resignations" were in the limited air time available for TV and radio news, "matters for the editors to decide."[27]

On February 26, 1988, Brig. Gen. Lee Hsien Loong told the Singapore Press Club that the press had to be "constructive" and "pro-Singapore," and "being for Singapore will often mean agreeing with the government . . . because the government is often right." And reiterated the threadbare refrain: "Our multi-racial society makes reporting on sensitive subjects a very delicate matter." Specifically rejecting the American press as a model, he said: "In our experience, an unrestrained babel leads to mayhem and riots rather than enlightenment." Inherent in the American model, which his audience ought to resist, was the journalistic "temptation to get involved, to take sides, the wish to influence events," and the desire to "be a player, even a major political force."[28]

Self-Censorship

Not surprisingly in the circumstances, and as a matter of commercial prudence and survival, the mass media practise self-censorship or restraint, mainly publishing news sensitive to government policies and action, and eschewing any letters, views, opinions or comments critical of government or which may displease it.[29] "The papers usually know how far they can go. . . . it is true that items of news which might embarrass the government are often either not made available or are suppressed by the newspapers themselves, knowing that the government would be displeased if they did publish these items."[30] *AWSJ* quoted William Giles, former editor of the *Singapore Sunday Monitor*[31] and now journalism professor, as saying: "The problem is that this sense of self-censorship and self-restraint encourages reporters and editors to censor even more than the authorities intended."[32] *Asiaweek's* Michael O'Neill, however, felt that the standard of Asian journalism would not improve as long as the journalists are "intimidated by their own self-censorship. . . . We have to put the possibility of the midnight knock on the door out of their minds."[33] Institute of Southeast Asian Studies (ISEAS) Fellow Russell Heng thought:

> The problem with self-censorship is that it is self-perpetuating. Edgy writers do not test those vague OB—out-of-bound—markers and therefore have to remain edgy.
> Self-censorship is not the only old habit which needs some changing. Between the writer curbing himself and an officialdom imposing the restrictions is another longstanding censorship machinery. Here, a publisher who will turn down a manuscript for its controversial theme. There, a distributor who will not stock a book because it is too sensitive.[34]

Given the media situation obtaining in Singapore, it comes as no revelation that presentations of news stories have a distinct slant or tilt in favour of officialdom. (See "Same Facts, but Different Slant."[35]) Consider the 1992 Marine Parade GRC—Group Representation Constituency—by-election in which the prime minister, Goh Chok Tong, in fulfillment of a foolish promise made to disbarred lawyer-politician J.B. Jeyaretnam, unnecessarily risked his political fortune by resigning his seat, thus calling a by-election in that GRC. Goh was returned with a slightly reduced majority from his 1988 election. But his electoral victory was bannered the next day on the front page of the *Sunday Times*: "A 73% Resounding Win for PM Goh." His win by a reduced majority, albeit minimal, was glossed over, although it was not without significance to political analysts.[36] Again, when the notorious defamation suit instituted by erstwhile prime minister Lee Kuan Yew against the former president of Singapore and longtime political comrade-in-arms, Devan Nair, was eventually settled through the mediation of their mutual Malaysian friend, the *Straits Times* tendentiously headlined it: "Nair Withdraws Remarks He Made About SM,[37] Withdrawal Accepted, Damages Waived."[38] And, for good measure, it revived the untrue hoary chestnut: "Mr Nair, 70, Singapore's third President, resigned . . . because of alcoholism"—when it was clearly shown that the prime minister had overstated the case. See C.V. Devan Nair's open letter to Lee Kuan Yew.[39] Its stablemate, the *Business Times*, lopsidedly headed the event: "SM Lee Drops Libel Suit Against Devan Nair."[40] In significant contrast, the Hongkong-based *South China Morning Post* on the same day dispassionately captioned the settlement:

"Singapore's Former Leaders Settle War of Words in Court." The settlement of the defamation suit, incidentally, was wholly unprecedented—all other previous settlements were invariably on Lee's terms and conditions.

An excellent, albeit different, example may be seen in this incident. Although no official directive was issued to the *Asiaweek* magazine's distributors to have a phrase descriptive of the prime minister deleted from an article entitled "So That's the Way It Was," the distributors decided, nevertheless, to take no chances, so fearful were they of the consequences of offending him, that they took it upon themselves to delete with black ink the adjectival phrase, "fire-breathing," from it. The article read in part: "In the heady days of Singapore's union with Malaysia in 1964–65, considerable pressure had built up on then Malaysian Prime Minister Tungku Abdul Rahman to put (deleted) Premier of Singapore Lee Kuan Yew under arrest."

Similarly, in 1977, the distributors of the *Review, ex abundanti cautela*, withheld circulation of a particular issue of the magazine, pending clearance by their lawyers that some articles therein and its editor's robust reply dismissing certain charges by the Singapore government did not constitute a libel on the government. This action was taken in great trepidation, notwithstanding the fact that the ministry of culture itself had indicated that it had no objection to its circulation in Singapore. In 1986, author Dennis Bloodworth recorded—among his anecdotes in the *Tiger and the Trojan Horse*, a book on Lee Kuan Yew and the communists—an observation of a minister made earlier to a foreign correspondent that Lee was "surrounded by 'sycophants and bumsuckers' and that, as result, he was becoming arrogant and testy." The Singapore publishers, Times Books International, were said to be "squeamish" at this particular inclusion. To resolve the impasse, Bloodworth sent the galley-proof to the prime minister, who responded with a note that it made "good and interesting reading."[41]

In August 1992, moved by moral rather than economic considerations, *Straits Times* editor-in-chief Cheong Yip Seng stopped the circulation of an issue of an SPH women's lifestyle magazine, *Her World*, because of an article on "flatting out"—a practice among young Singaporean couples, who take an Housing and Development Board (HDB) flat and live together without getting married, until the auspicious day allowed by their respective horoscopes. He had piously feared that the article would "sanctify something that may not be in our community's best interests." The costs of the stoppage were more than S$100,000, quite apart from the delivery delay. The interests of the shareholders, let alone of "intelligent and sophisticated" Singapore readers, were apparently of secondary or no consideration at all.[42]

An illustration of the absurd length to which the media in a closed society would go to avoid possible censure by the authorities is mirrored in the following incident. Some 85 percent of the population live in government-built flats. Following the disappointing loss of two electoral constituencies—Anson and Potong Pasir—to the opposition, the national development minister, Teh Cheang Wan, on March 21, 1985, made a shock announcement in parliament that henceforth the HDB's policy was to give priority to PAP MPs' constituencies on nonemergency services. The *Straits Times* carried out a telephone survey, and reported that the public's reaction to the ministerial proposal was generally adverse. The *Business Times*, on the other hand, published a direct and pungent editorial entitled "Feedback for Government."

On the night of March 22/23, 1985, the printing presses at Times House, where the *Business Times (BT)* was printed, came to an abrupt stop, and distributed copies of the *Business Times* were frantically recalled, and its leading article changed. Eleven thousand copies had been printed, and about 2,000 copies had already been distributed. News vendors were hastily recalled and instructed to collect them back. All but 30 copies were successfully retrieved. One of them strayed into the hands of opposition MP, J.B. Jeyaretnam. The *BT* leader read:

> If the PAP ever wanted feedback, it has now ensured it will get it. The bald stupidity of Teh Cheang Wan's statement in parliament regarding the way the HDB will treat the residents of Anson virtually makes it certain that the people of Singapore will cry "foul."
>
> Lessons must be learned the hard way. This is a fact of life as of politics. But where is the political sense or justification in punishing a whole constituency for the aggregate belief of all the voters. There are few who would deny that recalcitrant constituencies which willingly choose opposition MPs will not rank high in the regard of the ruling party. But to state in parliament, the bastion of democracy in Singapore, that residents of Anson will be at the bottom of the HDB's priority list as far as maintenance of the properties are concerned is to make the HDB the tool of the PAP. This cannot be. The HDB may well be the tool of the Government of Singapore, and it is not unfair that it should be used as such for government needs. However, it is a different kettle of fish for Mr. Teh to state openly that HDB will be used as a weapon of punishment against those who in aggregate preferred to be represented in parliament by someone other than a PAP representative.
>
> . . . All have seen that voting can swing substantially in elections. Whose turn will it be next, even if they continue as before to vote for the PAP?
>
> . . . There is an over-riding need for honesty in politics. But it would be naïve to suggest that this extends as far as to say that the party in power will openly disfavour those whom it thinks has offended it. It is not and never has been necessary to agree with what one's opponents say but it would be wrong to believe that we do not need to have the courtesy to respect the beliefs of others no matter how different from our own. And it certainly would be childish for a government to take the view that it should harness the powers of national institutions to revenge itself on those who voted the wrong way.

The *BT* leading article was swiftly replaced with a new editorial written, however, in more fulsome vein, under the same heading:

> The People's Action Party has never tried to hide its displeasure with those who chose to vote against it. It has always emphasized that just as there are benefits to be gained from voting PAP so is there a price to be paid for casting one's vote for the opposition. In particular, it has been clear for some years that Anson's voters would not have the PAP bending over backwards to accommodate them.
>
> In parliament on Thursday, the bones of general belief were fleshed with reality, and specific reality at that. As the minister in charge of the Housing and Development Board, Mr. Teh Cheang Wan, made it plain that as far as routine HDB servicing was concerned PAP constituencies would have priority over opposition constituencies. It is true that this is not a punishment that will have any markedly disadvantageous effects on HDB residents. Nor will it make PAP voters feel privileged. . . . Indeed, without forewarning, it is doubtful that the implementation of such a policy would ever have been noticed. Also, there are likely to be more occasions arising where one PAP constituency will be given priority over another.

But this is not the point. What Mr. Teh did, with the support of a few of his colleagues and Confucius, was to enshrine the concept that the PAP will not yield from its position that those who voted against it must be kept aware of the cost of having done so. . . .

We do not share the view that the might of a national institution should be harnessed in a political cause, even in so modest and inconsequential a manner, and notwithstanding that but for the PAP there would probably have been no HDB, or many new houses for that matter. But this is not the key issue either. There is no gainsaying the political honesty of the PAP and its consistency of belief is laudable. However, its admission of how it feels towards opposition voters, not in the heat of elections or the post-election trauma of a swing to the opposition, but coldly and openly in parliament, is another question.

It is our belief that many Singaporeans will cry "foul," not for fear that they too might earn the wrath of the ruling party but because their interpretation of Confucian "fairness" might be different from that of the PAP. Many will hold the opinion that magnanimity in victory is a more desirable trait in their leaders. Mr. Teh's statement has given the opposition parties an enduring platform from which they can bad-mouth the government. This in itself will hardly perturb the PAP. However, Singaporeans may choose to take the declared harshness of the PAP as a challenge rather than an admonition. In such an event, the government may find itself in receipt of feedback suggesting that a little more subtlety would not go amiss.

Shades of Confucius! Alas, how many times out of number has his venerable name been polluted and taken in vain? Howbeit, Jeyaretnam stirred a furious budget debate over the midnight sleight of editorial, when he asked in parliament whether the government had ordered the recall and editorial switch, or were the editors "so frightened that they took it upon themselves to withdraw the criticism. Either way you look at it, it's a scandal." The information minister of state, Dr. Tay Eng Soon, denied emphatically that the government had anything to do with the incident, that he was surprised to hear of it, and ventured to say that newspaper editors in Singapore were "independent" and "responsible," and "editorial decisions were entirely a matter of editorial freedom and editorial choice." And, to the incredible tongue-in-cheek reply, he added: "We have a press in Singapore, which is free, which reflects public opinion. . . . our press in Singapore is accurate, is informative and is credible."[43]

The next day, Peter Lim, *Straits Times* editor-in-chief, stepped into the breach to explain that, after reading the *BT* editorial, it was he who had decided on the recall and instructed the change, because ". . . the language used was unbecoming of a *Times* publication. I felt, too, that the editorial was missing a few salient points. . . . *Business Times* did not change its editorial line on the HDB's 'priority for PAP constituencies' policy. . . . But the language in *BT's* second editorial is classier."[44]

There is a lot to be said for direct, forthright speech. In any event, it is moot whether the language in the second leading article was classier, but the accent was decidedly different. And what were the "salient" points which the original editorial had allegedly missed? But, sad to relate, not all his sycophantic interception to please his political masters could save him when the axe finally fell.

Self-censorship can, also, be self-serving. Reference was made earlier to the publication by the *BT* of leaked information on flash estimates obtained from the ministry of trade and industry. An offended government ordered investigations, including raids on the *BT* and other offices in the city, to be carried out, not by the uniformed branch of the Singapore

Police Force, the Commercial Crimes Division, CID, or the Commercial Affairs Department, but by officers from the Internal Security Department. This was grave news, indeed. Neither the *Business Times* nor the *Straits Times* reported it, but instead maintained a studied silence until the news appeared in the *Asian Wall Street Journal.*

A sad reflection of the Singapore media and of its deep-seated fear of offending the political leadership is reflected in this melancholy incident. In March 1978, when a political detainee, Chan Hock Hua, died of cancer, no newspaper in Singapore was willing to carry an obituary notice from his family. That said, it does not mean that sensitive topics are never broached. As an insightful Holloway noted, the procedure adopted in such instances was:

> Where sensitive issues are involved, journalists must check with the relevant ministry press officers first to seek confirmation or further confirmation. If the officer says that the story cannot be run and the editors accept the reasons given for not printing it, the newspaper will abide by the decision. If the editors disagree—which is quite rare—they take it to higher levels and if the minister vetoes the report, the newspaper must weigh up the risks of ignoring him.[45]

The press coverage of the 1986 state visit of Israeli President Chaim Herzog is a good case in point. The official visit in June 1992 of South African President F.W. de Klerk is another. At an official briefing, Singapore journalists were reminded of "regional sensitivities and perceptions," and to be careful in their coverage of the visit as neighbouring countries might be "upset," and, according to *Asiaweek*: "The official word was: 'Play it down, don't highlight it on the front page, don't mention him playing golf with PM Goh, and stress that the visit is not political but to foster trade links.'" Editors and journalists dutifully complied with the instructions to the letter; but, nonetheless, they were "inadvertently" leaked out to South African newsmen accompanying President de Klerk, who was understandably chagrined that his historic visit to Singapore was being deliberately played down. News of his displeasure reached the ears of Singapore's officialdom, whose characteristic reaction was: "Find and shoot the messenger."[46]

"In the name of survival politics, the leadership expects the press to cultivate self-censorship and to conform to government-prescribed parameters."[47] Journalists, as a matter of prudence, make a mental list of verboten topics—or OB markers in golfing parlance—ranging from sexual harassment, certain aspects of homosexual behaviour to even the listing of golf club membership fees (because it could lead to friction between the haves and the have-nots). Other than the obvious, such as race or religious issues, journalists have to rely on their gut instincts, because even Brig. Gen. Yeo himself was hard put to list them all, except to fall back on a comparison with "the development of case law." And, as already noted, the criticisms on the performance of women PAP MPs in parliament, however honest and well-meant, appears to be part of this "development," even though the criticisms were actual quotations from the women observers interviewed.

After the furor over the *BT* editorial criticizing the gazetting of the *Time* magazine—to which reference has already been made—a practice was introduced for editorial writers from all newspapers in the group to meet in the chief editor's office for the same daily meetings at which news schedules were discussed. Writers put up drafts of leaders, etc., and circulate them among a committee of three or five persons for discussion and approval at the editorial conference. Wherefore, if an editorial or a leading article sometimes appears to the reader rather vapid, uninspiring or lacking in spontaneity or conviction, the plus side is that any political fallout is shared equally amongst the members of the editorial staff. "Two heads are better than one," and "safety in numbers" are not idle proverbs in Singapore's risky print media circles.

Given the cautionary tales herein, it is not surprising that self-censorship is also being practised by foreign publications because of the overhanging threat of restriction in circulation of their publication in Singapore, reinforced by a denial of a comfortable "perch" in Singapore to their correspondents from which they could watch and report on regional and Asian events.

The Tentacles of Censorship

Censorship, little publicized but still very real, also reaches out to the universities, the polytechnics and other institutions of learning and research in Singapore. We have already alluded to student publications. The same constraints apply to publications by the National University of Singapore (NUS) or even the Institute of Southeast Asian Studies (ISEAS). Visiting professors, lecturers and scholars are expressly advised to steer clear of "sensitive" areas of research. Race relations or religious issues are generally sensitive issues, but other topics, too, may be considered sensitive as where an article or paper advances contrarian views of Confucianism as a justification for authoritarian rule, or criticisms of Singapore's international posture on, say, Cambodia or Singapore's neighbours. For instance, an allusion to the military activities of an ASEAN member state in Cambodia was deleted from an ISEAS publication, even though the news item had already been carried elsewhere, thus distorting the sense and drift of the published paper, to the helpless frustration of its author. In another ISEAS publication, an author's personal observations in Cambodia were deleted allegedly due to "limitations of space." A reference to the approval given by the Phnom Penh government to an NUS academic delegation to visit Cambodia in December 1987 was suppressed because it was not considered politic at the time.

Articles, essays, opinions and theses are censored by the editors of academic journals, often with the reluctant consent of authors, who are presented with a Hobson's choice—if they do not agree to the deletions or alterations of passages deemed objectionable to or by the Singapore authorities, then their works would not be published by ISEAS or the institution concerned. In some cases, scholars were warned that their visas might not be renewed by the authorities. In one case, a scholar was told that nonconformity with such a directive would result in "dismissal" from the Institute of Southeast Asian Studies. These eager editors see censorship as necessary to bring scholarship into line with, if not support for, the official Singapore government's stand on those issues.

The Guild House of the National University of Singapore Society (NUSS)—an alumni graduate body—is situated within the Kent Ridge campus of the National University of Singapore. The Guild House was undergoing extensive renovations costing S$11 million. Since 1968, NUSS has been publishing *Commentary*, a journal which provides, albeit intermittently, an alternative forum for intellectual discussion. In 1994, the NUSS management committee—after agonizing over several days—decided to clamp down on the journal's mid-year issue—which had focused on culture—because it feared that it would "annoy" the government. "We can't afford to jeopardize the Society's future. We have to remember we're sitting on university land," said a fainthearted management committee member.[48] The editors resigned en bloc in protest.

The aborted *Commentary* issue had included essays on the performing arts, one of which defended the overall record of 5th Passage, a theatrical group reined in by the government early 1994 after it was linked with one Josef Ng's snipping of his pubic hair in public in the name of "performance art." Another article explained the role of forum theatre, which the government had stopped supporting because of fears that the interactive drama form could be abused. Before it went to press, the management committee, breaking with the convention of editorial freedom, decided to vet the proofs. Among the considerations which influenced the committee into taking the decision was an inane observation by Prime Minister Goh Chok Tong that NUSS "invites opposition MPs all the time" to its functions. However, an information ministry official, when contacted by a *Straits Times* reporter on the media fracas, purportedly replied that *Commentary* was "free to exercise its discretion about whether to publish or not."[49] But, in an uniquely Singapore coincidence, one of the editors, not long afterwards, lost his employment and privileged immigration status, and was declared *persona non grata*.

Two visiting senior lecturers at the National University of Singapore, Christopher Lingle and Kurt Wickman, published an article: "Don't Trust the Reports of Super-Charged Growth," which appeared in the opinion page of the *International Herald Tribune,* questioning China's impressive economic growth figures and highlighting alleged inconsistencies in those figures, and advised that "estimates of Chinese economic growth should be viewed with scepticism."[50] There was no official complaint from the Chinese government, but NUS authorities, apparently more sensitive than the Chinese themselves, summoned the two academics in and told them "not to write [further] this kind of article" nor "identify themselves with the university, when submitting future items to the international press." And as a reminder and record of that visit, they were given a memo specifying that future publications should first be cleared with the university.[51] Nothing of this appeared in the *Straits Times* or other local publications.

On December 6, 1994, an article appeared in the *Jakarta Post* by Dr. Bilveer Singh, an NUS political science lecturer, entitled "Singapore Faces Challenges of Success," which acknowledged that Singapore had made "very noteworthy" achievements in the areas of public housing, education, health and full employment. The article continued:

> But, despite the circumstances of plenty and great success, the country now faced internal political problems stemming from the growing frustrations among its people. . . . The rising cost of living had resulted in the cost of cars and housing rising beyond the reach of the majority of Singaporeans. . . . The proposed increase in ministerial pay had also been received badly by the public because of the general frustrations of costs which have hit the majority of the population. . . . Many, including the government, were profiteering as a result of the introduction of the Goods and Services Tax in April.
>
> What is now emerging in Singapore is a society that is faced with growing impoverishment even though a fortunate minority is still reaping profits and the queue for a Mercedes 320 is still very long. . . .
>
> What the statistics hide through the law of averages and generalization, is that the majority of Singaporeans are basically living hand-to-mouth and it is these Singaporeans, who

constitute the majority, that have become increasingly alienated with the government. . . . As a result, Singaporeans suffered from PAP fatigue. Failure to address these problems could lead over the years to a "point of no return" for the People's Action Party. This was the greatest danger facing the PAP and the Singapore state.

Singapore's charge d'affaires in Jakarta promptly replied, sharply rebuking the NUS academic, challenging him to substantiate his allegations or withdraw them. Dr. Bilveer Singh admitted it was a "gross error," apologized for the "negative impression" he had created about Singapore, and withdrew his allegations. It should not, however, be forgotten that Dr. Bilveer Singh has to live in Singapore, and his employer is the National University of Singapore.

In a forum on censorship and the arts organized by the NUS, a panelist, author and NUS lecturer, Kirpal Singh, pointedly remarked: "Race, language and religion are such touchy subjects here that writers self-censor their works even before the censors can get to them." Within those boundaries, academic freedom, apparently, may roam unmolested or undisturbed.

Letters to Editors

For reasons already noted, newspaper editors almost invariably decline as a matter of prudence to publish letters on controversial matters or topics for fear of offending the government. When nonconstituency member of parliament Dr. Lee Siew Choh drew the attention of the information minister, Brig. Gen. George Yeo, to the outrageous fact that the *Straits Times* "does not publish many letters from the public, especially when they were over controversial points made by ministers," he was brusquely told to direct his complaint to the paper concerned. Oppositionist Wee Han Kim, a prolific writer of thoughtful letters on the issues of the day—such as his observations on the conditional release of Amnesty International's prisoner of conscience, lawyer Teo Soh Lung, whose scandalous re-arrest and detention in 1988 rekindled world attention to the political antics of an authoritarian government—is often ignored by the *Straits Times* forum editor purportedly for "lack of space":

> I refer to your report (*Straits Times*, June 2, 1990, "ISD detainee Teo Soh Lung released on 3 conditions.")
>
> One of the three conditions on which Miss Teo has been released prohibits her from participating in political life. Yet the ISD statement concludes that she has been "rehabilitated enough to be released." If she has been "rehabilitated" why must her existence outside prison be conditional?
>
> Miss Teo sympathized with an opposition party (the Workers' Party) and worked for that party in Anson constituency where she was a resident when that constituency was represented in parliament by Mr J.B. Jeyaretnam. What the PAP government has done to her it can do to anyone sympathetic to an opposition party but who is not yet a member. People don't join political parties just like that. Obviously there is a waiting period when they get to know the party, what it stands for and its officers and members. They want to find out for themselves whether it is a decent outfit or whether it is made up of a bunch of crooks as the government would have them believe. Political opposition being a legitimate activity, the opposition would like to go about recruiting new members in as open a way as possible.

The Teo Soh Lung type detention and conditional release is one way of depriving opposition parties of all new blood. And I thought the government welcomed intelligent, rational and prudent people in opposition!

The letter subsequently appeared in the Workers' Party organ, *The Hammer*,[52] which published a collection of his unpublished letters to the *Straits Times*, entitle: *One Sweet Letter from You*, only to draw a cynical response from the *Straits Times*: "Who says writing to newspapers isn't a profitable business?"

Shortly after his return from an ambassadorial stint in France, Singapore's first chief minister, David Saul Marshall, wrote a letter to the editor of the *Straits Times* challenging the need for the death penalty, and questioning its "effectiveness" in Singapore. Marshall had always been against the death penalty. The editor refused to publish the letter on the feeble pretext that "it did not sponsor petitions and there was no evidence that death row was overcrowded." Outraged at this insouciance, Marshall remonstrated: "Where do we go to express our differences of views if we are not allowed to hold meetings or write to the press?" And, at a public forum, amplified his grievance at the suppression of his letter, by labelling the *Straits Times* as "either PAP wallahs or bootlickers," and local journalists as "pathetic [who] were only concerned about their own survival. They are running dogs of the PAP and poor prostitutes."[53] At first blush, the statement seemed rather intemperate, but, given the uncritical appreciation of official policies and the fawning posture it adopts towards officialdom, it is a well-deserved judgment.

It is common wisdom in Singapore that the names and addresses of correspondents of letters to the editors of the domestic media on controversial matters (whether they are published or not) are covertly noted down, and passed on by ISD moles or PAP supporters therein to the Internal Security Department for security screening and record. The screening of these correspondents and personalities extends beyond the domestic media to the foreign media, where correspondents who write on or about Singapore are quietly checked and their political background and reliability noted. Take this example. When a letter to the editor of the Hongkong-based *Review*, with a Singapore dateline, was published criticizing the Singapore government's use of the ISA against Roman Catholic activists as a violation of "basic human rights," the government ran a computer check on the writer's name with the National Registration Office—a department responsible for the computerized records of personal particulars of all Singaporeans, permanent and temporary residents—which soon found that he was not a Singaporean but a Hongkong student, against whom an order of prohibition of entry into Singapore was made. In other words, he was a prohibited immigrant.[54] Another correspondent's letter to the *Review*, also with a Singapore dateline, was compared, be it noted, with a letter, which he had written some three years earlier to the *Straits Times*. The press secretary to the minister for trade queried the writer as to his sudden misgivings on the way the Singapore government regarded its critics.[55]

There were understandably instances of writers giving fictitious names and addresses in letters, particularly on controversial matters to the offshore media. But another Singaporean correspondent, Chua Chuan Seah, whose credentials were similarly checked by the Singapore authorities, was paid a backhanded compliment for not using a nom de plume in his letter critical of the Singapore government to the *Review*. "The fact that so few are prepared to sign their names is part of the culture of Asia and particularly of the Chinese," wrote the press secretary to the minister for trade and industry.[56] If so, former senior minister, S. Rajaratnam, with his egregious yen for anonyms, must therefore be a notable Asian exception.

"After agonizing for months," *Straits Times* editor Leslie Fong informed readers in 1989 that he had decided with effect from July 1—save in exceptional circumstances, such as "when identification is likely to pose a very real threat to life and limb"—that letters to the editor would be published only if writers reveal their true names, addresses, home and office telephone numbers, "as they should be brave enough to state their views, and stand by them." With disarming simplicity, Fong promised readers to keep their personal particulars "confidential." The more pragmatic Chinese-language newspapers, however, did not follow suit, preferring the status quo. But, in October 1991, the PAP apologist-editor, "who makes no apologies for being pro-government," returned to the issue, urging his editorial colleagues in the three Chinese-language dailies to "phase out the use of pseudonyms, and not just in the letters they publish, but all opinion columns as well," and encourage their readers to "stand up for their views and so give political leaders a better feel of the Chinese ground."[57] Any apprehension felt by them was "misconceived," he said, if the experience of his own newspaper was anything to go by. But Chinese-educated Singaporeans are well envied for their keen instinct for survival in national politics.

As well he would, Lee endorsed the *Straits Times* decision as "correct." It may not be impertinent to recall that, during the 1959 general election campaign, Lee had urged his audience to send anonymous notes to his party of any critical comments by their European employers when they returned late from PAP lunchtime rallies, which he would arrange to have them read out to the people at subsequent rallies.[58] Depending upon the time, the place and circumstance, anonymity not only has its advantages but is recommended. According to the *Straits Times Forum '91 Roundup*, it received 7,270 letters, a 7 percent increase over the number received for 1990. But the percentage of letters published dipped from 26 percent of letters received in 1990 to 23 percent. Using the bench-mark of *eligible* letters received, one in three were published, while 35 percent of the letters were ineligible for publication because they had "no signature, name, address or contact telephone number."[59]

Investigative Reporting

Investigative reporting is not encouraged. As John Lent pertinently noted, "newspapers have been advised not to investigate matters that might be embarrassing to the authorities."[60] A seminar on "The Role of the Government and the Mass Media," attended by administrative officers and senior civil servants concluded, in a 1978 report, that "television news should be more investigative and newspapers contain more vigorous editorials and evaluative articles." But it surmised that the reason why investigative reporting had not been fully exploited was "probably because Radio and Television Singapore (RTS), being government-owned, may be disinclined to embarrass another government department." Newspapers, on the other hand, often contained editorials which merely repeat government policies and give only mild admonitions while news reports are "event-oriented" and "lack depth."[61] This report—which was a nine day wonder—is probably gathering dust in the archives of the National Library, and the reason for it is axiomatic.

The case of the venturesome *Business Times* illustrates the dangers of investigative reporting for journalists and editors alike, and the dilemma that confronts journalists in their quest for news and information.[62] On June 29, 1992, the *BT* carried a news report that "official flash estimates—quick, initial calculations—suggested that the economic growth in April and May fell below the first quarter rate of 5.1 percent." The information was leaked out from the ministry of trade and industry, whose minister was also the "rising son." Notwithstanding that the information neither endangered national security nor was embarrassing to the government, it ordered a probe into the leakage by the Internal Security Department. Deputy prime minister and minister for trade and industry, Brig. Gen. Lee Hsien Loong said: "An open government does not mean that you condone and accept leaks of sensitive official secrets which are price-sensitive. They have to be investigated."[63] As senior minister Lee remarked in sharp reproof of the occurrence, "it would never have happened on my watch," which informed Lee watchers interpreted as a rebuke to Goh of his stewardship of government affairs. "You can't run a government which is leaking all over the place," he added.[64]

On December 9, 1992, four persons, including the ambitious editor Patrick Daniel, were charged on nine counts of breaching the Official Secrets Act (OSA) in connection with the news report. The offences carry a maximum sentence of a $2,000 fine or two years gaol, or both. On June 18, 1993—just three days before the trial of the four was due to begin—*BT* technology editor Kenneth James was charged in court with receiving and passing on the information. The trial was adjourned pending consolidation of the charges.

Meanwhile, the New York-based Committee to Protect Journalists urged prime minister Goh Chok Tong to have the charges withdrawn, saying that "the use of the Official Secrets Act against Mr. Daniel is in violation of the internationally recognized right to 'seek, receive, and impart information,' as guaranteed in Article 19 of the United Nations' Universal Declaration of Human Rights." But, in view of the senior minister's sombre remarks, as noted above, it would take a brave prime minister to do so.

On March 31, 1994, all five accused persons were found guilty of breaching the OSA. Daniel was found guilty on two charges of receiving the data from James and communicating it to *BT* readers, and fined the maximum amount of S$2,000 on each charge. James was found guilty on two charges of receiving the data and communicating it to Daniel for which he was fined S$2,000 and S$1,500 respectively. After the trial, Cheong Yip Seng, the editor-in-chief of the Singapore Press Holdings' English/Malay newspapers division, opined that the convictions would not affect local journalists' "legitimate newsgathering" activities. But the statement of the PAP publicist MP Koo Tsai Kee—"If they knew it was a leak, they shouldn't have published the information"—seems to be the ascendant view.[65] This outlandish proposition is calculated to cause newspapers to fall back on official handouts, and dampen journalistic zest and zeal.

When the *Report of an Amnesty International Mission to Singapore* was released in 1980, criticizing the Singapore government for human rights abuses, Singapore newspapers only gave the government reaction with barely a hint of what the allegations were. Similarly, Asia Watch, in its 1989 *Report on Singapore and Human Rights Violations*, noted: "The coverage of potentially sensitive political issues usually appears to be designed to promote the government's position through extensive excerpts of official statements, pro-government commentary, and acceptance of the validity of government contentions and the accuracy of government assertions without question."[66]

Asia Watch experienced, at first hand, the Singapore "media's willingness to accept at face value government statements" in a front-paged article, captioned "Seow Reveals the Human Rights Connection, Amnesty and Asiawatch [sic] Knew Detainees Had Not Been Assaulted," when the *Sunday Times* reported: "When Amnesty International and Asiawatch [sic] accused the government of torturing detainees who had been arrested last year for involvement with a Marxist conspiracy, both organizations knew this to be untrue." The article was based on a government claim, which Asia Watch challenged as both "inaccurate and irresponsible."[67]

Opposition parties are generally given short shrift in terms of political news space except for negative coverage. In May and June 1987, no local journalists dared to seriously investigate the veracity of government accusations regarding the alleged Marxist conspiracy and its named conspirators. As one journalist disclosed to Asia Watch: "We knew more than we were reporting but we couldn't follow it up because we had to play it straight." Investigative zeal is not encouraged where the results might expose the weakness or falsity of the government's contention. When one journalist scooped an interview with Tan Wah Piow, the alleged overseas mastermind behind the Marxist conspiracy, the editor-in-chief of his paper refused to run the story.[68] Notwithstanding, when the level of his own political cognition momentarily slipped, Peter Lim, the once influential editor-in-chief of the *Straits Times* group, was eased out of his flagship to start a new afternoon newspaper, and, in addition, "voluntarily" took a pay cut. He had apparently allowed matters considered favourable to the opposition to be published in his stable of newspapers.

Cartoons, Caricatures and Editorial Humour

"A caricature is a portrait with an attitude, a likeness meant to provide recognition by its distortions. Although its purpose is often nothing more than to be a visual prank, caricature at its best has often been an acerbic and accessible form of social and political criticism. . . . a caricature should communicate an idea."[69] Long before the use of pseudonyms in letters was depicted as lacking in conviction and strength of character, Lee—whose facial features lend themselves admirably to caricature—had deprecated political cartoons and caricatures of Singapore political leaders in newspapers as being alien to Asian culture: "Our press cannot afford the luxury enjoyed in the West of being able to pillory presidents and prime ministers out of office or indulging in a little electoral skulduggery." In an address before the Institute of International Relations in Paris, Lee provided further insight into his political philosophy on cartoons, caricatures and media humour, when he commented on the Tiananmen demonstrations and their irreverent doggerels on China's paramount leader, Deng Xiaoping: "You cannot mock a great leader in an Asian Confucian society. If he allows himself to be mocked, he is finished.[70]

Echoing the master himself, information minister Brig. Gen. George Yeo, comparing the different way *Asiaweek* and its Chinese-language sister publication, *Yazhou Zhoukan*, reported news, stated the "Doonesbury approach" of pillorying political leaders is considered "very unseemly" because politicians are treated with respect in Eastern societies.[71] Political jokes and humour or lampoons at the expense of the political leadership, so beloved of the Western media, are similarly "non-U," or, in the metaphor of the day, politically incorrect. As former *Nanyang* general manager Lee Mau Seng said in Hongkong after his release from prison: "Humour is a dangerous business in Singapore. In other countries, a humourist gets $2,000 a month; in Singapore he gets two years."[72] Notwithstanding, cartoons and caricatures of Singaporeans generally, but sparingly of PAP leaders, are slowly reappearing in domestic newspapers. But they are rather pallid or cute efforts, quite safe and inoffensive, with none of the laser sarcasm of Pat Oliphant of Universal Press or the wry, biting humour of Morgan Chua of the *Review*.[73]

The Legal Weapon

Critical reporting on Lee and his government may attract one of two responses, namely, a civil or a criminal action for defamation or wilful contempt, and sometimes both of them, for example: an action for defamation at the personal suit of Lee or the relevant minister or wilful contempt of court at the instance of the attorney general, and, in some instances, prosecution for criminal defamation. It is apparent from the cases cited earlier that the Singapore courts tend to construe the laws of defamation and wilful contempt rather conservatively. However that may be, it is odd, in retrospect, that Lee himself was invariably the one who would spot or notice possibly defamatory statements in publications, which he would follow up with a memo to his affable law minister, E.W. Barker, for his and the attorney general's comments. The law minister—after penning a laconic sentence or two, usually "please see and advise" or "please see and take action," on the prime minister's memo—would pass it on to the attorney general's chambers for the necessary action. In borderline cases, the opinion of a Queen's Counsel in London, whose forte is the law of defamation, is usually sought.

Lee's proclivity for litigation is legendary. We have touched upon several of the libel actions which Lee brought against perceived denigrators in the course of this narrative. This may be a convenient place to discuss that notoriety and its contribution to the culture of fear in Singapore. The publishers of a possibly controversial book, *Singapore: The Ultimate Island (Lee Kuan Yew's Untold Story)*, resorted to the artifice of establishing a publishing business entity outside Singapore—Freeway Books, whose address was given as P.O. Box 292, Clifton Hill, 3068, Melbourne, Victoria, Australia. Letters sent to the address went unanswered until a check showed it was an accommodation address. Strange to tell, there was nothing in the book—written by T.S. Selvan—which was startlingly new or not already known to informed Singaporeans. Nonetheless, the author and the publishers felt it necessary to take all precautions. Perhaps, the blurb stating that the author was a former ISD officer—and, by implication, had access to secret or confidential or as yet untold information on Lee Kuan Yew, the government and its leaders—whetted the innate curiosity of Singaporeans and caused them to cross the causeway in droves to purchase it. But it is Selvan's difficulties with his Malaysian and other publishers in trying to get his book published which is of especial interest, for it presents, in microcosm, the problems of a writer, whose writings may be misconstrued by abulic publishers as critical of Lee and the Singapore government:

I took my manuscript across the causeway to interest a few publishers, big and small. None was keen. One publisher asked, this, even before reading the manuscript, whether I had been praiseworthy or critical of Lee and his government. Did it matter? Yes, it did. If you pleased Lee and his government, no one was bothered to read. Therefore, there was no money in it. If you were critical, it was not a nice feeling because you might end up with a writ on your desk. If that did not come about, your business interests in Singapore would "silently" suffer. . . . You see, he said, as he waved me on, Big Brother was everywhere. And he was a foreigner! The whole episode was irresistibly comic and frightening all at once.

I tried everywhere; I failed. In some instances I failed because I was not convincing enough. While in other cases the question was perennial: How do we get the book into the country? Lee was everywhere.[74]

A Candle or the Sun—a novel by Singapore surgeon Gopal Baratham, whose plot appears "like a fictionalized account of the Marxist conspiracy"—was rejected by "at least four" overly cautious local publishers, whose rejection was probably made, it was sarcastically suggested, "in the interests of the nation." Or was it for the fear of Lee? It was subsequently published in England,[75] and sold in book shops in Singapore. Another controversial book which was not banned, according to Russell Heng, had no such luck with local retailers because distributors were "rather cagey" about importing it. "The subtlety of book censorship in Singapore is too complex . . . In the final analysis, book publishers and distributors, like journalists, also have stories to tell of unidentified OB—out-of-bound—markers."[76]

Cartoonist George Nonis's modest collection of political cartoons, *Hello Chok Tong, Good bye Kuan Yew*, could not conceivably be said to be controversial, even though it contains some drawings of that famous visage. Nonetheless, the author tells of the difficulties he encountered in trying to have it published. Perchance, his wary publishers would have been more comfortable if the subject had looked more like Cary Grant. "It wasn't easy . . . I tried very hard. . . . At times, it seemed like I was risking life and limb."[77] Nonis's description of his quest for a publisher may seem a little exaggerated to some, but the essential truth is there. In his recent book, *Singapore, My Home Too*, Dr. Chee Soon Juan—a neuropsychologist, author and secretary general of the opposition Singapore Democratic Party—recounts his publishing difficulties with Singapore printers regarding an earlier book, *Dare to Change* (whose treatise was later adopted by his party—the SDP—as its political manifesto). No less than four printers turned him down for fear of offending the government; the eventual printer only accepted the assignment because she was a new arrival from Malaysia, unaware of Dr. Chee's political affiliations. About a fortnight later, her agitated employer rang up to say that they could not continue with the assignment as the book was "critical of the government," and that the company would willingly absorb the costs of production—even though it was virtually completed, save for the covers. After "hours of persuasion" that "although the book was critical it was not subversive," the proprietor reluctantly relented, and agreed to complete the assignment.

Even after its completion, Chee's problems were by no means over. They had just begun. No book shops were prepared to vend it—before he finally found one book shop which reluctantly agreed to do so. One irresolute bookseller, however, was not enough. Thus, on weekdays too, accompanied by loyal party supporters, he would stand at street corners to sell his book, during which Singaporeans would furtively approach him to buy a copy, thrust the money into his hands, quickly conceal it between the folds of their *Straits Times* newspaper or whatever other convenient objects they happened to be carrying at the time, and dash off with the guilt-ridden countenance of persons who had just purchased some illicit merchandise.[78] This tragicomedy, sadly enough, is still being repeated, not only with Dr. Chee and the SDP but also with Jeyaretnam and the Workers' Party in their attempts to sell or distribute their party newspapers. PAP ministers and supporters—long insensitive to the deleterious effects of the psychosis of fear pervading this "free and democratic" island nation—reportedly find tales of the misadventures of the opposition gleefully funny. (See the Undesirable Publications Act, Cap. 338, in the addendum.)

This author's own experiences with publishers for the publication of his book, *To Catch a Tartar: A Dissident in Lee Kuan Yew's Prison*, and the present monograph, tell more tales of this irrational ethos of fear. A United Kingdom publisher, perusing the first-draft manuscript of this work, declined publication, remarking:

> Lee Kuan Yew is clearly litigious and has successfully sued for libel, etc., various prominent media. While he is formally in retirement, neither he nor the present administration are going to like this report. . . . any publisher . . . must face the distinct possibility that Lee will sue one way or another.

But Yale University's Eugene Meyer Professor of Political Science, James C. Scott, saw the *Tartar* manuscript in a different light: "as an important historical document that people will be reading for a long time to come if they want to understand Lee's Singapore in its 'late' phase." It was a manuscript, which Yale SEA monographs "would be proud to do as a hard-bound and a paperback simultaneously," he said. Since then, it has seen two print runs. Notwithstanding the real fears that the book would be banned in Singapore, it was still eagerly awaited by numerous curious readers, including members of the Singapore government and the ISD. The impatient Singapore ambassador to Washington, D.C., had to be assured that he would be among the first to receive it when published. He was.

However that may be, when a consignment of the books arrived at the Select Book Shop, Tanglin Shopping Centre, Singapore, word soon spread among Singaporeans that "it" had finally arrived—and eager readers made a beeline for the book shop. But within days of the news, the book was hastily withdrawn, after ISD officers allegedly visited the shop, and had "a chat" with the proprietor, who reshipped them to the distributors. Notwithstanding, the demand was gratifyingly overwhelming. Yale SEA decided to give a Malaysian publisher reprint rights to bring out a Malaysian edition, which has also enjoyed two print runs, with a possible third. Most of the earnest buyers were from Singapore. The book is still not available in book shops in Singapore, although almost every other Singaporean has reportedly read it.

To round off this section, mention should be made of a well-known book entitled, *No Man Is an Island: A Study of Singapore's Lee Kuan Yew*,[79] by Australian Anglican minister and Oxford graduate, James Minchin, whose book is critical of Lee Kuan Yew and his government. For several years now, it is not available in book shops in Singapore, but is sold across the causeway in Malaysia where Singaporeans used to drive over to purchase it. Occasionally, on their return, overzealous Singapore customs officials confiscate the books if their gaze should fall on them.

Conclusion: The Next Lap

With his own personal and political agenda apparently completed and settled, on November 26, 1990, the prime minister ostensibly handed over the reins and trappings of office to his deputy Goh Chok Tong—who, he first made it known abroad, was "not his first choice" for the premiership—and, after some pregnant delay, the omnipotent PAP secretary-generalship as well. But Harry Lee Kuan Yew continues as senior minister in the Goh cabinet, and has not been bashful in stating many times over that he holds the power of override, a back-seat driver with powerful clout. There will, therefore, be little or no change in the political landscape of Singapore as long as he is still around. In this context, it is pertinent to note Lee's observations on China's aging leaders: "As long as the Long March veterans are there, the younger leaders are governing with the blessings of Deng [Xiaoping] and the veterans. The younger generation takes over only after the Long March heroes have gone."[80] That observation also applies with similar force to Singapore's younger leaders. In spite of all his bravado, Goh is in the unenviable position of always having to look over his shoulder. In a bold attempt to show that Singapore has a new captain of state, he promised, in emulation of U.S. President George Bush, "a kinder and gentler" Singapore: "There will be greater freedom for Singaporeans to make their own choices, and to express themselves, but this freedom is not extended to actions which rock the boat. We will not allow anyone to capsize Singapore. We will not brook interference from foreign newspapers in our domestic affairs. Those that do will be gazetted and have their circulation reduced."

On October 26, 1991, Professor Tommy Koh, director of the Institute of Policy Studies, at a forum on the role of the media in the "next lap," quoted information minister, Brig. Gen. George Yeo, that the government would allow journalists "more freedom, but would still draw the line between what the press could and could not do" and "the press to blossom and be more analytical, sophisticated and outward-looking." But where or what those lines are, nobody, not even the minister himself, knows. Some concerning race, language, religion and regional relations are fairly obvious. "I do not need the government to articulate that to me in so many words," said *Straits Times* editor Leslie Fong. Beyond the obvious, no one could really say with any certitude. Fong claimed that there was a general consensus between the press and the government about the parameters of media constraints. However, it was "impossible" to define the boundary lines, but journalists were expected to know them intuitively, prompting Professor Koh to interject that they, in truth, "must constantly work under a cloud of fear." But Yatiman Yusof, PAP MP for Tampines GRC and a former journalist, came up with a classic PAP disclaimer. Conceding that although there were no clearly defined boundaries, Yatiman maintained that "*senior journalists were nonetheless aware of them, through long experience and interaction with leaders behind closed doors. . . . What seemed like self-censorship was actually the result of this.*" [Author's emphasis] Describing the grim "realities of journalism in Singapore," Fong, in spite of himself, said: "The press laws and political culture are such that the government, with a vast array of powers at its disposal, will not countenance the press taking any determined stand against it on any issues that it considers fundamental."[81]

On July 27, 1992, Brig. Gen. Lee Hsien Loong vowed to journalists that "media controls would be relaxed over the long term." While his ministerial colleague Brig. Gen. Yeo, adopting a golfing metaphor, claimed that while the "fairways have been widened" under the Goh administration, the limits would be set as they go along, "rather like case laws." Be that as it may, group editor Cheong Yip Seng, at the 1992 *Straits Times* group annual awards to recognize journalistic excellence, said: "The future of our newspapers is best secured by a stable of stars, journalists who are informed, skilful and wise to the ways of the world, who are worth reading not just for news but for their insights."[82] Not once did he mention that they should also be free and independent.

The print media has come a long way from 1959, from a spiritedly independent voice of Singaporeans to a servile mouthpiece of Harry Lee Kuan Yew and his PAP government. It is a media with a credibility problem, characteristic of all media in thrall. The government is not unaware of the image problem. As the *Review* once pointed out: "Ministers want a corps of journalists which can produce periodicals that are pro-government but are sufficiently analytical to avoid being regarded by readers as propaganda. Sycophancy, the argument goes, breeds credibility problems and cynicism—hardly the raw materials needed to forge a national consensus."[83]

In trying to correct the course, the new team of ministers under its genial captain is experiencing acute political schizophrenia. While it recognizes, on the one hand, that the control should be relaxed so as to give the media scope for independent expression within certain guidelines (which they are still unable to work out), on the other hand, there is a morbid fear that such relaxation might open the floodgates of opposing views and criticisms, which, once opened, would be very difficult indeed to close again. Or, to use another metaphor, once a caged bird has been allowed to breathe the fresh, exhilarating air of freedom, it is impossible to lure it back into the cage, short of killing it. Casting a sombre shadow over the team's dilemma is their éminence grise whose ingenuity, skill and energy took over a decade to finally crush the independence of the media and bring it to his heel, for he knew "the hand that rules the press . . . rules the country." The press has become an indispensable tool for the political longevity of the PAP. Notwithstanding all the fancy rhetoric, it is unlikely that prime minister Goh Chok Tong or any member of his team of ministers will cause any dénouement of media control. Rather, one can expect a strengthening of PAP control over the media to ensure that only trusted editors, journalists and other such persons are appointed to the SPH editorial and corporate boards.

As it is, reporters and editors already know on which side their bread is buttered, and can usually be counted upon to anticipate the wishes of the political leadership. As British press baron Lord Northcliffe once superciliously declared, he never had to tell the editor what to write because the man he chose made this unnecessary. This is also the sad truth of the state of the Singapore media today. It is a media in thrall.

Notes

1. *Hansard,* Malaysian Parliamentary debates, December 18, 1964, col. 5076.
2. *Hansard,* Legislative Assembly debates, October 4, 1956, cols. 322–323.
3. But see David Marshall's outburst, "Today, Singapore's censorship is worse, broader and more strict than any time under British imperial rule," *Straits Times,* January 18, 1994.
4. *Straits Times,* April 23, 1959.

5. *Straits Times*, May 12, 1971.

6. Arabic script.

7. TV Singapura Malay press conference, August 11, 1965.

8. *Asiaweek*, April 6, 1990.

9. Roger Mitton, "The Long Story, What Role For the Press? Singapore's Answers," *Asiaweek*, September 25, 1992.

10. Nigel Holloway, "Government and press—a degree of trust," *Far Eastern Economic Review* (hereafter, *Review*), July 3, 1986.

11. *Sunday Times*, November 17, 1991.

12. Wee Han Kim, *One Sweet Letter From You*. Singapore: Hammer Publication, 1992.

13. *Straits Times,* Weekly Edition, February 1, 1992.

14. C.M. Turnbull, *Dateline Singapore: 150 years of the Straits Times*, Singapore: Singapore Press Holdings, 1995.

15. *The Australian*, June 10, 1971.

16. *Straits Times*, June 23, 1971. See also M. Coomaraswamy, "A Singaporean's disgust," *Review*, June 16, 1971. Gordon moved to Malaysia but was later banished by the Malaysian government for "activities prejudicial to the security and well-being of the country under the Banishment Act. She was allegedly involved in Palestinian politics: *Review*, May 6, 1974.

17. *Straits Times*, May 4, 1971.

18. Ambassador Tommy T.B. Koh, "Singapore Believes Freedom of Press Must Be a Two-Way Street," *New York Times*, March 14, 1987. See also remarks of S. Dhanabalan, minister for foreign affairs and culture quoted by Michael Antolik in "Singapore's Joust with Journalism," *Asian Profile*, vol. 19 no. 6, December 1991.

19. See also Cherian George, "The Press and the City," *Commentary*, vol. 10, December 1992.

20. Mitton, "The Long Story, What Role for the Press?" See also George, "The Press and the City."

21. Mitton, "The Long Story, What Role for the Press?"

22. Mitton, "What Role for the Press? Singapore's Answers."

23. Ibid.

24. Tan Teng Lang, *The Singapore Press: Freedom, Responsibility and Credibility.* Singapore: Times Academic Press for the Institute of Policy Studies, 1990.

25. Eddie C.Y. Kuo et al., *Mirror on the Wall: Media in a Singapore Election*. Singapore: Asian Mass Communication Research and Information Centre, 1993. See also George, "The Press and the City."

26. *Straits Times*, October 26, 1984.

27. *Hansard*, Parliamentary debates, January 12, 1988, col. 279.

28. *Straits Times*, February 27, 1988.

29. Letters, *Review*, January 14, 1988.

30. Alex Josey, *Singapore: Its Past, Present and Future*. Brisbane: University of Queensland Press, 1980.

31. Giles was at the *Monitor* during 1984–1985.

32. *Review*, July 3, 1986.

33. David DeVoss, "Southeast Asia's intimidated press," *Columbia Journalism Review*, March-April 1978.

34. Russell Heng, "Censorship: it can go either way," *Singapore*, July 1992, p. 18. See also Chee Soon Juan, *Singapore, My Home Too*. Singapore: Melodies Press Co., 1995.

35. *Straits Times,* February 27, 1988.

36. *Sunday Times,* December 20, 1992.

37. Senior minister: Lee's new designation in cabinet after he stepped down as prime minister in November 1990.

38. *Business Times,* April 20, 1993.

39. See Francis T. Seow, *To Catch a Tartar: A Dissident in Lee Kuan Yew's Prison,* New Haven: Yale Southeast Asia Studies, 1994. Appendix 5, for the full text of the open letter.

40. April 20, 1993.

41. *Straits Times,* Weekly Edition, December 7, 1991. See also July 25, 1992, issue.

42. Cf. *Life,* a report on the trend of single, educated women having babies outside marriage, either through artificial insemination or a temporary partner, caused some disquietude in parliament, *Straits Times,* March 4, 1992.

43. *Straits Times,* March 28, 1985.

44. Ibid.

45. *Review,* July 3, 1986.

46. Mitton, "The Long Story, What Role for the Press?"

47. Tan Teng Lang, *The Singapore Press: Freedom, Responsibility and Credibility.*

48. *Straits Times,* October 29, 1994.

49. Ibid.

50. *International Herald Tribune,* January 19, 1994.

51. *South China Morning Post,* February 2, 1994.

52. *The Hammer,* June 6, 1990.

53. *Straits Times,* January 18, 1994.

54. Letters, Gan Kim Yong, "Interpreting the fact," *Review,* August 13, 1987.

55. Letters, Gan Kim Yong, "Rights for critics," *Review,* October 15, 1987.

56. Ibid.

57. *Straits Times,* Weekly Edition, October 26, 1991.

58. *Straits Times,* May 19, 1959.

59. *Straits Times,* Weekly Edition, February 8, 1992.

60. John A. Lent, ed., *Newspapers in Asia: Contemporary Trends and Problems.* Hongkong: Heinemann Asia, 1982.

61. *Straits Times,* February 3, 1978.

62. Mitton, "The Long Story, What Role for the Press?"

63. *Straits Times,* Weekly Edition, November 7, 1992.

64. Mitton, "The Long Story, What Role for the Press?"

65. Mitton, "The Long Story, What Role for the Press?"

66. Asia Watch, *Silencing All Critics, Human Rights Violations in Singapore.* New York: Asia Watch, 1989.

67. *Sunday Times,* May 22, 1988. See Appendices B and C herein.

68. Asia Watch, *Silencing All Critics.*

69. Rosemary Ranck, reviewing *The Savage Mirror: The Art of Contemporary Caricature,* by Watson-Guptil. *New York Times,* January 31, 1993.

70. Speech, Institute of International Relations, May 23, 1990.

71. *Straits Times,* Weekly Edition, November 23, 1991. The *Yazhou Zhoukan* was sold to the Ming Pao Group of Hongkong in March 1994: *Straits Times,* Weekly Edition, December 30, 1995.

72. *Review,* December 3, 1987.

73. George Nonis, *Hello Chok Tong, Good bye Kuan Yew.* Singapore: Angsana Books, 1991.

74. T.S. Selvan, "Writer's Note," in *Singapore: The Ultimate Island (Lee Kuan Yew's Untold Story),* Melbourne: Freeway Books, 1990.

75. "Insight," *Straits Times,* Weekly Edition, March 7, 1992.

76. Heng, "Censorship: it can go either way."

77. George Nonis, *Hello Chok Tong, Good bye Kuan Yew.*

78. Chee Soon Juan, *Singapore, My Home Too.*

79. James Minchin, *No Man Is an Island: A Study of Singapore's Lee Kuan Yew.* 2nd ed., Sydney: Allen & Unwin, 1990.

80. Press interview, *Hongkong Standard*, November 21, 1989.

81. *Sunday Times*, October 27, 1991.

82. *Straits Times*, February 20, 1993.

83. *Review,* January 22, 1987. See also George, "The Press and the City."

Addendum
Relevant Legislation

A discussion on the print media would not be complete without reference to the other relevant legislation, which impacts upon the practice of journalism and its practitioners in Singapore. This addendum focuses on those specific sections of the law, other than the Newspapers and Printing Presses Act, and discusses the actual events or incidents in the light of the law.

Defamation Act, Cap. 75

Subject to any blasphemous, seditious or indecent matter or of any matter the publication of which is prohibited by law, a fair and accurate and contemporaneous report of proceedings publicly heard before any court is absolutely privileged, as well as any fair and bona fide comment thereon. See section 11. See, also, section 12 on the defence of qualified privilege available to newspapers in certain publications in an action for libel.

The Essential Information (Control of Publications and Safeguarding of Information) Regulations, 1966

The Emergency (Essential Powers) Act, 1964—a Malaysian Act—was extended to Singapore when Singapore was a constituent state within the Federation of Malaysia. It has to be read together with the provisions of the Republic of Singapore Independence Act. The act gives the president the power to make any regulations which he considers desirable or expedient for securing public safety, the defence of Singapore, the maintenance of public order and of supplies and services essential to the life of the community and, without prejudice to the generality of those powers, among other things, create offences and prescribe penalties (including the death penalty) which may be imposed for any offence against any written law (including regulations made under the act).

The Essential Information (Control of Publications and Safeguarding of Information) Regulations, 1966, were enacted after Singapore was separated from Malaysia. As already noted, the regulations were used to prevent discussion in print of the government decision to abolish jury trials for capital offences.

Protected information can only be disseminated if the consent of a competent authority has previously been obtained. A competent authority is any official designated by the minister for defence to be such, and a certificate by the minister "that an information is protected shall, until the contrary is proved, be deemed to be sufficient evidence of the fact."

Under regulation 4, a person is prohibited from obtaining or possessing or making records or copies of protected information. It also prohibits the dissemination of such information in any newspaper and the communication to any other person whether within or without Singapore.

Regulation 6 prohibits members of the armed forces from communicating, divulging or disclosing to the press, which is forbidden to print stories discrediting the military or discussing grievances against individual servicemen. If a publication prints a communication from a soldier, the ministry of defence is entitled to obtain the identity of the writer from the offending publication.

The regulations further state that "where any protected information is disseminated in a newspaper in contravention of regulation 4 of these regulations, every proprietor, editor, manager, printer, of such newspaper or any person responsible for reporting, publishing or printing the newspaper shall be guilty of an offence." The maximum punishment for this offence is a three-year jail term or S$10,000 fine, or both.

In June 1973, the *Nanyang Siang Pau* op-ed page editor, Goh Seow Poh, was fined S$500 for publishing an anonymous letter from a "group of soldiers" without the prior consent of the ministry of defence. The soldiers had inquired how they could obtain an earlier discharge from their national service to gain admission to universities.[1] It will be recalled that *Review* Singapore correspondent Ho Kwon Ping was found guilty of "disseminating protected information" in an article on the manufacture and export of M-16 rifles and the purchase of secondhand boats from the United States even though the information was widely known. Some further articles on other egregious aspects of the Singapore armed forces were taken into consideration in the sentence.

Judicial Proceedings (Regulation of Reports) Act, Cap. 149

This act regulates the publication of reports of judicial proceedings "in such a manner as to prevent injury to public morals" such as indecent matter or indecent medical, surgical or physiological details. Stories on matrimonial disputes can only contain basic details about the parties and witnesses; a concise statement of the charges; the defences and countercharges; submissions on any points of law arising therein; the court's decision and any observations made by it thereon. The penalty for infringement is S$1,000 or imprisonment for a maximum term of one year, or both.

Two Chinese editors of the *Lianhe Wanbao* and the *Shin Min Daily News* were fined S$700 and S$500 respectively for publishing investigative details of a television actress's movements in her husband's petition for divorce. A second similar charge for stories published on a subsequent day on the same divorce case was taken into consideration.[2] See section 50 (1) of the Children and Young Persons Act, Cap. 38, on the restriction on newspaper reports of proceedings in a Juvenile Court.

Internal Security Act, Cap. 143

The Internal Security Act (ISA) provides for the internal security of Singapore, preventive detention, the prevention of subversion, the suppression of organized violence against persons and property in Singapore and other incidental matters. The scope and use of the ISA has been discussed elsewhere in this book, and below. Under section 20 of the ISA, the relevant minister is also empowered to prohibit the printing, publication, and sale, inter alia, of subversive publications.

Another method of media control is seen in this repressive praxis, which through constant application the prime minister has elevated to an art form. Newspapers are discouraged from publishing matters anathema to government policy or plan through the disgraceful yet facile accusation that they are championing—or, a variant thereof, "glamourizing"—the cause of communism, chauvinism or communalism, as the case may be, or acting as proxies of foreign governments, whether friendly or otherwise, usually followed by the selective application of the ISA against targeted journalists, editors or proprietors. In this fearful atmosphere, it is a wise newspaper editor who avoids or refrains from publishing anything which might conceivably offend a prickly government. Among the detentions of other notable media personnel was former *Utusan Melayu* editor, Said Zahari. He was detained without trial under the ISA at Moon Crescent Centre and at other places of detention for nearly 16 years, and then exiled to the island of Ubin, off Singapore, for another nine months before he was finally released in August 1979. The case of nationalist journalist A. Samad Ismail is discussed elsewhere in this book.

A lesser-known case was that of a senior *Nanyang* reporter, Ngiam Thong Hai, whose detention was belatedly reported on October 18, 1966, in the *Straits Times* for "activities [allegedly] detrimental to the security of the Republic." He had been arrested by the ISD and detained for one week *before* the arrest was publicly made known. The official statement—one week into his arrest and detention—said:

> After protracted investigation by the ISD and corroborating evidence from a number of arrested persons connected with the underground organizations of the Communist Party of Malaya (CPM) in Singapore, the police have arrested Ngiam Thong Hai, who is deeply involved in activities detrimental to the security of the Republic. The government has a duty to protect the security of the country against illegal and unconstitutional activity and will ruthlessly pursue this aim irrespective of race, colour or creed.

A well-known but little-spoken fact is the ubiquity of ISD informers and agents in almost every facet of life in Singapore—from schools through the universities to the work-place. Therefore, it is a wise Singaporean who keeps his own counsel and the custody of his eyes. Nigel Holloway, in an excellent article, "Singapore Inc.'s Corporate Security Service," noted:

> The ISD has informers in every government department and is said to keep tabs on all senior civil servants and most cabinet ministers. It is also liberally represented in the media, including the *Straits Times* and the Singapore Broadcasting Corp. However its main worry seems to be religious and political organizations, judging by its crackdown on these groups over the past year.[3]

The editor of the *Straits Times* took offence at the article and, with touching naïveté, challenged him to name the ISD informers or agents within his organization.

The government's grip on the media was further tightened with the appointment of Tjong Yik Min, former ISD director—described by then prime minister Lee Kuan Yew as one of the ablest directors he had worked with—and permanent secretary to the ministry of communications to the board of directors of Singapore Press Holdings (SPH) in 1994.[4] He bids fair to succeed Lim Kim San, the aging and ailing loyalist leader of a vast media empire.

Official Secrets Act, Cap. 213

An act to prevent, amongst other things, the disclosure of official documents and information and to provide penalties for espionage. Depending upon the nature and gravity of the offence, a person may be liable on conviction to a fine not exceeding S$20,000 and to imprisonment for a term not exceeding 14 years. In this connexion, we have already discussed the case of *Business Times* editor, Patrick Daniel, and others, who were charged under the OSA.

Parliamentary (Privileges, Immunities and Powers) Act, Cap. 217

Sections 7 and 8 provide protection from any criminal or civil proceedings in respect of bona fide printing and publication of parliamentary proceedings without malice. See, also, Jeyaretnam and the Workers' Party organ, *The Hammer*, in chapter 6.

Penal Code, Cap. 224, Sections 449 to 500

Criminal defamation is committed where a person, by words intended to be read, makes or publishes any imputation concerning any person, intending to harm, or knowing or having reason to believe that such imputation will harm, the reputation of such person. It may amount to defamation to impute anything to a deceased person, if the imputation would harm the reputation of that person if living, and is intended to be hurtful to the feelings of his family or other near relatives. It may amount to defamation to make an imputation concerning a company, or an association or collection of persons as such. An imputation in the form of an alternative, or expressed ironically, may amount to defamation.

No imputation is said to harm a person's reputation unless that imputation directly or indirectly, in the estimation of others, lowers the moral or intellectual character of that person, or lowers the character of that person in respect of his caste or of his calling, or lowers the credit of that person, or causes it to be believed that the body of that person is in a loathsome state, or in a state generally considered as disgraceful.

Sedition Act, Cap. 290

The act prohibits speeches and publications with "seditious tendency," which includes inciting disaffection with the government and the judiciary among the people and between the races and classes. Inciting the people to change laws by means other than lawful ones is also deemed seditious.

Undesirable Publications Act, Cap. 338

The act first became law on September 16, 1938, as an ordinance, and was repealed and reenacted with amendments by the Undesirable Publications Act, 1967, "to prevent the importation, distribution, or reproduction of undesirable publications." The scope of the act extends to domestic as well as foreign publications, and vests in the relevant minister absolute discretionary powers to gazette a publication as undesirable. The definition of "undesirable" is as broad as it is vague. An undesirable publication is defined as one that is "prejudicial to public safety or public interest." As Indiana University librarian Cecil Byrd states: "This is so broad and general that under an irresponsible or repressive government or administration, publishing and book activity could be throttled or absolutely controlled."[5] The Undesirable Publications Act also covers publications printed unlawfully in Singapore.

There are no official criteria published for the guidance of importers regarding "undesirability," but it is easily deducible from a list of books and other publications which had previously been banned or disallowed entry. They fall into four main categories: political—communist or pro-communist literature; moral—literature relating to sex or violence; religious; and racially biased literature.

Foreign imported publications, and in particular Chinese-language publications, are examined under the act to ensure that they are not prejudicial to public safety and maintenance of public order in Singapore. Censorship is manifestly exercised. But, in 1971, the minister for culture assured the public that censorship of imported literature is based on "liberal principles" so that the people would be able to read various types of books and good publications.[6] English-language publications are also examined but on a selective basis with attention being paid as to their moral desirability. Publications which are refused entry are detained, and orders prohibiting their sale or circulation are published in the *Gazette*. Sexually oriented publications, such as the *Playboy* magazine, *Penthouse* magazine and other magazines falling within this genre, are gazetted as "undesirable."

In October 1991, three foreign publications—viz. an American adult comic book, *Deadline*, which consisted of "offensive illustrations and profane language"; an Australian women's magazine, *Cleo*, which carried "offensive illustrations of the male sexual organs"; and a special supplement to the British music magazine *Q*, which contained a "full-frontal nude photograph of an American punk rocker Iggy Pop"—were banned. The latter magazine was allowed to circulate without the supplement, but the distributors decided to withdraw it altogether. The distributors, however, were told that future issues of the magazines could circulate if they met with the approval of the ministry. Explaining the ban, a ministry's spokesman said: "Normally, we do not allow explicit displays of genitals. But we look at the pictures first to decide. It really depends on the way the picture is depicted. For instance, in a photographic magazine, we may be more liberal. But it varies. One cannot apply any hard and fast rules to this kind of thing. Publications which contain offensive material can be banned or the offensive parts can be blacked out or removed before distribution."[7]

The well-known magazine *Cosmopolitan* was banned in 1982 "for promoting promiscuous values." But encouraged by the Censorship Review Committee's recommendation that the government should consider easing restrictions on magazines that primarily feature text rather than photographs, the publishers, Australian Consolidated Press (Southeast Asia), in March 1993, approached MITA to bring out a special Singapore edition, which was refused after MITA had evaluated a more conservative South African edition on which it was supposed to be based. The ban on the magazine remains. In view of the continued prohibition, the Australian Consolidated Press (which publishes 70 titles in Australia and New Zealand) was reported to be reconsidering its plan to make Singapore its regional headquarters.[8] At about the same time, the March 1993 Singapore-edition of the French leisure-and-lifestyle monthly magazine, *Marie Claire*, was banned for carrying an article captioned "Sleeping with Celebrities: Three Women Confess," a confessional article "on casual sex and group sex." The publisher, Paul Beh of Magazines Incorporated, was directed by MITA to withdraw all copies and warned not to publish such articles in the future. "The publisher has the responsibility of ensuring that he does not publish materials that purvey permissive values and lifestyles." But the *Marie Claire* managing director said: "The aim of the magazine is to speak the facts and let the readers draw their own conclusions. This article was just raising issues, and not making a stand. Although the names of the women had been changed, they were all Singaporeans and their accounts were factual. We thought the article was within acceptable editorial limits. The magazine aims to be issue-oriented. But we do not understand the reasons for the ministry's concern." To ensure that future issues are not banned, the magazine's editors were reportedly considering clearing questionable articles with MITA.[9]

All major publishers and book importers of foreign publications, therefore, send as a matter of commercial prudence samples of publications to the ministry for culture—renamed the ministry of communications and information, and then the ministry of information and the arts—for clearance before exhibiting them for sale. This is done so that if a publication is found objectionable, a minimum financial loss would be suffered. Otherwise the publishers or importers risk having their "undesirable" literature banned or confiscated. Journalist-writer Alex Josey claimed, "Few books in English about Singapore, even the most critical written by pro-communists, have ever been prohibited."[10] This is not wholly true, as it does not state the true position.

Critical books on Singapore leaders, government or policy, although technically not banned, are simply not available in bookstores in the country. The authorities' usual disingenuous explanation for the nonavailability of such books is that the distributors have not brought the books into Singapore or that they have not yet complied with some regulation regarding publication or importation. We have already seen examples of this curious nonavailability of critical books. (See also "Legal Weapon," chapter 8.)

Notes

1. *Straits Times*, April 12 and June 8, 1973.
2. *Straits Times*, Weekly Edition, April 18, 1992.
3. *Far Eastern Economic Review*, June 30, 1988.
4. But see Cherian George, "The Press and the City," *Commentary*, vol. 10, December 1992.

5. Cecil K. Byrd, *Books In Singapore—A Survey of Publishing, Printing, Bookselling, and Library Activity*. Singapore: Chopmen Enterprises, 1970.

6. *Straits Times*, March 23, 1971.

7. *Straits Times,* Weekly Edition, November 30, 1991.

8. *Straits Times,* Weekly Edition, March 20, 1993.

9. Ibid.

10. Alex Josey, *Singapore: Its Past, Present and Future*. Brisbane: University of Queensland Press, 1980.

Appendix A

Newspaper Circulation*

No. of Copies Sold Per Day, 1984–1989

Language	1984	1985	1986	1987	1988	1989
Chinese	279,000	359,303	354,900	360,691	354,840	366,211
English	307,400	308,221	282,200	292,721	340,401	362,634
Total Circulation	630,600	713,866	684,298	700,925	743,334	777,052

*Sources: Singapore Yearbooks 1984–1989.

Appendix B

The *Sunday Times,* May 22, 1988

Seow Reveals Human Rights Connection
Amnesty and Asiawatch Knew Detainees Had Not Been Assaulted
BY LIAK TENG KIAT

WHEN Amnesty International and Asiawatch accused the Government of torturing detainees who had been arrested last year for involvement with a Marxist conspiracy, both organizations knew this to be untrue.

The two bodies had earlier learnt from detained lawyer Francis Seow who had interviewed several of them while they were in custody that they had not been assaulted.

This disclosure came from Seow's statutory declaration, parts of which were released by the Government on Friday.

Yesterday, the Government made public the full declaration, explaining in a press statement it had not done so earlier because it did not wish to "cloud the basic issue of foreign interference in Singapore's politics."

The portions released on Friday detailed Seow's relations with American diplomat E. Mason "Hank" Hendrickson and other unnamed State Department officials—whose identities have just been disclosed by the American embassy.

The previously omitted parts are not directly related to the case but were being released because "they are relevant to a full understanding of the affair," the press statement said.

Seow's sworn statement also related how he came to run for the presidency of the Law Society and his activities, many prompted by detainee Teo Soh Lung, after he won.

It also told of his participation, beginning the middle of last year, in a succession of human rights conferences abroad, viz.:

- THE biennial conference of Lawasia held in Kuala Lumpur in June/July 1987 to which he was invited by Param Cumaraswamy, a Lawasia Council member and President of the Malaysian Bar Council which was playing host;
- A WORKSHOP in Kuala Lumpur in October at the invitation of an unnamed official of the Asian Human Rights Commission;
- A CONFERENCE in Bangkok in December at the invitation of the International Commission of Jurists, which also invited him to another conference to be held next month in the Philippines; and
- THE Philippines International Law Conference in Manila in February at the invitation of Claudio Teehankee, the then Philippines Chief Justice.

Seow said he saw the conferences as an "opportunity to meet many luminaries of the judiciary and the legal profession."

"They avail me a forum to share my views . . . and to focus attention on some human rights problems in Singapore, such as the ISA arrests, so that concerned international organizations would bring pressure to bear upon the Singapore Government to release these detainees or put them on trial."

In addition, he said, the conferences "would give me an international profile as a human rights advocate" and were timely in view of his intention to run in the general elections.

He felt the ISA arrests would be an issue in the elections and an international profile "could give me a measure of immunity and preservation in the event of Government's action against me when I enter politics."

In an addendum to its press statement yesterday, the Government commented that it was "remarkable" that Seow, without any history of interest in politics or human rights, "should suddenly be in such great demand to address conferences. . . . "

"These invitations, arranged through the informal network of human rights organizations, appear to be part of the plan to build up Seow's reputation and credibility as an opposition figure of stature," it said.

Seow was contacted by and met representatives of Asiawatch, Amnesty International and the International Commission of Jurists, all of whom asked questions about the Marxist plot detainees.

In June, he agreed to meet an Udo Janz from Amnesty International who asked whether he had been allowed to interview the detainees, what he had observed of their physical well-being and the condition of their detention.

"I said that I was allowed to interview the detainees and they had told me that they were not assaulted," Seow wrote in this sworn statement.

He related a similar meeting in December with an Eric Schwartz of Asiawatch who had phoned him from New York.

"I do not know who referred him to me. It could well have been Hank Hendrickson," he said.

When they met in his office several days later, Schwartz also asked about the detainees.

"I replied that the three detainees, namely Lim Li Kok, Wong Souk Yee and William Yap, whom I interviewed had said they were not assaulted."

Despite this, the two organizations went on to accuse the Government of torturing the detainees and Seow himself issued two press statements in language he described in his declaration as "rather political and belligerent."

He said his purpose was to politicize the issue, and to generate pressure on the Government to release the detainees.

"In the process, I hoped I could build up my reputation as an ombudsman and help boost my political standing."

In addition, Seow talked of being sought for interviews by foreign correspondents.

He was "quite happy" to be interviewed, he said.

Besides generating publicity about the ISA issue, he "also felt that it would be useful for me to cultivate the friendship of these foreign journalists because, in the long-term, they could help publicize my views and this would be advantageous as I already had the intention to enter politics."

Appendix C
Asia Watch Response

June 20, 1988

To the Editor:

Asia Watch takes strong exception to a *Sunday Times* article ("Seow Reveals Human Rights Connection," May 22, 1988) in which your reporter alleged that our organization had knowingly made false accusations of government torture against detainees arrested under Singapore's Internal Security Act in May and June of last year. The article's allegation is both inaccurate and irresponsible.

The *Sunday Times* appears to have reached its conclusion based on an excerpt from lawyer Francis Seow's statutory declaration of May 16, in which Mr. Seow wrote that he had told Asia Watch that "the three detainees, namely Lim Li Kok, Wong Souk Yee and William Yap, whom I interviewed had said that they were not assaulted." However, Mr. Seow's declaration does not support the *Sunday Times*'s allegation.

First, because Mr. Seow's statement refers to only three of the 22 persons detained in May and June of last year, nothing in it contradicts what Asia Watch has written and stated publicly. As we have said before, we are convinced that detainees were subjected to various forms of mistreatment during detention, including physical assaults to the face and body, as well as prolonged interrogation and sleep deprivation in very cold rooms. In addition, detainees were repeatedly threatened during interrogation; among a number of threats, detainees were told that they would be detained indefinitely if they did not cooperate with their interrogators. Nearly all the detainees were subjected to one or more of such forms of mistreatment, and several of the 22 were physically assaulted. But contrary to the *Sunday Times*'s allegation, Asia Watch has never stated that every one of the 22 detainees was subjected to physical assaults. That Mr. Seow identifies three detainees who allegedly told him they were not physically assaulted thus in no way contradicts our statements on this issue.

Second, although Asia Watch did indeed speak with Mr. Seow during our visit in December, he is by no means the only person with whom our organization has discussed these issues. Over the past year, we have interviewed and received information from more than a score of Singaporeans knowledgeable about these cases, as well as Singapore-based diplomats from Europe, Asia and the United States, journalists who have followed these cases closely, and Singaporean diplomats based in Washington. We have reached our conclusions about mistreatment—including physical assaults—after carefully evaluating the information presented to us by *all* of these sources.

Third, while we will not now comment on the accuracy of Mr. Seow's statement because of the extremely vulnerable position in which he is being held by the government, we note that his statement was made under circumstances that we believe to have been coercive. Mr. Seow was subjected to incommunicado interrogation under the Internal Security Act (ISA), which permits indefinite detention without trial. As your newspaper has reported, former ISA detainees in Singapore have stated publicly that their releases were conditioned upon making statements that satisfied their interrogators. We do not know how Mr. Seow was treated under interrogation. We do know, however, that he was aware of the Internal Security Department practice of linking confessions, or other "satisfactory" statements by detainees, to releases. We also know that Mr. Seow was aware of the pattern of mistreatment against detainees who were not "cooperative." Under such circumstances, the accuracy of any statutory declaration is open to the most serious question. Indeed, the fact that detainees who had been freed renounced statements that they had made while in incommunicado detention underscores the unreliability of statements emanating from such coercive circumstances.

We are also disappointed that the *Sunday Times* did not attempt to contact us to obtain our comments before its story was published. We believe that this is a major departure from standard journalistic practice and helped to contribute to the inaccuracy of this article.

In conclusion, we must reiterate our concerns that detainees imprisoned in May and June 1987 were indeed subjected to mistreatment. Moreover, in light of consistent and credible reports to this effect, we call upon the government to initiate an independent investigation of the claims of mistreatment.

Sincerely,

Kenneth Roth, Esq.
Deputy Director
Human Rights Watch
(Asia Watch/Americas Watch/Helsinki Watch)
New York, N.Y.

Selected Bibliography

Books

Abu Hena Mustafa Kamal. *The Bengali Press and Literary Writing (1813–31)*. Dhaka: University Press Limited, 1977.

Amnesty International. *Report of an Amnesty International Mission to Singapore, 30 November to 5 December 1978*. New York: Amnesty International Publications, 1980.

———. *Singapore: Amnesty International Briefing*. 2d ed. New York: Amnesty International, 1978.

———. *Singapore: Detentions Without Trial Under the Internal Security Act*. New York: Amnesty International.

———. *Report of an Amnesty International Mission to the Republic of Singapore, 14–22 June 1987*. New York: Amnesty International, 1987.

Asia Watch. *Silencing All Critics, Human Rights Violations in Singapore*. New York: AsiaWatch, 1989.

Byrd, Cecil K. *Books In Singapore—A Survey of Publishing, Printing, Bookselling, and Library Activity*. Singapore: Chopmen Enterprises, 1970.

Bloodworth, Dennis. *The Tiger and the Trojan Horse*. Singapore: Times Book International, 1986.

Buckley, C.B. *An Anecdotal History of Old Times in Singapore*. 2 vols., Singapore: Fraser and Neave, 1902.

Caldwell, Malcolm. *Lee Kuan Yew—the Man, his Mayoralty, and his Mafia*. London: FUEMSSO, Spider Web, 1979.

Cheah Boon Kheng. *A. Samad Ismail: Journalism & Politics*. Comp. and ed. Kuala Lumpur: Singamal Publishing Bureau (M) Sdn Bhd, 1987.

Chee, Soon Juan. *Singapore, My Home Too*. Singapore: Melodies Press, 1995.

Chen, Mong Hock. *The Early Chinese Newspapers of Singapore 1881–1912*. Singapore: University of Malaya Press, 1967.

Dow Jones. *Lee Kuan Yew vs The News: A History*. New York: Dow Jones & Co., Inc., 1990.

George, T.J.S. *Lee Kuan Yew's Singapore*. London: Andre Deutsch, 1973.

Hamidah bte Haji Hassan. "A Consummate Actor," in *A. Samad Ismail: Journalism and Politics*, ed. Cheah Boon Kheng. Kuala Lumpur: Singamal Publishing Bureau (M) Sdn Bhd, 1987.

Husin Ali, S. "A Genuine Nationalist," in *A. Samad Ismail: Journalism and Politics*, ed. Cheah Boon Kheng. Kuala Lumpur: Singamal Publishing Bureau (M) Sdn Bhd, 1987.

Josey, Alex. *Singapore: Its Past, Present and Future*. Brisbane: University of Queensland Press, 1980.

Kesavan B.S. *Printing and Publishing in India*. 2 vols. India: National Book Trust.

Kuo, Eddie C.Y., Duncan Holaday, and Eugenia Peck. *Mirror on the Wall: Media in a Singapore Election*. Singapore: Asia Mass Communication Research and Information Centre, 1993.

Lee, Hsien Loong. "When the Press Misinforms," speech at 40th World Congress of Newspaper Publishers, Helsinki, Finland. Singapore: Ministry of Communications & Information, May 26, 1987.

Lee, Kuan Yew. "The Mass Media and New Countries," speech, General Assembly of the International Press Institute, Helsinki, Finland, in *Socialism That Works—The Singapore Way*, Singapore: Federal Publications, 1976.

Lent, John A. "Testimony," House of Representatives, Committee on Foreign Affairs, Subcommittee on Human Rights and International Organizations, July 7, 1988.

Lent, John A., ed., *Newspapers in Asia: Contemporary Trends and Problems.* Hongkong: Heinemann Asia, 1982.

Makepeace, Walter, Gilbert E. Brooke, and Roland St. J. Braddell (eds.). *One Hundred Years of Singapore.* 2 vols., London: John Murray, 1921.

Minchin, James. *No Man Is an Island: A Study of Singapore's Lee Kuan Yew.* 2nd edn. Sydney: Allen & Unwin Australia, 1990.

Ministry of Communications & Information. *The Right to Be Heard: Singapore's Dispute With TIME magazine & The Asian Wall Street Journal: The Facts.* Singapore: May 1987.

Morais, Victor J., ed. *Selected Speeches: A Golden Treasury of Asian Thought and Wisdom,* Kuala Lumpur: J. Victor Morais, 1967.

Nair, C.V. Devan, ed. *Socialism That Works—The Singapore Way.* Singapore: Federal Publications (S), 1976.

Nonis, George. *Hello Chok Tong, Good bye Kuan Yew.* Singapore: Angsana Books, 1991.

Parker, Elliott S. "Singapore," *World Press Encyclopedia,* edited by George Thomas Kurian. London: Mansell, 1982.

Priolkar, Anant Kakba. *The Printing Press in India: Its Beginnings and Early Development.* Bombay: Marathi Samshodhana Mandala, 1958.

Rajakumar, M. "Malaysia's Jean-Paul Sartre," in *A. Samad Ismail: Journalism and Politics,* ed. Cheah Boon Kheng. Kuala Lumpur: Singamal Publishing Bureau (M) Sdn Bhd, 1987.

Rosenberg, David et al. *Guided Press in Southeast Asia: National Development vs. Freedom of Expression.* ed. John A. Lent, Buffalo, Council on International Studies, State University of New York, 1976).

Selvan, T.S. *Singapore, the Ultimate Island: Lee Kuan Yew's Untold Story.* Melbourne: Freeway Books, 1990.

Sesser, Stan. *The Lands of Charm and Cruelty: Travels in Southeast Asia.* New York: Alfred A. Knopf, 1993.

Seow, Francis T. *To Catch a Tartar: A Dissident in Lee Kuan Yew's Prison,* Monograph 42. New Haven: Yale Southeast Asia Studies, Yale Centre for International and Area Studies, 1994.

Tan, Teng Lang. *The Singapore Press: Freedom, Responsibility and Credibility.* Singapore: Times Academic Press for the Institute of Policy Studies, 1990.

Taylor, John Calvin. "Lee Kuan Yew: His Rise to Power, 1950–1968," M.A. thesis. San Diego State University, 1976.

Turnbull, C.M. *The Straits Settlements, 1826–67.* London: The Athlone Press, 1972.

_____. *Dateline Singapore: 150 years of the* Straits Times, Singapore: Singapore Press Holdings, 1995.

Wee, Han Kim. *One Sweet Letter from You.* Singapore: A Hammer Publication, 1992.

Yeo, George. "Singapore and the Foreign Press: The Next Lap," speech to Foreign Correspondents' Association of Singapore, 1991.

Yong, C.F. *Tan Kah-Kee: The Making of an Overseas Legend.* Singapore: Oxford University Press, 1987.

Selected Articles

Antolik, Michael. "Singapore's Joust with Journalism," *Asian Profile,* vol. 19 no. 6, December 1991.

Asian Wall Street Journal. Editorial: "Jeyaretnam's Challenge" (October 17, 1985).

_____. Editorial: "Singapore's Trouble" (February 12, 1987).

_____. Editorial: "Matter of Regret" (October 15, 1990).

_____. Editorial: "The Singapore Raj" (October 18, 1990).

_____. Editorial: "White Man's Plot?" (October 29, 1990).

Asiaweek. "The Danse Macabre" (June 11, 1976).

_____. "Shake-Up and Merger in Singapore" (May 7, 1982).

_____. "A Distortion of Facts, You Say" (September 27, 1987).

The Australian. Editorial: "Singapore's tarnished image" (May 21, 1971).

Batterman, Nancy. "Singapore's Newspaper and Printing Presses (Amendment) Act 1986: A Bad News Bear?" *Lawasia, A Journal of the Law Association for Asia and the Pacific*, 1987.

Birch, E.W. "The Vernacular Press in the Straits," *Journal of the Straits Branch of the Royal Asiatic Society*, December, 1879.

Bowring, Philip. "Conflict of evidence," *Review* (March 25, 1977).

_____. "Free not to profit," *Review* (February 11, 1988).

_____. "When a copy is not a copy," *Review* (March 3, 1988).

_____. "The claims about 'Asian' values don't usually bear scrutiny," *International Herald Tribune* (August 2, 1994).

Casady, Simon. "Purging the Press," *Index on Censorship*, vol. 3 no. 4 (1975).

Cheong, Yip Seng. Letter: "Matter of fact," *Review* (February 12, 1987).

_____. Letter: "Board challenge," *Review* (March 5, 1987).

Das, K. "Malaysia: The enemies within," *Review* (July 2, 1976).

_____. "Malaysia's Samad: 'I did it my way'," *Review* (September 17, 1976).

_____. "Hussein gives Harun the Party nod," *Review* (November 5, 1976).

_____. "The purge from within," *Review* (November 12, 1976).

_____. "Succession struggle—round two," *Review* (November 26, 1976).

_____. "Switching on the confessions," *Review* (February 18, 1977).

_____. "The subtle art of subversion," *Review* (February 25, 1977).

_____. "Lee's TV chiller for Malaysia," *Review* (March 11, 1977).

_____. "Concern across the causeway," *Review* (March 25, 1977).

Davies, Derek. "Putting the Record Straight," *Review* (March 26, 1976).

_____. "Traveller's Tales," *Review* (March 25, 1977).

_____. "Putting the Record Straight," *Review* (March 25, 1977).

_____. "More in sorrow than anger," *Review* (March 25, 1977).

_____. "Postscript on Arun," *Review* (March 25, 1977).

_____. "Refuting the implications," *Review* (March 25, 1977).

_____. "Another 'confession' in Singapore," *Review* (April 29, 1977).

_____. "A Ban by any Other Name," *Review* (January 7, 1987).

_____. "Traveller's Tales," *Review* (May 14, 1987).

_____. "Traveller's Tales," *Review* (April 7, 1988).

D'souza, Edgar K. Letter: "What Yong told church delegation," *Review* (January 7, 1988).

DeVoss, David. "Southeast Asia's intimidated press," *Columbia Journalism Review*, March-April 1978.

Duthie, Stephen. "Singapore Exchange Puzzles Financiers," *Asian Wall Street Journal* (December 12–13, 1986).

Farrow, Moira. "Newsman says 'Fear rules'," *Vancouver Sun* (October 12, 1974).

Far Eastern Economic Review. "The Wong Way Out" (April 3, 1971).

_____. Editorial: "Wild about Harry," (May 29, 1971).

_____. "Regional Affairs: Mayday, Mayday, Mayday . . . " (May 22, 1971).

_____. Editorial: "Colour of their money" (June 5, 1971).

_____. A correspondent, "The Day a Man Cried" (June 5, 1971).

_____. Editorial: "A Lone Voice" (November 25, 1972).

_____. A correspondent, "Lee Kuan Yew's 'disincentives'" (December 9, 1972).

_____. A correspondent, "Predicting unrest" (December 3, 1973).

_____. A correspondent, "Pointing the finger" (March 4, 1977).

Fong, Leslie. Letter: "Undeserved slur," *Review* (August 4, 1988).

Fu, James Chiao Sian. Letter: "Rule No. 1: No Playing Games," *Review* (May 28, 1987).

_____. Letter: "Duty to be responsible," *Review* (January 7, 1988).

_____. Letter: "Singapore's side of the story," *Review* (January 21, 1988).

_____. "Advertisement: Telling it like it is?," *Review* (January 28, 1988).

George, Cherian. "The Press and the City," *Commentary*, vol. 10, December 1992.

Gibson-Hill, C.A. "The Singapore Chronicle, 1824–37," *Journal of the Malayan Branch of the Royal Asiatic Society*, vol. 26, pt. 1.

Haas, Michael. "The Politics of Singapore in the 1980s," *Journal of Contemporary Asia*, vol. 19 no. 1 (1989).

Heng, Russell. "Censorship: it can go either way," *Singapore* (July 1992).

Ho, Kwon Ping. "Union Chief sides with the State," *Review* (May 7, 1976).

_____. "Countering the communist sinister conspiracy," *Review* (May 14, 1976).

_____. "New student crackdown," *Review* (August 13, 1976).

_____. "Singapore Students: End of the lesson," *Review* (September 17, 1976).

_____. "Washington aids Asean buildup," *Review* (January 4, 1977).

Hoffman, Leslie C. "Threat to Freedom," *Straits Times* (April 21, 1959).

_____. "Fancy and Fact," *Straits Times* (April 30, 1959).

_____. "Think Again, Mr. Lee," *Straits Times* (May 20, 1959).

_____. "Bird of Passage, Mr. Lee? I stay," *Straits Times* (May 22, 1959).

Holloway, Nigel. "Government and press—a degree of trust," *Review* (July 3, 1986).

_____. "A fall from grace," *Review* (January 27, 1987).

_____. "Singapore's Inc.'s corporate security," *Review* (June 30, 1988).

Hongkong Standard. Editorial: "Chauvinism and Mr. Lee" (June 1, 1974).

Khaw, Ambrose. Editorial: "The Right to Live with Dignity," *Singapore Herald* (May 18, 1971).

Lent, John A. "Lee Kuan Yew and the Singapore Media: Protecting the People," *Index on Censorship*, vol. 4 no. 3, 1975.

_____. "True (?) Confessions—TV in Malaysia and Singapore," *Index on Censorship*, vol. 7 no. 2, 1978.

Levin, Bernard. "The law grossly misused," *Times* (London) (June 14, 1989).

_____. "A lively trade in vilification," *Times* (London) (August 24, 1989).

Lewis, Anthony. "A Respectful Press?" *New York Times* (March 14, 1987).

Li, Gladys. "A convenient scapegoat," *Review* (November 1, 1990).

Lim, Raymond. "Viewpoint, Will the Next Lap be a new era of intolerance?" *Straits Times, Weekly Edition* (February 1, 1992).

Lingle, Christopher. "The Smoke Over Parts of Asia Obscures Some Profound Concerns," *International Herald Tribune* (October 10, 1994).

_____, and Kurt Wickman. "Don't Trust the Reports of Supercharged Growth," *International Herald Tribune* (January 19, 1994).

Malik, Michael. "New Light on Detentions," *Review* (December 17, 1987).

Mitton, Roger. "The Long Story, What Role for the Press? Singapore's Answers, A Special Relationship," *Asiaweek* (September 25, 1992).

Morgan, James. "Medium, Not the Message," *Review* (May 15, 1971).

_____. "Low Profile in U.K.," *Review* (December 9, 1972).

Polsky, Anthony. "Lee Kuan Yew versus the Press," Pacific Community, *An Asian Quarterly Review*, vol. 3 nos. 1–4 (October 1971–July 1972).

Ranck, Rosemary. Review of *The Savage Mirror: The Art of Contemporary Caricature*, Watson-Guptil, *New York Times* (January 31, 1993).

Reece, Bob. Letter: "Why I left the Herald," *Straits Times* (June 9, 1971).

Rodan, Garry. "Symbolic Clash with International Press in Singapore," Asia Research Centre, Murdoch University, *Asiaview*, vol. 5 no. 1, 1995.

Scott, Margaret. "The right of reply," *Review* (June 11, 1987).

_____. "A Meeting of Minds," *Review* (October 27, 1988).

Senkuttuvan, Arun. "Singapore provides the connection," *Review* (July 2, 1976).

Smith, Colin. "The PM who fines you for not flushing the loo," *Observer* (December 10, 1989).

Smith, Patrick. "Pressed into wedlock," *Review* (April 23, 1982).

South China Morning Post. Editorial: "Spontaneous Reaction" (October 16, 1990).

Stockwin, Harvey. "The politics of detention," *Review* (July 2, 1976).

_____. "Transcending all races," *Review* (September 17, 1976).

Straits Times. Editorial: "*Herald* Affair" (May 24, 1971).

_____. "Saving the *Herald*" (May 25, 1971).

_____. "*Herald* Closes" (May 29, 1971).

_____. "This Freedom" (June 11, 1971).

Taylor, Stephen. "Liberalizing wind stirs in Singapore's press," *Times*, (London) (January 24, 1985).

Wall Street Journal. Editorial: "The Press and Mr. Lee" (April 20, 1988).

_____. "Singapore Scheme" (July 23, 1990).

_____. "Settlement in Singapore" (March 23, 1991).

Wallace, Charles P. "Singapore's grip," *Columbia Journalism Review*, November-December 1995.

Legal Cases

Associated Provincial Picture Houses Ltd. v Wednesbury Corporation [1947] 2 *All E.R.* 680

Lee Mau Seng v Minister of Home Affairs & anor [1971] 2 *Malayan Law Journal* (M.L.J.) 137

Attorney General v Pang Cheng Lian & Ors [1975] 1 *M.L.J.* 69

Workers' Party v Tay Boon Too; Workers' Party v Attorney General [1975] 1 *M.L.J.* 47

Tay Boon Too and anor v Workers' Party [1975] 2 *M.L.J.* 124 C.A.

Attorney General v Fred Zimmerman & Ors [1986] 1 *M.L.J.* 89

Dow Jones Publishing Company (Asia) Inc. Application [1988] 2 *M.L.J.* 416

J. B. Jeyaretnam v Law Society of Singapore [1988] 3 *M.L.J.* 425

Dow Jones Publishing Company (Asia) Inc. v Attorney General [1989] 2 *M.L.J.* 385.

Dow Jones Publishing Company (Asia) Inc. v Attorney General [1989] 3 *M.L.J.* 321

Lee Kuan Yew v Derek Davies & Ors [1990] 1 *M.L.J.* 390

Newspapers & Periodicals

Asian Wall Street Journal
Asiaweek
The Australian
Australian Financial Times
Bangkok Post
The Economist
Far Eastern Economic Review
International Herald Tribune
Manchester Guardian
New York Times
The Observer (London)
South China Morning Post
Sydney Morning Herald Tribune
Straits Times
Straits Times Weekly Edition
Times (London)
Time
Wall Street Journal

Other Publications

Asiaview
Columbia Journalism Review
Commentary
FBIS-East
Index on Censorship
Journal of the Malayan Branch, Royal Asiatic Society
Journal of the Straits Branch, Royal Asiatic Society
Singapore, a publication of the Singapore International Foundation, Chanson Press. September 1992; March 1993; March-April 1994.
Singapore Undergrad

Official Debates

Hansard, Singapore Legislative Assembly debates
Hansard, Singapore Parliamentary debates
Hansard, Malaysian Parliamentary debates

Official Papers

Report of the Singapore Riots Inquiry Commission 1951, Government Printer, 1951.
First Report of the Committee of Privileges, Complaints of Allegations of Executive Interference in the Judiciary, Parliament No 3 of 1987.

Official Publications

Singapore Facts and Figures, 1983–1985, Information Division, Ministry of Culture.
Singapore Yearbook, 1980–1990, Ministry of Communications and Information.
Singapore Yearbook, 1992, Ministry of Information and the Arts.
Singapore Yearbook, 1994, Ministry of Information and the Arts.

Index

A. Samad Ismail, a.k.a. Abdul Samad Ismail: adviser
to *Tun* Razak, 32; arrests, 28, 32, 111, 229;
awards, 35; *Laniaz*, 34; and Lee Kuan Yew,
28, 29, 31; newspapers, 28, 29, 30, 31,
34–36; and the People's Action Party (PAP),
29; and politicians, 28–29; prohibited
immigrant ban, 36; statement, 33; suspected
communist, 31, 32, 33, 34; and students, 28,
29; and trade unions, 29, 30; United Malays
National Organization (UMNO), 29, 30,
31–32, 33, 34, 35
Abdullah Ahmad, *Datuk*, 33
Abdullah Majid, 33
Abdullah Sudin, 33
Abdul Rahman Putra al-Haj, Tunku, 2, 31, 209
Abdul Razak bin Datuk Hussein, *Tun*: 32, 35, 178,
179, 197n; Razak Administration, 33
Abrams, Floyd, 146
Acts: Children and Young Persons Act, Cap. 38,
229; Defamation Act, Cap. 75, 228; Judicial
Proceedings (Regulation of Reports) Act,
Cap. 149, 229; Legal Profession Act, Cap.
161, 148; Parliamentary (Privileges,
Immunities and Powers) Act, Cap. 217, 230;
Printing Presses Act, Cap. 258, 20, 107, 158,
159; *See also* Ordinances
Adams, John, 4
Age, The (Melbourne), 59, 112, 195
Agence France-Presse, 102, 184, 190
Ahmad Ibrahim, 29
Ahmad Sebi, 28
American Business Council (ABC) in Singapore,
149–150, 153
American Society of Newspaper Editors, 149, 155,
177, 183
Amnesty International, 30, 142, 180, 215, 234,
235: 1980 *Report of an Amnesty International
Mission to Singapore*, 218
Anton Xavier, 146
ASEAN (Association of Southeast Asian Nations), 1
Asian Mass Communications Research and
Information Centre (AMIC), 207
Asian-Pacific Economic Cooperation (APEC),
159–163
Asian Wall Street Journal (*AWSJ*), 102, 143–145,
185–196: APEC, 162; association, guilt by,
183; banana-republic action, 152; cessation,
186, 187; circulation, 147; correspondents,
148, 160, 161, 162, 163, 182, 183; criticisms
on restrictions, 149–152; dispute with

government, 143–145, 149–156;
"engagements" in domestic politics, 155,
163; "model newspaper," 144; offered free,
154–155, 165–167; partial restoration, 162,
163, 170; refusal to print reply, 155;
restriction, 148; right of reply, 155, 158,
191–194; "slanted" reporting, 149; *WSJ*
editorial, 161
Asia Watch (New York), 218, 219, 234, 235,
236–237
Asiaweek, 26, 117, 127–128, 146, 147, 184, 208,
209, 219–220: circulation, 146, 164–165;
correspondents, 164, 184; coverage on
alleged Marxist conspirators, 164, 192
Association of Banks in Singapore, 153
Australian, 87, 101–102, 184
Australian Broadcasting Corporation, 77
Australian Consolidated Press (Southeast Asia),
232
Australian Financial Times, 175
Awanohara, Susumu, 181
Aw Boon Haw, 9
Aw Boon Par, 9
Aw Kow, *Datin*, 52, 54
Aw Kow, *Datuk*, 52, 54
Aw Sian, Sally: and Lee Kuan Yew, 65–66, 67,
69–70, 71–72, 93–94; IPI, Helsinki, 95; and
Singapore Herald, 40–41, 59–60, 65–66, 73,
74, 76, 83, 95
Aziz Ishak, 29
Azmi Mahmood, 31, 33

Baker, James, 161
Balakrishnan, N., 182
Bangkok Post, 59, 146, 161–162
Bank of China, 40, 52, 100
Baratham, Gopal, 221
Barisan Rakyat, 112
Barisan Sosialis (Socialist Front), 57, 75: premises
bugged, 130–131; publications, 128–131;
split from PAP, 1, 23, 31
Barker, E. W., 220
Bartlett, Vernon, 16
Bartley, Robert L., 153
Batterman, Nancy, 148
BBC (British Broadcasting Corporation), 89, 112
Beh, Paul, 232
Berita Harian, 30–31, 36, 39–40, 126: Chaim
Herzog's state visit, 127

Berita Harian (Malaysia), 111. *See also New Straits Times*
Berita Minggu. See Berita Harian
Bernard, Francis James, 6–7
Berthelsen, John, 182
Beyer, Lisa, 164
Birch, E.W., 10n
Bish, Jim, 88
Black operations, 39, 40, 43, 106, 101, 112: *Eastern Sun*, 52–54, 61; *Nanyang Siang Pau*, 43, 45, 46, 47, 50; *Singapore Herald*, 41, 58, 59, 61–62, 64, 68–70, 73, 75, 77, 79, 80, 83, 86, 89
Blackstone, Sir William, 6
Blom-Cooper, Louis, Q. C., 157, 159
Bloodworth, Dennis, 147, 185, 209
Bonham, Sir Samuel George, 6
Boon Hua Printing Press, 128
Boustead, Edward, 7
Bowring, Philip, 176, 183, 199n
Briggs, General Sir Harold, 179
British Labour Party, 102, 109
Buckley, Charles Burton, 7
Bush, President George, 161, 223
Business Day (Bangkok), 119. *See* Singapore Press Holdings
Business Times, 126–127: charge against editor and several others, 218; copies recalled/replaced, 210–211; editorial, 210–211; investigated by ISD under the OSA, 127, 206, 211–212; investigative reporting, dangers of, 217–219
Byrd, Cecil K., 231
Byrne, Kenneth M., 13

Caldwell, Malcolm, 109, 180
Callaghan, James, 109
Caricatures. *See* cartoons
Carroll, Bob, 59
Cartoons, 65, 122, 219–220
Casady, Simon, 55n, 109–110, 142
Catholic News, 135–137. *See also* Marxist conspiracy
Censorship: publications, 213–215; self-censorship, 215; visa withdrawal, 213, 214. *See also* Press
Censorship Review Committee, 232
Central Intelligence Agency (CIA), 89, 93
Chan Heng Chee, 137
Chan Hock Hua, 212
Chase Manhattan Bank (New York), 73, 76: rules on loans, 87–88
Chase Manhattan Bank (Singapore), 66–70, 73, 74–76, 81, 93: banking confidentiality, 66, 68, 72, 75, 87; bank licence threats, 88; foreclosure, 67–68, 70, 71, 72, 75, 88, 99–101; guarantors, 70, 74, 87–88, 93–94; overdraft, 67, 68, 71, 87–88, 94
Chauvinism: Chinese, 39, 41–42, 45, 46, 49, 51, 111, 229; Malay, 39, 43, 227. *See also Berita Harian; Nanyang Siang Pau; Sin Chew Jit Poh*
Cheah Boon Kheng, 30, 35
Chee Soon Juan, Dr., 129, 133, 171, 221. *See also* Christopher Lingle

Cheng Tong Fatt, 118
Cheng, Vincent. *See Catholic News*; Marxist conspiracy
Chen Hsien Tee, 45–46
Chen Mong Hock, 10n
Cheong Yip Seng, 117, 206, 209, 218, 224
Chern Sien Pao, 129, 130
Chiam See Tong, 126, 207
Chiang Kai Shek, 10
Chia Thye Poh, 130
China, People's Republic of, 51
China Democratic League, 9
Chinese Daily Journal of Commerce. See Nanyang Siang Pau
Chinese newspapers. *See specific Chinese newspapers*
Chin Lai Ching, Jenny, 132, 181
Chip Bee Press, 128
Cho Jock Kim, 88
Chou, Terence, 198n
Chowdhury, Amitabha, 78, 80, 84
Chua Chuan Seah, 216
Chua, Morgan, 220
Citizens' Paper, 96. *See also* Singapore Herald Cooperative Society
City Council, 13
Cleo, 231
Coleman, George Drumgold, 7
Commentary, 213–214
Commission of Inquiry, 74, 87, 106: calls for, 71, 73, 75, 76, 78
Committee of Privileges: allegations of executive interference in the judiciary, 145; *The Hammer*, 132
Committee to Protect Journalists, 146, 218
Commonwealth Press Union (CPU), 16, 50, 99, 187
Commonwealth prime ministers' meeting, 109
Communalism, 39, 45, 79–80, 229
Communism, 1, 33, 39, 46, 47–48, 51, 52, 230. *See also* Communist
Communist, 31, 40, 41, 49, 79, 89, 113, 134: activities, 31, 32, 33–34, 39, 70, 91–92; cause, 110; intelligence service, 53, 54; organization, 135; pro-communists, 110, 114; Socialist International front, 110; subversion, 40, 111
Communist Party of Malaya (CPM), 10, 179, 230
Confessions, 115, 164, 237: Foo Chin Yen, 135; Goh Lay Kuan and others, 110–111; Ho Kwon Ping, 114–115; Hussein Jahidin, 31; Kerk Loong Seng, 48; Lee Mau Seng, 46–47; Ly Singko, 46; Azmi Mahmood, 31; G. Raman, 113; Arun Senkuttuvan, 113; Shamsuddin Tung, 46
Confucius, 182, 211
Constitution, Malaysian, 25
Contempt of Court. *See specific newspapers and persons*
Coomaraswamy, M., 225n
Cooper Brothers, 79, 85

Copyright Act, Cap. 63, 166: Berne Convention on
Copyright, 198n; International Copyright
Convention, 198n
Corruption (Confiscation of Benefits) bill, 26
Cosmopolitan, 232
Counsel, access to, 46, 48, 50
Crawfurd, Dr. John, 5, 7
Cumaraswamy, Param, 235
Cuthbertson, John, 7

Daily Express (London), 18
Daily Journal of Commerce. See Nanyang Siang Pau
Daily Telegraph (London), 112
Daniel, Patrick, 127, 170, 206, 218, 230
Das, K., 33
Davies, Derek: and journalist staff, 180–181; and
Lee Kuan Yew, 114, 142–143; and the
Review, 32–33, 141, 192; ultimatum, 143.
See also Far Eastern Economic Review
Deadline, 231
Debates, inter-school, 45
Defamation. *See* Legal weapon; *persons; specific
newspapers*
de Klerk, F. W., 212
Democratic People's Republic of North Korea, 98
D'souza, Edgar Kenneth, 135, 136
Deng Xiaoping, 219, 223
Denisov, Vladimir I., 146
Devan, Janamitra, 196n
Development Bank of Singapore (DBS), 119, 123
Dhanabalan, S., 124, 132, 151, 180, 184, 225n
Dow Jones Inc., 102, 141, 143–144, 159–163: *Lee
Kuan Yew vs The News: A History*, 159;
withdrawal of appeal against Thean
judgment, 168; settlement, 169–170
Dow Jones Publishing Company (Asia) Inc., 144,
156: Application, 156, 157, 191; vs Attorney
General, 155, 156–157, 158
Drysdale, John, xii
Dutch Labour Party, 31, 102, 109, 110, 111
Duthie, Stephen, 149, 152

Eastern Daily Mail. See Newspaper, extinct
publications
Eastern Sun, 40, 52, 69, 70, 71, 75, 84, 88, 100:
closure and denial of press facilities, 54, 202;
commencement of, 53; editorial policy,
52–54, 69; loans to, 40, 52–53; management
of, 52–53
East India Company, The Honourable, 2, 4, 5, 6
Economist (London), 113, 167, 178, 183: Alwyn
Young's essay, 132–133; circulation restricted,
172; correspondents, 182; de-gazetted, 173;
GDP estimates, 170–171; readers' response,
172–173; right of reply, 172, 191; and the
Singapore government, 172–173
Elections: 1959 general election, 11–19; 1972
general election, 39–40; 1976 general
election, 111–117; 1981 Anson by-election,

117–119; 1984 general election, 125, 143;
1992 Marine Parade GRC by-election, 208
Elegant, Simon, 182–183
Elliott House, Karen, 169: and Goh Chok Tong,
160, 163
Emergency Regulations, 1948, 201
Essential Information (Control of Publications and
Safeguarding of Information) Regulations,
1966, 39, 112, 228–229
Eu Chooi Yip, 10
Eurasia Press, 134
Eurocommunist, 113. *See also* Communist

Fajar: University of Singapore, 134; banned, 134
Far Eastern Economic Review (Review), 72, 102, 110,
113, 146, 182, 184, 189, 224: circulation,
147, restricted, 160, 165, partial restoration,
170; distribution, cessation of, 165;
amendment to the NPPA, 165,
photocopying, 165–166, offer, free of charge,
166–167; official piracy, 166, 189; specific
copy, withheld, 209; letters column, 191,
192–193, 215–217; correspondents, 143,
180, 181, arrest of, 112, 114–115; coverage,
so-called Marxist conspiracy, 27, 115, 165;
Samad Ismail's TV confession, 32–33;
relations with Lee, 142, 143; ultimatum, 143,
190; libel, vs Derek Davies & Ors, 167–168;
Kann's statement on, 168; right of reply, 155,
158, 186
Farquhar, major later major-general William, 2, 7
Farrow, Moira, 55n
Fay, Michael, 184, 195
Financial Times (London), 113
Fong, Leslie, 126, 206, 217, 223
Foo Chin Yen, 135
Foreign Correspondents Association of Singapore,
101, 163–164, 178
Foreign Correspondents' Club, Hongkong, 168,
188, 190–191
Foreign media: access to government, 163; cartoons,
caricatures, 219–220; circulation, restriction a
sovereign right, 160, 193; correspondents,
182, expulsion of, 141, 142, 145, 178–184;
proposed ASEAN ban, 185; correspondents/
cameramen, accredited, 190, 195; coverage as
"outsiders for outsiders," 28, 101, 102, 193;
employment/work passes/permits, privilege,
161, 183, policy on granting, 142, 179, 180,
183, *local-itis*, 184; social visit passes, 183,
184; interviews of detainees, 113, 114;
legislation, NPPA, amendments, *raison d'être*,
141, 147–148, 154, 177–178; "engaging" in
domestic politics, definition of, 156, 158,
161, bond, *etcetera*, requirements, 185,
"offshore newspapers," definition of,
extended, 185; publications affected, 186,
190; exempted, 190; publications, popularity
of, 124, not banned, 183; right of reply, 155,

158, 186; operating principle, 191–194; matters *sub judice*, 192; Singapore, a salubrious perch, 188, 190–191; *See also* Media; *specific foreign publications*
Fraser, John, 7
Freedom of the press. *See* Press
Freeway Books, 220
Friedland, Jonathan, 182
Fu Chiao Sian, James, a.k.a. James Fu alias Andrew Fu, 23, 108: *amanuensis*, 141, 143, 146, 191, 192, 193, 194; *AWSJ*, 152; *Asiaweek*, 164; *Review*, 167, 181; Sing Tao group general manager, 198n; *Time*, 148
Fullerton, Robert, 7

"Gagging Act." *See* Indian press laws
Gan Kim Yong, 226
Gaspard, Armand, 18
Geiger, Matthew, 183
George, Cherian, 232
George, T. J. S., 19, 102
Ghafar Baba, 34
Ghazalie Shafie, *Tan Sri*, 32, 33, 34
Gibson-Hill, C.A., 10n
Giles, William, 208
Goh Chok Tong, 27, 36, 52, 171, 182, 218: correspondence with Elliott House, 160–161, 162–163; on Christopher Lingle, 174; *IHT*, 176; *local-itis*, 183; on NUSS, 214; "outrage" at Western media, 146–147; as prime minister, 221
Goh Keng Swee, Dr., 18, 57
Goh Lay Kuan, 110
Goh Seow Poh, 229
Goh Yew Heng, 198n
Goldstein, Carl, 182
Gorbachev, President Mikhail S., 146
Gordon, Shirle, 205, 225n
Government: British, 24; Indian, 2, 3, 4, 5, 6; Federal, 24, 25, 178, *See also* Malayan; Malaysian governments. Labour Front, 201; Malayan, 23; Malaysian, 31, 65, 70; PAP. *See* People's Action Party. U.S., 160, 163
Government Gazette, 5
Guardian. *See Manchester Guardian*
Gurney, Sir Henry, 179

Haas, Michael, 178, 194, 199n
Hahn, Jimmy, 60, 61, 64, 66–67, 68, 69, 70–71, 73, 78, 80, 86, 99; *Herald* takeover, 84, 85; notice of demand, 75–76
Hamid, Jumat, 29
Hamidah bte Haji Hassan, 29
Hammer, 131–133, 230. *See also* Marxist conspiracy
Handelsblatt, 181, 194
Harban Singh, 130
Harun Idris, 34
Hastings, Lord, 3
Heeda and Co., 40, 41, 57, 59, 65, 73. *See also Singapore Herald*

Heeda Ltd. *See* Heeda and Co.
Heng, Russell, 208, 221
Herald and Weekly Times Limited. *See Melbourne Herald*
Herzog, Chaim, 127, 212
Her World, 209
Hill, Suzanne, 198n
Hitler, Adolf, 137n
Ho Chee Onn, 142
Hoffman, Leslie, 14, 15–18, 30, 202
Ho Juan Thai, 111, 196n
Ho Kwon Ping, 112, 114–115, 229: release of, 115
Holloway, Lyndley, 123, 138n
Holloway, Nigel, 181, 212, 230
Hongkong Journalists' Association, 73
Hongkong Standard, 50, 73
Housing and Development Board (HDB), 47, 131, 209–211
Huo Bide, 143
Hussain bin Noordin, *Datuk*, 36
Hussein Jahidin, 23, 31, 33
Hussein Onn, *Datuk* later *Tun*, 32, 33, 35, 113, 114: Hussein Onn Administration, 33

Ih Shi Pao, 42
Indian press laws, 2–6: Act No XI of 1835, 5, 6, 19; "Gagging Act," 4
Industrial Workers' Union, 75
Institute of Southeast Asian Studies (ISEAS), 213
Internal Security Act (ISA), Cap. 143, 18, 21n, 40, 44, 48, 51, 53, 54: use of, 50, 100, 111, 114, 132, 134, 143, 180, 229–230, 235, 236–237. *See also* Preservation of Public Security Ordinance
Internal Security Council (ISC), 23
Internal Security Department (ISD), 31, 32, 34, 42, 44, 46, 87, 115, 124, 206: investigated by, 212; ISD director, 46; ISD factor, 216, 222; informers, 124, 230; screened by, 31, 216
International Commission of Jurists, 235
International Federation of Newspaper Publishers, 151
International Herald Tribune, 178, 185, 190: circulation, 173, not gazetted, 176; op-ed articles, Kishore Mahbubani, 173; Christopher Lingle, 173; contempt proceedings, 174–175; libel action, 174, 176
International Herald Tribune (Singapore) Pte Ltd, 175
International Press Institute (IPI), 13, 73, 74, 77, 80, 83: Australian committee, 18; General Assembly, Helsinki, 64, 77, 88, 101; keynote address by Lee Kuan Yew, 90–92; IPI resolution, 92–93
Investigative reporting, 217–219: on so-called Marxist conspiracy, 219. *See also Business Times*
Ismail bin Abdul Rahman, *Tun Dr.*, 33
Izvestia, 155

Jakarta Foreign Correspondents' Club, 77

James, Kenneth, 218

Janz, Udo, 235

Jawi Peranakkan. See Newspaper, extinct publications

Jayakumar, S., 165

Jek Yuen Thong, 44, 73–74, 76: and the Singapore Herald Co-operative rescue, 96; on amendments to the NPPA, 116

Jennings, Michael, 198n

Jeyaretnam, J.B., 117, 144, 145, 170, 197n, 207, 215: newsletters, 132; Committee of Privileges, complaints, 132, 144; disbarment, J.B. Jeyaretnam vs Law Society of Singapore, 157; and *Business Times*, 210

Johnson, Lyndon B., 130

Josey, Alex, 89, 101, 140, 232; expulsion from Malaysia, 178–179, 199n

Journal of Contemporary Asia, 180

Judicial Committee of the Privy Council: importance of, 39; abolition, 39, 157, 159, 167–168

Jury system, 38–39

Justice and Peace Commission. *See Catholic News*

Justus. See Catholic News

Kann, Peter, 168–169

Keasberry, Benjamin, 7

Keatley, Robert, 193

Kerala Bandhu, 19

Kerk Loong Seng, 42, 47, 48, 49, 51, 180

Khalil Akasah, 33

Khaw, Ambrose, 41, 59, 60, 64, 71, 77: letter to Rajaratnam, 62; press conference, 66, 68–69; printing permit, 86; Reece's resignation, 63–64

Khoo Kah Siang, Francis, 96, 97

Khoo, Michael, 145

Kirby, Justice Michael, 175

Koh, Adele, 62–64, 94. *See also Singapore Herald; Bob Reece*

Koh Beng Seng, 149, 154

Koh, Tommy T. B., 98, 152, 153, 192, 223

Koo Tsai Kee, 218

Krishniah, 69

Kuai Bao, 121–122

Kulkarni, V. G., 180–181

Kuomintang (KMT), 10, 43

Kwant, Hendrik J., 66–70, 74, 87, 88

Kyodo News Service, 184, 190

Lat Pau. See Newspaper, extinct publications

Law Society of Singapore, 27, 38–39, 136: critique on NPPA amendments, 148; restriction on, 148, 153

Lee Eu Seng, 107: arrest of 51; detention of 115; editorial directive, 47; *Nanyang Siang Pau*, owner-publisher, 40, 51; observations on *habeas corpus* judgment, 50; release of 116; statement on executives' arrests, 44, 45–46, 48

Lee, George, 9, 42

Lee Hee Seng, 123

Lee Hsien Loong, Brig.-Gen., 117, 127: *Jawi*, 203, racist remarks, 180; leaks, 218; media controls, 224; speech, World Congress of Newspaper Publishers, Helsinki, 1987, 192–193; Singapore Press Club, 1988, 27, 177, 207

Lee, Jackson, 84, 85

Lee, K. C., 17

Lee Kong Chian, 9

Lee Kuan Yew: and A. Samad Ismail, 28–29, 30, 31, 36; allegations of black operations, 40, 42, 43, 46, 52, 64, 68–70, 71, 75, 79, 89, 106; and the Anson by-election, 117–118, 125; and the art of gradualism, 38; Chinese chauvinist, 51; Chinese media, 39, 40, 41–42, 44, 106; crackdown on the media, 42, 78; and domestic media, 201–202, 203–204; English media, 9, 11–19, 40, 52–54, 58, 60, 65–70, 71, 73, 78, 79, 83, 89–90, 93–94, 202; and Indian media, 106; and journalists, 23, 25–26; Jury system, 38–39; and Malay media, 28–29, 31, 36, 39–40, 106; in the Malaysian parliament, 24; and 1959 general election, 1, 11; and 1972 general election, 39, 60–61, 106, 130; and 1976 general election, 111, 112, 122; and 1984 general election, 125, 144; as PAP Assemblyman, 201; press interviews with, 195; Privy Council, 39, 167–168; and the *Review*, 110, 142; as senior minister, 218; speeches, 39–40, 77, 88, 89, 90–92, 106–107, 168, 187–189. *See also* Communalism; Communism, Legal weapon; *specific publications*

Lee, Mary, 182

Lee Mau Seng, 43, 45, 46–47, 48–52: arrest of, 41, 42; *Hongkong Standard*, letter, 50, *Nanyang* official interference advice, 205. *See also Nanyang Siang Pau*

Lee Siew Choh, Dr., 129, 215: house bugged, 131; and Lee Kuan Yew, 131; media non-event, 130; press conference, 131

Lee Siew Yee, 35, 205

Lee Soo Ann, Dr., 96, 97

Legal weapon, 220–222: against Philip Bowring & Ors, 176; *Chern Sien Pao*, 129; Chia Thye Poh, 130; Derek Davies and Ors, 167; Dr. Chee Soon Juan, 171; Christopher Lingle, 173–174; C.V. Devan Nair, 208–209; Dr. Lee Siew Choh, 131; Dow Jones Publishing Company (Asia) Inc and Ors, 143–144; fear of, 220–222; Harban Singh, 130; Ho Kwon Ping, 112, 114–115; *International Herald Tribune* & Ors, 173–174; J.B. Jeyaretnam, 144; Leong Mun Kwai, 111–112; *Newsweek*, 141; Patrick Daniel and Ors, 127, 230; Peter Kann & Ors, 168–169; SDP printers, 129; *Star*, 146–147; Yeo Ah Ngoh, 130

Legislative Assembly, 50
Legislative Council, 6, 19
Lehner, Urban, 163
Lei Ren He, 192
Leifer, Michael, 164
Lent, Dr. John A., 109, 119
Leong Mun Kwai, 111, 112
Levin, Bernard, 145
Lewis, Anthony, 192
Li, Gladys, Q.C., 189–190
Li Vei Chen, 49
Lianhe Wanbao (United Evening News), 121, 126, 229
Lianhe Zaobao (United Morning News), 121, 126
Liberal Socialists, 12
Lim Boon Keng, Dr., 8
Lim, Catherine, 27
Lim Chin Siong, 29, 57
Lim Hock Siew, Dr., 129
Lim Kean Siew, 179
Lim Kim San, 118, 128, 206
Lim Li Kok, 235, 236
Lim, Peter: and *Business Times*, 211; editor-in-chief of *ST* group, 116–117; lending *New Nation* masthead, 120; ministerial calls, 205; *New Paper*, 127–128, 219; observations on Brig.-Gen. Lee's marksmanship, 117
Lim Pin, 47–48
Lim, Raymond, 204
Lim Siew Mei, 118
Lingle, Christopher, 173–176, 214
Loke Wan Tho, *Dato*, 8
Los Angeles Times, 184
Low, Patrick, 96
Ly Singko, 41–42, 43, 46, 47, 48, 49, 50–51

MacKee, Roy, 127
MacPherson, Sir Keith, 118
Mahadeva, A., 179, 199n
Mahathir Mohamad, *Datuk Seri* Dr., 34, 35, 185
Mahbubani, Kishore, 173
Makepeace, Walter, 6, 7
Malaya, Federation of, 1, 17, 38. *See also* Federation of Malaysia
Malaya Tribune, 8
Malay Mail, 35. *See also New Straits Times*
Malayan Chinese Association (MCA), 35, 41, 146
Malayan Communist Party (MCP), 16, 92. *See also* Communist Party of Malaya
Malayan New Democratic Youth League (MNDYL), 135
Malaysia, Federation of, 1, 15, 24, 25, 30, 34; Malaysia Agreement, 24
Malaysia Malayali. See Newspaper, extinct publications
Malik, Michael, 165, 167
Manchester Guardian, 88–89
Manila Times, 83
Mao Zedong (Mao Tse-Tung), 10, 22
Marcos, Ferdinand, 102, 143

Marie Claire, 232
Marshall, David Saul, 15, 18, 38–39, 49, 200, 216, 224n
Marxist conspiracy: arrests of alleged Marxist conspirators, 27, 103, 115; "do-gooders," 132; specifics of alleged conspiracy, 132, 135
Maurice, Brian, 113
McClean, Richard, 175
McDonald, Hamish, 181
Media: blackout, 207; control of, 19–20, 29, 41, 91, 146, 178–185, 190, 201–205, 210, 212, 223; criticisms by, 57–58, 61–62, 70, 75, 77, 78, 82, 125, 161, 211. *See also* Foreign media; ISA; Legal weapon; Press
Melbourne Herald, 112, 118
Merritt, Chris, 198n
Metcalfe, Sir Charles, 4
Meyer, Dr. Ernest, 73, 80
Min Pao Daily, 202
Minchin, James, 222
Mingguan Malaysia. See Utusan Melayu
Ministry of Home Affairs (MHA), 44, 45, 48, 103, 113–114, 115, 116
Mitton, Roger, 184
MND Holdings, 108, 123, 172
Mok Kwong Yue, 96
Monetary Authority of Singapore (MAS), 149, 151
Morgan, Ken, 193
Musa Hitam, 34

Nagle, Dominic, 59
Nair, C.V. Devan, 29, 203–204: Lee Kuan Yew's knight-errant, 78; legal suit, 208; NTUC secretary general, 78, 80; open letter to Lee Kuan Yew, 226n; as ouster, 144; PAP MP 117; president of Singapore, 10, 117; settlement, 208–209; Socialist International, 110–111, 115
Nair, I.V.K. *See* Newspaper, extinct publications
Nan Chiau Jit Pao. See Newspaper, extinct publications
Nanfang Evening Post, 19
Nanyang Siang Pau, 9, 18, 19, 51, 69, 75, 84, 106: allegations, 39, 43–44, 45, 46, 47, 51; circulation, 121, 125; denial of official press facilities, 49; editorials, 40, 44, 45, 47, 49; enforced merger with *Sin Chew Jit Poh*, 121; executives arrested, 40, 41, 46, 107; libel action, 89–90; ministerial interference, 49, 50, 204–205
Nanyang Siang Pau (Malaysia), 35
Napier, William, 7
Nathan, S.R., 118, 187
National Defense Fund, 96. *See also* Singapore Herald Cooperative Society
National Press Club (NPC), (Philippines), 77
National Trade Unions Congress (NTUC), 77, 80, 128
National Union of Journalists (NUJ) Malaysia, 182; *Utusan Melayu* chapel, 79

National University of Singapore (NUS), 171, 173, 213
National University of Singapore Society (NUSS), 213
Navijiwan, 126
Neave, David, 7
Nelson, William, 93
New Democrat, 133
New Nation, 80, 84, 118, 120
New Paper, 126, 204
New Statesman, 179
New Straits Times Press (Malaysia) Sendirian Berhad, 34, 35. *See also* the *Straits Times*
New York Times, 142, 145, 170, 171, 173, 184, 192
New World Hotel, 145, 181
Newspaper, 19, 20: extinct publications, 9–10; letters to editors, 215–217; permits, 19; right of reply, 155, 158, 186
Newspaper companies, 107–108: circulation, 52, 121, 125, 234 (appendix); control of, 116–117, 201–202; conversion into public companies, 100, 107, 108, 116, 124; divestiture of control, 9, 108, 115; restructure, 119–126. *See also specific newspaper companies*
Newspaper and Printing Presses Act (NPPA), Cap. 206, 21, 107–108, 116, 201: amendments, 116–117, 148, 156, 165–166; offshore newspapers, 185; requirements for bond, etc., 185
Newsweek, 141
Ng, Allan, 85
Ng, Josef, 214
Ngiam Thong Hai, 230
Nonis, George, 221

Odchimar, Marilyn, 145, 181
Official Secrets Act (OSA), Cap. 213, 127, 170, 171, 173, 218, 230
Oliphant, Pat, 220
O'Neill, Michael, 164, 208
Ong Eng Guan, 13, 23, 202
Ong Pang Boon, 20–21
Ong Teng Cheong, 207
Ooi, R. B., 52
Operation Cold Store, 1, 23–24, 30, 128, 129, 141
Operation Spectrum, 182. *See also* Marxist conspiracy
Ordinances: Preservation of Public Security Ordinance, 15, 16, 17, 18, 201; Printing Presses Ordinance, 1920, 19, 20; Printing Presses (Amendment) Ordinance, 1930, 20–21; Undesirable Publications Ordinance, 128. *See also specific acts*
Othman Wok, 29, 36
Overseas Union Bank (OUB), 119, 123

Parker, Elliott S., 122
Parliamentary (Privileges, Immunities and Powers) Act, Cap. 217, 230
Partai Rakyat, 19

Penal Code, Cap. 224, 230–231
Penthouse, 229
People, 19
People's Action Party (PAP), 1, 8, 11, 12, 15, 18, 19, 157, 179, 210: Socialist International, 102; withdrawal from, 110–111
People's Daily (China), 124
People's Front, 75, 111–112
Perreau, D.C., 8
Petir, 19
Pillai, M.G.G., 62
Playboy, 231
Plebeian: Plebeian Express. *See* Legal weapon; Political organs
Poh Soo Kai, Dr., 110
Political organs: *Battle for Merger*, 128; *Chern Sien Pau*, 129–130; *Hammer*, 131–133, 216; newsletters, 131; *Plebeian*, 129–131; *Plebeian Express*, 129; *Petir*, 128; printers, 128–129; publishing permits, 128, 129, 130, 134, 136; report on bugging incident, 131; *Wartawan*, 128. *See also* specific political organs
Polsky, Anthony, 55n, 142
Ponting, Clive, 171, 198n
Porter, David, 182
Pravda, 124
Press, 19–21, 106–107, 113, 205: censorship, 2–3, 6, 26, 91, 110, 126, 223; code of conduct, 3; self-censorship, 178, 187, 208–213; freedom, 2, 4, 6, 13–16, 17, 18, 20, 46, 74, 75, 77, 78, 79, 80, 82, 86, 92, 102, 115, 121, 124, 151; Indian legislation, 2–6; out-of-bound (OB) markers, 27, 208, 212; press laws, 19–21, 107–108. *See also* Media; Newspaper
Press conference, 66–72, 89: on arrest of *Nanyang* pressmen, 44; prelude to prime minister's conference, 65–66
Press Council, 108–109, 193
Press Foundation of Asia (PFA), 78, 80, 83–84
Printing Presses Act, 20–21
Printing Presses Ordinance, 19–20. *See also* Newspaper and Printing Presses Act
Pritt, D. N., Q. C., 134
Pura, Raphael, 181, 182
Puthucheary, Dominic, 113
Puthucheary, James, 57, 113, 134

Q, 231–232
Quayle, J. Danforth, 161, 182
Quek, Robert, 66

Radio and Television Singapore, 39, 45
Raffles, Sir Thomas Stamford, 2, 6–7
Rahamat bin Kenap, 36
Rahim Ishak, 29
Rajaratnam, Sinnathamby, 8, 11, 16, 18, 29, 44, 101: and *Eastern Sun*, 53; on foreign pressmen, 183; and *Malaya Tribune*, 8; and *Nanyang Siang Pau*, 44, 46, 52; Press Council, 108–109; pseudonyms, 216–217;

and *Singapore Herald*, 56–58, 59, 62–64, 65–66, 70, 71, 73, 78, 83–85, 94, 96, 97; and the *Singapore Standard*, 8, 13–14; on the SNPL and Straits Times group merger, 124; and the *Straits Times*, 8, 13–15, 16–18
Raman, G. (Gopalan Krishnan Raman), 113
Ranck, Rosemary
Razaleigh Hamzah, *Tengku*, 34, 35
Reece, Bob, 62–64, 94. *See also Singapore Herald*
Registrar of Companies, 80
Registrar of Societies, 98, 106
Renminribao, 155
Reporters' Advertiser. See Newspaper, extinct publications
Repression, 88, 89: technique in, 22, 102, 129, 201
Reyes, Alejandro, 164, 184, 199n
Reuters News Agency, 60, 64, 73, 145, 169, 181, 190
Richardson, Michael, 174, 175, 185
Right of Reply. *See specific newspapers*
Riots, Maria Hertogh, 91, 104n: Malay-Chinese, 91; May 13, 1969, 57, 64
Roces, Joaquin P., 78, 83, 84
Rockefeller, David, 73, 77, 87, 93
Rodan, Garry, 199n
Rodong Shinmun, 98
Rosett, Claudia, 189
Roth, Kenneth, 237
Rowley, Anthony, 181

Sabnani, Mano, 127
Said Zahari, 23, 30, 129, 179, 229
St. Clair, William Graeme, 7
Samani Mohamad Amin, 111
Sarangapany, G., 126
Schwartz, Eric, 235
Scott, James C., 222
Scott, Margaret
Seaward, Nick, 181
Sedition Act, Cap. 290, 36, 49, 231
Sedition Ordinance. *See* Sedition Act
See Ewe Lay, 9
Select Book Shop, 222
Selvan, T. S., 220
Senkuttuvan, Arun, 113, 115
Seow, Ashleigh, 198n
Seow, Francis T., 164, 184, 234–236, 236–237
SESDAQ (Stock Exchange of Singapore Dealing and Automated Quotation Market System), 149, 152, 153
Sesser, Stan, 195, 200n
Sheares, President Benjamin, 99, 112
Shelford, T., 7
Shenon, Philip, 184, 198n
Shin Min Daily News, 112, 120, 121, 126, 202, 229
Siebel, Norman, 64
Sikes, Jonathan, 183
Simmons, A.C., 108
Sin Poh group of newspapers, 53

Sin Chew Jit Poh (Malaysia), 35, 41–42
Sin Chew Jit Poh, 8, 19, 41–42, 52: cessation, 121; circulation, 121; enforced merger with *Nanyang Siang Pau*, 119–121. *See also Singapore Standard*
Sing Tao group, 198n
Singai Nesan. See Newspaper, extinct publications
Singapore, 1, 2: a salubrious perch, 188, 190–191; a "Third China," 46, 52
Singapore, 137
Singapore Chronicle, 5–7
Singapore Democratic Party (SDP), 129, 133, 221
Singapore Free Press, 6, 7, 19. *See also Straits Times*
Singapore Herald (defunct). *See* Newspaper, extinct publications
Singapore Herald, 40–41, 75, 103: Ambrose Khaw, 41, 62; assets valuation, 84–87; black operations, 42, 58, 59, 61–62, 64, 68–70, 71, 73, 75, 76, 78, 79, 86, 93; capitalization, 57, 59, 64, 79–80, 86; cartoon, 65; cessation, 86; circulation of, 70, 72; editorial posture, 40, 57, 58, 60, 62, 63, 64, 65, 68, 75, 100; foreclosure, 70–71, 75–76; Francis Wong, 41, 64–65, 89; guarantors 74; interference, 58, 203–204; investors, 41, 56, 57, 58, 59–60, 61, 65–70, 71–72, 73, 74, 76, 81–85, 118; job placement centre, 99; Lee Kuan Yew's hostility, 56, 71, 79, 83; management agreement, 58, 60, 73; notice of demand, 72, 75–76; official advice, 57, 58; official harassments, 41, 58–59, 201; overdraft, 69; passes/permits, 62–64, 81, 83–86, 87, 89, 95, 99; postscript, 102; rally of support, 75, 76, 77–78, 81, 95–96; receiver appointed, 81, 84–85, 98, 99; "Save the *Herald*" campaign, 72–73, 74, 75, 76–78, 83, 102; "Save the *Herald*" charade, 80–85; Stock Exchanges of Singapore and Kuala Lumpur, listings on, 75; trust fund, 95, 96; winding-up, 99–100
Singapore Herald Co-operative Society, 96–99: licence/permit, 96, 97–98, 99; pro-tem committee, 96
Singapore International Foundation (SIF), 137
Singapore Journal of Commerce. See Straits Times
Singapore Journalist, 16
Singapore Manual and Mercantile Workers' Union, 166
Singapore Merchant Bankers' Association, 153
Singapore Monitor, 120, 122, 123, 124, 125: closure, 125
Singapore Monitor (Private) Limited, 119–121. *See also Singapore Monitor*
Singapore National Union of Journalists (SNUJ), 25, 74, 79, 119, 141: *Wartawan*, 199n; Times chapel, 78
Singapore News and Publications Limited (SNPL), 119–126
Singapore People's Alliance (SPA), 11, 12, 19

Singapore Polytechnic Students' Union, 73, 80, 135
Singapore Press Club, 177: 1972 speech by Lee
    Kuan Yew, 26–27, 106–107; 1988 speech by
    Lee Hsien Loong, 27, 207
Singapore Press Holdings Ltd (SPH): companies
    within SPH, 128, 172; corporate board, 206,
    207, 230; demonstrations against, 123–124;
    denial of government involvement in, 124,
    125, 138n; foreign press holdings, 119;
    merger between SNPL and Straits Times
    group, 122–124; opposition to, 124; rules of
    merger, 123
Singapore Standard, a.k.a. the *Tiger Standard*, 8, 11,
    13, 15, 19, 52
Singapore Stock Exchange, 123, 153, 204
Singapore Technocrat, 135
Singapore Undergrad, 134
Singapore Union of Journalists, 74. *See also*
    Singapore National Union of Journalists
    (SNUJ)
Singapore Yearbook: 1983, 1989, 1990, 1992, 1994,
    121
Singh, Bilveer, 214–215
Singh, Kirpal, 215
Sinnathuray, T. S., 112, 130, 169
Siow Long Hin, 137n
Smith, Colin, 102
Smith, Patrick, 143
Socialist International, 31, 113: expulsion of PAP
    from, 109–111, 115
South China Morning Post, 119, 168, 184, 187,
    208–209. *See also Straits Times*
Spackman, Jack, 72–73
Special Branch: black operations, 112; Malaysian,
    32, 33
Singapore, 43, 45, 130–131
Speech, freedom of, 6, 46, 82, 101, 134, 135, 160,
    174
Spurr, Russell, 113
Stankard, Francis, 76, 87–88
The Star (Malaysia), 146–147
Stephens, Donald (Fuad), *Tan Sri Datuk*; and Lee
    Kuan Yew, 60, 61; interview, 73; investment
    in *Singapore Herald*, 41, 56, 57, 60, 64–65,
    69, 70, 73–74, 82, 83, 93, 94; size of, 100.
    See also Singapore Herald
Stewart, Ian, 184
Stock Exchanges of Singapore and Kuala Lumpur,
    75
Stolbach, Charles, 166, 167
Straits Advocate. See Newspaper, extinct publications
Straits Guardian. See Newspaper, extinct
    publications
Straits Intelligence. See Newspaper, extinct
    publications
Straits Produce. See Newspaper, extinct publications
Straits Settlements (SS), 2, 4, 5, 6, 19,
Straits Times, 7: British interests in, 88, 94; during
    Ong Eng Guan mayoralty, 202; editors, 8,

94, 105n; Foreign investments, 54, 58, 60,
    88, 100, 118–119; incorporation, 8, 14, 19,
    35, 121–123; leader writers, 94, 105n; letters,
    215–216; and 1959 general election, 11, 12,
    14, 15, 16, 17–18, 20; and *Nanyang*
    executives' arrests, 44–45; relocation, 19; and
    Singapore Herald, 80, 86–87, 95, 103
Student Christian Movement of Singapore (SCMS),
    75, 103. *See also* Marxist conspiracy
Sun Tzu, 109, 169
Sunday Mail, 19, 202
Sunday Monitor. See Singapore Monitor
Sunday Nation. See Nation
Sunday Observer (London), 102
Sunday Times, (London), 183
Sunday Times, 219, 234–236, 236–237. *See also*
    Straits Times

Tamil Murasu, 19, 126
Tan Boon Teik, 48
Tan Chin Har. *See Nanyang Siang Pau*
Tan Chin Tiong, Brig.-Gen., 135
Tan Kah Kee, 9, 10
Tan Ken Sin, 35
Tan Sai Siong, 127
Tan Tee Seng, 132
Tan Teng Lang, 26
Tan Wah Piow, 219
Tang Fong Har, 27
Tasker, Rodney, 182
Tay Boon Too and anor v Workers' Party. *See*
    Workers' Party
Tay Eng Soon, Dr., 211
Tay Kheng Soon, 96
Taylor, Stephen, 125–126
Teehankee, Claudio
Teh Cheang Wan, 146, 209, 210, 211
Temasek Holdings Limited, 108, 123, 172
Teo Soh Lung, 215–216, 234
Tham, Peter, 204
Thean, L.P., 167
Time, 109, 189: circulation restriction, 127, 148;
    restored, 149; right of reply, 148, 155
Times (London), 77, 113, 145–146
Times Books International, 209
Times Printers Pte Ltd, 167, 172
Tsai Tan. *See* Tan Sai Siong
Tsang, Kenneth, 132, 182
Temasek Holdings Limited
Thomas, Margaret, 126
Thomson of Fleet, Lord, 100
Tjong Yik Min, 230
Toh Chin Chye, Dr., 12, 13, 124, 179
Tung Tao Chang, Shamsuddin, 43, 50: arrest, 41,
    42; detention, 46; *habeas corpus application*,
    48, 49; *incommunicado*, 48; *Nanyang Siang*
    Pau, 41, 45; opposition candidate, 111–
    112
Turnbull, C. M., 120, 205

Undesirable Publications Act, Cap. 338, 222, 231–232
United Malays National Organization (UMNO), 29, 30, 31–35, 111, 179
United National Party, 73
United Overseas Bank (UOB), 119, 123
UPI (United Press International), 112, 190
University of Singapore Democratic Socialist Club, 75
University of Singapore Socialist Club, 134
University of Singapore Students' Union (USSU), 73
US News and World Report, 167
U.S. State Department, 95, 150–151, 174, 192
Utusan Malaysia, 31
Utusan Melayu, 10, 28, 30, 77, 179: and A. Samad Ismail, 28–29; and Lee Kuan Yew, 28, 29, 36, 205 relocation, 36
Utusan Zaman. See Utusan Melayu

Vancouver Sun, 55n
Vittachi, Nury, 167
Voice of America (VOA), 152
Voice of the People, 19

Wallace, Charles, 184
Wartawan. See SNUJ
Washington Post, 173
Wee Cho Yaw, 84–85, 96, 97, 119
Wee Han Kim, 204, 215
Wellesley, Lord, press censorship, 2–3
Westerhout, Alexander W., 8
Western media. *See* Foreign media
Westlake, Michael, 181–182
Westminster Press Group, 59
Wickman, Kurt, 214
Wilson, Harold, 109
Woman's Affair, 204
Wong, Francis: and Dr. Goh Keng Swee, 57; editor of *Sunday Mail*, 202; founder-editor of *Singapore Herald*, 41, 201; "half-politician,"

57, 58, 94; and James Puthucheary, 57; and Lee Kuan Yew, 79; letter to *Singapore Herald*, 64–65; and Lim Chin Siong, 57; official advice, 57–58; official interference in, 204; printing permit, 81, 86; resignation from, 41, 59, 60; and S. Rajaratnam, 57; and S. Woodhull, 57
Wong Kan Seng, 149, 181, 183, 196–197n
Wong Lin Ken, Dr., 44
Wong Souk Yee, 235, 236
Woodhull, S., a.k.a. Sandrasegeram s/o Woodhull, 57
Woods, Robin Carr, 8
Workers' Party, 18: media blackout, 207; publications, 131–133, 216. *See also* the Marxist conspiracy
Workers' Party vs Attorney General, 141
Wright, Peter, 171

Yap, William, 235, 236
Yatiman Yusuf, 183, 223
Yatron, Gus, 187
Yazhou Zhoukan, 219–220, 226n
Yeh Sai Fu, Julius, 53
Yeo Ah Ngoh, 130
Yeo, Brig.-Gen. George, 27: *AWSJ*, 163, 169; cartoons, 219–220; defining OB markers, 212, 223; foreign media, 103, 178, 181, 185; *Hammer*, 132; as information minister, 205, 206; Press Councils, 109; right of reply, 194; SPH, 126; *Straits Times*, 215
Yeo Ning Hong, Dr., 155, 165
Yeong Yoon Ying, 198n
Yong, Archbishop Gregory, 135, 136
Yong, C. F., 10n
Yong Nyuk Lin, 12
Young, Alwyn, 132
Yung, Frank, 118
Yusuf Ishak, 28–29. *See also Utusan Melayu*

Zecha, Adrian, 67
Zhonglian, 136
Zimmermann, Fred, 149, 154, 191

About the Book and Author

Once a proud and independent institution, the Singapore press was brought to its knees by threats, arbitrary arrests and detentions, general harassment, and litigation during Prime Minister Lee Kuan Yew's administration. Singapore's former solicitor general, Francis T. Seow, tells this story, documenting the demise of the *Eastern Sun,* the *Nanyang Siang Pau,* and the *Singapore Herald* (among other news publications), as well as the severe curbs placed on foreign journalists reporting on Singapore.

By the early 1980s, Singapore's entire press establishment had been restructured; with founding owners forced to divest their holdings of newspaper companies. Since then, as Seow substantiates the press has become the mouthpiece of the state, using invidious self-censorship to distort the news.

Francis T. Seow, now a fellow at Harvard Law School's East Asian Legal Studies Program, held several key posts in Singapore's government, including service as the solicitor general in 1967–1971. Arrested in 1988 on allegations that he illegally received funds in support of opposition politics, he was detained (though never formally charged) for 72 days, and Amnesty International named him a prisoner of conscience. In November 1988, he was invited by Human Rights Watch to visit the United States, where he has since remained in exile.